EDUCATION AND SOCIAL SECTOR
Issues and Challenges

EDUCATION AND SOCIAL SECTOR

Issues and Challenges

Editors

DR. IMRAN SALEEM
M.Com. (Gold Medalist), Ph.D.
Department of Commerce
Aligarh Muslim University, Aligarh (U.P.)

ASHRAF IMAM
PGEDP, MFC
Department of Commerce
Aligarh Muslim University, Aligarh (U.P.)

REGAL PUBLICATIONS
New Delhi - 110 027

EDUCATION AND SOCIAL SECTOR
Issues and Challenges

ISBN 978-81-8484-181-7

Typeset by
RAHUL COMPOSERS
358, Pocket-B, Phase-2, Sector-16 B, Dwarka, New Delhi - 110 075

Printed in India at
MAYUR ENTERPRISES
WZ Plot No. 3, Gujjar Market, Tihar Village, New Delhi - 110 018

Published by
REGAL PUBLICATIONS
F-159, Rajouri Garden, New Delhi - 110 027 • Phone : 45546396
E-mail : regalbookspub@yahoo.com

Contents

Preface

Education is decisive for both economic growth and development. Evidences from the developing world show that universal primary education contributes strongly to growth and development of country. As economic growth continues so the importance of secondary and higher level education, particularly of technical and vocational nature, will increase. In fact, education is the social institution that reaches the largest segment of the population with the goal of guiding it through a systematic learning process. Crucial Issues to be addressed by Education: Poverty, Gender, Health and Unemployment.

The primary aim of this book is to provide readers with a clear understanding of the various terminologies, definitions, trends, and issues associated with the education and social sector issues. It is written in simple, easy-to-understand language. It provides examples, case studies, lessons learned, and best practices that will help planners and decision-makers in addressing pertinent issues and crafting policies and strategies appropriate for the social sector development. We hope that all will find this book to be of tremendous value and a resource guide. It is design to cover all aspects of education and its role for social sector issues and its development.

Finally, we thank all who have been involved with this book, i.e. contributors, writers, researchers, peer reviewers and the production team.

IMRAN SALEEM
ASHRAF IMAM

List of Contributors

Amit Joshi, Assistant Professor in Economics, Swami Vivekanand Night College of Arts and Commerce, Dombivli (Maharashtra).

Ashraf Imam, Ph.D. Scholar at Aligarh Muslim University, Aligarh (U.P.).

Benard Nyakweba Oyagi, Research Scholar of Mohanlal Sukhadia University, Udaipur (Rajasthan).

Chander Parkash, Faculty Member, GHS Modia Khera, Sirsa (Haryana).

Dr. **Arun Bhadauria**, Assistant Professor, Amity University Uttar Pradesh, Lucknow Campus, Lucknow (U.P.).

Dr. **Asma Parveen**, Associate Professor, Department of Psychology, A.M.U., Aligarh (U.P.).

Dr. **Azkiya Waris**, Lecturer, Regency Teachers' Training College, Sitapur (U.P.).

Dr. **Garima Sharma**, Lecturer, Communication Skills, Mangalayatan University, Aligarh (U.P.).

Dr. **Iftekhar Ahmed**, Assistant Professor, Department of Political Science, N.R.E.C. College, Khurja (U.P.).

Dr. **Jamil Ahmad**, Department of Economics, Aligarh Muslim University, Aligarh, Aligarh (U.P.).

Dr. **Kiran Lata Dangwal**, Assistant Professor, Department of Education, University of Lucknow (U.P.).

Dr. **Mirza Shahab Shah**, Associate Professor and Head, Faculty of Commerce, K.S. Saket P.G. College, Ayodhya, Faizabad (U.P.).

Dr. Mohammad Parvez, Associate Professor, Department of Education, Aligarh Muslim University, Aligarh (U.P.).

Dr. Mohd. Shamim, Assistant Professor, Department of Commerce, Aligarh Muslim University, Aligarh (U.P.).

Dr. Mushtaq, A. Siddiqi, Associate Professor, The Business School, University of Kashmir, Kashmir (J & K).

Dr. N.N. Pandey, Principal, Dalmia College and Research Guide, JJTU.

Dr. Naga Raju Alluri, Assistant Professor, Department of Commerce, P.G. Courses and Research Centre, D.N.R. College, Bhimavaram, W.G. District (A.P.).

Dr. P. Khicha, Head of Department of Business Administration in B.N. PG College, Udaipur (Rajasthan).

Dr. R. Madhavi, Faculty Member, Department of Communication Studies, University of Pune, Pune (Maharashtra).

Dr. Rajesh Kumar, Department of Political Science, AMU, Aligarh (U.P.).

Dr. Reshu Agarwal, Associate Professor and Dean Academics, Techno Institute of Management Sciences, 331, Near Indira Canal, Faizabad Road, Lucknow (U.P.).

Dr. S. Venkateshwar Rao, Lecturer, University P.G. College, Nirmal, Kakatiya University, Vidyaranyapuri, Warangal (A.P.).

Dr. Shekhar Rajpoot, Psychiatric Social Worker-Institute of Mental Health and Hospital, Agra (U.P.).

Dr. Sunil Kumar, Associate Professor in Political Science, Shyam Lal College (Evening), University of Delhi, Delhi.

Dr. Surendra Singh, Post-Doctoral Fellow, D.U., New Delhi.

Faheema Afzal, Periyar University, Salem (T.N.).

Fozia Chowdhary, Research Scholar, Department of Commerce, Aligarh Muslim University, Aligarh (U.P.).

G. Prasad Babu, Ph.D. Scholar at NDRI, Karnal (Haryana).

G. Srinivas, Asst. Professor, Jyothismathi Institute of Technology and Science, Karimnagar (A.P.).

G.P. Sahu, Motilal Nehru National Institute of Technlogy, Allahabad (U.P.).

Ghazala Rashid, Research Scholar, Department of Education, AMU, Aligarh (U.P.).

Himmat Singh Deora, Ph.D. Scholar (Political Science), JNU, New Delhi.

Iram Feroz, Research Scholar, Department of Psychology, A.M.U., Aligarh (U.P.).

Javed Khan, Research Scholar, Department of Commerce, Aligarh Muslim University, Aligarh (U.P.).

Jnanjyoti Sarmah, Mathematics Department, Morigaon College (Assam).

K. Chandrasekar, Assistant Professor, Alagappa Institute of Management, Alagappa University, Karaikudi (T.N.).

Kamran Mohammad Khan, Lecturer, ACN College of Engineering and Management Studies, Aligarh (U.P.).

Krishna Kumar, Research Scholar, Faculty of Commerce, Banaras Hindu University, Varanasi (U.P.).

Kusum Lata Kapoor, Research Scholar, klkapoor1967 @gmail.com

M. Sayeed Alam, Assistant Professor, Department of Business Administration, East-West University, Dhaka (Bangladesh).

Mohammad Awais, Research Scholar, Department of Agricultural Economics and Business Management, Aligarh Muslim University, Aligarh (U.P.).

Mohammad Muqeet Khan, Research Fellow, Department of Geography, Aligarh Muslim University, Aligarh (U.P.).

Mohammad Rauf, Research Scholar, Faculty of Law, A.M.U., Aligarh (U.P.).

Mohd. Shakir, Junior Research Fellow, Department of Education, A.M.U., Aligarh (U.P.).

Mohd. Taqi, Research Scholar, Department of Commerce, Aligarh Muslim University, Aligarh (U.P.).

Ms. Asha A. Jindal, Associate Professor, Department of Statistics, K.C. College, Mumbai (Maharashtra).

Ms. Sadaf Khan, Research Fellow, Department of Commerce, A.M.U., Aligarh (U.P.).

Naheen Haider Zaidi, P.G. Student, Centre for Women Studies, Aligarh Muslim University, Aligarh (U.P.).

Narendra Pal Singh, Research Scholar, Department of Sociology, Babasaheb Bhimrao Ambedkar University (A Central University), Lucknow (U.P.).

Nida Siddiqui, Research Scholar, Department of Sociology and Social Work, A.M.U., Aligarh (U.P.).

Nizamuddin Khan, Associate Professor, Department of Geography, Aligarh Muslim University, Aligarh (U.P.).

Nyakundi K. Ruth, Student of Mahendra Arts and Science College, Kalipatti (T.N.).

Omar Faruq, Assistant Professor, Department of Business Administration, East-West University, Dhaka (Bangladesh).

Osman Bin Salam, Asst. Professor, Jyothismathi Institute of Technology and Science, Karimnagar (A.P.).

P.A.L.N.S. Kalyani, Associate Professor, Department of Management Studies, Sphoorthy Engineering College, Hyderabad (A.P.).

Prabir Panda, Motilal Nehru National Institute of Technlogy, Allahabad (U.P.).

Pradeep Kumar Singh, Asst. Professor, Department of Mechanical Engg. (Delhi Institute of Tech., Mgt. and Research. Faridabad), (Haryana).

Preeti Sharma, Thesis submitted in English Language Teaching from A.M.U., Aligarh (U.P.).

Prof. A.P. Pandey, Professor, Department of Economics, Bhu, Varanasi (U.P.).

Qurratul Aein Ali, Research Scholar, D/O Sociology and Social Work-A.M.U., Aligarh (U.P.).

Rizwan Alam, MCA (final Year), A.M.U., Aligarh (U.P.).

Rohit C. Pawar, Research Student, Department of Communication Studies, University of Pune, Pune (Maharashtra).

S.K. Bhardwaj, Asst. Professor, Department of Mechanical Engg. (Delhi Institute of Tech., Mgt. and Research, Faridabad), (Haryana).

Sabina Sharmin, Assistant Professor, Department of Statistics, Biostatistics and Informatics, University of Dhaka, Dhaka (Bangladesh).

Sachin Garg, Department of Computer Science and Application, Aggarwal College, Ballabgarh (Haryana).

Sadaqat Ali, Research Scholar, Department of Commerce, Aligarh Muslim University, Aligarh (U.P.).

Saliha Khatoon, Research Scholar, Department of Education, Gulbarga University, Gulbarga (Karnataka).

Sandeep Jain, Department of Computer Science and Application, Aggarwal College, Ballabgarh (Haryana).

Shabnam, Assistant Professor in Psychology, Department of Humanities and Management, NIT, Jalandhar (Punjab).

Shailendra Kumar Singh, Ph.D. Scholar, Department of Economics, Bhu, Varanasi (U.P.).

Sharmila, Lecturer, J.G. College of Education, Sirsa (Haryana).

Shazia Tabassum, Research Scholar, Department of Commerce, A.M.U., Aligarh (U.P.).

Simarekha Bhagowati, Mathematics Department, Morigaon College (Assam).

Smriti Nagi, Research Scholar, Department of Education, Singhania University, Jhunjhunu (Rajasthan).

Talata C. Ratnayake, Ph.D. Scholars at NDRI, Karnal (Haryana).

Zahid Raza Khan, Research Scholar, Magadh University, Gaya (Bihar).

CHAPTER

1

Education Through Participation

An Avenue for Security of Sustainable Livelihood

ARUN BHADAURIA

ABSTRACT

The policy design and execution through available infrastructure, is in the redesigning mode. Innovative designs are being ushered in to create most appropriate resource-base for education through participation. The response and success so far is satisfactory, however, it is seldom enough to notice rural education as driving force for sustainable rural development and sustainable livelihood security. Rural livelihood security is absolutely a separate issue so far as looked upon by common village inhabitants. The rural elites in the past have propagated a thought, i.e. 'work is beyond education. More educated means more difficult to find employment in the area'. Such kind of thoughts, beliefs, misconceptions are needed to be addressed with adequate blend of employment, economic activity and learning by doing.

They (adults) will not be asked to join for education only but to come for job and 'learning by doing' with the assurance of getting employment and for minors adequately monitored education equipped with functional student database hub. Livelihoods can be made up of a range of on-farm, off-farm and extra-territorial activities which together provide a variety of procurement strategies for food, cash, shelter, recognition, satisfaction, grooming, growth and development. Thus, each individual can have several possible sources of entitlement which constitute its livelihood. These entitlements are based on the resource endowment and its position in the legal, political and social fabric of society.

Keywords: Sustainable, Livelihood, Security, Student, Data, Hub, Participation, Transformation.

INTRODUCTION

In the recent times as per the recommendations of Education Commission, participatory education mode is sought as a indispensable application to make Public Private Partnership (PPP)—a successful model of Education, which is much hyped for accomplishment of 'education for all'—dream project of Government of India (GoI). The policy design and execution through available infrastructure, is in the redesigning mode. Innovative designs are being ushered in to create most appropriate resource base for education through participation. The response and success so far is satisfactory however it is seldom enough to notice rural education as driving force for sustainable rural development and sustainable livelihood security. Rural livelihood security is absolutely a separate issue so far as looked upon by common village inhabitants. The rural elites in the past have propagated a thought, i.e. 'work is beyond education. More educated means more difficult to find employment in the area'. Such kind of thoughts, beliefs, misconceptions are needed to be addressed with adequate blend of employment, economic activity and learning by doing. They (adults) will not be asked to join for education only but to come for job and 'learning by doing' with the assurance of getting employment and for minors adequately monitored education equipped with functional student database hub. MNREGA however doing good job in this regard, it is suffering from corruption as this programme is politically motivated and activities are forcefully created for villagers. The said activity does not provide sustainable means of livelihood security as it does not has business opportunities, competition and business characteristics.

Business Opportunities are created by absolute and free participation of all the communities, physical infrastructure and Government Bodies. While role of government is of regulator and facilitator—which is being performed through MNREGA type programmes to create physical infrastructure, the other segment, i.e. community—Business Community and Household both are required to show interest in the utilization of the created infrastructure. This objective may be accomplished only through Public Private Partnership but through Participation of people, which constitute '4P' Model. This model though is not in action but it needs to be on priority for sustainable livelihood security.

This paper comprises four sections and first section highlights the current issues pertaining to livelihood security, second section bring out the concept of livelihood security intone with employment through participation and education, third section is based on the innovative application-oriented sustainable livelihood security system.

I. CONCEPTUAL SHIFT IN THE MEANING OF LIVELIHOOD SECURITY

Livelihood security is defined as adequate and sustainable access to income and resources to meet basic needs (including adequate access to food, potable water, health facilities, educational opportunities, housing, time for community participation and social integration). Livelihoods can be made up of a range of on-farm, off-farm and extra-territorial activities which together provide a variety of procurement strategies for food, cash, shelter, recognition, satisfaction, grooming, growth and development. Thus, each individual can have several possible sources of entitlement which constitute its livelihood. These entitlements are based on the resource endowment and its position in the legal, political and social fabric of society (Drinkwater and McEwan, 1992). The risk of livelihood failure determines the level of vulnerability of an individual to income, food, and health, nutritional, political, social and psychological insecurity. Therefore, livelihoods are secure when individual have secure ownership of, or access to, resources and income earning activities, including reserves and assets, to offset risks, ease shocks and meet contingencies (Chambers, 1989). A livelihood is sustainable, when it "can cope with and recover from the stress and shocks, maintain its capability and assets, and provide sustainable livelihood opportunities for the many generation to come (Chambers and Conway, 1992)". Unfortunately, not all households are equal in their ability to cope with stress and repeated shocks. Poor people balance competing needs for asset preservation, income generation and present and future food supplies in complex ways (Maxwell and Smith, 1992). Thus, food and nutritional security are subsets of livelihood security; food needs are not necessarily more important than other basic needs or aspects of subsistence and survival within households. Food-insecure households juggle among a range of requirements, including immediate consumption and future capacity to produce.

1.1 Current Issues and Fundamental Parameters of Livelihood Security

1. The structural vulnerability of livelihood systems in Less Developed Countries (LDCs) such as skewed distribution of resources, sub-division and fragmentation of land holdings, poor connectivity and of course low level of awareness and education, backward and inhibitory approach towards developmental processes led to poor, non-livable, economically weaker and unsustainable dwellings;
2. Focusing and deliberating upon improved technology of production and processing to stabilize yields through diversification into agro-ecologically appropriate crops, natural resource management, and filing up of voids in economic and political distribution system, cost effective and business-oriented measures are brazenly required. (e.g. soil and water conservation);

3. Operational approach to Create alternative income-generating activities for the purpose of attainment the goal of self-sustained system (e.g. activities to develop small enterprise);
4. Need of reinforcing coping strategies that are economically, environmentally, globally and of course locally sustainable (e.g. seasonally appropriate off-farm employment);
5. Improvement in on-site inventory management and implementation capacity to increase the availability of buffer stocks in order to provide cushions from shocks; and
6. Improvement through community participation in common property and logistics management.

1.2 Components of Household Livelihood Security

1. Security of Business Opportunity and development
2. Economic security (income, skills, time)
3. Nutritional security (Shelter, Mother and child care Health including water and sanitation)
4. Environmental Awareness Security
5. Educational Participatory security
6. Community participation (gender, ethnic group, religious affiliation)
7. Habitat security
8. Food security
9. Health security
10. Political and Legal Security

Livelihood Security requires strengthening the capacity of masses and political system mapping out key issues, providing guidance on necessary priority actions leading to economic well-being, determining populations most at risk, and building community and household resilience through awareness raising activities with the functional and effective association with community volunteer organization.

Southern Sudan and surrounding areas such as Abyei, the Nuba Mountains and Blue Nile may be taken as illustration where food security is addressed through development of an integrated food security strategy and by leveraging Title II and Disaster Assistance funds in a complementary manner that emphasizes the transitions taking place in livelihoods, education, health, nutrition, institutions and security.

OXFAM's livelihoods program in Tazikistan revolves around to identify problems, potential solutions, partnerships, and interventions are appropriate to address the complex issues of food and livelihood security thereby trying to develop a five year strategic framework and a proposal for a sustainable livelihoods program at national and regional levels.

World Food Programme (WFP) in rural Bangladesh aims to create socio-economic profiles and determine levels of vulnerability and food security in operational areas. The disaggregating by socio-economic status enabled a more nuanced and descriptive analysis of food security and vulnerability issues, allowing WFP to design their programmes accordingly.

2. ISSUES OF LIVELIHOOD SECURITY ARE ADDRESSED WITH 'EMPLOYMENT THROUGH PARTICIPATION AND EDUCATION' APPROACH

Education is a key component in the conceptualization of the 11th Five Year Plan (FYP). As per draft of FYP Nine working groups and Four steering committee are constituted for education in which larger emphasis has been laid upon Development of Education of SC/ST/Minorities/Girls/and other Disadvantaged Groups, Technical Education, Higher Education, Language Development and Book Promotion, Secondary and Vocational Education, Sports and Physical Education, Adolescents' Development and Sports and Youth Affairs, Basic/Elementary Education and Literacy, Art and Culture. The whole gamut of actions and policy-making under the aegis of Planning Commission is deviating from employment-oriented, participatory and livelihood security-based sustainable education system. No doubt that Government of India has done commendable work in the field of primary and higher education. Despite of some good work over past 50 years by the governing bodies, the literacy rate is dismally low at 61%. The country, which ranks 2nd in the terms of population and is one of the fastest growing economies, ranks disappointing 144th in ranking of countries based on literacy rate. One of the largest countries in the world in terms of population has one of the lowest literacy rates in the world. The country being claimed to emerge as next superpower is lagging far behind in Human Development Index.

"Education is the most critical element in providing employment to people with appropriate skills and knowledge and giving them access to participate in creation and establishment of productive employment activities in the future. The 11th Plan should pay special attention to this area. An ideal we should strive for is that all inhabitants should be able to get as much participation in employment generation activities and education as they are capable of getting, irrespective of their socio-economic, ethical, religious and psychological profile."

2.1 Dropouts and Participation Policy

One of the main reasons for low mental and personality grooming despite constant thrust from government is inability to track a student's progress and to keep them concerned with all round priority over hunger and life. If there is a consolidated place where all the student information is available then it becomes easier to analyze the performance of various initiatives taken by Ministry of HRD. This may help in monitoring student's participation in all the activities which in one or other way will help them to grow mentally and physically.

Some of the major objectives that are important and are in line with Planning Commission's objectives are mentioned below:

1. Education for Poor.
   - (a) Not just enrolment but education on economical security.
   - (b) Sharp reduction in drop-outs through pulling back mechanism.
2. Inclusion of excluded groups—SCs, STs, OBCs, Minorities and Girls on the basis of various levels of participation.

3. Development of national standards and norms for educational and learning levels.
4. Active participation of community in management of schools—move from highly centralized system to a decentralized system and finally resorting to self-sustained system of education and economy.
5. Assisting disadvantaged, destitute and deprived children.
6. Universalization of Secondary Education for the knowledge driven world.
7. Removal of disparities in education and skills.
8. Accountability for delivery of education—public, private and self-established.
9. Merit-*cum*-Means-based loan and scholarship programs through SHG and other similar micro-credit systems.
10. Student data validation for admissions, testing and grading—both domestic and migrating (see Notes about success stories and recommended student data hub).
11. Ensure continuous and growing supply of quality manpower to the services sector and industries.
12. Increase Technical/Vocational Education and Skill Development.
13. Increase adult literacy through continuing education programs.
14. Enlarging the pool of scientific manpower—identify and nurture bright young students to take up higher studies for pursuing scientific research as a career.

2.2 The "Student Data Hub"

The "Student Data Hub" can assist the Planning Commission and various Stakeholders to understand the lifelong education of the entire student population across all sectors past, present and future with a complete longitudinal profile Integrated with all administrative systems, institutions and agencies and leverage this for learning, analysis, planning and administration of the Indian Education System.

3. EDUCATION IS ENSURED THROUGH PARTICIPATION IN ECONOMIC AND LIVELIHOOD EARNING ACTIVITIES

3.1 Sherry Arnstein (1969) Described a Ladder of Participation with Eight Steps

First is Manipulation and second is Non-participative Therapy aims to cure or educate the participants. The proposed plan is best and the job of participation is to achieve public support by public relations. Third and most important step to legitimate participation is information. However, there is needed to lay lesser emphasis on a one way flow of information ignoring any channel for feedback. Fourth is Consultation, i.e. Attitude surveys, neighbourhood meetings and public enquire. Fifth is Placation—Co-option of hand-picked 'worthies' onto committees. Sixth is Partnership in which Power redistributed through negotiation between citizens and power holders. Planning and decision-making responsibilities are shared. Seventh and eighth is Delegated power and Citizen Control. Citizens are holding a clear majority of seats on committees with delegated powers to make decisions. Public now has the power to assure accountability of the program to them. Have nots handle the entire job of planning, policy-making and managing a program.

3.2.1 Initiation and Process

Participation doesn't just happen, it is initiated. Someone then manages a process over time, and allows others involved some control over what happens. The process is described during four phases: Initiation—Preparation—Participation—Continuation.

3.2.2 Control

The initiator is in a strong position to decide how much control for. This decision is equivalent to taking a stand on the ladder—or adopted a stance about the level of participation.

3.2.3 Power and Purpose

Understanding participation involves understanding power: the ability of the different interests to achieve what they want. Power will depend on who has information and money. It will also depend on people's confidence and skills. Many organizations are unwilling to allow people to participate because they fear loss of control. However, there are many situations when working together allows everyone to achieve more than they could on their own. These represent the benefits of participation.

3.2.4 Role of the Facilitators

Facilitators control much of what happens. It is important they constantly think about the part they are playing.

3.2.5 Stakeholders and Community

A stakeholder is anyone who has a stake in what happens. Who will be affected by any project, who controls the information, skills and money needed, who may help and who may hinder? Everyone affected does not have an equal say. Use the ladder to think about who has most influence. The community which participates depends on the project as different people are interested in different issues.

3.2.6 Partnership

Useful when a number of different interests willingly come together formally or informally to achieve some common purpose. The partners don't have to be equal in skills, funds or even confidence, but they do have to trust each other and share some commitment. Building trust and commitment takes time.

3.2.7 Commitment

Commitment is the other side of apathy: committed people want to achieve something, apathetic don't. But what leads to commitment? Not telling people "You ought to care," inviting them to public meetings or bombarding them with glossy leaflets. People care about what they are interested in, and become committed when they feel they can achieve something. Hard selling won't achieve that. If people are apathetic about your proposals, it may simply be that they don't share your interests or concerns.

3.2.8 Ownership of Ideas

People are most likely to be committed to carry something through if they have a stake in the idea, or allow people to say "We thought of that." In practice, that means running brainstorming workshops, helping people think through the practicality of ideas, and negotiating with others a result which is acceptable to as many people as possible. Apathy is directly proportional to the stake people have in ideas and outcomes.

3.2.9 Confidence and Capacity

Putting ideas into practice depends on people's confidence and skills. Many participation processes involve breaking new ground. It is unrealistic to expect individuals or small groups suddenly to develop the capability to make complex decisions and become involved in major projects. They need training or the opportunity to learn formally and informally, to develop confidence, and trust in each other.

3.3 Economic Inequalities Leading to Emergence of Deprived Class

In British economy many people in low and middle income jobs have seen either little or no improvement in their earnings over the last three decades. Ironically, wages have grown by almost 100 percent for rich minority such as Judges, Barristers, and Solicitors, etc., while they fell by 5 percent for truck drivers, packers, and bottlers in the same period (see Notes). Wages grew by over 100 percent for a "rich minority" of judges, barristers and solicitors, while they fell by 5 percent for forklift truck drivers and 3 percent for packers and bottlers in the same period (AFP Report, 2011).

Their participation is forbidden and the rift has been increasing between and within nations, regions and cities, but questions of redistribution have to some extent been displaced by those of recognition, empowerment and diversity in urban and regional inquiry and policy. Such things have happened due to lack of participation. Participation is certainly a necessary condition for moving towards a more egalitarian society, current policies are valuable but limited in terms of the degree of representation and the extent of control. They are part of an affirmative agenda—that is, they tackle symptoms but not causes of destitution. It has been suggested that artificial measures like reservation may only ensure quantitative participation it does not guarantee educational, political, economical and administrative empowerment. Along with a favorable political will, a number of complementary interventions need to be initiated to overhaul protection-based socio-economic structure. This calls for an organized and sustained mass movement to adequately represent masses' interests. The ongoing experiments and experiences suggest that periodic training, orientation and sensitization can help people's representatives perform their assigned functions in a better way. In this regard, they are to be supported by institutions like the Non-Government Organizations (NGOs), Community level associations and organizations and above all the political parties which may politically enlighten the masses especially on the issues like integrated development mechanism.

4. TRANSFORMATION OF SOCIETIES INTO GROUP OF RATIONAL CITIZENS

Social and cultural dimensions have always been important for accomplishment of long-term national goals. Had our freedom fighters not followed Mahatma Gandhi, freedom certainly would not have been restored. Similarly, transformation of social groups into open-minded, rational, educated and development-oriented groups can do miracles in livelihood security and development. Perhaps this is the reason behind numerous failures encountered when development is given an exclusively techno-economic orientation, provide the basis for a new search to give meaning to hitherto neglect socio-cultural norms. This search is all the more relevant in this era of globalization that set into momentum the tendency to homogenize social and cultural specificity. The sustainability of any society will depend in large measure on the degree of diversity and self-reliance that it is able to maintain with regard to reproducing its social and cultural concomitants. At the core of this are issues pertaining to the food and livelihood security of its people. Society may address this issue through comprehensive approach of participation and dialogue.

Participation is the only key to open the plethora of opportunities for the self-sustainable development and management system. The mix of technology and participatory tool brings forth revolutionary changes in the socio-economic and security aspects of the masses. In the response of this mechanism application of participatory economic activities led education which is self-sustained leading to the highest preference to the attendance and maintenance of need-utilization-regeneration records through data hub, as mentioned in the notes, is the need of the hour.

References

The study claims the incomes of lower-paid workers have risen by just 27 percent in real terms over the past 30 years. In contrast, it suggests the top 10 percent of earners are the only group whose incomes have risen in line with gross domestic product since 1978, increasing four times more than the lower-paid group over that period. The report found a "sharp divide" in earnings growth between professions, and warned that the current income squeeze could continue as wages trail behind inflation for years. While medical practitioners saw a 153 percent rise since the late 1970s, bakers' wages fell 1 percent.

Daya Bai, an aspiring nun from Kottayam, transformed into Daya Bai, social activist deep inside the villages of Madhya Pradesh, has already become history. She is staying in Barul village and working with the villagers since 1995. She had tried to empower the villagers to avoid exploitation and also done experiments to revamp the traditional methods of agriculture. "It is a huge task, as most of the villages have switched to soya bean cultivation. They get support from the government and also money-lenders for that. Especially, with a big soya oil mill functioning in the neighboring district. However, I could make some aware that extensive soya cultivation will deplete the life of the soil." Daya Bai tried to bring about the change by community-based primary education. Even though she could get results, with many batches of students coming out with good results, Daya Bai is not all that optimistic about the future. "The community has a very low self-esteem and it is easy for others to misguide them. All the good work done till now could be easily derailed. For example, they do not prefer to use their own language. Their dialect of Bhojpuri is fast being replaced with Hindi." Daya Bai is now attempting to counter this by sharing her experience with a wider world through a book, and her street theatre. And also attempting to move beyond her village.

Currently, Kerala, which is one of the smaller provinces in India, has more than 2,200 Common Service Centres (CSCs) and these centres, set-up through public-private partnerships offer a variety of services in wide spectrum of areas such as agriculture, e-governance, education, and e-payment.

Arun Varma, vice-president, Infrastructure Leasing and Financial Services Limited, said ICT technologies are very important for accelerating economic and social development of developing nations. Countries which use ICT technologies effectively can leap frog and attain economic development and social empowerment in a shorter timeframe than that took developed countries to prosper in the past. Technical Centre for Agricultural and Rural Cooperation (CTA), the ground-breaking initiative, whose theme is "Social and Economic Development using Information and Communications Technologies (ICTs)", is meant to enhance participants' knowledge on how India has harnessed ICT to promote its overall growth. Collaborators for the study visit in India include Infrastructure Leasing and Financial Services Limited (IL and FS), Kerala State IT Mission (KSITM) and SREI-Sahaj Corporate. Taking its advantage in IT skills, India has embarked upon some of the most ambitious plans for welfare and governance. For instance, the National e-Governance Plan (NeGP), which is currently being implemented, aims to set-up more than 100,000 rural tele-centres to deliver government services. The participating countries in the study visit include Burkina Faso, Burundi, Cameroon, Congo, Cote d'Ivoire, Ethiopia, Ghana, Kenya, Niger, Rwanda, Tanzania, Uganda, Zambia and Zimbabwe. CTA (Technical Centre for Agricultural and Rural Cooperation) is an ACP-EU institution established in 1984, based in Wageningen, The Netherlands, working in the field of information for development. CTA develops and provides services to improve access to information for agriculture and rural development and strengthens the capacity of ACP stakeholders to acquire, produce, exchange and utilize information in this area. CTA views ICTs as a major technological intervention for faster growth. Infrastructure Leasing and Financial Services Limited (IL and FS) is one of the largest program management and consultancy institution that focuses on infrastructure development. The company is promoted by large financial institutions like the Life Insurance Corporation of India and HDFC Ltd. IL and FS, has been appointed by the Government of India as the program managers for setting up 100,000 Common Services Centres for the delivery of Government to Citizen (G2C) and Business-To-Customer (B2C) services in rural India. This project is considered to be the largest ICT-driven citizen-centric scheme in the world. IL and FS is implementing the scheme through its Education and Technology Services subsidiary. Till now, the company has facilitated setting up of over 55,000 centres under the Public Private Partnership.

Sahaj e-village Limited is a subsidiary of SREI Finance, mandated to set-up Common Service Centres and bring government and business to rural India, within the Aegis of the National E-Governance Plan. Aimed at bridging the undemocratic urban-rural divide, Sahaj has delved into Infrastructural Development to set-up, operate and manage as many as 30,000 CSCs across India under the Public Private Partnership framework. Already about 27 services G2C and B2C services have been rolled out through these CSCs, including government form submission, agricultural soil testing, e-Learning, electric bill collection, mobile top ups, railway reservation, insurance premium collection, and rural job portal.

Kerala State Information Technology Mission (KSITM) is the nodal agency for developing IT infrastructure in the state of Kerala. KSITM is credited with successfully creating a conducive eco-system for taking Information Technology to the common people. KSITM started the "e-Litaeracy for All" campaign through the Akshaya telecentres. Akshaya centres have grown in strength and have added more services later. There are over 2000 Akshaya Centres in the state today. KSITM is set-up by the Government of Kerala.

Rwanda Telecentre Network (RTN) has decided to take the lead of eliminating the digital gap and promoting digital opportunities in rural Rwanda by creating 1,000 Teleservice centres by the year 2015. This will be possible by implementing a unique business model that RTN is already familiar with and which was successfully implemented by Nyamata Teleservice Centre since 2004 in Eastern province of Rwanda. This model is unique in a sense that more emphasis is put on local content and services rather than infrastructures. The core idea is to enable ICT access point to move from traditional-oriented services to a wide range of online services.

Muralidharan, Karthik (2009): "Public-Private Partnerships for Quality Education in India", Journal entitled 'Public-Private Partnership Model in India: Concepts, Issues and Outlook' January http://www.aarkstore.com/reports/Public-private-Partnership-Model-in-India-Concepts-Issues-and-Outlook- 12634.html

Crul Ruud Barera Paul (2009 and 2010): 'Rwanda to adopt Public-Private Partnership (PPP) model in Telecentre project Day 1'; *Study Tour India*, Monday, 30 November, and Tuesday, 26 January.

Reporter, B.S. (2008): 'PPP model will boost education infra'; Report/ New Delhi, November 26, 0:49 IST.

Kurien, John (2000): 'Factoring Social and Cultural Dimensions into Food and Livelihood Security Issues of Marine Fisheries: A Case Study of Kerala State, India'; Paper provided by Centre for Development

Studies, Trivendrum, India in its series Centre for Development Studies, Trivendrum Working Papers with number 299. Feb.

Sen, Payel Datta Prabhat (2009): 'Women in Urban Local Governance: Empowerment Through Participation'; *Journal of Governance and Public Policy*, Vol. 4, Nos. 3 and 4, pp. 48-61, September and December.

Fleming, Ben (2009): 'Participation Is the Key to Empowerment'; http://www.scn.org/cmp/modules/par-ben.htm

Hiremath, B.K. and Mishra, H.K. (2009): Enahancing Livelihood Security of Tribal Farmers through Agribusiness: Successful Experiences from Gujarat'; Institute of Rural Management, Anand, livelihood_gujarat.pdf

Frankenberger, T.R. and McCaston, M.K. (1998): 'The household livelihood security concept FNA/ANA 22.

Riess, Armin (2005): 'Is the PPP Model Applicable Across Sectors?'; Economic and Financial Studies, EIBEIB Conference on Economics and Finance Luxembourg, 20 January,

Velez, Eduardo (2006): 'Education for Rural People: Compensatory Programme in Rural America'; Meeting of International Working Group on Education (IWGE), Rome, 12-15 June; evelezbustillo@worldbank.org

Development of Food and Livelihood Security Tools for a Pandemic Influenza Preparedness and Response Toolkit; Oct. 2008-Oct. 2009 Under the AI.COMM project, TANGO.

Sudan Food Assistance Transition Study (2007): TANGO in Collaboration with USAID's FANTA Project; Sept. 2007-Nov. 2007.

OXFAM Tajikistan (2007): Sustainable Livelihoods Project Design for Tajikistan, Jan. 2007-Feb. 2007

Anand, Haridas (2010): 'Empowering Villagers through Education'; *The Hindu*: Online edition of India's National Newspaper; Saturday, Feb. 06.

Report (2011): 'Most Wages have Stagnated over Past 30 Years: TUC, AFP, June 07.

CHAPTER

2

Raising Interest in Economics Subject

An Inspiring Activity

AMIT JOSHI

INTRODUCTION

Education is one of the most important Macro-Economic Indicator of Economic Development. It is a process of continuous thinking, reasoning and analyzing. Education is a route to enlightens and tool for empowerment. If carried out effectively, Education can transform our youth into a huge human Capital and make our country one of the most powerful nations of the world. The teachers of the country therefore have a unique opportunity of empowering nearly half of the Indian population that would be of young capable age at a time when most of the people in developed countries would past their productive age. If Education is an important indicator of Human Development then teachers are the tools that will enable the learners to enrich themselves with knowledge. It is going to be the eminence of teachers that will determine the quality of education and empowerment of students in India. The entire educational system of our country is in the process of change. NAAC has recognized the importance of teaching and learning in improving the quality of education. Consistent Innovation and Up-gradation in the delivery of knowledge mechanism is significant in this process. Efficient and good teachers always try to introduce new ideas and techniques and practices in classroom transaction, curricular or co-curricular activities. The National policy on education also recognized that teachers should have freedom to innovate, to devise appreciate methods of communication and activities relevant to the needs of and capabilities of and the concerns of community. After a series of interaction with key industry players, academicians and a bit of introspection some teachers from the college affiliated to Mumbai University felt that there has to be some different way of learning thereby making it and enjoyable experience for the students and this is how the idea of Arthmanthan which has become major economic festival of Mumbai cropped up in 2001.

RATIONALE FOR ARTHMANTHAN

We most of the teachers were from Economics Department and therefore we felt that initially Arthmanthan an Economic festival can encourage innovative practices among students and teachers. Moreover these innovative practices won't be very costly for colleges to undertake and even first generation learners would benefit from these practices. Economic liberalization introduced in the early 1990's has catapulted the Indian Economy to the high growth orbit. High growth rates witnessed in sectors such as financial services and IT brought huge employment opportunities, for the educated youth. Subsequently, sector such as telecom and airlines have witnessed reforms progress quickly resulting in vast business and employment opportunities. In the last two decades, we have seen success stories of new Indian MNCs such as Infosys and Bharat which did not exist in the late 1980's.

At the same time the fact is that there still exist a deep skill gap where on the other hand the corporate sector is desperately seeking out talented youth to fill the ever increasing job positions created from their expanding operations; while on the other hand a large number of university graduates or degree holders still cannot find a job because they do not possess the requisites skills. Most of the times the social and economic status of the students do not allow them to perform their best. The world over, economic professors, lecturers and teachers and practicing economist play a key role in policy-making. Ben Bernanke, the fed chairman and other key administrators in westerns countries are economists and often come form Economics background, however. In India, the subject is often marginalized and sometimes even ignored. And even in Mumbai, India's commercial and financial capital, the role of Economics and Economists is barely recognized. Therefore in order to bring the subject in limelight and make it popular among the students and to increase the scope of the subject beyond merely teaching among the teachers Arthmanthan was introduced. The festival has completed a decade. Arthamanthan has been a platform for Innovative practices for learning subjects of Economics and Management. The purpose of arthmanthan is not only confined to 2 days festival but we expect it to be innovative practices to be continued on regular basis by all the institutions. It is also imperative that the benefits of innovative methods should also reach the economic and socially deprived population.

COST EFFECTIVENESS

The cost effectiveness of Arthmanthan lies in the innovative tools used under arthmanthan that requires minimum cost of operation which an average institution can incur.

Basic Requirement

- LCD Projector.
- Computers with internet connections.
- Basic stationary materials, etc.

It is equally important to note that these requirements should be supplemented by the various new and inspirational ideas from the teachers.

ACTIVITIES UNDER ARTHMANTHAN

In today's era, knowledge is power and to equip the students with that power, Innovative practices in teaching and learning are powerful instruments. It is necessary to make learning an enjoyable experience. I would like to share my personal experience about how innovative practices in education can make teaching and learning joyful and pleasant. I am from Economics stream and therefore would like to share my experience with reference to that subject. The keyword of my presentation will revolve around "Academic festival". In the year 2001, the Economics Department of Acharya Marathe College, Mumbai came with an idea of educating the younger generation through academic festival. We often use to hear students complaining that Economics is boring, dull and very theoretical subject and there is nothing much appealing about it. In order to make the subject live and fruitful, the economics department decided to bring the subject beyond classroom by organizing Economic festival called *Arthmanthan*. We knew that we can create global leaders in Economics only if our young minds are motivated to think the economist way! To start off they must be urged to broaden their horizons and think beyond the classroom! And The Economics Festival was a step towards this...The mission of Arthmanthan was to attract and enhance student's interest in and enthusiasm towards Economics by bringing subject to life.

OBJECTIVES OF ARTHMANTHAN

- Enhance the learning process by introduction of "Action-oriented" learning.
- Promote an active student-centred and student-friendly approach to learning.
- Encourage students to think like global leaders in economics.

- Show that economics can be a fascinating and lively subject dealing with real life problems rather than just abstract theories being currently taught in classrooms.
- Encourage the students to apply economic concepts to real life.

We initially started with a very low profile but students and educationists applauded the festival all over Mumbai. I being a member of the organising committee have seen this festival growing. The contents of the festival were modified every year by addition of innovative even. Over the years, the festival has received wide coverage in the media and has inspired many other colleges to introduce similar festivals. It has in fact become a forum for industry-academia interaction. The festival is today the largest festival of its kind in India! I would like to throw light on the events of this festival, which all the students have started enjoying.

INNOVATIVE TOOLS

The innovative tools were the events which were not only cost effective but they also ensured that learning can be a great fun, provided that they such tools are adopted in the regular teaching and learning mechanism.

(1) Global Leaders Meet

It is an event where the participating teams play the role of economic advisers of the various world countries allotted to them in advance. They analyse the current economic policies of their country and discuss on measures to improve the standard of living of their country. Well, students also had to truly represent the country allotted to them—dressing up like them and speaking a bit of the native language too! The objective is to make students study the economy of various countries in the world.

(2) Business Plan

This event is aimed at saluting the rising spirit of Indian entrepreneurs. Entrepreneurship lies at the heart of a successful economic model. Hence, we need to revive the spirit of entrepreneurship, which existed in India. We encouraged students who have an idea, an interesting business plan, or have the knack of sniffing out business opportunities... to come ahead and present their idea, the business model and the action plan to make their dream a reality. Students were asked to put on their thinking hats and come up with a business.

(3) Budding Economists

Budding Economist' is an attempt to bring out the economist in students! Students analyze and make presentations on various Economic Issues given to them.

(4) Admasters Competition

This is an advertising event in which participating teams are given a product each, for which they prepared and presented a logo, jingle and television advertisement.

(5) Skit Competition

Here various economic issues are given in advance. Student should take up any one of these issues and prepare a skit. The students will be judged on various parameters including presentation of the issue at hand, innovative thinking, acting skills effective use of props, costumes and music.

(6) Quiz-Wiz

For those interested in testing their Economic Quotient there is a Quiz Competition in which questions based on Economists and their contributions, Currencies, International trade and various sectors of the Economy and Financial data and Statistics are asked.

(7) Economics Songs

This event, which was introduced last 4 years ago, was meant for those students who are tired of same old lectures in Economic and wished that economic classes could be as interesting as their favorite songs. The objective was to make Economics more fun. Under this event students prepare their own Economic songs. This year the songs on global financial crisis, inflation, promises made by the Finance minister, critical evaluation of fiscal and monetary policy were harmonic by the students. The idea was very innovative and it became one of the most popular events of the festival as told to us by the organizers. Some songs were truly original while some of them were inspired from some interesting songs posted at You Tube. Some of the Economic songs will be shown in presentation.

Apart from these events there was debating, elocution, Poster, Cartoon and Essay Competitions on various Economic themes and issues, thematic speeches from various Economist in industry and academics. So in one or the other way Arthmanthan has made learning Economics a very pleasant experience. Today the festival has started cropping up and the outcomes are really very positive. Most of the Colleges have started similar kind of festivals. The organizers are fully convicted about the value the festival is adding to the knowledge of the students. The success of this festival is its student-friendly and student-centric approach. The report of this festival was also presented at an International Conference on Education at Cambridge, U.K.

SIGNIFICANCE OF THIS FESTIVAL

The festival has been very significant with the theme of the Conference. In India we see big Institutions and Business schools on in the big towns and cities. Some of the good institutions do really frame their curriculum with respect to teaching and learning to cater the needs of the industry. But it is difficult for the socially and economically deprieved section of the society to meet the educational expenses. The tool used in these festivals requires minimum operation cost which can be beared by any average institutions across the country. As far as our Mumbai experience is concerned around 10 colleges have already started similar kind of festival. The Researcher strongly feels that there is a need to develop an interlinkage model among such institutions where a group of institutions can take initiatives to promote innovative activities and educate other institutions in the remote area institutions of the state.

References

Yadav, S., Innovation in Teachers' Education, *University News*, Association of Indian Universities, Vol. 48, No. 40, Oct. 04-10.

NCERT (2006), National Focus Group on Teachers' Education for Curriculum Renewal, *NCERT*, New Delhi.

Kurhade, M.S., February 2007, "In Search of Touchstone", *Sanskar Sarjan Education Society*, Mumbai.

Pathan, S.N., 2005, "Quality Improvement Programme in Higher Education through NAAC : A Success Story of Maharashtra", *Intellectual Book Bureau*, Bhopal.

Madhukar, I. (2007), "Changing Contexts of Higher Education", Authors Press, New Delhi.

Kamat, A. (1968), "Two Studies in Education", Asia Publishing House, Bombay.

http://www.arth-manthan.org

CHAPTER

3

Micro Finance

A Tool for Poverty Alleviation and Women Empowerment

P.A.L.N.S. KALYANI

"Micro credit is about much more than access to money. It is about women gaining control over the means to make a living. It is about women lifting themselves out of poverty and vulnerability. It is about women achieving economic and political empowerment within their homes, their villages, their countries."

ABSTRACT

Micro finance aims at providing the rural and urban poor, especially women, with savings, credit and insurance and aims to improve household income security. The micro finance programmes undertaken by NGOs do provide access to credit for the poor, enable them to undertake income generation programmes, and contribute to higher recovery rates.

Responsibilities such as development of economic infrastructure and providing bank finance to micro finance groups must be undertaken by the Government, as only micro finance programmes cannot alleviate poverty. Self-help group (SHG) is a self-governed peer controlled small informal association of the poor, usually from socio-economically homogenous families, who are organized around savings and credit activities.
Key words: Feminist empowerment paradigm, financial self-sustainability paradigm, Poverty alleviation paradigm

INTRODUCTION

India falls under low income class according to World Bank. It is second populated country in the world and around 70% of its population lives in rural area. 60% of people depend on agriculture, as a result there is chronic underemployment and per capita income is only $ 3262. This is not enough to provide food to more than one individual. The obvious result is abject poverty, low rate of education, low sex ratio, and exploitation. The major factor account for high incidence of rural poverty is the low asset base. According to Reserve Bank of India, about 51% of people house possess only 10% of the total asset of India. This has resulted low production capacity both in agriculture (which contribute around 22-25% of GDP) and Manufacturing sector. Rural people have very low access to institutionalized credit (from commercial bank).

Poverty is the lack of basic human needs, such as clean water, nutrition, health care, education, clothing and shelter, because of the inability to afford them. Poverty is widespread in India, with the nation estimated to have a third of the world's poor. World Bank estimates, 80% of India's population lives on less than $ 2 a day. According to a 2005 World Bank estimate, 41% of India falls below the international poverty line of US $ 1.25 a day; having reduced from 60% in 1981.

Poverty reduction has historically been a result of economic growth as increased levels of production, such as modern industrial technology, made more wealth available for those who were otherwise too poor to afford them. Today, economic liberalization includes extending property rights, especially to land, to the poor, and making financial services, notably savings, accessible. Inefficient institutions, corruption and political instability can also discourage investment. Aid and government support in health, education and infrastructure helps growth by increasing human and physical capital.

Since independence, various governments in India have experimented with a large number of grant and subsidy-based poverty alleviation programmes. These programmes were based on grant/subsidy and the credit linkage was through commercial banks only. As a result, these programmes became unsustainable, perpetuated a dependant status on the beneficiaries and depended ultimately on the government employees for delivery. This not only led to misuse of both credit and subsidy but banks never looked at it as a profitable and commercial activity as well.

Hence was adopted the concept of micro credit in India. Success stories in neighboring countries, like Grameen Bank in Bangladesh, Bank Rakiat in Indonesia, Commercial and Industrial Bank in Philippines, etc., gave further boost to the concept in India in the 1980s. India thus adopted the similar model of extending credit to the poorest sector and took a number of steps to promote micro financing in the country.

Micro finance is the provision of financial services to low-income clients or solidarity lending groups including consumers and the self-employed, who traditionally lack access to banking and related services.

More broadly, it is a movement whose object is "a world in which as many poor and near-poor households as possible have permanent access to an appropriate range of high quality financial services, including not just credit but also savings, insurance, and fund transfers." Those who promote micro finance generally believe that such access will help poor people out of poverty.

Micro finance is a broad category of services, which include microcredit. Microcredit can be defined as the provision of credit services to poor clients.

Micro finance programmes not only give women and men access to savings and credit, but reach millions of people worldwide bringing them together regularly in organized groups. Although no 'magic bullet', they are potentially a very significant contribution to gender equality and women empowerment, as well as pro-poor development and civil society strengthening. Through their contribution to women ability to earn an income these programmes have potential to initiate a series of 'virtuous spirals' of economic empowerment, increased well-being for women and their families and wider social and political empowerment. Micro finance services and groups involving men also have potential to question and significantly change men's attitudes and behaviors as an essential component of achieving gender equality.

There is evidence of significant potential for micro finance to enable women to challenge and change gender inequalities at all levels if there is a strategic gender focus. There have also been many important recent innovations in products and services to enable women to better benefit. Nevertheless benefits cannot be assumed and even financially sustainable micro finance if it is gender blind may seriously disempowered women and increase inequality. It is clear that most micro finance programmes have a long way to go before they make their full potential contribution to gender equality and empowerment. Many of the strategies promoted for financial sustainability may exacerbate the negative impacts of debt, because of over rapid expansion, rigid product design inappropriate to women's economic activities, cutting of necessary support services

Women are not a minority, but the 'marginalized majority'. This is not only a women's human right, but necessary for any serious agenda for poverty reduction, economic growth and civil society strengthening.

NEED FOR THE STUDY

Micro finance is hailed by many as an important tool for poverty alleviation. The potential for reaching and assisting low-income households in meeting their basic financial needs, for protecting against risks, and for developing social and economic empowerment on a sustainable basis have precipitated donor funding into micro finance in the late 90's causing the sector to rapidly expand.

Most institutions providing financial services to the poor operate under a corporate mission who includes poverty reduction, and donors have allocated increasing amounts of funding to micro finance on this basis. Micro finance programmes have burgeoned in many developing countries as part of their efforts to reduce poverty. The portion of poor clients served by micro finance institutions has been rapidly growing at a rate of 25 to 30 percent annually over the past five years. It is estimated that tens of millions of low-income people now have access to financial services.

The need of micro finance arises because the rural India requires sources of finance for poverty alleviation, procurement of agricultural and farms input.

- Micro finance is a programme to support the poor rural people to pay its debt and maintain social and economic status in the villages.
- India is agriculture based economy so micro finance may be a tool to empower the farmers and rural peoples to make agriculture profitable.

The research study is highlighting a picture rural India as a profitable segment for micro finance institutions.

IMPORTANCE OF THE STUDY

India's GDP ranks among the top 15 economies of the world. However, around 300 million people or about 80 million households are living below the poverty line, i.e. less than $2 per day according to the World Bank and the poorest are which earns $1 per day. It is further estimated that of these households, only about 20% have access to credit from the formal sector. Out of these 80 million house hold, 80% takes credit from the informal sources i.e. local Zamidars, Chit Funds, etc. With about 80 million households below MFIs include non- governmental organizations (NGOs), credit unions, non-bank financial intermediaries, and even a few commercial banks. The present study aims at offer suggestions to Government, Banking and Non-Banking Financial Organizations, Non Governmental organizations, Policy-makers, Rural poor, Unemployed, self employed and Women in particular to throw some insights about Problems in the possession of Micro Credit and various models for poverty alleviation and women empowerment.

The study attempts to answer the following question:

- How Micro Finance is used as a tool for poverty alleviation and Women Empowerment?

OBJECTIVES

- To study the importance and role of micro finance in poverty alleviation and Women empowerment.

NEED FOR WOMEN EMPOWERMENT

Empowerment is now increasingly seen as a process by which the one's without power gain greater control over their lives. This means control over material assets, intellectual resources and ideology. It involves power to, power with and power within. Some define empowerment as a process of awareness and concretization, of capacity building leading to greater participation, effective decision-making power and control leading to transformative action. This involves ability to get what one wants and to influence others on our concerns. With reference to women the power relation that has to be involved includes their lives at multiple levels, family, community, market and the state. Importantly it involves at the psychological level women's ability to assert themselves and this is constructed by the 'gender roles' assigned to her specially in a cultural which resists change like India.

Empowerment of women is a commitment for PACS and some others strategic programmes, while developing strategies for empowering women some programmes are sensitive to recognizing women's contribution and their knowledge as the first step. The appreciate that women require principally social support to fight their sense of inadequacy and fears to enhance their self-respect and dignity. Empowering women means control over their bodies and becoming economically independent, controlling resources like land and property and reduction of burden of work. A society or programme which aims at women's empowerment needs to create and strengthen sisterhood and to promote overall nurturing, caring and gentleness. PACS emphasis on emphasis on women SHG's as a collective is one such efforts.

WOMEN EMPOWERMENT THROUGH SELF-HELP GROUPS

PACS programme has largely utilized SHG's as an empowering instrument. More than 80% of these are exclusively for women. The fifth national synthesis report (Draft) reports that official perception has changed as SHG's are firmly raising voices and SHG's are being used to achieve RTI awareness:

- Women members are elected as PRI representatives.
- SHG/PRIs are regularly organising Gram Sabha as a forum for public appraisal.

Anecdotal accounts suggest that women are economically empowered those suffering. Domestic violence is given legal reference and awareness to prevent child marriage promotes girls education and prevent dowry marriage and alcoholism.

Self-help groups have emerges as an important strategy for empowering women and alleviating poverty. SHG's are based on idea of dialogic small groups, which shall function at developing collective consciousness. Linked with micro credit these groups are able to access credit and subsidy to meet crisis needs as well as developmental needs reducing their dependence on moneylenders. There is fair amount of evidence to suggest that PACS SHG's have successfully ensured people's entitlements including women. Statistically PAC's initiatives in realizing entitlements show that—In Balika Samriddhi Yojana 189 females have been benefitted realizing 2572400 Rs. in Employment Guarantee Scheme 55397 women have been provided, 1271 girls enrolled and 9524 women provided Indira Awas Yojna. Kanya Vidya Dhan has been availed by 131 girls while Mahila Samridhi Yojana has benefited 7 women. Maternity benefits have reached 2943 women and NFE educated 862 women. Old age pension went to 7774 women while no woman benefited from the Pradhan Mantri Awas

Yojna. Sam Vikas Yojna benefitted 975 women compared to 467 men Bridge courses benefitted 740 girls. Widow pension was ensured to 2948 women and 217 women get yellow cards.

ROLE OF MICRO FINANCE IN POVERTY ALLEVIATION AND WOMEN EMPOWERMENT

There are a range of contrasting views on the relationship between micro finance and Empowerment. These views are captured in three key 'paradigms:

- Feminist empowerment paradigm
- Financial self-sustainability paradigm
- Poverty alleviation paradigm

Each paradigm has its own interpretation of concepts like 'sustainability' and 'participation' as well as it own priorities in micro finance delivery, complementary services and organizational structure. These different interpretations and priorities create underlying tension between supporters of the different paradigms, leading to obvious implications for the acceptance and adoption of empowerment approaches in MFIs.

The feminist empowerment paradigm is firmly rooted in the development of some of the earliest micro finance programs in the South, including the Self-Employed Women's Association (SEWA) in India. Its underlying concerns are gender equality and women's human rights. Micro finance is promoted as an entry point in the context of a wider strategy for women's economic and socio-political empowerment that focuses on gender awareness and feminist organization. Under this paradigm, micro finance must be:

- Part of a sectoral strategy for change that identifies opportunities, constraints and bottlenecks within industries which, if addressed, can raise returns and prospects for large numbers of women. Possible strategies include linking women to existing services and infrastructure, developing new technology such as labor-saving food processing, building information networks, shifting to new markets, and policy level changes to overcome legislative barriers and unionization.

- Based on participatory principles to build up incremental knowledge of industries and enable women to develop their strategies for change.

Many organizations go further than interventions at the industry level to include gender specific strategies for social and political empowerment. Some programs have developed very effective means for integrating gender awareness into programs and for organizing women and men to challenge and change gender discrimination. Some also have legal rights support for women and engage in gender advocacy. These interventions to increase social and political empowerment are seen as essential prerequisites for economic empowerment. Economic empowerment itself is defined in more than individualist terms to include issues such as property rights, changes intrahousehold relations and transformation of the macro-economic context.

The financial self-sustainability paradigm (often referred to as the financial systems approach or sustainability approach) has very different views on many of these issues. Its definitions of empowerment are in essentially individualist terms with the ultimate aim being the expansion of individual choice or capacity for self-reliance. The paradigm assumes that increasing women's access to micro finance services will in itself lead to individual economic empowerment through enabling women's decisions about savings and credit use, enabling women to set-up micro-enterprises, and increasing incomes under their control. It is then assumed that this increased economic empowerment will lead to increased well-being of women and also to social and political empowerment.

The ultimate aim of this paradigm is large programs that are profitable and fully self-supporting in competition with other private sector banking institutions and able to raise funds from international financial markets rather than relying on funds from development agencies. The main target group, despite claims to reach the poorest, is the 'bankable poor': small entrepreneurs and farmers.

Policy discussions have focused particularly on setting of

interest rates to cover costs, separation of micro finance from other interventions to enable separate accounting and program expansion to increase outreach and economies of scale, reduction of transaction costs and ways of using groups to decrease costs of delivery. Recent guidelines for CGAP funding and best practice focus on production of a 'financial sustainability index' that charts progress of programs in covering costs from incomes.

This emphasis on financial sustainability is seen as necessary to create institutions that reach significant numbers of poor people in the context of declining aid budgets and opposition to welfare and redistribution in macro-economic policy.

Within this paradigm, gender lobbies have been able to argue for targeting women on the grounds of high female repayment rates and the need to stimulate women's economic activity as a hitherto underutilized resource for economic growth. They have had some success in ensuring that considerations of female targeting are integrated into conditions of micro finance delivery and program evaluation. Alongside this focus on women, the term 'empowerment' is frequently used in promotional literature.

The poverty alleviation paradigm also differs in many of its interpretations and understandings of empowerment in micro finance. Poverty alleviation under this paradigm is defined in broader terms than market incomes to encompass increasing capacities and choices and decreasing the vulnerability of poor people. The main focus of programs as a whole is on developing sustainable livelihoods, community development and social service provisions like literacy, healthcare and infrastructure development. There is not only a concern with reaching the poor, but also the poorest.

Policy debates have focused particularly on the importance of small savings and loan provisions for consumption as well as production, group formation and the possible justification for some level of subsidy for programs working with particular client groups or in particular contexts. Some programs have developed effective methodologies for poverty targeting and/or operating in remote areas.

Gender lobbies have argued for targeting women because

of higher levels of female poverty and women's responsibility for household well-being. However, although gender inequality is recognized as an issue, the focus is on assistance to households and there is a tendency to see gender issues as cultural and hence not subject to outside intervention. Although the term 'empowerment' is frequently used in general terms, often synonymous with a multi-dimensional definition of poverty alleviation, the term 'women's empowerment ' is often considered best avoided as being too controversial and political. Poverty alleviation and women's empowerment are seen as inherently synergistic. The assumption is that increasing women's access to micro finance will enable women to make a greater contribution to household income and thus, together with other interventions to increase household well-being, will translate into improved well-being for women and enable women to bring about wider changes in gender inequality.

One of the reasons why gender issues, particularly women's empowerment, frequently become marginalized in micro finance institutions is because of perceived conflicts between women's empowerment and the development aims of the financial self-sustainability and household level poverty alleviation paradigms. In the financial self-sustainability paradigm, women's empowerment strategies are seen as entailing unacceptable costs as the paradigm's explicit aim is to develop fully financially self-sufficient MFIs. In the poverty alleviation paradigm, women's empowerment is seen as an external imposition by Western-influenced middle-class feminist elite with little relevance to the needs of poor women. It is also seen as politically sensitive and involving conflicts within households and communities that may undermine organizational sustainability.

CONCLUSION

Micro finance programmes has sustainable impact on the empowerment of women. SHGs, where a majority of groups are linked with the help of NGOs that provide support in financial services and specialized training, have a greater ability to make a positive impact on women empowerment. If women empowerment is to be pursued as a serious objective. by SHG programmes in particular and the larger micro finance community in general, greater emphasis needs to be placed on training, education and creating awareness in order to achieve a larger and more lasting empowerment.

References

D. Nagayya, and D. Koteswara, Rao (2009), Micro Finance and Support organistions in the Southern states of India, *Journal of Rural Development*, Vl. 28, No. 3.

Daley-Harris, Sam (2002), Pathways Out of Poverty: Innovations in Micro finance for the Poorest Families; "Improving the Social and Empowerment Impact of Micro Finance", pp. 264-5, 2002, Bloomfield, CT: Kumarian Press.

Daley-Harris, Sam (2002), Pathways Out of Poverty: Innovations in Micro finance for the Poorest Families; "Micro finance Impacts Directly and Significantly on Economic Poverty" p. 22, 2002, Bloomfield, CT: Kumarian Press.

EBFB (2004), Why focus on environmental SMEs?" www.ifc.org (accessed 4 September, 2004.

Financial Sector of the World Bank Group (2002), "Rural and Micro finance SMEs", www.worldbank.org (accessed 4 September, 2004).

H.S. Shylendra, Samapati Guha and Veerasekhara (2010), The role of SHGs on MFI Intermediaries—A study of Sabarkantha District of Gujarat, *Journal of Rural Development*, Vol. 29, No. 4, Satya Sundaram (2007), Micro finance in India.

International Finance Corporation (2004), Sustainable Financial Markets Facility, www.ifc.org (accessed 4 September, 2004)

J. Fedrick (2010), Rle of Micro Finance in Poverty Alleviation—An empirical Analysis, *Indian Economic Panorama*, Vol. 20, No. 3.

K. Srinivasa Rao (2008), Micro Finance—A tool for Poverty Alleviation and Women Empowerment, *The Management Accountant*, Vol. 43, No. 2.

K. Raji Reddy, H. Sateesh (2008), Micro Finance in Rural India, *Business Vision*, Vol. 4, No. 3.

K.G. Karmakar (2008), Micro Finance in India.

K.K. Tripathy and Sudhir K. Jain (2010), Micro finance and rural Self employment through Self Help Groups: A Study of select districts in Orissa and Haryana, *Journal of Rural Development*, Vol. 29, No. 2.

K.R. Lakshmy Devi and Uma, P., (2010), Development Programme and Women's Empowerment; Kerala Experience, *Journal of Rural Development*, Vol. 29, No. 3.

N. Srinivasan (2009), Micro Finance in India : State of the Sector Report 2009.

R.K. Maheswari and Ekta Rastogi (2010), Critical Appraisal of Micro Finance in India (Special Reference to UP), *The Management Accountant*, Vol. 45, No. 1.

Robinson, Marguerite S. (2002), "The Micro Finance Revolution: Sustainable Finance for the Poor".

Rubinstein, Joel (1993), Micocredit : A Poverty Eradication Strategy that Works", www.action.org/microjoel.html (accessed 4 September, 2004).

Subramanian (2010), Empowerment of Women through Self-Help Groups in Tirunelveli Dist., T.N.—A Swot Analysis, *Prabhandhan, Indian Journal of Management*, Vol. 3, No. 3.

Sam Daley Haris (2002), Pathways out of poverty: Innovations in Micro Finance for Poorest Families, Kumarian Press, Inc.

Sangram Panigrahi (2010), Self-Help Groups-Bank Linkage Programmes: Focusing on the Inclusion of Financially Excluded People, *Indian Journal of Finance*, Vol. 4, No. 10.

V. Gopalan (2011), MFIs, Why the Hurly Barly?, *The Management Accountant*, Vol. 46, No. 1.

Yunus, Muhammad (1994), Extracts from the keynote address delivered at 85th Rotary International Convention help in Taipei, Taiwan, on June 12, 1994.

Yunus, Muhammad (1994), Grameen Bank, "Major Uses of Loan Funds", Bangladesh (1994).

CHAPTER

Literacy and Fertility in Uttar Pradesh

A Statistical Analysis

Asha A. Jindal and N.N. Pandey

ABSTRACT

This paper examines the relationship between female literacy rate and mean number of births per ever married woman at district level for Uttar Pradesh using Census 2001 data. This paper also attempts to examine the possible impact of the educational attainment of female on their fertility behavior in Uttar Pradesh.

INTRODUCTION

Female literacy is becoming important as mothers play a central role in supporting children's education. Literate and educated mothers not only push their children to go to school, but are also able to help them with their school work when they do go to school. Therefore, it is argued, literate mothers are a strong weapon in the fight against illiteracy. Secondly, women have economic potential just as men do. If women remain illiterate, some of that economic potential is lost (as it is for men). Therefore, for a people or a nation to achieve development ideals, it is necessary that their female population be educated as well. Third point is that educated women tend to have fewer children than illiterate women.

Socio-economic development particularly education plays a key role in reducing fertility and mortality. But in recent years, question is that at what extents the socio-economic development linked with fertility in Indian context or is there over time attributed to some other factors. Some Study shows determinants of fertility are female literacy rate, urbanization, per capita income, regional variation and female work participation, etc. Numerous explanations are given to reduce fertility. It is suggested that literacy will lead to delay in marriageable age. This leads to better understanding of contraceptive use which in turn reduces fertility.

DATA AND ANALYSIS

The population census of India, conducted every ten years, is the most comprehensive source of information on the size, distribution, living conditions and demographic characteristics of the population. For estimation of Female Literacy Rate and Mean Number of Births per ever married woman at district level, Census 2001 is used. Besides this, for estimation of Age-Specific Fertility Rate (ASFR), Total Fertility Rate (TFR), General Fertility Rate (GFR), Census 2001 data is used. With regard to educational level of women, they have been classified into 7 groups, namely, Illiterate, Literate, Literate but below primary, Primary but below middle, Middle but below matric or secondary, Matric or secondary but below graduate, Graduate and above in respect of total, rural and urban. The scope of the study is limited to 2001 census data as only provisional total are declared for 2011 census data.

Female literacy rate and mean number of births per ever married women are inversely linearly related. The correlation coefficient between two rates is -0.419 which is significant as per Table 1.

TABLE I
Correlations

		FLR_2001	*MNB*
FLR_2001	Pearson Correlation	1	-.419**
	Sig. (2-tailed)		.000
	N	70	70
MNB	Pearson Correlation	-.419**	1
	Sig. (2-tailed)	.000	
	N	70	70

**Correlation is significant at the 0.01 level (2-tailed).

Table 2 presents the data on age-specific fertility by literacy status of females in the Uttar Pradesh. The general fertility rate is 112 for illiterate women and 71 for literate women. The difference between these two groups is 41 points whereas this difference is 33 points in rural area and 37 points in urban area. However, GFR is high for women with educational attainment of Graduate and above as well as ASFR is also high for age group of 25-29 which is natural phenomena.

As for age specific fertility rates, literate woman in all age groups have low fertility then their illiterate sisters and this ASFR decreases as educational attainment of female increases in total, rural and urban areas of Uttar Pradesh.

CONCLUSION

Literacy is inversely linearly related to fertility levels of woman in Uttar Pradesh. Government programmes aimed at reducing fertility through the provision of services in respect of family planning methods which would not be of much help as long as female literacy rate is low. Therefore, every effort must be made to promote literacy among females. But these efforts

TABLE 2

Age-Specific Fertility Rate by Literacy of Women in Uttar Pradesh

Age-Specific Fertility Rate for Total

Age Group	*Illiterate*	*Literate*	*Literate but below primary*	*Primary but below middle*	*Middle but below matric or secondary*	*Matric or secondary but below graduate*	*Graduate and above*
(1)	*(2)*	*(3)*	*(4)*	*(5)*	*(6)*	*(7)*	*(8)*
15-19	0.035	0.012	0.013	0.016	0.012	0.007	0.000
20-24	0.167	0.120	0.156	0.157	0.149	0.092	0.055
25-29	0.176	0.141	0.170	0.159	0.151	0.128	0.101
30-34	0.144	0.098	0.132	0.110	0.096	0.079	0.068
35-39	0.100	0.056	0.085	0.064	0.052	0.039	0.031
40-44	0.065	0.034	0.053	0.040	0.030	0.022	0.013
45-49	0.047	0.031	0.040	0.034	0.030	0.022	0.012
GFR	112	71	86	82	72	54	59
Total Fertility Rate	3.672586	2.461435	3.246384	2.901253	2.594811	1.942547	1.406095

(Contd.)

TABLE 2 (*Contd.*)

Age-Specific Fertility Rate for Rural

Age Group	*Illiterate*	*Literate*	*Literate but below primary*	*Primary but below middle*	*Middle but below matric or secondary*	*Matric or secondary but below graduate*	*Graduate and above*
(1)	(2)	(3)	(4)	(5)	(6)	(7)	(8)
15-19	0.037	0.015	0.014	0.018	0.014	0.010	0.000
20-24	0.171	0.144	0.166	0.165	0.159	0.115	0.084
25-29	0.180	0.159	0.178	0.167	0.160	0.143	0.128
30-34	0.149	0.113	0.140	0.117	0.105	0.093	0.085
35-39	0.105	0.070	0.092	0.071	0.060	0.052	0.043
40-44	0.069	0.044	0.058	0.044	0.035	0.030	0.023
45-49	0.049	0.038	0.042	0.037	0.033	0.027	0.020
GFR	116	83	91	88	80	68	86
Total Fertility Rate	3.796246	2.910359	3.454236	3.086635	2.830271	2.352858	1.917505

Age-Specific Fertility Rate for Urban

Age Group	*Illiterate*	*Literate*	*Literate but below primary*	*Primary but below middle*	*Middle but below matric or secondary*	*Matric or secondary but below graduate*	*Graduate and above*
(1)	*(2)*	*(3)*	*(4)*	*(5)*	*(6)*	*(7)*	*(8)*
15-19	0.020	0.005	0.007	0.010	0.006	0.003	0.000
20-24	0.135	0.075	0.115	0.122	0.112	0.062	0.043
25-29	0.150	0.110	0.138	0.132	0.121	0.107	0.092
30-34	0.117	0.073	0.106	0.088	0.073	0.064	0.064
35-39	0.076	0.038	0.065	0.048	0.039	0.031	0.028
40-44	0.046	0.021	0.039	0.029	0.023	0.017	0.012
45-49	0.037	0.023	0.034	0.028	0.026	0.020	0.011
GFR	86	49	66	61	51	39	51
Total Fertility Rate	2:907007	1.725746	2.521085	2.285566	2.00305	1.520777	1.252489

are not very encouraging despite the fact that a constitutional obligation exists for enrolment of all the children up to age of 14 years in primary and middle schools but good proportion of children are still outside. Hence it is important to make all possible efforts to promote literacy among girls without much delay.

REFERENCES

Alka Saxena, Socialisation of Women education, Rajat Publication, New Delhi, 2002, pp. 267-312.

Anuradha Sharma, Status of Female Literacy in Punjab: Facts and Views, *Indian Journal of Education*, No. 38, July-September 2007, pp. 26-33.

Andrew, F. Sigel, Practical Business Statistics, fourth edition, Irwin, McGraw-Hill, 2000, pp. 468-542.

Asha Jindal, Low Birth Weight Among Babies and Factors Related to it: A Statistical Analysis, *Entire Research-National Journal*, Issue II, Vol. III, Oct. 2010.

Asha Jindal, Female Literacy : A Success Story of Maharashtra, *Variorum-Multidisciplinary e-Journal*, Vol. II, 2010.

Ashok Kumar, Declining Sex Ratio in India, Women in Contemporary Indian Society, Volume I, 1993, pp. 33-45.

C.P. Yadav and Arun Kumar, Female Students in India, Women in Contemporary Indian Society, Volume I, 1993, pp. 144-52.

Damodar Gujarathi, Sangetha, Basic Econometrics, McGraw Hill Companies, Fourth edition, 2010, pp. 1-517.

Darren George and Paul Mallery: SPSS for Windows, Dorling Kindersley Pvt. Ltd., Licensees of Pearson Education in South Asia, 2009.

Divya Rao, Gendered Inequality in Educational Transitions, *Economic and Political Weekly*.

en.wikipedia.org/wiki/Literacy_in_India

Harish, Factors Influencing Female Participation, Women in Contemporary Indian Society, Volume I, 1993, pp. 242-75.

H.P. Joshi, Educational Infrastructure for Women, Women in Contemporary Indian Society, Volume I, 1993, pp. 127-43.

http://www.censusindia.gov.in/2011-prov-results/prov_data_products_up.html

M.V. Vaithilingam, K. Praveen Kumar and D.N. Vidhate, Impact of Female Literacy on Vital Rates Among Indian States and Union Territories, *Indian Journal of Population Education*, July-September 2007, pp. 51-60.

Mc Clamroch Kristi (1996): Total Fertility Rate, Women Education and Women's Work; What are the Relationships?; *Population and Environment*; 18(2); NewYork, USA, pp. 172-86.

Michael S. Lewis Beck, Regression Analysis, International Handbooks of Quantitative Applications in the Social Sciences, Volume 2, Sage Publication, 1993.

N. Sreekumaran Nair, P. Raman Kutty, Das Acharya, Shalini Chandrasekhar and R.S. Phaeendra Rao, Female Literacy as a determinant of socio-demographic status and infant survival, *Health and Population—Perspectives and Issues*, 18(4); 1995, pp. 190-202.

CHAPTER

5

Levels of Educational Development

A Case Study of Changing Scenario

NAHEEN HAIDER ZAIDI AND MOHAMMAD AWAIS

INTRODUCTION

The foundation of every state is the education of its youth
—Diogenes Laertius

The concept of education is like a diamond which appears to be of a different colour when seen from a different angle. The word development reflects positive change. The term development is the state of change from a given situation of a region to become a better one within the given period of time. Education is perhaps the most vital requirement for the inclusive growth, empowering individual and society, opening up opportunities and promoting true public participation in the development process. It is an important factor that fuels both social change and economic growth.

India has the second largest education system in the world after China. In the context of globalization, education assumes greater meaning. Greatness of a nation should not be measured by its ranking in global economic order, but by its ability to provide quality education. The last two decades have shown enormous improvement in the literacy scene country as reflected by the average literacy figures. The scenario of educational progress in India began to change rapidly due to the new thrusts given by the government's New Policy of Education (1986) and the Programme of Action (1992), which aimed at improving learning achievements for all children between 6-14 years of age. A host of major initiatives by the government, and the mobilization of external resources for primary education, had a deep impact on the status of primary education in India.

According to census 2001, the average literacy rate of India accounted for 64.8 percent. While the literacy rate of Uttar Pradesh in 1991 was registered as 40.71 percent and 57.56 percent in 2001. The literacy rate in Bijnor district was registered as 40.55 percent in 1991 which increased to 59.37 percent in 2001. Against this backdrop, this study has been undertaken with following objectives:

OBJECTIVES

1. To examine the spatial distribution of educational facilities in the district.
2. To present a detailed account of changing scenario of student enrolled in educational levels.
3. To analyze the changing figure of teacher-student ratio.
4. To review the schemes running by Government to promote education status.

METHODOLOGY

The study is confined within the Bijnor district and is based on secondary source of data. The district Bijnor is comprised of 11 development blocks. The data and information were collected from Sankhiyiki Patrika of Bijnor district 1991 and 2001. For the assessment of changing scenario data were converted into weighted value of indicators such as:

1. Number of students per 1000 of population.
2. Number of schools per 1000 of students.
3. Number of teachers per 1000 of students.

Data were analyzed by using simple percentages and averages.

RESULTS AND DISCUSSION

1. Number of Students per 1000 of Population

It is indicated from the Table 1 that in the category of class I to V, the highest ratio of student per 1000 population is registered in Kiratpur block, i.e. 276 followed by Nehtaur 267 and Seohara 265.08. The above figures are higher than the district ratio of 230 in 2001. The blocks which scored the lowest ratio in the district are Najibabad, i.e. 205.62 followed by Jalilpur 213.57 and Kotwali 207.54. As the Table 1 reveals data of 1991 and 2001, some blocks registered under poor student ratio and some have remarkable growth in student enrolment in the primary schools.

In the category of class VI to VIII, above table shows the fact that the average ratio of district was 117 in 2001 while 62.98 in 1991. The highest ratio of student per 1000 population was registered in block Seohara, i.e. 175.27. The comparison of data 2001 with 1991 reveals that in each block number of students augmented in senior basic schools.

From the Table 1 data of class IX to XII point outs that on average 39 students got admitted per 1000 population in the district which shows the enrolment in this category is very low. The highest ratio was registered in block Dhampur 27.84 in 1991 and 59.78 in Seohara in 2001. Comparison shows ratio grew drastically.

2. Number of Schools per 1000 of Students

Table 2 examines the number of schools per thousand

TABLE I

Number of Students per 1000 of Population (1991-2001)

Sl. No.	*Blocks*	*Class I to V*		*Class VI to VIII*		*Class IX to XII*	
		1991	*2001*	*1991*	*2001*	*1991*	*2001*
(1)	*(2)*	*(3)*	*(4)*	*(5)*	*(6)*	*(7)*	*(8)*
1.	Najibabad	88.00	205.62	100.51	97.47	5.48	20.01
2.	Kiratpur	124.70	275.99	104.68	032.02	2.66	35.54
3.	Mohdpur Devmal	97.95	228.51	73.88	106.45	14.40	48.74
4.	Haldaur	111.28	238.83	71.58	136.17	19.34	33.00
5.	Kotwali	69.05	207.54	56.57	88.72	5.61	28.28
6.	Afzalgarh	116.62	231.18	96.04	127.38	18.71	29.75
7.	Nehtaur	118.87	266.84	83.71	116.05	9.67	35.36
8.	Dhampur	106.66	218.91	90.69	145.20	27.84	48.03
9.	Seohara	137.50	265.08	105.91	175.27	11.06	59.78
10.	Jalilpur	96.31	213.57	79.97	118.66	11.21	38.85
11.	Noorpur	119.69	223.28	75.57	94.95	5.28	52.01

Source : Computed from the data of *Zila Sankhiyiki Patrika*, Bijnor, 1991 and 2001.

TABLE 2

Number of Schools Per 1000 of Students (1991-2001)

Sl. No.	*Blocks*	*Primary School*		*Junior High School*		*Intermediate School*	
		1991	*2001*	*1991*	*2001*	*1991*	*2001*
(1)	*(2)*	*(3)*	*(4)*	*(5)*	*(6)*	*(7)*	*(8)*
1.	Najibabad	5.35	5.08	0.89	0.96	0.85	1.76
2.	Kiratpur	4.93	4.29	1.07	1.31	3.24	1.70
3.	Mohdpur Devmal	5.26	4.85	1.45	1.12	1.24	1.59
4.	Haldaur	6.01	5.03	1.65	1.30	0.33	1.59
5.	Kotwali	6.92	5.16	1.35	1.05	1.51	1.81
6.	Afzalgarh	5.33	4.18	0.88	0.92	1.74	1.98
7.	Nehtaur	5.47	4.48	2.17	1.14	1.44	1.78
8.	Dhampur	5.35	4.84	1.22	0.92	1.46	1.94
9.	Seohara	4.94	4.13	1.50	0.73	2.17	1.87
10.	Jalilpur	4.80	4.46	0.86	0.92	2.06	2.23
11.	Noorpur	4.77	4.46	1.45	2.04	5.05	1.61

Source : Computed from the data of *Zila Sankhiyiki Patrika*, Bijnor, 1991 and 2001.

students in the Bijnor district. The analysis is based on three levels of institutions these are Primary Schools, Junior High Schools and Intermediate Schools for the years 1991 and 2001.

Primary Schools per 1000 students in the district are lower than the previous decade. On an average which was 6 schools per thousand students. The maximum number of schools in the category of Primary Schools was in block Kotwali, i.e. 6.92 in 1991 followed by Haldaur (6.01) however in some blocks there are number of schools are less like in Noorpur (4.77). In the year of 2001, data reveals that the maximum of schools observed in block Kotwali (5.16) followed by Najibabad (5.08) but lower ratio of schools found in Seohara (4.13).

In the category of Junior High Schools, the ratio for the year 1991 depicts that the maximum number of schools found in block Nehtaur (2.17) followed by Haldaur (1.65). As far as lower ratio is concerned, it was observed in Jalilpur (0.86). The highest ratio was registered in block Noorpur (2.04) followed by Kiratpur (1.31). Lower ratio found in Seohara (0.73) during the period of 2001. The reasons for the decline of ratio are as: (i) faster population growth in this age group, (ii) drop-out, (iii) closing of older schools due to poor infrastructure facilities.

During the year 1991, the maximum number of Intermediate Schools was observed in block Noorpur (5.05) followed by Kiratpur (3.24) but minimum ratio was in Haldaur (0.33). The highest number of schools was registered in Jalilpur (2.23) followed by Afzalgarh (1.98) while lowest in Haldaur (1.59) in the year of 2001.

3. Number of Teachers per 1000 of Students

Table 3 shows the number of teachers per 1000 students during the year of 1991 and 2001. In the class of 1 to 5 analysis reveals that the ratio of number of teachers in 1991 was highest in block Seohara (14.05) followed by Kotwali (12.20) and Haldaur (11.88) and lowest in Kiratpur (6.97) as compared to 2001 the maximum ratio was in Noorpur (10.77) and minimum also in Kiratpur (7.28). Number of teachers per 1000 of students decreases due to population increase at very alarming rate. Those who are educated they have migrated to cities or other metropolis.

TABLE 3

Number of Teachers per 1000 of Students (1991-2001)

Sl. No.	*Blocks*	*Class I to V*		*Class VI to XII*	
		1991	*2001*	*1991*	*2001*
1.	Najibabad	7.20	7.88	19.31	31.99
2.	Kiratpur	6.97	7.28	22.54	17.16
3.	Mohdpur Devmal	10.32	9.66	24.51	35.70
4.	Haldaur	11.88	9.58	32.71	16.72
5.	Kotwali	12.20	7.80	20.74	17.49
6.	Afzalgarh	9.41	8.60	20.13	19.84
7.	Nehtaur	9.53	8.48	28.66	22.94
8.	Dhampur	11.69	9.29	26.76	25.13
9.	Seohara	14.05	8.02	26.60	23.70
10.	Jalilpur	9.64	8.30	31.25	28.66
11.	Noorpur	10.92	10.77	25.09	14.73

Source : Computed from the data of *Zila Sankhiyiki Patrika*, Bijnor, 1991 and 2001.

The number of teachers in class 6 to 12 is more or less similar in 1991 and 2001. In 1991, the maximum ratio of teachers was registered in block Haldaur (32.71) followed by Jalilpur (31.25) and Nehtaur (28.66) while minimum in Najibabad (19.31). During the period of 2001, the highest ratio of teachers was in Mohdpur Deomal (35.70) followed by Najibabad (31.99) whereas lowest in Noorpur (14.73). The ratio of number of teachers at block level is high or low due to uneven distribution of educational facilities.

SCHEMES AND PROJECTS

The Government of India, as part of its Constitutional commitment, has initiated a number of programmes to achieve the goal of universalization of elementary education in a time bound manner. Some of the major initiatives have been the Operation Blackboard (1986), Non-formal Education Scheme (1986), the Shiksha Karmi Project (1987), Mahila Samakhya

(1989), the District Primary Education Programme (1994), the Mid-Day Meal Scheme (1995), School Chalo Abhiyan (2000) and the Sarva Shiksha Abhiyan (2001) and the most recently introduced The Right of Children to Free and Compulsory Education Act or The Right to Education Act (RTE), which has come into force from April 1, 2010 ensuring free education to school children aged 6-14.

Some of the schemes and projects are being running in the district Bijnor, these are:

> Under Basic Education Department mid-day meal scheme, scholarships scheme, Area intensive programme running in these projects children under age groups 6 to 11 and 11 to 14 are being benefited.

1. *Mid-Day-Meal Scheme*: Under this scheme all the children up to class V are given three kg. wheat free of cost every month.
2. *Scholarship Scheme*: Under this scheme the students from 1 to 5 class belonging to the category S.C./ O.B.C./minorities get scholarships worth Rs. 300 per year whereas the students sending in class VI to VII get Rs. 480 per month. This grant is realized from Samaj Kalyan/Minorities Kalyan Department.
3. *Non-Formal Education Programme*: Under this scheme free education is imparted to the children 6 to 11 age group. This scheme is running in 08 Blocks in the district.
4. *School Chalo Abhiyan*: Under the scheme of D.P.E.P. School Chalo Abhiyan was being conducted from 01/ 07/2000 to 31/07/2000. Efforts have been made to get all the children admitted.
5. *Special Health Checkup*: All the children of all the primary schools in this district have been medically examined from 15.8.2000. Health Department has given full Co-operation in this respect.

At the senior level there is a detail of some programmes and schemes for the development of educational status in the Bijnor district:

1. *Vocational Education*: Under the schemes of vocational education, the students of Class 9-12 are to provide the practical knowledge of following trades: (1) Photography, (2) Automobile, (3) Nursery, (4) Dress Designing, (5) Handicraft, and (6) Cooking.
2. *Computer Education*: The students of G.I.C. are being provided the practical knowledge of computer education.
3. Establishment of girl's schools.

CONCLUDING REMARKS

From the above discussion it is concluded that the Bijnor district came in backward category in terms of educational facilities as it is characterized by low number of schools, low teacher student ratio. Government schools are poorly maintained and drop-out cases are alarming. It becomes even serious as we move from primary level to the higher levels. Children have been sent to the schools only to receive scholarship and mid-day-meal. Most of the children are forced to earn money by their parents largely due to poverty. Quite often, children's scholarship and their earned money are being misused for drinking and gambling by their father. So there is dire need of better infrastructures in schools and awareness programme to impart education at grass-root level. Serious effort should be made to minimize drop-out cases of children especially the girl child.

References

Hazra, Anupama (2010), "Rural Literacy in India: The Changing Scenario", *Kurukshetra*, Vol. 58, No. 11 , September, pp. 3-5.

Zila Sankhiyiki Patrika, District Bijnor, 1991.

Zila Sankhiyiki Patrika, District Bijnor, 2001.

bijnor.nic.in.

http://bijnor.nic.in/dios.htm

http://bijnor.nic.in/bsa.htm.

http://www.upeducation.net/Facts/Facts%26figures/.

CHAPTER

6

Health is a Key Component of the Human Development

P. KHICHA, BENARD NYAKWEBA OYAGI
AND NYAKUNDI K. RUTH

ABSTRACT

Health is a key component of the human development index. This paper looks at how health is measured, how the level of health across countries is converging, and which countries are outliers to this global trend. We argue that conceptually health measures should account for illness as well as mortality. However, in practice we show that population mortality and illness measures tend to move closely together, allowing us to use life expectancy as a reasonable proxy for population health. Overall health is improving, and over the last 40 years life expectancy has been converging, with larger gains taking place in countries that initially had lower levels of life expectancy. We show, however, that a detailed analysis gives a more complex picture. Rather than a long-term pattern of global convergence we see two distinct groups of countries in the data, clustering around different long-run levels of life expectancy.

We consider outliers from the general picture found in cross-country analysis. HIV/AIDS plays a large role in explaining the poor nealth performance of some countries particularly in Sub-Saharan Africa. HIV/AIDS has meant that from 1990 on the process of convergence in health has stopped and is being reversed.

Finally we argue that health improvements do not have to wait for national income to rise. Many countries have experienced large health gains without prior income gains, and in countries not affected by HIV/AIDS the last 40 years have largely been a success story in terms of achievements in health.

Keywords: Health, Life expectancy, Human development.

INTRODUCTION

There is wide-spread agreement that heath is an important component of human development. Health was identified as a component of human development in the Human Development Report 1990 (United Nations Development Program 1991) and is a central part of the Human Development Index. The World Bank has shifted from an emphasis on promoting economic growth (e.g. Commission on International Development, 1969) to include a focus on health, education, and social exclusion (see World Development Report, 2001). The Millennium Development Goals, adopted at the Millennium Summit of the United Nations in September 2000 focused on poverty, mortality, education, health, gender equality and environment as the key measures of development. More recently. The Commission on the Measurement of Economic Performance and Social Progress (2009) put forward eight distinct spheres of well-being in addition to consumption and wealth: health, education, personal activity, political voice and governance, social connectedness, environmental conditions, personal insecurity, and economic insecurity. It also argued for a focus on inequality in these indicators as well measures of their average levels.

While there seems to be general agreement that health is an important component of human development there is an issue about how exactly we should measure health. To some extent this is a question of the conceptual underpinning of the development measure we seek. Our theory of what development is, and of well-being, should dictate the appropriate health measure. On the other hand we have the consideration that at present we only have few internationally comparable measures of health and in practice must base comparisons on these. While it is true we are limited in the set of health variables we can use, it is useful to discuss how well these measures correlate with the more meaningful underlying measure of health we would like to use. This gap between theory and measurement is partly a matter of a conceptual gap—the health measure we use may be trying to measure something that is different for the measure we would wish in theory. However, we also have measurement error; we may not perfectly capture the construct we are trying to capture. The measure of health currently used in the Human Development Index is life expectancy. The period 1970-2005 has seen large improvements in life expectancy in most countries and convergence in life expectancy, with countries that had lower life expectancy in 1970 seeing larger gains in life expectancy subsequently. However, when we look at the data in more detail a more complex picture emerges. Instead of uniform convergence to a high level of life expectancy, there appear to be two separate groups of countries. One group has low life expectancy while the other has high life expectancy. Among the high life expectancy countries we see modest and fairly uniform gains in life expectancy over time. Among countries with low initial life expectancy increases in life expectancy are not a uniform and smooth catch up. Rather some countries that initially have low life expectancy seem to jump to join the high life expectancy regime, while others stagnate with low or little in the way of life expectancy gain, and sometimes even falling life expectancy.

As well as the general trends outlines above we have some countries which are outliers to the process. One set of outliers are the Sub-Saharan African countries with high levels of HIV/AIDS. The general patterns of pattern relative failure of countries with initially low life expectancy is exacerbated by the large number of HIV/AIDS deaths in Sub-Saharan but the phenomenon is not entirely due to HIV/AIDS; these countries are outliers to the process outlined above. The countries with high prevalence rates of HIV have seen little in life expectancy improvement and indeed some have seen absolute declines relative to 1970 levels. The other area in which there has been a relative failure to improve life expectancy has been in the former Soviet Republics. In contrast to these we have a number of success stories, countries with life expectancy gains far in excess of our model's predictions and sometimes involving a jump to low level health regime to the high level regime.

We also discuss the interrelationship between health and income. Income per capita is also part of the human development index and across countries higher levels of health and income go together. However, the relationship is not close enough to take one as a proxy measure of the other. In addition, over the years 1970-2005 we see much larger improvements in health around the world than we would expect based solely on the increases in income over the period.

Countries, even very poor countries, can improve their population health using direct health interventions even when incomes are not rising. It is important to realize that health improvements can be achieved with first waiting for income to rise.

In most countries life expectancy has risen and the relatively faster rise in countries with initially low levels of health means that in these countries their human development index, relative to the leading country, will be rising. The great worry is the health crisis, particularly in Sub-Saharan Africa, being brought about by the high prevalence of HIV/AIDS.

2. THE CONCEPT OF HEALTH

Life expectancy is the health measure used in the Human Development Index. We begin by considering the issue of whether life expectancy is the right measure of population health on conceptual grounds. Mathers *et al.* (2003) also consider this issue. It is clear that a longer life span is preferable to a shorter lifespan, but the quantity of lifespan says nothing about the quality of life. There are a number of approaches to adjusting life years lived by health status to get a better measure that accounts for illness. One approach is to use quality adjusted life years (QALYs) where individuals express the their preferences by valuing a the quality of a life year lived in a state of ill-health as the fraction of a year lived in full health that would give them the same utility. Another is to use disability adjusted life years (DALYs) where a life year lived with disability is considered equal to a fraction of a year lived in full health, with the adjustment being made by an expert panel.

To some extent these two approaches to adjusting life years for ill health represent different ways of thinking about of welfare. One way is to use a utilitarian social welfare function. In this approach social welfare is defined as the sum of individual utilities. This leads to using QALYs. However, in the capabilities approach to measuring development we can think of welfare as being measured by the size of the choice set rather than the utility of what is chosen. In the capabilities approach we can think of healthy life span as a basic constraint that limits people's choice, and we want to measure the objective size of the choice set, independently of how people value the choices.

The estimates of life expectancy against healthy life expectancy for 192 countries in 2002 using data from the World Health Report, 2004 (World Health Organization, 2004). We see a very close association between the two measures, with healthy life expectancy rising linearly with life expectancy. A regression of healthy life expectancy, HL, on life expectancy, L, using this data gives :

$$\begin{aligned} HL &= -3.859 + 0.936\ L \\ &\quad\ \ (0.424) \quad (0.006) \\ N &= 192\ \ R = 0.991 \end{aligned}$$

where we have standard errors of the estimates in parentheses.

The intercept is significantly different from zero and the coefficient on life expectancy is significantly lower than one. This implies that healthy life expectancy is not simply a proportion of life expectancy. For example, according to this linear relationship, when life expectancy is 40, then healthy life expectancy is 33.6 and the proportion of years in ill-health is 0.16. In contrast, when life expectancy is 70 then healthy life expectancy is 61.6 so the proportion of years in ill health is 0.12. The fraction of life spent in disability is relatively constant across countries with life expectancy below 60, but for countries where life expectancy is above 60 years the proportion of years in disability appears to decline as life expectancy rises.

In plot the expected years in disability against life expectancy. This shows that people living in countries with higher life expectancy expect more years of disability, up to a life expectancy of about 70. For life expectancies above 70 however, increased life expectancy seems to be associated with and lower number of years lived with disability. It appears that at low levels of health, as health improves, in terms of longer life spans, the onset of disability is also pushed back proportionately, so that the fraction of life spent in disability stays relatively constant. However, at very high levels of life expectancy we see a "compression of morbidity", longer life spans are associated with a compression of the number of years spent disabled. In most developed countries we have time series data showing this compression of morbidity (Fries, 2003). When life expectancy increases, healthy life expectancy increases more than proportionately, compressing the number of years lived with disability into a shorter fraction of the lifespan. This means that life expectancy increases in developed countries are generally very good news since they go hand in hand with greater healthy life expectancy and delays in the average age at which disability occurs. Unfortunately we lack similar time series evidence on how expected years in disability changes when life expectancy increases in developing countries. The cross-country evidence to the expected age of onset of disability rising proportionately with life expectancy in these countries making life expectancy a fairly good proxy for healthy life expectancy.

In cost effectiveness studies in which health gains are measured in QALYs or DALYs we usually discount gains to future life expectancy by a social discount rate (often a rate of 3% per annum is used). We could apply the same logic to measures of life expectancy at birth and argue that survival at birth, which comes in the immediate future, is more valuable than survival at older ages which comes in the distant future.

However, discounting in this way has several problems. Firstly, we may not want discount health at the same rate as money, and secondly, it is unclear that the discount rate used by individuals in deciding between present and future consumption is appropriate as social discount rate for comparing across generations born at different times (see Kaplow, 2007 for a discussion of these issues).

In addition, life expectancy is not measured for a cohort born today over its future. It is actually a synthetic measure constructed from current period age specific mortality rates, and is the life span a person would, one would expect if they were exposed to this age specific mortality. If we think of life expectancy simply as a summary statistic, capturing current age specific mortality rates in a single number, there is no need to discount. However, thinking of it as a summary measure of current mortality rates does raise the issue that it is more sensitive to changes in the infant mortality rate than to changes in mortality at older ages, since the "cost" of a death in terms of life expectancy foregone declines with age (Vaupel, 1986).

There is also the issue of inequality in life spans. A particular level of life expectancy can represent very different age specific mortality patterns. For example, in one country everyone could live to age 70 while in another half the people could live to age 50 and the other half to age 90. Both these populations will have life expectancy 70, on average, but one has equal life spans while the other has very unequal life spans. We could think of the variation in life spans as undesirable inequality if different life spans are identified with different groups in the population.

Alternatively if everyone has the same life expectancy the different life spans actually experienced could be viewed as undesirable risk (Edwards, 2008). In either case we might want a measure that considered not just life expectancy but also the spread of life span outcomes experienced by the population. When we consider inequality and risk we will be concerned with the joint distribution of health, income and education, since the welfare impact of deprivation are unlikely to be simply additive. In addition to the issue of getting the right measure of health there is the issue of how health should be weighted in constructing the human development index. At present health, income and education get equal weights on one third each. If we take a social welfare approach to measuring human development we can ask how people value health improvements in terms of money units to get a sense of the relative importance of health and income in welfare. Becker, Philipson, and Soares (2005) estimate the money value of health improvements in each country based on estimates of willingness to pay for additional life years (Viscousi and Aldy 2003). They find that the value of life expectancy improvements between 1960 and 2000 were, on average, about the same as the value of income improvements. This implies that we should weight a countries health improvements roughly equally with is income improvements when thinking about total welfare and is in line with the current weighting of income and health in the human development index.

3. ESTIMATES OF LIFE EXPECTANCY

The human development index currently uses life expectancy as its measure of health. In this section we assume that life expectancy is the right measure and ask how well it is measured by current statistics. In theory, life expectancy can be calculated directly from age specific mortality rates. However, when direct measures of age specific mortality are not available, or are unreliable, there are also indirect methods of estimating life expectancy. Demographic indicators such as population growth rates, and the age distribution, are closely linked to mortality rates and life expectancy, and data on such demographic indicators can be used to make inferences on the level of life expectancy. The United Nations constructs reasonable estimates of life expectancy that are consistent both with the direct evidence and with indirect indicators, using information from a variety of data sources in each country.

Measurement of mortality rates and demographic indicators can be based on vital registration data, age distributions in the census, and nationally representative survey information on infant mortality and deaths of other family members. All of these data sources have potential problems, due, for example, to under-reporting of deaths in vital registration, under-enumeration of the population and age misreporting in census data, and survey data may suffer from error due to small sample sizes. The complete set of estimates of life expectancy across countries and over time includes some interpolated or extrapolated data, particularly prior to 1980 (Bos, Vu, Stephens, Patience, 1992).

The introduction of the World Fertility Surveys in the 1970s, which were followed by the Demographic and Health Surveys from the mid 1980s onwards, have led to improved estimates of infant and under five mortality in many developing countries. Data on adult mortality rates are often less reliable in these countries (Hill, 2003). When the availability of relevant direct data are limited, model life tables are used to provide indirect estimates life expectancy. For example when there is data only on infant mortality available model life tables can be used to impute life expectancy. This means that life expectancy estimates for developing countries are sometimes based on a simple transformation of their infant mortality rates (Deaton, 2007). These transformations, have changed over the last few years to take into account the change in age specific mortality pattern due to HIV/AIDS.

The underlying data on infant and under five mortality rates from household surveys may be less reliable if they are used to estimate child mortality retrospectively. While questions on births and child survival asked of mothers (conditional on these mothers still being alive) over the last five years are usually thought to be reasonable, calculating infant mortality rates on longer recall periods may be subject to recall bias. Issues of methods and measurement in estimating life expectancy are discussed in detail in Lopez *et al.* (2003). Even the best estimates are subject to a range of uncertainty and Daponte *et al.* (1997) discuss how to quantify this uncertainty. Given the imperfection of the estimates, Bayesian methods that impose some prior knowledge of the structure of the data may lead to improved mortality estimates; this approach is used by Girosi and King (2008).

In Tables 1 and 2 we plot under five mortality rates for Guatemala. Guatemala had Demographic and Health Surveys (DHS) in 1987, 1995 and 1998. These surveys tell a fairly consistent story, rates calculated using recall in a later DHS tend to match fairly closely the rates found at the time in an

TABLE I

Outliers-based as Life Expected Gain and Expected Gain 1970-2005

Countries	*Life expectancy in 1970*	*Gain life exp. 1970-2005*
Afghanistan	35.5	7.9
Niger	38.1	11.5
Nigeria	40.4	6.9
Western Sahara	42.0	22.9
Nepal	42.6	22.6
Congo (RD)	43.0	3.8
Rwanda	44.4	4.0
Tanzania	46.7	7.0
India	48.8	13.9
Oman	49.5	25.5
Kenya	52.2	.3
South Africa	52.8	-1.0
Iran	53.9	16.7
Zimbabwe	54.9	-13.2
Brazil	54.6	10.5
Malaysia	61.3	13.1
China	62.0	12.4
Singapore	68.8	10.8
Germany	70.8	8.5
Italy	71.5	9.3
U.K	71.7	7.3
France	71.8	8.6
Japan	72.2	10.2
Spain	72.2	8.1
Canada	72.5	7.7
Netherland	73.2	3.6
Norway	74.1	5.9
Sweden	74.4	6.1

Table 2

Life Expected Gain and Regime Prediction : 1970-2005

Countries	*Life exp. 1970*	*Gain life exp. 1970-2005*	*In regime exp. gain*	*1 regime exp. gain*	*2 probability of regime 1 given 1970 life exp.*	*Probability regime 1 given gain 1970-2005*
(1)	*(2)*	*(3)*	*(4)*	*(5)*	*(6)*	*(7)*
Afghanistan	35.5	7.9	16.4	26.4	1.00	1.00
Niger	38.1	11.5	14.0	24.7	0.99	1.00
Nigeria	40.4	6.9	12.3	23.5	0.98	1.00
W. Sahara	42.0	22.9	11.0	22.0	0.95	0.77
Nepal	42.6	22.6	10.6	22.3	0.94	0.71
Congo (RD)	43.0	3.8	9.6	21.6	0.90	1.00
Rwanda	44.4	4.0	9.2	21.3	0.88	1.00
Tanzania	46.7	7.0	7.2	19.9	0.73	1.00
India	48.8	13.9	5.8	18.9	0.60	0.73
Oman	49.5	25.5	5.3	18.6	0.55	0.08
Kenya	52.2	0.3	3.3	17.1	0.33	1.00
South Africa	52.8	-1.0	2.8	16.9	0.29	1.00
Iran	53.9	16.7	1.9	16.2	0.22	0.02

(Contd.)

TABLE 2 (*Contd.*)

(1)	(2)	(3)	(4)	(5)	(6)	(7)
Zimbabwe	54.9	-13.2	1.2	15.6	0.16	1.00
Brazil	54.6	10.5	-1.6	13.6	0.04	0.00
Malaysia	61.3	13.1	-3.7	12.1	0.01	0.00
China	62.0	12.4	-4.2	11.8	0.01	0.00
Singapore	68.8	10.8	-9.5	8.1	0.00	0.00
Germany	70.8	8.5	-11.6	7.0	0.00	0.00
Italy	71.5	9.3	-11.6	6.5	0.00	0.00
U.K.	71.7	7.3	-11.7	6.8	0.00	0.00
France	71.8	8.6	11.8	6.4	0.00	0.00
Japan	72.2	10.2	-12.1	6.2	0.00	0.00
Spain	72.2	8.1	-12.1	6.2	0.00	0.00
Canada	72.5	7.7	-12.3	6.0	0.00	0.00
Netherland	73.2	3.6	-13.2	5.4	0.00	0.00
Norway	74.1	5.9	-13.5	5.2	0.00	0.00
Sweden	74.4	6.1	13.8	5.0	0.00	0.00

older DHS. In addition, Guatemala has a vital registration and figures on under-five mortality from the registered deaths match the DHS estimates quite closely. There are a few very high estimates of under-five mortality in the 1960's but these are not matched by the vital registration data. While the consistency of the data from different sources is encouraging it does not mean that the mortality estimates derived from them are correct; in principle there could be the same bias occurring in each source.

In the estimates of under-five mortality based on data from Demographic and Health Surveys for Nigeria in 1990 and 2003 as well as mortality data from the World Fertility Survey (WFS) in 1981. While the different surveys agree quite well over time, the data for Nigeria for under-five mortality-based on the three surveys differ markedly. In comparing the data from the 2003 DHS survey in Nigeria with data from the 1990

DHS survey we have the problem that when the data cover the same years they do not overlap.

This may be due to recall bias in the later survey, or to one of the surveys not being representative of the overall population. We also have the problem that the recall estimates from the 1990 DHS survey are generally higher than those found at the time in the 1981 World Fertility survey. We are left of the problem of constructing a consistent time series for infant mortality in Nigeria from surveys that give conflicting evidence. Given the large role that under five mortality rates play in determining life expectancy (Vaupel, 1986) these examples demonstrate the type of issues that have to be addressed when constructing life expectancy estimates. In developed countries mortality at older ages plays a larger role in variations in life expectancy (White, 2002). These caveats on data quality mean that we should not draw too much in the way of inference from small differences in estimated life expectancies. The data may however be sufficiently reliable to discern some broad movement in health. Until the advert of HIV/AIDS, infant mortality rates were falling, and life expectancy was rising worldwide, even in countries with little or no growth in income (Ahmad, Lopez, and Inoue, 2000, Cutler, Deaton and Lleras-Muney, 2006). In the following sections we shall investigate to what extent this represents convergence in health and what factors are driving these health gains. Overall, our analysis points to some possible improvements in the measurement of health as a human development indicator. Conceptually there is a strong argument for using healthy life expectancy, adjusting life expectancy downward for years lived with disability, as our health metric. However this would require a major new data collection effort to collect data on the prevalence of disability. The strong linear relationship suggests that life expectancy, which depends only on mortality and not morbidity, may in practice capture a large portion the actual variation in population health. We might also consider how to improve our life expectancy measure to adjust for inequality, or risk, due to the variance of life span outcomes.

There is scope for improvement in data quality, particularly in developing countries where life expected is often modeled based on very sparse data rather than estimated from actual age specific mortality rates.

4. IMPROVEMENT AND CONVERGENCE IN LIFE EXPECTANCY

The general consensus in the literature is that while income per gaps have been fairly constant over the last 50 years, health status is low health countries has been improving faster than in high health countries leading to a convergence in population health levels around the world (Deaton, 2004). The issue of convergence is important for the human development index since countries are measured relative to the leading country. Uniform improvements with no convergence will mean that average value of the human development index across countries will remain the same. However, if there is convergence the average value of the index will rise as countries close with the leader.

In this section we discuss three challenges to this consensus of convergence. First, the picture of convergence depends on which health measure we take, and is sensitive to transformation of the health measure. For example, log life expectancy may not be converging while life expectancy does converge. We show this dependence on functional transformation is fundamental and means we should use a conceptually correct measure of health so we are talking about convergence of interesting, meaningful, variables. Secondly, we show that convergence holds from 1970 to 1985 but since 1990 there has been large scale divergence. Thirdly, if we measure population health in terms of life expectancy we show that the picture is of two convergence clubs rather than uniform convergence over the period 1970-2005. All countries that had good levels of health in 1970, and some countries that had low levels, are converging towards a common high level of life expectancy. However, there is a substantial group of countries, whose health status was low in 1970, that are converging together towards a much lower level of life expectancy.

Health, as measured by life expectancy, has been improving in most countries over the last fifty years. In addition to this evidence of improvement on average, there is evidence that life expectancy is rising fastest in countries that had low life expectancy in 1970, leading to the view that life expectancy gaps between countries are narrowing, with the prospect of convergence in health in the long-run (Deaton, 2004; Neumayer, 2003; Sab and Smith, 2002; Hobijn and Franses, 2001).

Consider again Tables 1 and 2 showing the distribution of life expectancy across countries 1970 and again in 2005 using a kernel estimator. The striking feature of these plots is the twin peaks in the distribution of life expectancy. Some countries are clustered around a low level of life expectancy while others cluster around a high level of life expectancy, with very few countries being in the middle between these two clusters. Over time, the modal life expectancy in each cluster has moved to the right. However, in addition, some countries appear to have "jumped" from the low life expectancy cluster, reducing its height, to the high life expectancy cluster, increasing the size of its peak. "high life expectancy" regime) than in regime 2 (the "mortality trap"). Countries are more likely to be the mortality trap regime if their initial life expectancy is low, but there have a chance of "jumping" to the high life expectancy regime, with a probability that depends on their initial income level.

We assume that in each regime there is a linear relationship between initial life expectancy and the improvement in life expectancy. This will generate β-convergence within each regime. The probability of being in a particular regime depends on initial life expectancy (we assume the likelihood is a linear function of initial life expectancy, translated to a probability by the cumulative normal distribution). We estimate model 2 by maximum likelihood. Estimation and hypothesis testing using model 2 is not straight forward since the model does not satisfy the usual regularity conditions used in statistical modeling. Our estimation methods require a grid search over possible parameter values, while hypothesis testing requires Monte Carlo methods to estimate the distribution of test statistics. The statistical problems of these types of models, and methods we can use to overcome them, are described in detail in Bloom, Canning and Sevilla (2003).

The results of our estimation of model 2 are shown in columns 2 and 3 of Table 1. We estimate two regimes each with β-convergence, but with different slopes. The "mortality trap" regime gives smaller improvements in life expectancy at each level of live expectancy. The results in Table 1 show that the probability of being in the "mortality trap" regime decease as initial life expectancy rises. Countries with life expectancy above 55 in 1970 are almost certain to be in "high life expectancy" regime. However, for countries with life expectancy below 55 in 1970 there is a probability of being in the good regime and a probability of remaining in the mortality trap. A likelihood ratio test (based on bootstrapped critical values) of the two regime model against a single regime decisively rejects a single regime; the two regimes fit the date better. The two regime model also fits better than a more complex single regime models that allows for a non-linear relationship.

We find that the data rejects the model in which all countries follow the same process in favor of the convergence club approach. Our results include a number of countries that have seen substantial declines in life expectancy since 1990 due to HIV/AIDS. However, our conclusions do not depend on the presence of HIV/AIDS; we obtain similar results using data on life expectancy that exclude the effect of HIV/AIDS mortality, though in this case the performance of the "mortality trap" regime is not as bad as when we include AIDS mortality (Bloom and Canning 2007). The twin peaks in the distribution of life expectancy are very similar to the twin peaks in income reported in Quah (1996). This raises the idea that development is not a smooth process, but involves a trap with low income and poor health. Some countries, however, manage to escape this trap and once they have broken free they converge quickly to the high level equilibrium. This means that we see some countries clustered around the low level trap, while others are clustered around the high level equilibrium, with only a few countries in transition between the two "clubs".

5. OUTLIERS

The two regime model set out in Table 1 captures the overall picture of movements in life expectancy but some individual countries deviate from the predictions of the model. In Table 2 we list the countries in our dataset in order of their life expectancy in 1970 shown in column 1. In column 2 we show the actual gain in life expectancy in the country over the period 1970-2005. Column 3 shows the expected gain in the country over the period if it is in the "mortality trap" regime. Column 4 shows the expected gain in the high life expectancy regime. Column 5 gives the probability that a country is in the mortality trap regime given its life expectancy in 1970. Column 6 gives the probability that it is in the mortality trap regime given its 1970 life expectancy and the gain in life expectancy seen over the period 1970-2005. We calculate the posterior probability of the regime given the data on its performance over the period 1970-2005 using Bayes' rule. We highlight countries in that appear to have jumped out of the mortality trap over the period, while we highlight in those who seem to have jumped from the high life expectancy regime into the mortality trap. Four countries seem to have jumped out of the mortality trap. Indonesia, Viet Nam, Oman, and Maldives all had low life expectancy in 1970 and based on this, the probability we assigned to them being in the mortality trap in column 5 was greater than one half. However, as we can see each of these countries experienced a rapid increase in life expectancy over the period 1970-2005. This rapid gain was in each case much closer to the rapid gain predicted by the high life expectancy regime than the mortality trap. The posterior probability of being in the mortality trap regime given this good performance, shown in column 6 of Table 2, is in each of the four cases less than one half. The countries like, Myanmar, Kenya, Namibia, South Africa, Congo, Botswana and Zimbabwe, all had reasonably high life expectancy in 1970 and we assign them on this basis to being in the high life expectancy regime (their probability of being in the mortality trap in 1970, shown in column 5, is less than one half). However, their performance over the period 1970-2005 was poor, indeed South Africa, Congo, Botswana and Zimbabwe all saw decreases in life expectancy. Given this poor performance the posterior probability they are in the mortality trap regime, shown in column 6, exceeds one half. Considering performance relative to that predicted by the initial regime, and looking for jumps between regimes is just one way of thinking about outliers.

However, outliers in absolute magnitude of their performance come from across the distribution. Bhutan, Western Sahara and Nepal appear to be in mortality trap but had very large gains in life expectancy, though not sufficient to move them out of the trap. On the other hand Indonesia, Viet Nam and Oman are all once again outliers with large gains in life expectancy relative to what we would predict given our model. Swaziland, Zambia, Lesotho, Uganda, Kenya, South Africa, Congo, Botswana and Zimbabwe all had life expectancy gains more than 10 years lower than our model predicts, which can explained by HIV/AIDS. The former Soviet Union also performed very poorly relative to our prediction, though in this case the causes are related to the collapse of employment, stress, and alcoholism (Shkolnikov *et al.*, 2001).

6. DETERMINANTS OF HEALTH

There are a number of factors that lead to health improvements. The proximal determinants are factors that affect nutrition and the disease environment, together with preventive and curative medical interventions. Improvements in nutrition strengthen the immune system and reduce susceptibility to disease. Access to clean water and sanitation can reduce the transmission of fecal contamination and the spread of infection. Preventive interventions, such as vaccination, can immunize against disease. Medical treatment can cure disease. The epidemiological transition sets out a model where countries transition from a high burden of infectious disease to a greater burden of non-infectious disease, though countries can have a dual burden with noninfectious diseases becoming prevalent while the infectious diseases have not been eliminated.

There is a debate about the relative importance of the different factors that affect health. Fogel (2004) emphasizes the historical effect of improving nutrition while Preston (1975) and Deaton (2006) put more weight technological progress and new health interventions. There is evidence of the on public health measures such as clean water and sanitation in cities (Cultler and Miller, 2005), as well as a role for medical treatment in modern populations (Cutler and McClellan, 2001). The relative importance of these mechanisms clearly varies in different times and places, and the interaction between them makes a precise accounting difficult.

An alternative to looking at these proximal determinants of health is to look at more distal determinants. We can think of health as being determined my income and education (Lleras-Muney, 2005). Income provides the means to purchase nutrition and health inputs and so leads to better health. Although there is a strong case for the direct effect of income on health due to nutrition and health interventions becoming more affordable, it may be that income is also acting as a proxy for a wider measure of socio-economic status and development and that the causal effect is due to other mechanisms. Another possible explanation for the link between income and health at the individual level is that it is relative, and not absolute, income that matters (Lynch *et al.*, 2000, Martikaien *et al.*, 2002, Marmot and Wilkinson, 2001, Marmot, 2002). A low position in the social hierarchy may induce psychosocial stress that is linked to increased behaviors that put people at risk of ill health and to physiological reactions in the immune system that directly lead to worse health. The relative income hypothesis suggests that inequality has a direct negative effect on health but the evidence for such a direct effect is contested (Deaton, 2002, 2003).

Preston (1975) showed that, across countries, life expected was correlated with income per capita, but that the relationship changes over time. However, the relationship changes over time. For a country with a fixed level of income per capita, life expectancy in 2005 will on average be about eight years higher than in 1970. Preston showed that about three quarters of life expectancy increase can be explained by the upward movement of the curve, and about one quarter by countries getting richer and moving along the curve. The curvature of the relationship between income and health (implicit in our use of log income suggests that a policy of redistributing income from the rich to the poor will improve average health outcomes since the gains in health of those with low incomes will outweigh the losses of those with high incomes. The World Health Organization's Commission on Social Determinants of Health (2008) argues that in order to improve health inequalities countries and global institutions need to tackle the inequitable distribution of money, power, and resources in the world. The U.K. government recently commissioned a report on effective evidence-based strategies for reducing health inequalities in England from 2010. The resulting Marmet Review (2010) advocates a policy of focusing on investment in childhood health and education, and reducing the gradient in living standards through a more progressive tax system. However, this policy prescription depends on the relationship being causal rather than income merely acting as a proxy for some broader notion of socio-economic status, and needs to be balanced against the negative incentive effects of redistributive taxation (Deaton, 2003).

References

Acemoglou, D., Johnson, S., Disease and Development: The Effect of Life Expectancy on Economic Growth, *National Bureau of Economic Research*, 2006, Working Paper No. 12269.

Ahmad, Omar B., Alan D. Lopez, and Mie Inoue, 2000, The decline in child mortality: a reappraisal, Bull World Health Organ, Vol. 78, No. 10: 1175-91.

Becker, G.S., Philipson, T.J., and Soares, R.R. (2005), *American Economic Review,* 95, 277-91.

Bloom, David E. and David Canning, "Mortality Traps and the Dynamics of Health Transitions," Proceedings of the National Academy of Sciences of the United States of America, 2007, Vol. 104(41), pp. 16044-49.

Bloom, D.E., Canning, D. Cumulative Causality, Economic Growth and the Demographic Transition, in Population Matters: Demographic Change, *Economic Growth,* and Poverty in the Developing World, N. Birdsall, A.C. Kelley, and S.W. Sinding eds., 2001, Oxford University Press, New York: 165-97.

Bloom, D.E., Canning, D., Sevilla, J. The Effect of Health on Economic Growth: A Production Function Approach. *World Development,* 2004; 32: 1-13.

Bos, E., Vu M.T., Stephens, P.W., Patience, W. (1992), Policy Research Working Paper Series (World Bank, Washington, DC), No. 851.

Commission on the Measurement of Economic Performance and Social Progress (2009), Report of the Commission on the Measurement of Economic Performance and Social Progress, www.stiglitz-sen-fitoussi.fr/en/index.htm.

Commission on Macroeconomics and Health, Macroeconomics and Health: Investing in Health for Economic Development, 2001, Geneva, World Health Organization.

Commission on Social Determinants of Health, Closing the gap in a generation: health equity through action on the social determinants of health: final report of the commission on social determinants of health, 2008, Geneva, *World Health Organization.*

Commission on International Development (1969), Partners in Development: Report, Praeger.

Cutler, D.M., Miller, G. The Role of Public Health Improvements in Health Advances: The Twentieth-Century United States, Demography, 2005; 42: 1-22.

Cutler, D.M., McClellan, M. Productivity Change in Health Care, *American Economic Review,* 2001; 91: 281-86.

Deaton, Angus, 2004, "Health in an Age of Globalization", Brookings Trade Forum, 2004, pp. 83-130, Brookings Institution Press.

Deaton Angus, 2007, Global Patterns of Income and Health: Facts, Interpretations, and Policies, WIDER Annual Lecture UNU World Institute for Development Economics Research, Helsinki.

Deaton, A. "The Great Escape: A Review Essay on Fogel's The Escape from Hunger and Premature Death, 1700-2100, *Journal of Economic Literature,* 2006; 44: 106-14.

Deaton, A. Health, Inequality, and Economic Development, *Journal of Economic Literature,* 2003; 41: 113-58.

Deaton, A. Policy Implications of the Gradient of Health and Wealth", Health Affairs 2002; 21:13-30.

Edwards, Ryan D., The Cost of Uncertain Life Span (June 2008). NBER Working Paper Series, Vol. w14093.

Fogel R.W. The Escape from Hunger and Premature Death, 1700-2100: Europe, America, and the Third World. Cambridge: Cambridge University Press, 2004.

Girosi, Federico and Gary King, Demographic Forecasting, Princeton University Press, 2008.

Hill, K. (2003) Adult Mortality in the Developing World: What We Know and How We Know It, Population Division, Department of Economic and Social Affairs, United Nations, New York.

Hobijn, B., Franses, P.H. Are Living Standards Converging? Structural Change and Economic Dynamics, 2001; 12: 171-200.

Kaplow, Louis, 2007, "Discounting Dollars, Discounting Lives: Intergenerational Distributive Justice and Efficiency," *The University of Chicago Law Review*, Vol. 74, No. 1, pp. 79-118.

Lleras-Muney, A., The Relationship Between Education and Adult Mortality in the United States, *Review of Economic Studies*, 2005; 72: 189-221.

Lynch, J., Davey Smith, G., Kaplan, G.A., House, J.S., Income Inequality and Mortality: Importance to Health of Individual Income, Psychosocial Environment, or Material Conditions, *British Medical Journal*, 2000; 320: 1200-04.

Lopez, A.D., Ahmad, O.B., Guillot, M., Ferguson, B.D., Salomon, J.A., Murray, C.J.L., Hill, K.H. Life tables for 191 countries for 2000: data, methods, results. In: Murray, C.J.L., Evans, D.B., eds. Health systems performance assessment: debates, methods and empiricism. Geneva, World Health Organization, 2003: 335-53.

Mathers, C.D., Salomon, J.A., Murray, C.J.L., Lopez, A.D. Alternative Summary Measures of Average Population Health. In: Murray, C.J.L., Evans, D.B., eds. Health Systems Performance Assessment: Debates, Methods and Empiricism. Geneva, World Health Organization, 2003: 319-34.

McMichael, A.J., McKee, M., Shkolnikov, V., Valkonen, T. Mortality Trends and Setbacks: Global Convergence or Divergence? Lancet, 2004; 363: 1155-59.

Martikainen, P., Bartley, M., Lahelma, E. Psychosocial Determinants of Health in Social Epidemiology, *International Journal of Epidemiology*, 2002; 31:1091-93.

Marmot, M., Wilkinson, R.G. Psychosocial and Material Pathways in the Relation between Income and Health: A Response to Lynch *et al.* *British Medical Journal*, 2001; 322: 1233-36.

Marmet Review (2010), Strategic Review of Health Inequalities in England post-2010, the Marmot Review.

Molina, George Gray and Mark Purser, 2010, Human Development Trends Since 1970.

Neumayer, E. Beyond Income: Convergence in Living Standards, Big Time. Structural Change and Economic Dynamics, 2003; 14: 275-96.

Preston, S. (1975), "The Changing Relation between Mortality and Level of Economic Development", *Population Studies*, Vol. 29, No. 2, pp. 231-48.

Schultz, T.P. Productive Benefits of Health: Evidence from Low Income Countries, in Health and Economic Growth: Findings and Policy Implications, G. Lopez-Casasnovas, B. Riveras and L. Currais eds., 2005, MIT Press, Cambridge, MA.

Strauss, J., Thomas, D., Health, Nutrition, and Economic Development," *Journal of Economic Literature*, 1998; 36: 766-817.

Vaupel, J.W., 1986, "How Change in Age-specific Mortality Affects Life Expectancy", *Population Studies*, Volume 40(1): 147-57.

Viscusi, W.K., and J.E. Aldy, 2003, The Value of a Statistical Life: A Critical Review of Market Estimates from Around the World, *The Journal of Risk and Uncertainty*, 27: 5-76.

White, K.M. Longevity Advances in High-Income Countries, 1955-96. *Population and Development Review*, 2002; 28: 59-76.

World Health Organization (2004), World Health Report, 2004, Geneva.

World Bank (2001), World Development Report 2000/01—Attacking Poverty, New York.

CHAPTER

7

The Role of ICT in Education

Chander Parkash and Sharmila

ABSTRACT

Information and Communication Technology has permeated in every walk of life affecting the technology fields such as launching satellites, managing businesses across the globe and also enabling social networking. The convergence of computer, communication and content technologies, being known as ICT, has attracted attention of academia, business, government and communities to use it for innovative profitable propositions. Year by year it is becoming simpler to use devices such as desktop palm top, iPod, etc. 21st century is characterized with the emergence of knowledge-based society wherein ICT plays a pivotal role. The National curriculum framework, 2005 (NCF, 2005) has also highlighted the importance of ICT in school education. With this backdrop, major paradigm shift is imperative in education characterised by imparting instructions, collaborative learning, and multidisciplinary problem-solving and promoting critical thinking skills. Nowadays the role of Information and Communication Technology (ICT), especially internet in the education sector plays an important role in the process of empowering the technology into the educational activities. Education sector can be the most effective sector to anticipate and eliminate the negative impact of ICT. Technology (internet) in another side can be the most effective way to increase the student's knowledge.

The main purpose of the Strategy for Information and Communication Technology Implementation in Education is to provide the prospects and trends of integrating information and communication technology (ICT) into the general educational activities. Government of India has announced 2010-20 as the decade of innovation. Reasoning and Critical thinking skills are necessary for innovation. Foundation of these skills is laid at school level. It is desirable that affordable ICT tools and techniques should be integrated into classroom instructions right form primary stage so as to enable students develop their requisite skills. Most of the tools, techniques and tutorials are available in Open domain and accessible on web. At Primary and Upper Primary level, focus may be on simple access to information and trying to compile different views and analyse them to conclude in one's own way. At the Secondary level, gathering and structuring of data and computing to arrive at some reports may be taken up in any subject not necessarily Science and Mathematics. At the Senior Secondary level, when students are so exposed, they will get highly motivated to use ICT tools for taking up complex, multidisciplinary problems such as biochemistry, bioinformatics, environmental science, forensic science, nanotechnology, business intelligence, etc. This may necessitate computing tools and techniques of generic nature as well as domain-specific. This is the time when the students and the teachers together will work in global competitive environment. The schools affiliated to the CBSE have been at the forefront of adopting the most modern innovations and practices to ensure there is a continuous enhancement in the overall quality of teaching and learning. The CBSE believes that it must bring the immense benefits of ICT and computing technology to every classroom across its fraternity of affiliated schools to improve academic outcomes of learners and to enhance the productivity of teachers in classrooms. This can be done by encouraging the use of technology in classroom teaching—e-learning and instant assessments which shall also go a long way in supporting its CCE initiative as well. CCE in the right spirit entails periodic assessments which are integrated effectively in the classroom teaching and learning. Infact all assessments must inform teaching and using technology helps to create interest among learners as for example a quiz may be done online as part of formative assessment. Technology can greatly assist teachers in classrooms to teach difficult and abstract subject matter concepts effectively if the right digital instruction materials, supporting technology infrastructure and intensive training is provided to the teachers to support instruction.

Being aware of the significant role of ICT (internet) in our life, especially in the educational activities, education authorities should be wise enough in implementing the strategies to empower ICT in supporting the teaching and learning process in the classroom. ICT is not just the bloom of the educational activities, but also it will be the secondary option to improve the effective and meaningful educational process. There are some unavoidable facts in the modern education:

- The ICT has been developing very rapidly nowadays. Therefore, in order to balance it, the whole educational system should be reformed and ICT should be integrated into educational activities.
- The influence of ICT, especially internet (open source tool) cannot be ignored in our student's lives. So, the learning activities should be reoriented and reformulated, from the manual source centered to the open source ones. In this case the widely use of internet access has been an unavoidable policy that should be anticipated by schools authorities.
- The presence of multimedia games and online games by internet has been another serious problem that should be wisely handled by the educational institutions. The students cannot be exterminated

from this case. They can have and do with it wherever and whenever they want. Schools, as a matter of fact, do not have enough power and time to prevent or stop it after school times. Meanwhile, most parents do not have enough times to accompany and control their children. So, the students have large opportunities to do with multimedia games or online games or browsing the negative and porn sites. Having been addicted, the students will have too little time to study, and even do not want to attend classes.

In such situation, education institutions play an important role to eradicate these problems. One of which is by facilitating the students to do edutainment or educational games. Schools can let their students be familiar with educational games adjusted by their teachers. Besides, they can also support and facilitate their students to have their own blogs in the internet. In their blogs, the students can create and write something, like an article, poem, news, short stories, features, or they can also express their opinion by an online forum provided in the internet. They are able to share experiences throughout their blogs to others from all over the world. it will lessen their time to visit the negative or porn sites existed.

- The implementation of ICT in education has not been a priority trend of educational reform and the state paid little attention to it. Therefore, there should be an active participation, initiative and good will of the schools and the government institutions to enhance ICT implementation at school.
- The teachers should be the main motivator and initiator of the ICT implementation at schools. The teachers should be aware of the social change in their teaching activities. They should be the agent of change from the classical method into the modern one. They must also be the part of the global change in learning and teaching modification.

References

Goel, D.R. (2002), Information and Communication Technology in Education: Changes and Challenges. *University News.*

Muller, Max. (2007), In Encyclopaedia Britannica. Retrieved August 15, 2007, from Encyclopaedia Britannica Online: http:/www.britaninica.com

Rosenberg, M.J. (2001), e-Learning: Strategies for Delivering Knowledge in the Digital Age. NY: McGraw-Hill. Venkatasubramanian, K. (2003).

Development as a Knowledge Society. *University News.*

National Staff Development Council and National Institute for Community Innovations (2001), E-learning for educators: Implementing the standards for staff development.

CHAPTER

Health Education and Investment in India

Awareness Towards Strategic Initiatives

K. CHANDRASEKAR

ABSTRACT

The world is more concerned with the health of the people, as productivity directly depends on the health and well-being of the people. Every organisation tries to maximise their productivity through their human resource by making good investment in the healthcare aspects of the employees. Rapid economic growth in some key Asian countries (led by the world's most populous nation China) and pro-poor policies have, no doubt, combined to reduce the number of the poor; yet, income disparities have considerably widened in this region. Struggling to cope with the challenges thrown by this disparity, governments are constantly exploring ways and means to raise the living standards of those at the bottom of the pyramid.

Organisations look forward to invest greatly in the healthcare aspects. This has emerged the health investment market to spread across fields and functions, as per the needs of the people. This has created an impact in the minds of the different people to study and explore about the prospects of Health Education and investment. This paper looks into the aspects of the growing market for health investment and the prospective issues relating to investing in healthcare sector. The problems of the investment in health are also highlighted to give a vivid picture about the Health education and the investment market in India.

Keywords: Health education, Health investment, Health insurance, Healthcare sector, Medical Tourism, Rural Health

INTRODUCTION

Living is beautiful in this world as long as you are healthier. Health is the most important aspect for every human being, as they wish to live their days without any disturbances due to diseases. Today, the world is more concerned with the health of the people, as productivity directly depends on the health and well-being of the people. Every organisation tries to maximise their productivity through their human resource by making good investment in the healthcare aspects of the employees. Organisations look forward to invest in the healthcare aspects such as medical insurance, health cover, precautionary safety measures, etc. This has emerged the health education and the investment market to spread across fields and functions, as per the needs of the people.

HEALTH EDUCATION AND INVESTMENT—A MUST

What has the world come to in the last many decades? Despite tremendous advances in science and technology, huge gains on the economic front and, more recently, a globalising world, today, one out of every six in the world or close to 1.25 billion are mired in poverty and hunger.

A large majority of the world's poor (typically earning less than $ 1 per day) are in developing countries, concentrated mainly in Africa and Asia. India is home to a large number of poor. Most of India's poor are homeless, under-fed and under-clothed.

Admittedly, Asia's contribution to poverty reduction has been noteworthy. Rapid economic growth in some key Asian countries (led by the world's most populous nation China) and pro-poor policies have, no doubt, combined to reduce the number of the poor; yet, income disparities have considerably widened in this region. Struggling to cope with the challenges thrown by this disparity, governments are constantly exploring ways and means to raise the living standards of those at the bottom of the pyramid.

WHO—ROLE IN HEALTH AWARENESS

The mission of the Office, which opened in 2003, is to provide an evidence-based, systematic and accountable approach to the full integration of the social and economic determinants of health into development strategies of countries in the WHO European Region.

The Office Fulfils Two Interrelated Functions

- Providing a portfolio of services to Member-States to increase their capacity to invest in health promotion by addressing and integrating into development agendas the policy implications of the social and economic determinants of health; and
- Monitoring, reviewing and systematizing the policy implications of emerging research findings on the social and economic determinants of health.

Essential to the execution of both functions are activities to develop skills and know-how, designed for policy-makers, practitioners and representatives of non-governmental organizations, academia and programmes of WHO and other United Nations agencies. The Office was established through a Memorandum of Agreement between the Government of Italy (the Ministry of Health and the Veneto Region) and WHO/Europe. Other Member-States, WHO collaborating centres and other partner institutions provide additional support. A scientific advisory board, whose members are nominated by the WHO Regional Director for Europe, advises the Office on its work.

INVESTMENT IN HEALTH—THE CONTRIBUTION TO ECONOMIES

The Commission on Macroeconomics and Health of World Health Organization concluded that ill-health was contributing to the low level of economic growth in poor countries. The landmark report showed that investment in some basic health interventions would lead to substantial economic growth. Production in poor countries—for example, from agriculture and mining—is much more obviously affected by physical well-being. In addition, the measures to improve health in poor countries, such as immunisation and access to essential drugs, are less complex than those needed to manage the large burden of non-communicable disease in rich countries. Understanding the role of health as a driver of economic growth is important, given the stated commitment of the governments of WHO's member-countries in March 2000 to make themselves the most competitive and dynamic knowledge-driven economy by 2010.

THE ECONOMIC INFLUENCE OF HEALTH INVESTMENT

Healthier individuals might affect the economy in four ways:

- They might be more productive at work and so earn higher incomes
- They may spend more time in the labour force, as less healthy people take sickness absence or retire early.
- They may invest more in their own education, which will increase their productivity.
- They may save more in expectation of a longer life—for example, for retirement—increasing the funds available for investment in the economy.

In particular, it is important to take account of the possibility that people health is influenced by their employment status, as there may be financial or other benefits associated with being more or less healthy than you actually are. Measures such as employment or income and health can work in both ways and both measures can be influenced separately by other factors.

Finance ministers are more interested in whether the value of human health translates into national gains. The current economic wealth of rich countries owes much to previous health gains. For example, about 30% of economic growth in the United Kingdom between 1790 and 1980 has been estimated to be attributed to better health and dietary intake. Better health meant that British workers increased their ability to convert energy into productive work by over 50% during this period. A study in 10 industrialised countries during the century to the mid-1990s found that better health increased the rate of economic growth by about 30%.

Studies that have looked at only poor countries or all countries have consistently found that better health, typically measured by life expectancy, is a significant determinant of subsequent economic growth, in some cases contributing more than improved education.

Firstly, life expectancy is not a good way to compare health in rich countries because it varies relatively little. In contrast, death rates from cardiovascular disease among the population of working age vary substantially between rich countries. For example, the death rate from ischaemic heart disease among people under 65 in the Australia, despite having fallen steeply in the past two decades, is still twice as high as in USA. In an analysis of 26 rich countries during 1960 to 2000, reductions in cardiovascular mortality emerge as a robust predictor of subsequent economic growth. In one model, a 10% fall in cardiovascular mortality is associated with a 1% increase in per capita income. Although this may not seem large, it amounts to a substantial contribution over the long-term.

Secondly, existing analyses fail to take account of the scope to increase the official retirement age. A recent simulation exercise in UK showed how an increase in the age of retirement that was consistent with gains in life expectancy would mitigate many of the adverse economic consequences attributed to ageing of societies.

IMPRESSIVE GROWTH NUMBERS

In each of the last four years, India registered robust GDP growth (in excess of 8 percent a year, with the highest recorded at 9.4 per cent in the last fiscal 2006-07). In the Ninth Plan (1997-98 to 2001-02), the annual average GDP growth rate was a decent or not-inconsiderable 5.4 percent.

These impressive growth numbers should have automatically translated to more widespread income generation among populations across the country. But it has not been the case, unfortunately. The benefit of economic growth has not flowed evenly to the entire population of the country. Both the industry and services sector have registered double-digit growth. Income in the hands of those engaged in these two high growth sectors have risen and continue to rise.

However, these two sectors employ only one-third of the country's workforce. In other words, incomes in the hands of a third of the workforce continue to rise fast. It is this section of the population (representing some 60 million families or about 30 percent of the 195 million families at present in India) with higher disposable income, which is now driving the demand for goods and services—be it food, clothing, housing, health or education. A majority of these families is concentrated in the urban and peri-urban areas.

THE RURAL HEALTH—RALLY ON EDUCATION

What is the fate of the other two-third of the population? Most of them are engaged—directly or indirectly—in agriculture and related activities, and live in the rural areas. While industry and services sectors both demonstrate impressive growth, agriculture has languished. Annual average growth in farm and related activities in the last ten years—1997 to 2006—was a woeful 2.3 percent. In other words, income in the hands of a vast majority of rural population has grown at an extremely modest rate. This tardy income growth has crippled their financial capacity to access goods and services.

While India's overall growth story unfolds impressively and the world watches with amazement the dazzling economic performance, the soft underbelly of the economy—agrarian distress—goes largely unnoticed. Even top government functionaries look uncomfortable talking about the poor and hungry. Whether the discomfort is out of ignorance or indifference or guilt is hard to tell. The media continues to chase sensational stories relating to the glamour beats of the stock market (the rise and rise of the Sensex), wealthy corporate moghuls, foreign investor interest, high fashion and entertainment and so on.

NUTRITION SECURITY—THE PERVASIVE PROBLEM

One of the most sinister aspects of the country's current state of affairs is pervasive malnutrition and under-nutrition, especially among women and children. As important as food security is nutrition security. The country is slowly turning nutrition insecure. This is because a significant number of people have inadequate access to adequate quantities of food. There has been a decline in per capita foodgrains availability.

It is the question of access and affordability. Access to food is restricted as the public distribution system does not cover the entire universe of poor or financially vulnerable people. Rising food prices of recent years—due to shortages, market distortions, high international prices—further reduce the quantum of food intake. Those in whose hands incomes are rising—about a third of the population—are in a position to consume more because they enjoy both access and affordability. It is not the case with poor people.

'A sound mind in a sound body' is a dictum more relevant to the country today than at anytime. In addition to food and nutrition, the young population of today needs education. Again access to and affordability of education will determine the mental quality of the young population in the years to come. Therefore, investment in education, training and development of skills is the need of the time.

THE NATIONAL HEALTH INITIATIVES

The Government launched the National Rural Health Mission (NRHM) in 2005. It aims to provide quality healthcare for all and increase the expenditure on healthcare from 0.9 per cent of GDP to 2-3 per cent of GDP by 2012. During the 2009 interim budget, the government allocated US $ 2.42 billion for NRHM. For example, the Tamil Nadu government has allocated US $ 698.16 million for health and family care for the year 2009-10, up from US $ 564.34 million a year ago. The increased budget includes creating a mega blood bank—Asia's largest—in Chennai and upgrading several hospitals, besides launching a new insurance scheme.

The government has announced a US$ 63.2 million initiative to promote domestic manufacture of medical devices such as stents, catheters, heart valves and orthopedic implants that will lead to lower prices of this critical equipment.

Amidst the global financial crisis, the Left Front government is trying to woo investment in the healthcare sector. "The two most important areas in health which require immediate attention are the sectors of pharmacy and medical equipment, both of which have potential for investment," said Health Minister Surjya Kanta Misra.

At a Healthcare Summit organised by the Indian Chamber of Commerce on Wednesday, Misra stressed on the importance of addressing the current situation where the government has to deal with the shifting scenario in healthcare from communicable to non-communicable diseases. Once again the government reiterated the potential of the private-public partnerships in this sector.

HEALTH INVESTMENT—AREAS OF OPPORTUNITY

The fast growth in the Indian healthcare sector has created various pockets of opportunities for investors. A recent FICCI-Ernst and Young report highlights several such areas within the healthcare sector.

- Medical infrastructure forms the largest portion of the healthcare pie. Beds in excess of one million need to be added to reach a ratio of 1.85 per thousand at an investment of US $ 77.9 billion.

- The medical equipment industry is around US $ 2.17 billion and is growing at 15 per cent per year. It is estimated to reach US $ 4.97 billion by 2012.
- The medical textiles industry is projected to double to reach US $ 753 million by 2012.
- Clinical trials have the potential to become a US $ 1 billion industry by 2010 and the health services outsourcing sector has the potential to grow to US $ 7.4 billion by 2012, from US $ 3.7 billion in 2006.

Notwithstanding the current economic slowdown, the US $ 2.26 billion Indian wellness services market is expected to grow at about 30-35 percent for the next five years on the back of rising consumerism, globalisation and changing lifestyles, according to a FICCI-Ernst and Young study. The report classified wellness industry into seven core segments of allopathy, alternative therapies, beauty, counselling, fitness/ slimming, nutrition and rejuvenation. While rejuvenation services such as spas, alternative therapies, ayurveda treatments and beauty services are expected to grow by as much as 30 per cent, fitness comprising gyms and slimming centres are expected to grow by more than 25 percent.

THE PROGRESSIVE HEALTH INVESTMENT MARKET

Healthcare, which is a US $ 35 billion industry in India, is expected to reach over US $ 75 billion by 2012 and US $ 150 billion by 2017, according to Technopak Advisors in their report—'India Healthcare Trends, 2008'. The sector offers immense potential to healthcare players as the country witnesses a rise in the incidence of lifestyle-related and other diseases. A growing elderly population and rise in income levels are also pushing for better facilities in the country.

To meet this growing demand, the country needs US $ 50 billion annually for the next 20 years, says a Confederation of Indian Industry (CII) study. India needs to add 3.1 million beds by 2018 to the existing 1.1 million, and requires immediate investments of US $ 82 billion, as per the Technopak Advisors report. Adds a FICCI-Ernst and Young report, India needs an investment of US $ 14.4 billion in the healthcare sector by 2025, to increase its bed density to at least two per thousand populations.

According to a latest report by McKinsey, driven by strong local demand, Indian healthcare market is expected to continue growing close to previously projected rates of 10 to 12 percent. With average household consumption expected to increase by more than 7 percent per annum, the annual healthcare expenditure is projected to grow at 10 percent and also the number of insured is likely to jump from 100 million to 220 million.

India's healthcare industry registered 42.44 per cent growth in net profit during April-June 2009, according to the Associated Chambers of Commerce and Industry (ASSOCHAM). In the healthcare sector, the leading 10 companies posted a growth of 23.94 percent in total income and 21.37 percent in total expenditure during the quarter.

HEALTH INSURANCE AND INVESTMENTS IN HEALTH

Currently only 10 percent of the Indian population has health insurance, which means that there is tremendous scope for growth in this area. The Indian health insurance business is growing at 50 percent. The sector is projected to grow to US$ 5.75 billion by 2010, according to a study by the PHD Chamber of Commerce and Industry.

The sector has been attracting huge investments from domestic players as well as financial investors and private equity (PE) firms. Funds such as ICICI Ventures, IFC, Ashmore and Apax Partners invested about US $ 450 million in the first six months of 2008-09 compared with US $ 125 million in the same period a year ago, according to an analysis carried out by Feedback Ventures. Feedback Ventures expects PE funds to invest at least US $ 1 billion in the healthcare sector in the next five years. In February 2009, India Venture invested almost US $ 18 million in Tamilnadu-based Kavery Medical while in June, IFC invested US $ 30 million in Max India, Piramal Life Sciences, the research and development (R&D) arm of Piramal

Group is investing US $ 41.17 million in the next two years' period to discover and develop new chemical entities and novel drug delivery systems. The Hinduja Group will invest up to US $ 72 million in increasing capacity of its hospital in Mumbai by 350 beds in the next four years through expansion of existing facility and setting up of a new unit. As part of its 'Healthymagination' initiative, GE will spend US $ 3 billion over the next six years on research and development, provide US $ 2 billion of financing over the next six years to drive healthcare information technology and health in rural and underserved areas, and invest US $ 1 billion in partnerships, content and services.

The government, along with participation from the private sector, is planning to invest US $ 1 billion to US $ 2 billion in an effort to make India one of the top five global pharmaceutical innovation hubs by 2020. The Ajay Piramal Group-owned private equity (PE) firm, India Venture Advisors, will launch its second US $ 150 million healthcare fund next year.

MEDICAL TOURISM—THE FLOURISHING HEALTHCARE

In 2007, India treated 450,000 foreign patients ranking it second in medical tourism. According to a study by McKinsey and the CII, medical tourism in India could become a US $ 2 billion industry by 2012 (from US $ 350 million in 2006). Credit Suisse estimates medical tourism to be growing at between 25-30 per cent annually.

The key selling points of the medical tourism industry are its cost effectiveness and its combination with the attractions of tourism. Treatment cost is lowest in India—20 per cent of the average cost incurred in the US, Singapore, Thailand and South Africa. Besides world class medical facilities, India is also trying to promote its traditional medicine such as ayurveda.

One best example of Indian medical tourism is the Ayurvedic Treatment provided in Kerala. Kerala has become a hub for many foreigners, who wish to undertake best treatment in ayurvedic.

FOREIGN INVESTMENT IN HEALTH SECTOR

India has invited Canadian investments in its booming health sector and offered world class affordable treatment for patients from Canada to avoid long waiting time at home. "There are tremendous opportunities for transfer of technology and investment in booming health sector in the country. Besides, India can offer developed world class treatment at a fraction of the cost," Preeti Saran, Consul General of India said. India has well-trained doctors and modern medical facilities, and Canada has innovative research and exemplary services. Synergy between these countries could be used for mutual benefits.

THE CHALLENGE AHEAD

India needs to set-up a real-time infectious disease surveillance system, improve public health infrastructure and pursue universal health coverage, according to experts.

The absence of an effective public healthcare system has contributed to the resurgence of a range of infectious diseases such as malaria and tuberculosis (TB). Others, such as cholera and typhoid, are continuing to rise, Jacob John, a fellow at the Christian Medical College, Vellore, said.

Scientists emphasised how India's recent economic growth must now be matched by the implementation of a universal healthcare system by 2020. The reports paint a dismal picture of India's health system. The country has the world's highest number of maternal and child deaths, with 1.8 million children under five and 68,000 mothers dying each year.

In 2009, India had two million new cases of TB, the highest of any country worldwide. Diseases such as visceral leishmaniasis, filariasis, cholera, and dengue are severely neglected, with little monitoring and surveillance, leading to repeated outbreaks. The country is also facing a crisis of chronic diseases such as heart ailments, diabetes, and cancer that are set to worsen over the next few decades.

Much of the problem lies in India's fragmented healthcare system, with states differing widely in their health policies. A severe shortage of health workers in remote areas and clogged supply chains of drugs and vaccines leave millions with no access to healthcare. Much of India is too poor to pay for health—half of its population lives on less than a dollar a day. High out-of-pocket payments to private doctors are sending many families into crippling debt.

It is time India moved towards a universal health care system, with its national rural health mission, initiated in 2005, offering a good starting point. The mission is starting to decentralise health planning, increase funding and community involvement in rural areas, and integrate vertical health programmes. Noting a huge challenge in financing a universal healthcare system for India's one billion population, experts suggested a hike in public spending on health from one per cent to six per cent of the national wealth, through a variety of taxes.

CONCLUSION

Health sector is one of the largest sectors which will make a healthy society. Investment in health may brings high social value also many of the entrepreneurs invests in health inorder to help the society. This rate is increasing now days. This will be the good sign for developing a good society. Health education and health investment will prosper not individually but with every other industry and fields, as 'Health' is the most crucial element of life. Thus, organisations aspire to maximize their returns through good investments in Health.

References

Gray, Hillel, "New Directions in the Investment and Control of Pension Funds", Investor Responsibility Research Center, 1983, pp. 36-37.

WHO Report, European Office for Investment for Health and Development, Venice.

Jackson, Kevin T., "Building Reputational Capital: Strategies for Integrity and Fair Play that Improve the Bottom Line", Oxford University Press, 2004.

Rajagopalan, M.S., "Health and Nutrition Profile of India", Health Education in South-East Asia, Vol. XV, No. 1, 2000.

Richardson, Benjamin J., "Socially Responsible Investment Law: Regulating the Unseen Polluters", Oxford University Press, 2008.

Mishra, M.S., "Health Policy and Management of Health Care Delivery Services in India—Issues and Challenges", Public Health in India—Five decades. A commemorative volume (Calcutta : AIIPH and PH), Vol. 1, 1998.

Marrewijk, M.N.A. and T.W. Hardjono, 'The Social Dimensions of Business Excellence', Corporate Environmental Strategy, 2001.

Young, Lauren, "A Social Fund's Strategic Shift", *Business Week Online*, 2006.

http://www.socialinvest.org/resources

http://en.wikipedia.org/wiki/Health_investment

http://www.bmj.com/cgi

http://www.thelancet.com/india-towards-universal-health-coverage

CHAPTER

9

Persisting Effect of Unemployment on Social and Professional Well-being

Importance of Communication Skills in Getting Good Jobs

GARIMA SHARMA, AZKIYA WARIS AND PREETI SHARMA

Unemployment means that while the people are willing to work, they have no work to do. The most important reasons of India's poverty and backwardness are her problem of unemployment. In today's fast growing world, unemployment is only a disaster for the people who are made unemployed as for the remainder fortunate enough to not be affected. Ignorance of good communication skills plays a major role in not getting the good employment. People do not be able to get the jobs of their dreams just because of the basic knowledge of English language. English has and will play a vital role in establishing our access to scientific and non scientific learning at the advanced level and will bring our younger generations closer to the level where they will find it easy to achieve what they choose to. The painful spectacle of English being treated with a chauvinistic intolerance at the hands of people, for whom it has opened up vistas of advanced learning in science and technology, commerce and industries, politics and judiciary, is no more witnessed. As a source language, it is the only language which is fully equipped with vernaculars and it renders adequately the entire corpus of technical terms and scientific jargon. This state of affairs necessitates a compulsive resort to this language for the people who come out of the institutions of Higher Learning to find jobs of their own liking.

Every employer is looking for a specific set of skills from job-seekers that match the skills necessary to perform a particular job. But beyond these job-specific technical skills, certain skills, i.e. Communication skills are nearly universally sought by employers. The better news is that job-seekers with weaknesses in these areas can improve their skills through training, professional development, or obtaining coaching/ mentoring from someone who understands these skills. And without these skills a person is in efficient in getting good employment.

In general, the higher one's level of education, the better one's chances of getting and keeping a good job. For example, according to the *New York Times'* website this past week, women with a college degree have only about half the rate of unemployment (right now during this recession) that women with only a high school diploma have (I believe the numbers were 4.2% compared to 8.8). In most careers, communication skills are vital. If a person is unable to communicate well in a society or in his/her professional career, he/she will not be able to move forward in his/her life. In order to get to a position of responsibility, you need to be able to communicate (again, depending on your career) with bosses, subordinates, customers, co-workers and others. Education is one of the most important factors in landing a better job. This is why more and more people are attending schools of higher education. In my opinion, colleges in particular and schools in general do two things well. First, they help a person think critically. So, even if you don't actually use what you have learned in college in the real world, school will help. How many times have you heard people say, "I've never use that in the real world!" Sure, a person may not use certain equations, etc., but the process of learning is what is important. It develops a person's mind. This is key. Second, colleges and schools in general help people interact with one another. The better a person's social skills are, the better the chance for success. Why? We will inevitably deal with people. So, in this sense, language skill is extremely important. Perhaps, one more point. In an information age such as ours, language skill may be even more important.

The more education, training, and specific skills a person can bring to a job interview, the more likely he or she will be to obtain employment. People get paid for what they know and what they can do. In the marketplace, a job applicant simply must have something to sell to an employer to meet that employer's needs. As for the importance of communication skills (both written and oral), it would be hard to overemphasize their importance in the workplace, regardless of the job. Miscommunication creates errors, wastes time, and reduces effectiveness and productivity. Also, poor communicators who deal with the public make a bad impression for their companies. Employers understand the importance of clear and professional communications. Several years ago I taught a college night class in oral and written communications. My students were bank employees, and their banks paid their tuition. That makes a convincing argument in favor of communication skills being very important in the workplace. Education enables a person to acquire specific knowledge and skills. Education is definitely very helpful in getting jobs that require use of such knowledge and skill. Education is also helpful in improving general mental capabilities of a person, and therefore education is also contributing factor in getting jobs where the education may not be directly related to the job. For example, many companies recruit fresh graduates and post-graduates from diverse academic fields and train them to take up managerial responsibilities not directly related to their educational specialization. However, people can also be over qualified for a job. A person, who is highly educated, tends to get bored in jobs that do not require application of his or her mental capabilities and therefore unable to perform the job effectively. For this reason companies avoid recruiting people who are over qualified. Communication skill is something that people may have in degrees that are mostly unrelated to their education. Communication is the ability to understand other and to make them understand you. This kind of skill is useful in most of the jobs excepting some very few jobs like a research scientist working independently. Therefore, communication skill is a definitely plus point in getting jobs and in performing well in one's job.

Effective communication and managers' communication skills are an extremely important issue for effective organizational behaviour.

Effective business must succeed in all its aspects in order to both correspond to the newest market trends, and satisfy customers' demands.

Lack of effective communication may lead to:

- Misunderstandings
- Lack of information
- Decrease in employees' performance
- Increase in company's turnover, as a result

Ineffective or poor communication is frustrating for employees, and becomes a source of a conflict. Managers' inability to clearly express their thoughts, ideas and demands leads to employees' inability to perform work well, according to the company's demands.

Such a situation may take place when an employee is not truly aware of what is requested of benefits of effective communication of workplace.

If a manager is able to communicate their ideas clearly, so that employees definitely know what is asked of them, the subordinates will, consequently, perform their jobs correspondingly. On contrast, an aggressive way of managing reports results in employees' getting more and more frustrated, often guessing what their real faults were. This decreases the satisfaction an employee gets from the job.

CONCLUSION

A good style of management, as well as a positive approach to communication, ensures that an employee and a supervisor understand each other, and are more effective at the workplace. Effective communication in the workplace provides employees with a clear understanding of what is demanded from them, with knowledge of what to do and what to expect. For organizations, such a communication style creates effective performance of the staff, and, consequently, increases customer loyalty and profit. It is very clear that if a person wants himself/herself professionally and socially sound, he/she must have a strong command over the four skills, i.e. are listening, reading, writing, and most importantly speaking.

References

ADMIN (2010), Professional Etiquettes for that first good impression, Oct. 22.

How does education affect chances of attaining a job? And what role does communication skills playing a career?

Randall, S. Hansen and Katherine Hansen, What do employers really want? Top skills and values employers seek from job-seekers.

CHAPTER

10

Women's Empowerment and Gender Equality to Promote Education

A Review

JAMIL AHMAD

ABSTRACT

Women empowerment means empowering women socially, economically and politically so that they can break away from male domination and claim equality with them. Its aim at increasing women's power in terms of their self-reliance and internal strength to determine choices in life includes both controls over resources and over ideology. Women empowerment means not only greater external control but also growing inner capability as greater self-confidence and inner transformation of one's consciousness that enable one to overcome external barriers to access resources and changing the traditional ideology for social, economic and political

development of women. Empowerment is therefore clearly concerned with power and particularly with the power relations and the distribution of power between individuals and groups (Kahlon, 2004, S. Batliwala, 1994: 17). Empowerment is a multidimensional process, which should enable the individuals or a group of individuals to realize their full identity and power in all spheres of life. Despite the progress made by the Indian women, the life of average Indian women from birth through infancy, childhood, adolescence, marriage, motherhood is a long journey of battle against discrimination are deprivation that is due to socio-culture structure of the society that decides women's all round development. Hence the economic empowerment of women is essential for achievement gender equality in all spheres. The purpose of this paper is to identify the key links between education and women empowerment. Knowing the fact that education provides the critical foundation from which further empowerment flows, the main objectives of this study is to review the status of women in India in present scenario. This paper also evaluates the growth of sex-wise enrolment by stages in the different period.
Key Words: Women Empowerment, Education, Gender Equity.

I. INTRODUCTION

Women empowerment means empowering women socially, economically and politically so that they can break away from male domination and claim equality with them. Its aim at increasing women's power in terms of their self-reliance and internal strength to determine choices in life includes both controls over resources and over ideology. Further, Women empowerment is not only greater external control but also growing inner capability as greater self-confidence and inner transformation of one's consciousness that enable one to overcome external barriers to access resources and changing the traditional ideology for social, economic and political development of women. Empowerment is a multidimensional process, which should enable the individuals or a group of individuals to realize their full identity and power in all spheres of life.

Despite the progress made by the Indian women, the life of average Indian women from birth through infancy, childhood, adolescence, marriage, motherhood is a long journey of battle against discrimination are deprivation that is due to socio-culture structure of the society that decides women's all round development. Hence, the economic empowerment of women is essential for achievement gender equality in all spheres.

Empowerment is an ongoing and dynamic process, which enhances women's and any other marginalized and alienated groups ability to change the structure and ideologies that keep them subordinate. It is a process of making present power structure more inclusive, including all men and women, senior citizens, dalits, indigenous people and people with disabilities (Bhasin and Dhar, 1998). Empowerment is therefore clearly concerned with power and particularly with the power relations and the distribution of power between individuals and groups (Kahlon, 2004, S. Batliwala, 1994: 17).

II. OBJECTIVE AND METHODOLOGY

The purpose of this paper is to identify the key links between education and women empowerment. Knowing the fact that education provides the critical foundation from which further empowerment flows, the main objectives of this study is to review the status of women in India in present scenario. This paper also evaluates the growth of sex-wise enrolment by stages in the different period. The data that we use to examine the gender inequality and empowerment of women are taken from the various issues of National Family Health Survey (NFHS-3), Ministry of Health and Family Welfare, Government of India, World Development Reports, World Development Indicators of World Bank and Human Development's Reports of UNDP.

III. THE STATUS OF WOMEN IN INDIA : PRESENT SCENARIO

Eliminating gender differences in access to education and educational attainment are key elements on the path to attaining gender equality and reducing the disempowerment of women. In recognition of the pivotal role of education in development and of persistent gender inequalities in access to education, the elimination of gender disparity in primary education is one of the Millennium Development Goals. The achievement of universal primary education has been a key goal of Indian planning since Independence. Almaz Negash (2006) highlighted the discrepancies between men and women in the contemporary world with the supporting statistics that: (i) There are 135 million children in the world between 7 and 18 who are not receiving any education at all, of which approximately 60 percent are girls, (ii) Of the girls who do begin primary school, only 1 in 4 is still in school four years later, (iii) The gender gap increases at higher levels of education, (iv) Two-thirds of the 880 million illiterate adults around the world are women, (v) When women's income increases, money is more likely to be channeled back into families and they are more likely to educate daughters, and (vi) Each additional year in school raises a woman's earnings by about 15 percent compared to 11 percent for a man.

The continuous emphasis on female education, literacy-mission-drive and adult female literacy drive, etc., all these have contributed in minimizing the gender gap in India. Table 1 show the literacy rate for the age groups 7+ and 15+ for the census years 1961 to 2001.

The literacy rate of the population aged 7+ recorded 28.3 per cent in 1961, 34.5 per cent in 1971, 43.6 per cent in 1981, 52.2 per cent in 1991 and 65.4 per cent. It shows that the literacy rate increased by 13.2 percentage points between 1991 and 2001, whereas it had increased only by 8.6 percentage points between 1981 and 1991. It can also be observed that male literacy of the population aged 7+ increased by 35.5 percentage points between 1991 and 2001, whereas female literacy has increased even more rapidly by 38.8 percentage points during the same period. For the population aged 15+ similar patterns was recorded. Accordingly, the male-female gap in the literacy rate of the population aged 7+ has declined from 25 percent to 21.7 percent and of the population aged 15+ from 28.3 percent to 24 percent between 1961 and 2001. The growth during 1991-2001 exceeded that of every previous decade and it can be considered as a great achievement. State-wise Literacy Rates and Decadal Difference in Literacy Rates by Sex are shown in Table 2. A perusal of this table reveals that the

TABLE I

Literacy Rate of the Population in the Age Groups 7+ and 15+ 1961 to 2001

Year	Literacy Rate (Age 7+)			Literacy rate (Age 15+)			Gender difference (M-F)	
	Male	Female	Total	Male	Female	Total	Age 7+	Age 15+
(1)	(2)	(3)	(4)	(5)	(6)	(7)	(8)	(9)
1961	40.4	15.4	28.3	41.5	13.2	27.8	25.0	28.3
1971	46.0	22.0	34.5	47.7	19.4	34.1	24.0	28.3
1981	56.4	29.8	43.6	54.9	25.8	40.9	26.6	29.1
1991	64.1	39.3	52.2	61.3	34.1	48.2	24.8	27.2
2001	75.9	54.2	65.4	71.1	47.1	59.4	21.7	24.0

Source : Census of India, 2001, Government of India.

TABLE 2

State-wise Decadal Difference in Literacy Rates by Sex in India : 1991-2001

India/States/ Union territories	*1991*				*2001*				*Change in Literacy Rate (1991 to 2001)*		
	Total	*Males*	*Females*	*Gap in Literacy rate*	*Total*	*Males*	*Females*	*Gap in Literacy rate*	*Total*	*Males*	*Females*
(1)	*(2)*	*(3)*	*(4)*	*(5)*	*(6)*	*(7)*	*(8)*	*(9)*	*(10)*	*(11)*	*(12)*
India	52.2	64.1	39.3	24.8	65.5	76.0	54.3	21.7	13.3	11.9	15.0
J and K	N.A	N.A	N.A	N.A	54.46	65.75	41.82	23.93	—	N.A	N.A
Himachal Pradesh	63.94	75.41	52.26	23.16	77.13	86.02	68.08	17.94	13.19	10.61	15.82
Punjab	58.51	65.66	50.41	15.26	69.95	75.63	63.55	12.08	11.45	9.97	13.14
Chandigarh	77.81	82.04	72.34	9.70	81.76	85.65	76.65	9.00	3.94	3.61	4.31
Uttaranchal	57.75	72.79	41.63	31.17	72.28	84.01	60.26	23.75	14.53	11.22	18.63
Haryana	55.85	69.10	40.47	28.62	68.59	79.25	56.31	22.94	12.74	10.16	15.84
Delhi	75.29	82.01	66.99	15.02	81.82	87.37	75.00	12.36	6.53	5.36	8.01
Rajasthan	38.55	54.99	20.44	34.55	61.03	76.46	44.34	32.12	22.48	21.47	23.90
Uttar Pradesh	40.71	54.82	24.37	30.46	57.36	70.23	42.98	27.25	16.65	15.40	18.61
Bihar	37.49	51.37	21.99	29.38	47.53	60.32	33.57	26.75	10.04	8.95	11.58

(*Contd.*)

TABLE 2 (*Contd.*)

(1)	(2)	(3)	(4)	(5)	(6)	(7)	(8)	(9)	(10)	(11)	(12)
Sikkim	56.94	65.70	46.76	18.94	69.68	76.73	61.46	15.27	12.73	11.03	14.70
Arunachal Pradesh	41.59	51.45	29.69	21.76	54.74	64.07	44.24	19.83	13.15	12.62	14.55
Nagaland	61.65	67.62	54.75	12.87	67.11	71.77	61.92	9.85	5.46	4.15	7.17
Manipur	59.89	71.63	47.60	24.03	68.87	77.87	59.70	18.17	8.97	6.24	12.10
Mizoram	82.27	85.61	78.60	7.01	88.49	90.69	86.13	4.56	6.22	5.08	7.53
Tripura	60.44	70.58	49.65	20.93	73.66	81.47	65.41	16.06	13.22	10.89	15.77
Meghalaya	49.10	53.12	44.85	8.27	63.31	66.14	60.41	5.73	14.21	13.02	15.56
Assam	52.89	61.87	43.03	18.84	64.28	71.93	56.03	15.90	11.39	10.06	13.00
West Bengal	57.70	67.81	46.56	21.25	69.22	77.58	60.22	17.35	11.52	9.77	13.66
Jharkhand	41.39	55.80	25.52	30.28	54.13	67.94	39.38	28.57	12.74	12.14	13.86
Orissa	49.09	63.09	34.68	28.41	63.61	75.95	50.97	24.98	14.52	12.86	16.29
Chhattisgarh	42.91	58.07	27.52	30.54	65.18	77.86	52.40	25.46	22.27	19.79	24.87
Madhya Pradesh	44.67	58.54	29.35	29.19	64.11	76.80	50.28	26.52	19.44	18.26	20.93
Gujarat	61.57	73.39	48.92	24.47	69.97	80.50	58.60	21.90	8.40	7.11	9.68
Daman and Diu	71.20	82.66	59.40	23.26	81.09	88.40	70.37	18.03	9.89	5.73	10.97
Dadra and Nagar Haveli	40.71	53.56	26.98	29.58	60.03	73.32	42.99	30.32	19.33	19.76	16.01
Maharashtra	64.87	76.56	52.32	24.24	77.27	86.27	67.51	18.75	12.39	9.71	15.20

Andhra Pradesh	44.09	55.13	32.72	22.42	61.11	70.85	51.17	19.68	17.02	15.72	18.45
Karnataka	56.04	67.26	44.34	22.93	67.04	76.29	57.45	18.84	11.00	9.03	13.12
Goa	75.51	83.64	67.09	16.55	82.32	88.88	75.51	13.37	6.81	5.24	8.42
Lakshadweep	81.78	90.18	72.89	17.29	87.52	93.15	81.56	11.59	5.74	2.98	8.67
Kerala	89.81	93.62	86.17	7.45	90.92	94.20	87.86	6.34	1.11	0.58	1.69
Tamil Nadu	62.66	73.75	51.33	22.42	73.47	82.33	64.55	17.78	10.81	8.58	13.22
Pondicherry	74.74	83.68	65.63	18.06	81.49	88.89	74.13	14.76	6.75	5.21	8.50
Andaman and Nicobar Islands	73.02	78.99	65.46	13.53	81.18	86.07	75.29	10.78	8.16	7.08	9.83

Source : Census of India, 2001, Government of India.

gender gap in literacy rate was highest in top five states namely, Rajasthan with 34.55 percent, Uttaranchal with 31.17 percent, Chhattisgarh with 30.54 percent, Uttar Pradesh with 30.46 percent and Jharkhand with 30.28 percent in 1991. But in 2001, out of the above five states only Rajasthan had gender gap of 32.12 percentage points and rest have recoded less than 30 percentage points. During 1991-2001, four States/Uts namely, Kerala with 0.58, Lakshadweep with 2.98, Chandigarh with 3.61 and Nagaland with 4.15 had values of decadal difference in male literacy rates less than five. Six States/UTs namely Rajasthan with 21.47, Chhattisgarh with 19.79, Dadra and Nagar Haweli with 19.76, Madhya Pradesh with 18.26, Andhra Pradesh with 15.72 and U.P. with 15.4 registered top positions in decadal difference in male literacy rates. Decadal difference (1991-2001) in female literacy rates was registered lowest in first four States namely, Kerala with 1.69, Chandigarh with 4.31, Nagaland with 7.17 and Mizoram with 7.53, whereas the same was recoded highest in Chhattisgarh with 24.87, Rajasthan with 23.9, M.P. with 20.93, Uttaranchal with 18.63 and U.P. with 18.61 percentage points. Analyses reveal that many States have made significance progress in minimizing the gender gap in literacy rates. All these suggest that concerted efforts must be made for increase in enrolment as well as retention of girls in poor performing States.

IV. GROWTH OF ENROLMENT

In the school year 2005-06, 71% of children age 6-17 attended school—77% in urban areas and 69 percent in rural areas (IIPS and Macro International, 2007). As Figure 3.1 shows, 66% of girls age 6-17 attended school, compared with 75% of boys in the same age group. The sex ratio of children 6-17 attending school in the 2005-06 school year is 889 girls per 1,000 boys.

While gender differentials in school at-attendance are minimal among children age 6-10, they increase with age. In fact, the sex ratio of girls attending school per 1,000 boys attending school declines from 957 in the age-group 6-10, to 884 in the age-group 11-14, and then to a low of only 717 in the age-group 15-17. In addition to the gender differential in school attendance among children age 15-17, the low absolute levels of school attendance for both girls and boys in this age group is also of concern. Less than half of boys and about one-third of girls age 15-17 attend school.

FIG. 1

Percentage of Boys and Girls Attending School in 2005-06 School Years

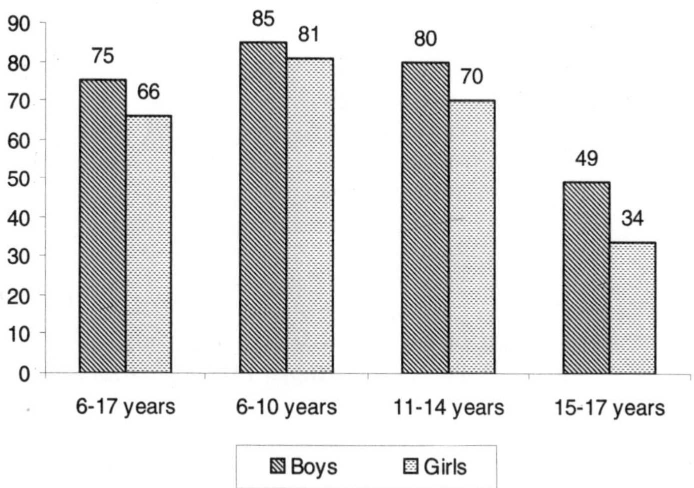

An examination of the data on school attendance by age, however, reveals that gender disparity in school attendance is largely a rural phenomenon (Figures 2 and 3). In urban areas, about equal proportions of boys and girls attend school at each age; however, in rural areas, gender inequality in attendance is evident in every age group and increases with age. Notably, even in urban areas, only about half the children age 15-17 attend school.

Both supply and demand-side factors play a role in whether children attend school or not. Key supply-side factors include the availability, accessibility, and quality of schools—factors for which no information is available in NFHS-3. The demand-side factors include the level of education of

Fig. 2
Percentage of Boys and Girls Attending School in 2005-06 School Years NFHS-3, India

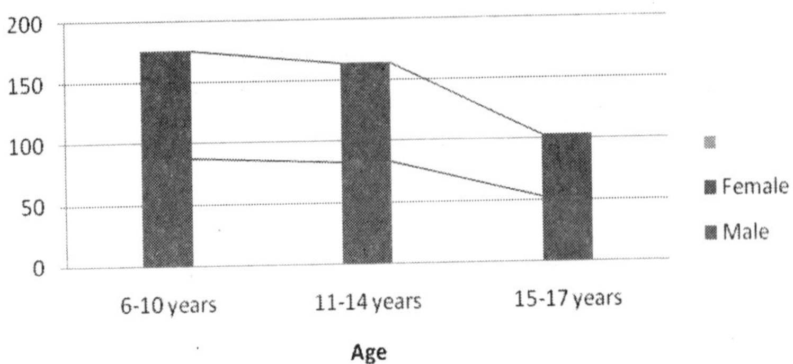

Fig. 3
Percentage of Boys and Girls Attending School in 2005-06 School Years NFHS-3, India

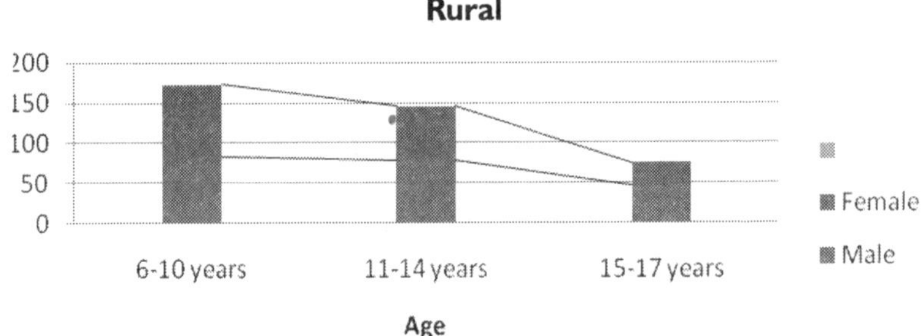

household members and household wealth—factors whose influence can be examined using NFHS-3 data. Adults who are educated are more likely to ensure that their children are educated. Wealth enables access to education by providing the resources needed to buy quality education and by reducing the opportunity cost of children's time. For poorer households, children's time spent in school is time not spent in contributing to the economic sustainability of the household.

The following are the strategies adopted by the Government to check drop-out rates: (i) Creating parental awareness, (ii) community mobilization, (iii)economic incentives, (iv) Minimum Levels of Learning (MLL), (v) District Primary Education Programme (DPEP), (vi) National Programme of Nutritional support to Primary Education (Mid-day Meals Scheme), (vii) The 83rd Constitutional Amendment Bill was introduced in Rajya Sabha to make the Right to Elementary Education a fundamental right and a fundamental duty, (viii) National Elementary Education Mission, (ix) A National Committee of State Education Ministers has been set-up with the Minister of Human Resource Development as the Chairperson of the committee, (x) Media publicity and advocacy plans, and (xi) Sarva Shiksha Abhiyan, etc.

VII. CONCLUSION

In this study an attempt has been made to assess the current size of the gender gap by measuring the extent to which women in India have achieved equality with men in terms of educational attainment. For the overall development of the country, educated, healthy, enlightened and empowered women are very much essential. An educated mother will always provide light to her children. The findings of the study indicate that the gender disparities in literacy among the women has widen. Men still continue to dominate the women depriving them of many crucial needs of the life. The experience of the developed countries and India clearly shows that the gender gap is more in India in comparison to developed countries where the gap is so minimum that it may be ignored. Indicators for measuring women's power sharing level must include her freedoms and ability to influence the decision about her and other's at all level. As who wields the real power depend not only on economic and political structure but also on social ideology. There is some other hidden factors such as undervaluation of women's work, over burden with work, stress and responsibility of women that need to be qualified and should receive the special consideration to increase the gender equality. If gender equality is indeed to be achieved, there is need to pay attention to the interest of women. Now it is a well-established fact that education is the most significant factor that has highest degree of positive correlation with Social and Economic development. A renewed focus on achieving total literacy is required, with a special emphasis on female literacy. Reducing the gender gap at all level of education would be a focus area.

References

Acharya, Meena (1997) : "Gender Equity and Empowerment of women, A Status report", UNFPA, Kathmandu, Wanthor Pushpa Acharya.

Acharya, Meena, Ghimire, Pushpa (2005) : "Gender Indicators of Equity, Inclusion and Poverty Reduction", *EPW*, Oct., 29.

Batliwala, S. (1994) : Women's Empowerment in South Asia: Concept and Practices in Exchange Change, 1(2).

Bhasin, K. and S. Dhar (1998) : "Joining Hands to Developed Women Power", a report of a South Asian Workshop on Gender and Sustainable Development, Koitta, Bangladesh.

Chaudhry, M. (1993) : "Indian Women's Movement: Reform and Revival", Radiant Publisher, New Delhi.

Human Development Report (1990, 1995, 2004, 2005) : UNDP, Oxford University Press, New York.

IBRD (2001) : "Attacking Poverty, World Development Report", Oxford University Press, New York.

Kahlon, P. (2004) : 73rd Amendment and Women's Empowerment: A Punjab Study, Paper Presented in the seminar on 'Rural Empowerment and Economic Empowerment in South Asia at G.B. Pant Social Science Institute, Allahabad, India.

Sen, Amartya (2001) : "Many faces of Gender Ineqality", *Frontline*, Nov. 9.

Singh, Shrawn Kr. (2003) : "Political empowerment of women still a Dream in India", Third World Impact.

Almaz Negash (2006) : "Economic Empowerment of Women": http://www.scu.edu/ethics/practicing/focusareas/global_ethics/economicempowerment.html

Anand, Sudhir, and Amartya Sen (1995) : Gender inequality in human development: Theories and measurement. Occasional Paper 19. United Nations Development Programme, Human Development Report Office.

Bhargava, P.K. (2002) : http://educationforallinindia.com/page174.html

Census of India (2001) : Provisional Population Totals. Office of the Registrar General of India, Government of India, 2001.

Chiang, Lan-hung Nora (1998) : "Women and Development in Taiwan." *Asian Journal of Women's Studies*, 4(4)

Choudhury, Usha Ranee (1999) : "Political Awareness and Women's Participation in Politics."Gender Perspective: Participation, Empowerment and Development. ed. Anil Dutta Mishra. New Delhi: Radha Publications: pp. 131-39.

Das, Gupta, Monica, Jiang Zhenghua, Li Bohua, Xie Zhenming, Woojin Chang, and Bae Hwa-Ok. (2003) : "Why is Son Preference So Persistent in East and South Asia?" Working Paper No. 2942, The World Bank.

Das, Gupta, Monica and P.N. Mari Bhat (1998) : 'Intensified Gender Bias in India: A consequence of Fertility Decline', in M. Krishnaraj, R. Sudarshan and A. Shariff (eds.) Gender, Population and Development, Oxford University Press, N. Delhi.

Dreze Jean and Amartya Sen (1996) : India, Economic Development and Social Opportunity, Oxford University Press, New Delhi.

Haq, Mahbub ul. (1995) : Reflections on Human Development. New York: Oxford University Press.

IndiaStat.Com (2005) : Electronic database. www.indiastat.com, last accessed May 15, 2005.

Kochak, Ajani K., (2005) : "Development Indices: A comparative study of India and China", Institute of Chinese Studies, Occasional Studies Series, No. 4, June 2005.

Mahendra K. Premi (2002) : http://educationforallinindia.com/page172.html

Sen, Amartya (1989) : "Development as Capability Expansion." *Journal of Development Planning*. New York, 19: 41-58.

Sen, Amartya (1999) : Development as Freedom. New York: Anchor Books.

Sen, Samita (2000) : "Toward a Feminist Politics? The Indian Women's Movement in Historical Perspective." Policy Research Report on Gender and Development, Working Paper Series No. 9.

Shariff, Abusaleh (1998) : India Human Development Report, National Council of Applied Economic Research, Oxford University Press, N. Delhi.

Sharma, Kumud (2000) : "Power and Representation: Reservation for Women in India." *Asian Journal of Women's Studies*. 6(1).

Srivastava, A.B.L. (2002) : http://educationforallinindia.com/page171.html

UNDP (United Nations Development Programme). (1990): Human Development Report, 1990. New York: Oxford University Press.

UNDP (2001) : Human Development Report, 2001. New York: Oxford University Press.

United Nations (2005) : "Convention on the Elimination of All Forms of Discrimination against Women." Last updated February 2005. www.un.org/womenwatch/daw/cedaw/, accessed May 3, 2005.

United Nations (2005) : "Convention on the Political Rights of Women." Last updated 2004.http://www.un.org/womenwatch/asp/user/list.asp?ParentID=10741, accessed May 3, 2005.

United Nations Development Fund for Women (UNIFEM) (2002) : Progress of the World's Women, 2002 : Gender Equality and the Millennium Development Goals, Volume 2. New York: United Nations Development Fund for Women.

Visaria, Leela (2000) : "Violence Against Women: A Field Study", *Economic and Political Weekly*, Vol. 35, No. 20, May 13th-19th.

Wolff, Brent, *et. al.* (2000) : "Who decides? Women's Status and Negotiations of sex in Uganda." Culture, Health and Sexuality, 2(3): 303-22.

World Bank, Gender and Development Group (2003) : Gender Equality and the Millenium Development Goals. http://www.mdgender.net (10 Oct 2004).

UNDP (1990) : Human Development Report, New York.

———, (1995) : Human Development Report, New York.

———, (2000) : Human Development Report, New York.

———, (2005) : Human Development Report, New York.

Websites

http://www.flonnet.com/fl2218/stories/20050909000607300.htm

http://www.thehindu.com/thehindu/br/2006/08/01/stories/2006080100181500.htm

http://en.wikipedia.org/wiki/Economy_of_India

http://presidentofindia.nic.in/scripts/palatest1.jsp?id=7

http://en.wikipedia.org/wiki/Education_in_India

http://www.education.nic.in/htmlweb/stateeduprofile.htm

http://www.womenexcel.com/education/education.htm

http://www.literacyonline.org/products/ili/webdocs/alshi.html

http://educationforallinindia.com/page172.html

CHAPTER

11

Pioneering Dreams for Improving Quality in Higher Education

With Special Reference to India

MIRZA SHAHAB SHAH AND KRISHNA KUMAR

ABSTRACT

Of course higher education in India has been in the news for many reasons. The new HRD Minister Kapil Sibal has been busy drafting new bills and formulating new policies to give a big push to higher education and to open up the higher education sector to foreign universities and their affiliates. In this scenario, two issues have been the major focus. Only 10 percent of eligible young students enroll in colleges in India Though the official enrolment ratio in India is about 11 per cent, if we go by how many of these students are really learning anything in logically well–equipped colleges, my guess is that the ratio will be down to alarmingly low level of about 5 per cent. For example, in the US and Europe, the enrolment ratio is more than 60 percent. Even in China, our favorite competitor these days, the ratio is about 19 percent. Second, the need to urgently improve the quality of higher education in the country to make it more competitive globally and to emerge 'global knowledge hub' in the near future. However, any meaningful discussion on these two issues has to recognize two alarming features of higher education system in the country. Improving educational performance ranks high on the national agenda, with educators and policy-makers focusing on testing, accountability, curriculum reform, teacher quality, school choice, and related concerns. Though extensive literature exists that links school facilities to the quality of education and to teacher morale and teacher, clearly absent has been an examination of how school conditions affect teaching and learning. To gain a milestone for a successful education system, one needs a high quality teaching staff. Attracting and retaining high quality teachers is thus a primary requirement for an educational institution. For the development of teachers and students there are some points to improve higher education conditions.

Teachers and students hold the main responsibility for improving higher education. But they need a lot of help. College and university leaders, state and federal officials, and accrediting associations have the power to shape an environment that is favorable to good practice in higher education. This paper is a summary of some principles for Good Practice in Higher Education as compiled in a study supported by the American Association of Higher Education.

Key words: Education, Policy-maker, curriculum reform, teacher quality.

INTRODUCTION

India has one of the largest Higher Education systems in the world Central Government is responsible for major policy relating to higher education in the country. It provides grants to UGC and establishes central universities in the country. The Central Government is also responsible for declaration of Education Institutions as 'Deemed to be University' on the recommendation of the UGC. Since the establishment of formal universities at Calcutta, Bombay and Madras in the year 1857. The western system of higher education has been progressing every year. There have been many committees colonial India. Their recommendations were not give due importance by the colonial rulers. After independence, there have been attempts to review the progress of higher education and to suggest measures to be taken for its speedier progress.

A little more than half a century has passed since the Government initiated a planned development of higher education in the country with the establishment of University Grants Commission in 1953. The policy for the development of higher education has been mainly governed by the "National Policy on Education" of 1986 (as modified in 1992) and its Program of Action, 1992. The 1986 policy and Action Plan of 1992 were based on the two land mark reports namely, the "University Education Commission Report" of 1948-49 (popularly known as Radhakrishnan Commission), and the "Education Commission Report" of 1964-66, (popularly known as Kothari Commission). These two reports, in fact, laid down the basic framework for the National Policy of 1986 for higher education in the country. The Radhakrishnan Commission on University Education had set-up goals for development of higher education. While articulating these goals, the Commission put it in following words: "The most important and urgent reform needed in education is to transform it, to endeavor to relate it to the life, needs and aspirations of the people and thereby make it the powerful instrument of social, economic and cultural transformation necessary for the realization of the national goals. For this purpose, education should be developed so as to increase productivity, achieve social and national integration, accelerate the process of modernization and cultivate social, moral and spiritual values." The National Policy on Higher Education (1986) translated the vision of Radhakrishnan Commission and Kothari Commission in five main goals for higher education, as enumerated below; which include Greater Access, Equal Access (or Equity), Quality and Excellence, Relevance and Value-based Education.

- Greater Access requires an enhancement in the education institutional capacity to provide opportunities to all who deserve and desire higher education.
- Equity involves fair access to the poor and the socially disadvantaged groups.

- Quality and Excellence involve provision of education by accepted standard so that students receive available knowledge of the highest standard and help them to enhance their human resource capabilities.
- Relevance involves promotion of education so as to develop human resources keeping pace with the changing economic, social and cultural development of the country.
- Value-based Education involves inculcating basic moral values among the youth.

QUALITY CONTROL IN THE 21ST CENTURY THROUGH HIGHER EDUCATION

Over the last twenty years, a new paradigm of the function of higher education in society has emerged. While universities still maintain their role as the "conscience of society", more pragmatic roles have been evolving over time: universities no longer pursue knowledge for its own sake; rather they provide qualified manpower and produce knowledge. With this new economically-oriented paradigm, comes accountability. Higher education will be judged in terms of outputs and the contributions it makes to national development. Criteria to assess the quality of the work and of the teams which carry out research in this new university will differ from those of more traditional, disciplinary science. In the past, quality was determined through peer review. Control was maintained by careful selection of those judged competent to act as peers, which was in part determined by their previous contributions to their discipline. In the new university additional criteria are added through the context of application which now incorporates a diverse range of intellectual interests as well as other social, economic or political ones. To the criterion of intellectual interest and its interaction, further questions are posed, "Will the solution be competitive in the market? Will it be cost effective? Will it be socially acceptable, Quality assurance will be more complex as universities move to broaden the range of their knowledge missions? Until now, quality control in teaching and research has been exercised through essentially the same type of peer review system. Quality has been a matter for academics and academics alone. It has been up to them to determine when quality in both teaching and research has been achieved. Hybridization of the disciplinary structure is likely to Quality Assurance in Higher Education continued to be the main mode of expansion in teaching provision in the future. If new research practices diffuse more widely throughout universities, entirely new assurance mechanisms will be necessary for the problem-oriented teaching that will accompany it. One can expect to see the development of new bench-marking methodologies and the production of a range of benchmarking studies across the higher education sector. These studies will help rank universities according to various quality indicators by region, by country and even globally; not only according to teaching and research but across the entire range of knowledge missions (Schofield, 1998). In the quality assurance processes which are now emerging, a much wider range of factors is being considered. Universities will not be able to insist on criteria which reflect their intellectual interests alone rather they will be one actor among several and the challenge for them will be to ensure that their legitimate interests survive the negotiation process.

GOVERNANCE IS A KEY ISSUE IN HIGHER EDUCATION

Governance is currently a key issue not only for higher education institutions but for society as a whole. The way organizations are managed, the directions they take and the values they hold send clear signals about their role and functions in society. For this reason, the governance structures of universities were unquestioned for most of the twentieth century. Yet in the final decades of that century significant changes were starting to be felt. The most important of these changes related to the way universities were viewed by governments. In particular, the role of universities in contributing to national economies was being recognized. Greater accountability and more intense scrutiny from the outside meant that the traditional values of universities were being challenged. The task of universities, and for society as a whole, is to develop strategies that will retain the best of what universities have traditionally stood for while responding positively to new pressures and priorities. The principle of partnership, therefore, is not simple rhetoric. It underscores a set of relationships that need to be reflected in the governance structures of universities in the twenty-first century. There is no doubting the potential of universities to contribute to national economies but equally there is no doubting their record as significant social institutions. Unfettered managerialism is not the answer for universities of the future. Certainly, modern universities need to be managed but that management needs to involve the 'academic heartland' as much as it needs to be guided by broader social purposes. The management of universities in this century needs to be encased in structures that rely on guidance from above in the form of governing bodies and from below in the form of academic staff. These bi-directional processes influencing management have the potential to re-engage an alienated academy and re-establish the broader purposes of universities. It is not too difficult to imagine the kind of structures that will reflect these principles and it would not be difficult to accept different configurations across national systems. In the end, it will be these governance partnerships that will determine not only who and who will not be involved in university decision-making, but the very identity of the modern university itself. There is a choice confronting governments and policy-makers and it is a choice about the future. Let us hope that it will be made wisely and let us hope that it will focus on the inclusion and participation of key players rather than their exclusion and marginalization.

PRINCIPLES OF GOOD PRACTICE FOR ASSESSING STUDENT LEARNING

Teachers and students hold the main responsibility for improving higher education. But they need a lot of help. College and university leaders, state and federal officials, and accrediting associations have the power to shape an environment that is favorable to good practice in higher education. These nine principles, which were created by a panel of assessment experts and revised in 1996, provide a fundamental basis and starting place to assist in the design of an assessment plan for an academic program."This document was developed under the auspices of the AAHE Assessment Forum with support from the Fund for the Improvement of Post-secondary Education with additional support for publication and dissemination from the Exxon Education Foundation. Copies may be made without restriction."

1. *The assessment of student learning begins with educational values.* Assessment is not an end in itself but a vehicle for educational improvement. Its effective practice, then, begins with and enacts a vision of the kinds of learning we most value for students and strive to help them achieve. Educational values should drive not only what we choose to assess but also how we do so. Where questions about educational mission and values are skipped over, assessment threatens to be an exercise in measuring what's easy, rather than a process of improving what we really care about.
2. *Assessment is most effective when it reflects an understanding of learning as multidimensional, integrated, and revealed in performance over time.* Learning is a complex process. It entails not only what students know but what they can do with what they know; it involves not only knowledge and abilities but values, attitudes, and habits of mind that affect both academic success and performance beyond the classroom. Assessment should reflect these understandings by employing a diverse array of methods, including those that call for actual performance, using them over time so as to reveal change, growth, and increasing degrees of integration. Such an approach aims for a more complete and accurate picture of learning, and therefore firmer bases for improving our students' educational experience.
3. *Assessment works best when the programs it seeks to improve have clear, explicitly stated purposes.*

Assessment is a goal-oriented process. It entails comparing educational performance with educational purposes and expectations—those derived from the institution's mission, from faculty intentions in program and course design, and from knowledge of students' own goals. Where program purposes lack specificity or agreement, assessment as a process pushes a campus toward clarity about where to aim and what standards to apply; assessment also prompts attention to where and how program goals will be taught and learned. Clear, shared, implementable goals are the cornerstone for assessment that is focused and useful.

4. *Assessment requires attention to outcomes but also an equally to the experiences that lead to those outcomes.* Information about outcomes is of high importance; where students "end up" matters greatly. But to improve outcomes, we need to know about student experience along the way—about the curricula, teaching, and kind of student effort that lead to particular outcomes. Assessment can help us understand which students learn best under what conditions; with such knowledge comes the capacity to improve the whole of their learning.
5. *Assessment works best when it is ongoing not episodic.* Assessment is a process whose power is cumulative. Though isolated, "one-shot" assessment can be better than none, improvement is best fostered when assessment entails a linked series of activities undertaken over time. This may mean tracking the process of individual students, or of cohorts of students; it may mean collecting the same examples of student performance or using the same instrument semester after semester. The point is to monitor progress toward intended goals in a spirit of continuous improvement. Along the way, the assessment process itself should be evaluated and refined in light of emerging insights.
6. *Assessment fosters wider improvement when representatives from across the educational community are*

involved. Student learning is a campus-wide responsibility, and assessment is a way of enacting that responsibility. Thus, while assessment efforts may start small, the aim over time is to involve people from across the educational community. Faculties play an especially important role, but assessment's questions can't be fully addressed without participation by student-affairs educators, librarians, administrators, and students. Assessment may also involve individuals from beyond the campus (alumni/ae, trustees, employers) whose experience can enrich the sense of appropriate aims and standards for learning. Thus understood, assessment is not a task for small groups of experts but a collaborative activity; its aim is wider, better-informed attention to student learning by all parties with a stake in its improvement.

7. *Assessment makes a difference when it begins with issues of use and illuminates questions that people really care about.* Assessment recognizes the value of information in the process of improvement. But to be useful, information must be connected to issues or questions that people really care about. This implies assessment approaches that produce evidence that relevant parties will find credible, suggestive, and applicable to decisions that need to be made. It means thinking in advance about how the information will be used, and by whom. The point of assessment is not to gather data and return "results"; it is a process that starts with the questions of decision-makers, that involves them in the gathering and interpreting of data, and that informs and helps guide continuous improvement.

8. *Assessment is most likely to lead to improvement when it is part of a larger set of conditions that promote change.* Assessment alone changes little. Its greatest contribution comes on campuses where the quality of teaching and learning is visibly valued and worked at. On such campuses, the push to improve educational performance is a visible and primary

goal of leadership; improving the quality of undergraduate education is central to the institution's planning, budgeting, and personnel decisions. On such campuses, information about learning outcomes is seen as an integral part of decision-making, and avidly sought.

9. *Through assessment, educators meet responsibilities to students and to the public.* There is a compelling public stake in education. As educators, we have a responsibility to the public's that support or depend on us to provide information about the ways in which our students meet goals and expectations. But that responsibility goes beyond the reporting of such information; our deeper obligation to ourselves, our students, and society is to improve. Those to whom educators are accountable have a corresponding obligation to support such attempts at improvement.

A FOCUS FOR IMPROVEMENT

These principles are not Ten Commandments shrunk to a twentieth century attention span. They are intended as guidelines for faculty members, students, and administrators—with support from state agencies and trustees—to improve teaching and learning. These principles seem like good common sense, and they are : because many teachers and students have experienced them and because research supports them. They rest on 50 years of research on the way teachers teach and students learn how students work and play with one another, and how students and faculty talk to each other. While each practice can stand on its own, when all are present, their effects multiply. Together, they employ six powerful forces in education:

- Activity
- Diversity
- Interaction
- Cooperation
- Expectations
- Responsibility

Good practices hold as much meaning for professional programs as for the liberal arts. They work for many different kinds of students—white, black, Hispanic, Asian, rich, poor, older, younger, male, female, well-prepared, under-prepared. But the ways different institutions implement good practice depends very much on their students and their circumstances. In what follows, we describe several different approaches to good practice that have been used in different kinds of settings in the last few years.

In addition, the powerful implications of these principles for the way states fund and govern higher education and for the way institutions are run are discussed briefly at the end. As faculty members, academic administrators, and student personnel staff, we have spent most of our working lives trying to understand our students, our colleagues, our institutions, and ourselves. We have conducted research on higher education with dedicated colleagues in a wide range of schools in this country. We draw the implications of this research for practice, hoping to help us all do better. We address the teacher's how, not the subject-matter what, of good practice in undergraduate education. We recognize that content and pedagogy are present, their effects multiply. Together, they employ six powerful forces in education.

FUTURE DEVELOPMENTS IN THE AREA OF GRADUATE QUALITIES

This is identified strong and weak positions of institutional commitment to developing, assessing and recording the qualities of the graduates of an institution. It contends that there are changes set in train by the fact that a mass higher education system is developing an increasingly competitive market for graduates. These changes involve providing information that differentiates between graduates of an institution and also between graduates of different institutions. This information will include specifying the attainments of individual graduates in 'employment-related skills' so that graduates are valued as potential employees in fields that are not necessarily in the field-specific area of their degree. It is contended that, where institutions can present credible information about their commitment to developing qualities in graduates and students can provide evidence of the attainment of these qualities, both the institution and its students will be advantaged in a buyer's market for graduates.

CONCLUSION AND SUGGESTIONS

Teachers and students hold the main responsibility for improving higher education. But they need a lot of help. College and university leaders, state and federal officials, and accrediting associations have the power to shape an environment that is favorable to good practice in higher education. What qualities must this environment have?

- A strong sense of shared purposes.
- Concrete support from administrators and faculty leaders for those purposes.
- Adequate funding appropriate for the purposes.
- Policies and procedures consistent with the purposes.
- Continuing examination of how well the purposes are being achieved.

There is good evidence that such an environment can be created. When this happens, faculty members and administrators think of themselves as educators. Adequate resources are put into creating opportunities for faculty members, administrators, and students to celebrate and reflect on their shared purposes. Faculty members receive support and release time for appropriate professional development activities.

The role of improved schooling, a central part of most development strategies, has become controversial because expansion of school attainment has not guaranteed improved economic conditions. This reviews the role of education in promoting economic well-being, focusing on the role of educational quality. It concludes that there is strong evidence that the cognitive skills of the population rather than mere school attainment are powerfully related to individual earnings, to the distribution of income, and to economic growth. New empirical results show the importance of both minimal and high-level skills, the complementarily of skills and the quality of economic institutions, and the robustness of the relationship between skills and growth. International comparisons incorporating expanded data on cognitive skills reveal much larger skill deficits in developing countries than generally derived from just school enrolment and attainment. The magnitude of change needed makes it clear that closing the economic gap with industrial countries will require major structural changes in schooling institutions.

References

Adelman, C. (Ed.). Assessment in American higher education: Issues and contexts. Washington, DC: Office of Educational Research and Improvement, U.S. Department of Education, 1985.

Angelo, T.A. (Ed.). Classroom Research: Early Lessons from Success, New Directions for Teaching and Learning, No. 46, Jossey-Bass Publishers, San Francisco (1991).

Astin, A.W. Assessment for Excellence: The Philosophy and Practice of Assessment and Evaluation in Higher Education, Oryx Press, Phoenix (1993).

Astin, A.W.; Banta, T.W.; Cross, K.P.; El-Khawas, E.; Ewell, P.T.; Hutchings, P.; Marchese, T.J.; McClenney, K.M.; Mentkowski, M.; Miller, M.A.; Moran, E.T.; Wright, B.D. Nine principles of good practice for assessing student learning. AAHE Assessment Forum, July 25, 1996. http://www.aahe.org/principl.htm

Banta, T.W., *et al.*, Making A Difference: Outcomes of a Decade of Assessment in Higher Education, Jossey-Bass Publishers, San Francisco (1993).

Braskamp, L.A., Ory J.C., Assessing Faculty Work: Enhancing Individual And Institutional Performance, Jossey-Bass Publishers, San Francisco (1994).

Brookhart, S.M., The Art and Science of Classroom Assessment: The Missing Part of Pedagogy, 1999; 27(1). ERIC Reports.

Centra, J.A., Reflective Faculty Evaluation: Enhancing Teaching and Determining Faculty Effectiveness, Jossey-Bass Publishers, San Francisco (1993).

Cyrs, T.E., Teaching and Learning at a Distance: What it Takes to Effectively Design, Deliver, and Evaluate Programs, New Directions for Teaching and Learning, No. 71, Jossey-Bass Publishers, San Francisco (1997).

Diamond, R.M., Designing and Assessing Courses and Curricula—Revised Edition, Jossey-Bass Publishers, San Francisco (1998).

Edington, S., Hunt, C., Teaching Consultation Process Sourcebook, New Forums Press, Inc., Stillwater, OK (1996).

Gaff, J.G., New Life for the College Curriculum: Assessing Achievements and Furthering Progress in the Reform of General Education, Jossey-Bass Publishers, San Francisco (1991).

Gardiner, L.F. Redesigning Higher Education: Producing Dramatic Gains in Student Learning , 2nd Printing (Vol. 23, No. 7). ISBN 1-878380-63-X, 149, pp. ERIC Reports.

Glassick, C.E, Huber, M.T, Maeroff, G.I. Scholarship Assessed: Evaluation of the Professoriate. An Ernest L. Boyer project of the Carnegie Foundation for the Advancement of Teaching. Jossey-Bass Publishers, San Francisco, 1997.

Halpern, D.F., Student Outcomes Assessment: What Institutions Stand to Gain, Jossey-Bass Publishers, San Francisco (1987).

Hanna, G.S., Better Teaching Through Better Measurement, Harcourt Brace Jovanovich, Inc. (1993).

Jacobi, M., Astin, A., Ayala, F., College Student Outcomes Assessment: A Talent Development Perspective. ASHE-ERIC Reports, 1987; 16 (7). ISBN 0-913317-42-X, p. 143, Softcover.

Jacobs, L.C., Chase, C.I., Developing and Using Tests Effectively: A Guide for Faculty, Jossey-Bass Publishers, San Francisco (1992).

Keig, L., Waggoner, M.D., Collaborative Peer Review: The Role of Faculty in Improving College Teaching, The George Washington University, ASHE-ERIC Higher Education Report No. 2, Washington, DC (1994).

MacGregor, J. (Ed.). Student Self-Evaluation: Fostering Reflective Learning, New Directions for Teaching and Learning, No. 56, Jossey-Bass Publishers, San Francisco (1993).

McMillan, J.H. (Ed.). Assessing Students' Learning, New Directions for Teaching and Learning, No. 34, Jossey-Bass Publishers, San Francisco (1988).

O'Neil, C., Wright, A., Recording Teaching Accomplishment: A Dalhousie Guide to the Teaching Dossier, Office of Instructional Development and Technology, Dalhousie University, Halifax, NS, Canada (1993).

Ory, J.C., Ryan, K.E., Tips for Improving Testing and Grading, Sage Publishers, Inc., Newbury Park, CA (1993).

Palomba, C.A., Banta, T.W., Assessment essentials: Planning, implementing, and improving assessment in higher education. Jossey-Bass, San Francisco, CA, 1999.

Paulson, M.B., Feldman, K.A., Taking Teaching Seriously: Meeting the Challenge of Instructional Improvement, The George Washington University, ASHE-ERIC Higher Education Report No. 2, Washington, DC (1995).

Ratcliff, J.L., *et al.*, Realizing the Potential: Improving Post-secondary Teaching, Learning, and Assessment, Prepared for U.S. Department of Education, Office of Educational Research and Improvement,

National Institute on Post-secondary Education, Libraries, and Lifelong Learning, by The National Center on Post-secondary Teaching, Learning, and Assessment, University Park, PA (1995).

Richlin, L., Manning, B., Improving a College/University Teaching Evaluation System, Alliance Publishers, Pittsburgh, PA (1995).

Schilling, K.M., Schilling, K.L., Proclaiming and Sustaining Excellence: Assessment as a Faculty Role. 1998; 26(3). ERIC Reports.

Seldin, P., Changing Practices in Faculty Evaluation: A Critical Assessment and Recommendations for Improvement, Jossey-Bass Publishers, San Francisco (1985).

Seldin, P., *et. al.*, How Administrators Can Improve Teaching: Moving from Talk to Action in Higher Education, Jossey-Bass Publishers, San Francisco (1990).

Seymour, D. (Ed.). Total Quality Management on Campus: Is it Worth Doing? Jossey-Bass Publishers, San Francisco (1994).

Simerly, R.G., *et. al.* Strategic Planning and Leadership in Continuing Education: Enhancing Organizational Vitality, Responsiveness, and Identity, Jossey-Bass Publishers, San Francisco (1989).

Stark, J.S., Thomas, A., Assessment Program Evaluation, Simon and Schuster Custom Publishing, Needham Heights, MA (1994).

Stark, J., Lattuca, L.R., Shaping the College Curriculum: Academic Plans in Action, Allyn and Bacon/Simon Schuster Co., Needham Heights, MA (1997).

Theall, M., Franklin, J. (Eds.). Student Ratings of Instruction: Issues for Improving Practice, New Directions for Teaching and Learning, No. 43, Jossey-Bass Publishers, San Francisco (1990).

Theall, M., Franklin, J. (Eds.). Effective Practices for Improving Teaching, New Directions for Teaching and Learning, No. 48, Jossey-Bass Publishers, San Francisco (1991).

Travis, J., Models for Improving College Teaching: A Faculty Resource, Association for the Study of Higher Education (ASHE), ASHE-ERIC Higher Education Report, No. 6, Washington, DC (1995).

Vella, J., Berarinelli, Burrow, J., How Do They Know They Know, Jossey-Bass Publishers, San Francisco.

Walvoord, B.E., Anderson, V.J., Effective Grading: A Tool for Learning and Assessment, Jossey-Bass Publishers, San Francisco (1998).

Weimer, M., Parrett, J.L., Kerns, M.M., How Am I Teaching? Forms and Activities for Acquiring Instructional Input, Magna Publications, Inc., Madison, WI (1988).

Wolverton, M., A New Alliance: Continuous Quality and Classroom Effectiveness (Vol. 23, No. 6). ISBN 1-878380-62-1, p. 91, ERIC Reports.

Wright, W.A., *et al.*, Teaching Improvement Practices: Successful Strategies for Higher Education, Anker Publishing Company, Bolton, MA (1995).

CHAPTER

12

An Outlook of Educational Attainment and Literacy in Rural India

A Case Study

MOHAMMAD MUQEET KHAN
AND NIZAMUDDIN KHAN

INTRODUCTION

Right to Education is the primary right of every citizen of India, whether a child resides in a high profile society or in a far away not so developed secluded village. Schools in rural areas are promoted to raise the level of education and literacy in rural India. The main aim of running these types of schools in India is to increase the rates of literacy in rural areas. More than 40 percent of India's population is illiterate and cannot read or write. In addition, schools in rural areas are inadequate and often equivalent to being non-existent. Thus, government's initiative to set-up schools in rural areas came into picture. The conditions of rural education in India, is improving steadily and the government is also providing full support and providing with many initiatives. The fee structure in these schools is also very low so that every child can study and afford it.

Parental education has a strong positive influence on schooling outcomes and in particular for the girl child. The impact of mother's education is more pronounced for the girl child than for boys. Secondly, the economic well-being of the household as measured by income or wealth indicators affects the likelihood of going to school. Poorer households are prone to income shocks and unable to insure themselves. Credit constraints prevent them from borrowing. They are less likely to send their children to school and more likely to pull the children out of school in the event of an adverse shock. Hence, there is also a link between the occupation of the household head and the likelihood of going to school. Thirdly, sibling rivalry too is important. Girls are likely to be pulled out of school in order to help with household chores (Grootaert and Patrinos, 1999). The key factors affecting child labour are household size and composition, education and employment status of the parents, household's ability to cope with income fluctuations, functioning of the labour market and the prevailing production technology. They find that even after conditioning on household characteristics, financial constraints increase the probability of child labour. They argue that since poor families are unable to insure themselves against adverse (income) shocks, children's labour is important for their ability to cope with the shock. This is true since children's wages comprise a large share of the family budget. Hence, it is also recognized that child labour and child schooling is not an either or decision and that the two are not mutually incompatible.

In the Indian context, analysing the National Council of Applied Economic Research (NCAER) data, Duraisamy (2002) concludes that parental education, family income, and availability of middle schools within the village have a significant positive effect on child school enrolment decisions in India. Dreze and Kingdon (2001) and Leclercq (2001a, 2001b) find similar results for north India. However, they stress school quality as the key determinant of enrolment and grade attainment. Chin (2002), addressing one aspect of Operation Blackboard in India (change from one-teacher to two teacher schools), finds that changes in school quality have a bigger impact on school completion and literacy among girls than boys. Kochar (2001) proxies for school quality by student-teacher ratio and finds that this affects the probability of going to school.

Though there are very few schools in rural areas, children and their parents are showing interest and availing school facilities in these remote locations. Children have to walk miles to reach their school. Rural schools pay special attention to children in these locations so that each child gets an equal and important opportunity. They promote reading, writing and enhanced basic education. These schools also provide study material to every student apart from meals during school hours, uniforms, etc. They not only provide kits for hands-on-learning, but also notebooks, textbooks and pencils to poor children. Apart from that, they also give scholarships to deserving students regularly, who wish to study ahead. They create community awareness, about the need for education and world literacy. Many indirect benefits of a basic rural education include poverty reduction, disease control, enhanced employment opportunities and increasing rate of literacy. The curriculum includes English, Mathematics, General Knowledge and Drawing. With the help of rural education, every family and child has excess to basic primary education. Individual's special talents are recognized. The teaching methodology ensures that each and every student is exposed to educational experience in an active and dynamic learning environment, so that they can achieve excellence. The primary objectives of rural schools is to ensure that every child in rural India receives quality education which prepares them to compete in the competitive global environment.

UNDERSTANDING THE CONCEPT OF LITERACY AND EDUCATION

- *Literate*: A person age 7 years and above who can both read and write with understanding in any language is taken as literate. A person who can only read but cannot write is not literate. It is not necessary that to be considered as literate, a person should have received any formal education or passed any minimum educational standard. Literacy could also have been achieved through adult literacy classes or through any non-formal educational system. People who are blind and can read in Braille are treated as literates.
- *Literacy rate*: Literacy rate of the population is defined as the percentage of literates in the age group seven years and above. For different age groups the percentage of literates in that age group gives the literacy rate.
- *Educational level*: The highest level of education a person has completed.

STUDY AREA

For the study, the district of Ambedkarnagar in the North Indian state of Uttar Pradesh has been selected as study area, taking into consideration its economic backwardness, agricultural base as well as presence of large number of rural population. It forms a part of Ghagra basin and lies between 26° 09′ N and 26° 40′ N latitudes and between 82° 12′ E and 83° 05′ E longitudes. The study area occupies an area of 2,361 sq. km. and has a population of 2,026,876. About 91% population lives in villages whose main occupation is agricultural farming. Administratively, the district has 4 sub-divisions (tehsils) and 9 development blocks.

STATE OF LITERACY IN THE DISTRICT

In the district, about 58.4 percent population is literate. The literacy is 72.5 percent in urban areas and 57.0 percent in rural areas. The male literacy is higher at 71.4 percent as against 45.3 percent female literacy, and therefore the gap in male/female literacy rate is 26.1 percentage points. In rural areas among 10 CD Blocks, the highest literacy is at 63.3 percent in Atrauli and lowest at 54.3 percent in Akbarpur. The literacy among males in rural areas is 70.5 percent in comparison to 43.4 percent among females. The lowest female literacy of 39.9 percent is in Bhiyaon CD Block. The gap in male/female literacy rate is highest in Bhiyaon CD Block which is 30.6 percent. In 42.4 percent of villages covering 47.0 percent of rural population the literacy range is 51 to 60. Among urbanites in the district, as much as 79.4 percent males are literates as against 65.1 percent females. The highest urban literacy is in Jalalpur (81.1 percent) and lowest in Ashrafpur Kichhauchha at 57.1 percent. The maximum males literacy is also found in Jalalpur at 87.1 percent and lowest at 67.8 percent in Ashrafpur Kichhauchha. The highest female literacy is also in Jalalpur at 75.0 percent and lowest at 46.0 percent in Ashrafpur Kichhauchha. Still, the maximum gap in male-female literacy rate at 21.8 percentage points is found in Ashrafpur Kichhauchha. The literacy among Scheduled Castes is 47.5 percent, in the countryside and 54.7 percent in towns. The percentage of literacy among Scheduled Tribes is 54.7 percent at district level. Only 6.8 percent females among Scheduled Tribes population are found literate in the district.

District and tehsil-wise literacy rates besides the number of literates and illiterates for total, rural and urban areas are given in Table 1. The literacy rates are worked out by excluding population of 0-6 years. As per 2001 Census, the proportion of literates to total population excluding 0-6 years comes to 58.4 per cent in the district. This proportion in rural area is 57.0 per cent against 72.5 per cent in urban areas. In the district the literacy rates of male (71.4 per cent) is much higher than that of females (45.3 per cent). Among the tehsils, Tanda tehsil tops with 61.0 per cent literates followed by Allapur tehsil (59.1 per cent). Akbarpur tehsil with 55.9 per cent literates stands at the bottam in the district. Out of 4 tehsils, the literacy rates of Tanda, Allapur and Jalalpur Tehsils are higher than that of district average. It is observed that in urban areas of district the literacy rates are higher than the rural areas. The gap between

TABLE I

Number and Percentage of Literates and Illiterates by Tehsils, 2001

Sl. No.	Name of Tehsil	Total/ Rural/ Urban	Number of literates and illiterates						Percentage of literates			Gap in male-female literacy rate
			Number of literates			Number of illiterates						
			Person	Males	Females	Person	Males	Females	Person	Males	Females	
(1)	(2)	(3)	(4)	(5)	(6)	(7)	(8)	(9)	(10)	(11)	(12)	(13)
1.	Tanda	Total	251,957	151,864	100.093	261,099	110,990	150,109	61.0	71.8	49.7	22.2
		Rural	184,680	113,064	71,616	210,825	88,504	122,321	58.4	70.2	46.1	24.2
		Urban	67,277	38,800	28,477	50,274	22,486	27,788	69.8	77	61.9	15.1
2.	Allapur	Total	178,888	109,964	68,924	199,342	77,784	121,558	59.1	73.9	44.9	29.1
		Rural	178,888	109,964	68,924	199,342	77,784	121,558	59.1	73.9	44.8	29.1
		Urban	0	0	0	0	0	0	0	0	0	0
3.	Jalalpur	Total	217,812	134,074	83,738	242,433	97,373	145,060	58.7	72.2	45.1	27.1
		Rural	197,694	123,091	74,603	232,915	93,230	139,685	57	71.1	43	28.1
		Urban	20,118	10,983	9,135	9,518	4,143	5,375	81.2	87.1	75	12.1

(*Contd.*)

TABLE 1 (*Contd.*)

(1)	(2)	(3)	(4)	(5)	(6)	(7)	(8)	(9)	(10)	(11)	(12)	(13)
4.	Akbarpur	Total	305,880	191,150	114,730	369,465	151,754	217,711	55.9	69.1	42.5	26.6
		Rural	284,821	179,152	105,669	356,618	146,057	210,561	54.9	68.4	41.2	27.3
		Urban	21,059	11,998	9,061	12,847	5,697	7,150	74.5	81.1	67.2	14.0
	Districts Total	Total	954,537	587,052	367,485	1,072,339	437,901	634,438	58.4	71.4	45.3	26.1
		Rural	846,083	525,271	320,812	999,700	405,575	594,125	57	70.5	43.4	27.2
		Urban	108,454	61,781	46,673	72,639	32,326	40,313	72.5	79.4	65.1	14.3

Source : District Census Handbook, Part XII-A and B (Series 10), Uttar Pradesh, Census of India, 2001.

male and female literacy is very high which comes to 26.1 per cent in the district, as a whole. The situation at tehsil level is not much different. However, this gap in urban literacy is low which comes to 14.3 points against the rural areas, where the gap between male and female literacy is 27.2 points.

The Table 2 reveals number of literates, illiterates and the literacy rates in rural areas at C.D. block level in the district. 57.0 per cent of the total rural population excluding the age-group of 0-6 years literates in the district. The corresponding proportion of male and female literates comes to 70.5 and 43.4.per cent respectively which shows very wide gap of 27.2 per cent in male and female literacy. At C.D. block level, Atraulia C.D. block has the highest rural literacy rate of 63.3 per cent while 76.5 per cent males and 49.6 per cent females are literates in this block. The lowest literacy rate in rural areas is noted in Akbarpur C.D. block (54.3 per cent). There are wide variations in male and female literacy in all the C.D. blocks of the district. The maximum difference of 30.6 points is found in Bhiyaon C.D. block.

Table 3 gives the distribution of villages by literacy rate ranges in the district. There is no such type of villages in the district, which have all the literate or illiterate population. 710 villages accounting for 42.4 per cent of the total villages are in the literacy range of 51-60 per cent and 508 villages (30.3 per cent) fall in the literacy range of 61-70 per cent. The lower literacy rate of 1 to 50 per cent observed in 334 villages (19.9 per cent) of the district. The higher literacy ranges of 71 to 100 per cent covers 123 villages (7.4 per cent). The range of 51-70 have the maximum number of 1218 villages forming 72.7 per cent of the total inhabited villages.

Table 4 shows number and percentage of Scheduled Castes literates and illiterates by sex in CD blocks 2001. In rural areas of the district proportion of literates is 47.5 per cent in which 62.2 males and 32.9 females. Thus, the gap in male and female literacy rates is 29.3 per cent. Among 10 CD blocks, Ramnagar CD block has the highest literacy rate and Bhiti CD block has the lowest literacy rates. The gap in male/female literacy rates in Atraulia CD block is highest and this gap is lowest in Akbarpur CD block.

Table 2
Number and Percentage of Literates and Illiterates by Sex in C.D. Blocks, 2001

Sl. No.	Name of Tehsil	Number of literates and illiterates						Percentage of literates			Gap in male-female literacy rate
		Number of literates			Number of illiterates						
		Person	Males	Females	Person	Males	Females	Person	Males	Females	
(1)	(2)	(3)	(4)	(5)	(6)	(7)	(8)	(9)	(10)	(11)	(12)
1.	Tanda	103,615	64,133	39,133	122,389	122,389	51,919	57.1	68.7	44.7	24.0
2.	Baskhari	81,065	48,931	32,134	88,436	36,585	51,851	60.1	72.3	47.8	24.5
3.	Ramnagar	85,748	52,782	32,966	98,596	38,878	59,718	58.3	72.8	44.2	28.6
4.	Jahangirganj	76,992	47,237	29,755	85,300	32,731	52,569	59.3	74.7	44.6	30.1
5.	Jalalpur	121,035	74,689	46,346	135,140	54,989	80,151	58.5	71.6	45.1	26.4
6.	Bhiyaon	76,659	48,402	28,257	97,775	38,241	59,534	54.9	70.5	39.9	30.6
7.	Bhiti	67,552	42,845	24,707	82,129	33,016	49,113	55.7	70.2	40.9	29.3
8.	Katehari	80,346	50,508	29,838	99,363	40,061	59,302	55.4	69.5	41.2	28.3
9.	Akbarpur	136,923	85,799	51,124	175,126	72,980	102,146	54.3	66.9	41.2	25.7
10.	Atraulia	16,148	9,945	6,203	15,446	6,175	9,271	63.3	76.5	49.6	26.9
	District (Rural Total)	846,083	525,271	320,812	999,700	405,575	594,125	57.0	70.5	43.4	27.2

Source : District Census Handbook, Part XII-A and B (Series 10), Uttar Pradesh, Census of India, 2001.

TABLE 3

Distribution of Villages by Literacy Rate Range, 2001

Range of literacy rate for villages	*Number of inhibited villages*	*Percentage distribution of Villages*	*Population*	*Percentage distribution of population*
0	0	0.0	0	0.0
1-10	3	0.2	726	0.0
11-20	5	0.3	1.628	0.1
21-30	14	0.8	5,714	0.3
31-40	54	3.2	45,266	2.5
41-50	258	15.4	312,354	16.9
51-60	710	42.4	868,351	29.3
61-70	508	30.3	540,342	29.3
71-80	106	6.3	68,242	3.7
81-90	16	1.0	3,054	0.2
91-99	1	0.1	106	0.0
100	0	0.0	0	0.0

Source : District Census Handbook, Part XII-A and B (Series 10), Uttar Pradesh, Census of India, 2001.

The Table 5 presents the distribution of villages by literacy rate range for Scheduled Castes population at the 2001 census. In majority of inhabited villages which from about 77.9 per cent of total rural Scheduled Castes population the literacy range is 41 to 60 percentages. In the district, there are 1,533 inhabited villages with Scheduled Castes population with about 47.5 per cent of literacy rate.

The Table 6 brings out the number and percentage of Scheduled Tribes literates and illiterates by sex in CD Blocks at the 2001 census. The number of illiterates is more than literates in the district and CD Blocks, with exception to Atraulia CD Block. The literacy rate of the Scheduled Tribes population at about 29.1 per cent is less than the corresponding rate it about 47.5 per cent in case of Scheduled Castes community. The gap in male and female literacy rates at about 37.1 per cent is higher than what it is in case of the Scheduled Castes

TABLE 4

Number and Percentage of Scheduled Castes Literates and Illiterates by Sex in C.D. Blocks, 2001

Sl. No.	Name of C.D. block	Number of literates and illiterates						Percentage of literates			Gap in male-female literacy rate
		Number of literates			Number of illiterates						
		Person	Males	Females	Person	Males	Females	Person	Males	Females	
(1)	(2)	(3)	(4)	(5)	(6)	(7)	(8)	(9)	(10)	(11)	(12)
1.	Tanda	25,350	16,651	8,699	41,859	17,598	24,261	47.8	61.4	33.5	28.0
2.	Baskhari	16,848	10,856	5,992	26,555	10,963	15,592	49.4	63.8	35.1	28.7
3.	Ramnagar	19,181	12,276	6,905	30,049	11,903	18,146	49.8	65.6	34.9	30.7
4.	Jahangirganj	17,359	11,386	5,973	28,453	10,968	17,485	48.5	65.9	32.2	33.7
5.	Jalalpur	27,875	18,106	9,769	45,973	19,097	26,876	47.7	61.7	33.6	28.1
6.	Bhiyaon	17,546	11,412	6,134	28,939	11,399	17,540	48.0	64.2	32.6	31.6
7.	Bhiti	11,507	7,813	3,694	22,897	9,687	13,210	42.0	56.5	27.2	29.3
8.	Katehari	15,627	10,279	5,348	27,414	11,356	16,058	45.5	60.0	31.0	28.9
9.	Akbarpur	25,898	16,706	9,192	43,071	18,037	25,034	47.2	60.5	33.7	26.8
10.	Atraulia	2.625	1.766	859	4,071	1,645	2,426	49.5	66.4	32.4	34.0
	District (Rural Total)	179,816	117,251	62,565	299,281	122,653	176,628	47.5	62.2	32.9	29.3

Source : District Census Handbook, Part XII-A and B (Series 10), Uttar Pradesh, Census of India, 2001.

TABLE 5

Distribution of Villages by Literacy Rate Range for Scheduled Castes Population, 2001

Range of literacy rate for villages	*Number of inhibited villages*	*Percentage distribution of Villages*	*Scheduled Castes Population*	*Percentage distribution of population*
0	10	0.7	95	0.0
1-10	2	0.1	139	0.0
11-20	17	1.1	2,195	0.5
21-30	68	4.4	11,959	2.5
31-40	250	16.3	73,558	15.4
41-50	575	37.5	217.379	45.4
51-60	484	31.6	155,493	32.5
61-70	107	7.0	17,543	3.7
71-80	15	1.0	677	0.1
81-90	3	0.2	51	0.0
91-99	0	0.0	0	0.0
100	2	0.1	8	0.0
District Total	1,533	100.0	479,097	100.0

Source : District Census Handbook, Part XII-A and B (Series 10), Uttar Pradesh, Census of India, 2001.

community (about 29.3 per cent). The literacy rate of highest in Atraulia CD Block and lowest in Bhiti CD Block. The gap in male/female literacy rate in Atraulia CD Block is in favour of the females.

The Table 7 gives the distribution of villages by literacy rate range for the Scheduled Tribes population at the 2001 census. In the district the Scheduled Tribes population is found in 11 villages out of which in 2 villages the literacy range is 100 per cent. However, the maximum (31.5 per cent) of the Scheduled Tribes population is found in only 3 villages with literacy range from 11 to 20 percentages.

Table 8 depicts that, out of 1,675 inhabited villages in the district 1,047 villages (62.5) per cent have been provided with

TABLE 6

Number and Percentage of Scheduled Tribes Literates and Illiterates by Sex in C.D. Blocks, 2001

Sl. No.	*Name of C.D. block*	*Number of literates and illiterates*						*Percentage of literates*			*Gap in male-female literacy rate*
		Number of literates			*Number of illiterates*						
		Person	*Males*	*Females*	*Person*	*Males*	*Females*	*Person*	*Males*	*Females*	
(1)	*(2)*	*(3)*	*(4)*	*(5)*	*(6)*	*(7)*	*(8)*	*(9)*	*(10)*	*(11)*	*(12)*
1.	Tanda	9	8	1	37	22	15	25.7	36.4	7.7	28.7
2.	Jalalpur	10	10	0	28	11	17	34.5	52.6	0.0	52.6
3.	Bhiti	6	5	1	31	13	18	23.1	38.5	7.7	30.8
4.	Katehari	1	1	0	2	1	1	33.3	50	0.0	50.0
5.	Akbarpur	5	5	0	13	6	7	31.3	50	0.0	50.0
6.	Atraulia	1	0	1	0	0	0	100	0	100.0	-100.0
	District (Rural Total)	32	20	3	111	53	58	29.1	43.9	6.8	37.1

Source : District Census Handbook, Part XII-A and B (Series 10), Uttar Pradesh, Census of India, 2001.

TABLE 7

Distribution of Villages by Literacy Rate Range for Scheduled Tribes Population, 2001

Range of literacy rate for villages	*Number of inhibited villages*	*Percentage distribution of Villages*	*Scheduled Tribes Population*	*Percentage distribution of population*
0	2	18.2	5	3.5
1-10	0	0.0	0	0.0
11-20	3	27.3	45	31.5
21-30	1	9.1	37	25.9
31-40	1	9.1	15	10.5
41-50	2	18.2	39	27.3
51-60	0	0.0	0	0.0
61-70	0	0.0	0	0.0
71-80	0	0.0	0	0.0
81-90	0	0.0	0	0.0
91-99	0	0.0	0	0.0
100	2	18.2	2	1.4
District Total	11	100.0	143	100.0
Literacy rate for District Rural :		29.1		

Source : District Census Handbook, Part XII-A and B (Series 10), Uttar Pradesh, Census of India, 2001.

the education facilities of one type or the other. Table also shows that the number and proportion of rural population served by different kind of amenities. Out of total rural population of 1,845,783 persons in the district, 1,513,522 (82.0 per cent) have educational facility of one or the other type.

Table 9 presents distribution of villages not having certain amenities within the village at district level. They have to go out of their village to avail these facilities. Such villages have been presented according to various distance ranges in this table. 659 villages do not have primary school in their villages and out of these villages, children of 568 villages have to travel

Table 8

Distribution of Villages and Population According to Availability of Educational Facility, 2001

Sl. No.	*C. D. Block*	*No. of inhabited villages*	*No. of villages having educational facility*	*Total population of inhabited villages*	*Population availing educational facility*
(1)	(2)	(3)	(4)	(5)	(6)
1.	Tanda	242 (100)	131 (54.1)	226,004 (100)	168,224 (74.4)
2.	Baskhari	121 (100)	90 (74.4)	169,501 (100)	153,018 (90.3)
3.	Ramnagar	174 (100)	105 (60.3)	184,344 (100)	147,786 (80.2)
4.	Jahangirganj	224 (100)	109 (48.7)	162,292 (100)	119,751 (73.8)
5.	Jalalpur	168 (100)	152 (90.5)	256,175 (100)	245,296 (95.8)
6.	Bhiyaon	140 (100)	94 (67.1)	174,434 (100)	146,267 (83.9)
7.	Bhiti	175 (100)	103 (58.9)	149,681 (100)	115,962 (77.5)
8.	Katehhri	181 (100)	97 (53.6)	179,709 (100)	133,118 (74.1)
9.	Akbarpur	224 (100)	156 (69.6)	312,049 (100)	263,607 (84.5)
10.	Atraulia	26 (100)	10 (38.5)	31,594 (100)	20.493 (64.9)
	District Total	1,675 (100)	1,047 (62.5)	1845,783 (100)	1,513,522 (82.0)

Source : District Census Handbook, Part XII-A and B (Series 10), Uttar Pradesh, Census of India, 2001.

TABLE 9

Distribution of Villages Not Having Certain Amenities, Arranged By Distance Ranges from the Places where these are Available, 2001

Village not having the amenity of	*Distance range of place from the villages where the amenity is available*			
	Less than 4 kilometers	*5-10 kilometers*	*10+ kilometers*	*Total (Col. 2-4)*
1. Education				
(a) Primary School	568	86	5	659
(b) Middle School	972	419	26	1,417
(c) Degree College	406	592	660	1,658

Source : District Census Handbook, Part XII-A and B (Series 10), Uttar Pradesh, Census of India, 2001.

less than 5 km for schooling, out of 1,675 inhabited villages as many as 1,417 are deprived of middle school and 1658 of degree college. Of these 972 avail the facility of middle school at a distance of less than 5 km, 419 at a distance of 5-10 km and the remaining 26 at a distance of 10+ km. In respect of degree college 406 avail this facility at a distance of less than 5 km, 592 between 5 to 10 km and rest 660 villages at a distance of 10+ km.

Table 10 deals with the distribution of villages according to distance from the nearest statutory town and availability of different amenities within the village. Out of total 1,675 inhabited villages in the district, there are 201 villages which have nearest towns upto a distance of 5 km. Of these only 130 villages forming 64.7 per cent of these total villages, are having the educational facilities of one type or the other. There are 966 inhabited villages in the district which fall in the distance range of 5-15 km, of these 611 villages constituting 63.3 per cent have been provided with the educational facilities. Whereas 366 villages fall in the distance range of 16-50 km of these, 64.2 per cent villages have educational facility. Furthermore, there are only 8 villages in the district which are situated beyond 50 km from the nearest town and out of these 5. (62.5 per cent) enjoy

TABLE 10

Distribution of Villages According to the Distance from the Nearest Statutory Town and Availability of Educational Facility, 2001

Distance range from the nearest staturoty town (in kilometres)	*Number of inhabited villages in each range*	*Type*
		Education
Less than 5	201 (100.0)	130 (64.7)
5-15	966 (100.0)	611 (63.3)
16-50	366 (100.0)	235 (64.2)
51+	8 (100.0)	5 (62.5)
Unspecified	134 (100.0)	66 (49.3)
District Total	1,675 (100.0)	1,047 (62.5)

Source : District Census Handbook, Census of India, 2001.

the education facility in the village itself whereas there are 134 villages whose distance ranges from the nearest statutory town have not been given. Such villages have been grouped under the unspecified category. 66 (49.3 per cent) villages have the educational facility of one or other type.

EDUCATIONAL CENTRES OF THE DISTRICT

The presence of large number of educational centres in any region is an important indicator of socio-economic development in that region. Good educational facilities in any region will boost the literacy rate, which will ultimately increase the quality and efficiency of man-power.

Table 11 shows the distribution of different educational centres in different blocks of Ambedkarnagar district. There are 1585 junior basic schools in the district, which varies between 8.58 percent (Bhiti) and 15.46 percent (Akbarpur), followed by

TABLE 11

Block-wise Number of Recognized Educational Centres in Ambedkarnagar District, 2001

Sl. No.	Blocks	No. of Junior Basic Schools	No. of Senior Basic Schools	No. of Higher Sec. Schools	No. of Optical Educational Centres	No. of Degree Colleges	No. of Master Degree Colleges	No. of Industrial Training Centers
(1)	(2)	(3)	(4)	(5)	(6)	(7)	(8)	(9)
1.	Bhiti	136	38	19	2	2	—	—
2.	Katehhri	163	56	20	2	2	—	—
3.	Akbarpur	245	86	26	9	9	2	1
4.	Tanda	211	58	27	4	4	2	1
5.	Baskhari	172	56	15	2	2	—	—
6.	Ramnagar	165	53	10	1	1	—	—
7.	Jahangirganj	149	42	11	1	1	1	—
8.	Jalalpur	201	70	30	5	5	—	—
9.	Bhiyaon	143	49	24	3	3	—	—
	Total	1585	508	182	29	29	5	2

Tanda (13.31), Jalapur (12.68), Ramnagar (10.41), etc. The total number of senior basic schools in the district is 508, out of which 16.93 percent are occupied by Akbarpur whereas only 7.68 percent by Bhiti block. The total number of higher secondary schools in the district is 182 with great regional variations among different blocks of the district. Akbarpur block has highest number of degree colleges in the district, 2 each in Akbarpur and Tanda, and 1 in Jahangirganj block. There are only 2 industrial training centres in the whole district, which impart industrial and technical training to the needy students.

PROBLEMS IN PRESENT SCENARIO

In India, condition of rural education is still improving, the conditions of these rural schools is still very poor. Most of the schools do not have proper infrastructure. They do not get most of the facilities such as computer education, sports education and extra-curricular activities. There are very few schools in the rural areas and children have to travel far away distances to avail these facilities and most schools in these locations do not provide drinking water. There are no proper transport facilities so children don't like to travel miles to come to school. The quality of education is also very poor. The teachers get very less income so, most of the time the teachers are either absent or there is a possibility that teachers give less attention to children. There is no excess to supplemental education. There are many initiatives taken by the government, but they are not implemented in the schools, so the present scenario remains the same.

CONCLUSION

Despite encouraging leaps in literacy and current school attendance over the 1990s, the situation at the start of the twenty-first century leaves much to be desired. It is clear that a lot remains to be done to achieve universal elementary education. The central government's new emphasis on elementary education under its Sarva Shiksha Abhiyan initiative the promise of continuation of the enabling conditions of the 1990s give grounds for optimism in the medium-term. However, even if progress towards universal elementary education is rapidly achieved, education of a decent quality for all will remain a challenging goal. In particular, developments such as the increasing employment of para-teachers in small or marginal communities and the rapid growth of private education give rise to concerns about 'hierarchies of access', with those who are poorer and subject to discrimination being frequently left with the lower quality options in primary schooling. The achievement of better education for all will require still greater social action and public commitment than has been given to education so far.

References

Chin, A., 2002, "The Returns to School Quality When School Quality is Very Low: Evidence from Operation Blackboard in India", Manuscript, Department of Economics, University of Houston.

District Census Handbook, 2001, Part XII-A and B (Series 10), Uttar Pradesh, Census of India.

District Statistical Magazine, 2010, Economic and Statistical Office, Ambedkarnagar District, U.P.

Drèze, J. and Geeta Gandhi Kingdon, 2001, "School Participation in Rural India". *Review of Development Economics*, 5(1), 1-24.

Duraisamy, M., 2002, "Child Schooling and Child Work in India". NCAER, Working Paper 84.

Grootaert, C. and Patrinos, H.A., (eds.), 1999, The Policy Analysis of Child Labour: A Comparative Study. New York, NY: St Martin's Press.

Kochar, A., 2001, "Emerging Challenges for Indian Education Policy". Working Paper 97. Center for Research on Economic Development and Policy Reform, Stanford University.

Leclercq, F., 2001a, "Household Structures and School Participation: Is there Sibling Rivalry in Rural North India?" Mimeo.

Leclercq, F., 2001b, "Patterns and Determinants of Elementary School Enrolment in Rural North India". Mimeo.

www.justindianschools.com/articles/108-review-of-rural-education-in-india.html

CHAPTER

13

Perceived Supports and Effectiveness of IQAC Functionaries

MUSHTAQ A. SIDDIQI

ABSTRACT

Most of the workshops, conferences and seminars on IQAC have tended to focus only on the potential role, responsibilities of IQAC as a tool for institutional excellence. Very little seems to have been done to identify the environmental barriers that hamper its effectiveness and process of realizing its goals for quality enhancement and sustenance. In view of the growing concern among the educational managers, teachers, NAAC functionaries, research scholars in general and IQAC functionaries in particular about the barriers, the author draws on the management literature and offers a framework with an aim to offer a way out for the same. The article supports that several supports like Perceived Management or Government Support, Perceived Student Support, Perceived Coworkers

Support, are some of the perquisites to enhance the effectiveness of IQAC. Emphasizing the supports for IQAC functionaries, the article also proposes a positive relationship between cognitive assessment of IQAC functionaries about these supports, their involvement and IQAC effectiveness. This simple conceptual framework will not only help IQAC become more relevant but also may shape future agendas for research in IQAC-related issues.

Key Terms: Perceived Management Support, Perceived Student Support, Perceived Coworker Support, IQAC Functionary's Involvement, IQAC effectiveness.

INTRODUCTION

Owing to liberalization, privatization, and globalization, the socio-economic and technological changes are more vivid than ever before. Education is, undoubtedly, the single largest contributor to change potential of societies and nations. Moreover, in the present 'knowledge era' where skills and knowledge become quickly obsolete, no country can ensure its substantial development without providing quality education to its citizens. This necessitated the establishment of NAAC (National Assessment and Accreditation Council) in 1994 by UGC with an aim to make quality a defining element of nation's higher education. The country's premier quality assurance agency, NAAC has been engaged in improving higher education through the process of self and external quality evaluation of institutions, promotion and sustenance initiatives.

In education there seems to be no static practice that contributes to its quality for ever. Some practices may be good at a certain time but not at another due to environmental changes and its impact. As a matter of fact quality assurance is a continuous process and an integral part of the functioning of an institution. Accordingly, assessment, accreditation and sustenance initiative is not a one time job. It is an ongoing and dynamic process of improving policies, procedures, practices to achieve educational excellence. It is in fact, a beginning of the process of quality enhancement aimed at institutional excellence. In consistent pursuit of this quality, NAAC emphasizes the promotion of internal quality assurance system through establishment of Internal Quality Assurance Cell (now IQAC henceforth in this article) in higher education institutions.

IQAC does not simply act as a conduit in between the respective institution and NAAC. It contributes meaningfully in the post-accreditation phase. It is a part of an institution's system to work towards realizing its goals for quality enhancement and its sustenance. The cell fine tune its activities in accordance to the specific environment in which it operates, channelise the efforts towards the attainment of academic excellence, works out plans, ensures its implementation and consequently develops a quality culture in HEIs.

Despite the fact that IQAC has made a significant contribution to the institutional quality improvement, there is a growing concern that IQAC suffers from certain structural, operational and functional limitations. The varying environment in the country pose diverse operational-challenges (environmental-barriers) to IQAC. The present article draws attention towards one of the components of the environment in which IQAC operates and believes that if improved, can go a long way in improving effectiveness of IQAC. More specifically, this article proposes several supports like Perceived Management Support, Perceived Student Support, Perceived Coworkers Support, are some of the preconditions to enhance the IQAC functionaries' commitment and consequent operational efficiency of IQAC.

PERCEIVED MANAGEMENT SUPPORT

An IQAC functionary in an institution volunteers to engage in various initiatives, activities aimed at improving quality and its sustenance in their institution. It is based on individual initiative and reflects the teacher's macro-level interest in the institution as a whole. Although, these tasks are not formally rewarded by the institution, yet they perform them for attaining institutional excellence. These IQAC functionaries can hardly play their expected role unless they score high in attendance, diligence, commitment, innovation, compliance and sense of belongingness toward their institutions. The relevant literature supports that service employees' cognitive assessment about supervisory support is positively related to their attitudinal responses like attendance, diligence, commitment, innovation, compliance (Eisenberger *et. al.*, 1990); service efforts (Mohr and Bitner, 1995); and sense of obligation toward their organisation (Shore and Wayne, 1993). Thus, ensuring management support (head of the institute, administration, Government, etc.) to IQAC is the need of the hour to sharpen these desired attitudinal responses among IQAC functionaries. These IQAC functionaries desired responses, in turn add to their commitment and consequently improve IQAC effectiveness.

Base on the above discussion the author offers two propositions as:

P1 The IQAC functionaries' Perceived Management Support is positively related to their involvement.

P2 The IQAC functionaries' involvement mediate the relationship between management support and IQAC-effectiveness.

Countless empirical studies support that top management support for quality is most influencing factor in quality improvement. IQAC may consciously select quality initiatives, given the knowledge of opportunities as well as threats to their institution. However, IQAC cannot implement it unless the

FIG. 1

IQAC Functionaries Perceived Supports and its Direct and Indirect Impact on IQAC Effectiveness

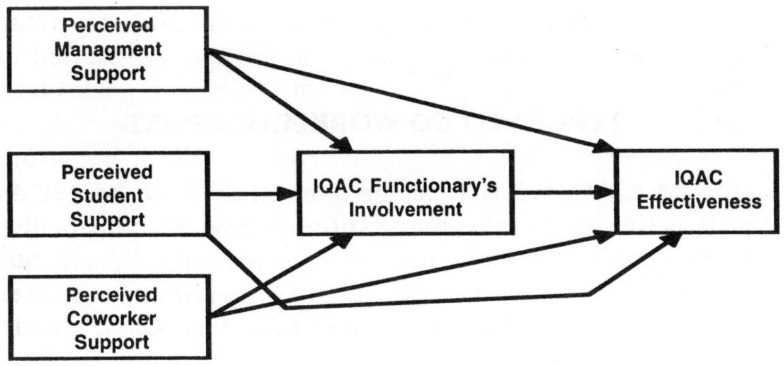

government provides visible quality leadership, places resources for its implementation and understands it as a part top management's culture to reap the fruits of IQAC initiatives. Stated differently:

P3 The IQAC functionaries' Perceived Top Management Support is directly and positively related to IQAC effectiveness.

PERCEIVED STUDENT SUPPORT

In human service settings, customers who are referred as partial employees invariably have a substantial, direct influence on service outcomes (Lengnick-Hall, 1995). If the inputs provided by the consumer are inadequate and/or inappropriate, this results in service problems and failures. Likewise, in education where a student is an integral part of educational service delivery system, inappropriate or inadequate input can be for instance his failing to follow the time schedules, rules and regulations of the institution, to give feedback for system improvement, to demand quality education and demonstrate commitment to quality education, to do the necessary advance preparation for tutorials and ask appropriate questions, to keep patience during lectures, to participate in the quality assurance activities and so on. Base on above the author proposes:

P4 The IQAC functionaries Perceived Students' Support is positively related to their involvement.

P5 The IQAC functionaries Perceived Students' Support is directly and positively related to IQAC effectiveness.

PERCEIVED CO-WORKER SUPPORT

The IQAC, being a change agent, has to go beyond the usual activities to take the institution towards the path of excellence. Multiple operations and people with different skill sets are to be involved to make sure that everything beyond the regular activity is implemented to improve and sustain quality on all operational fronts. It requires IQAC functionaries to establish and create a culture of teamwork and performance, and resolve conflicts that otherwise hamper employees who want to implement the IQAC plans. This is in view of the fact that team work, cooperation and effective collaboration with coworkers are vital to service quality improvement.

Zeithaml *et. al.* (1988), one of the quality gurus referred service performance gap as the disparity between the desired service quality specifications and the actual service delivery. The authors found that one of the key factors that contribute to this disparity is lack of cooperation among coworkers. The cooperative atmosphere and good coworker's relationship at work lead into practice of citizenship behaviours. It refers to employees' voluntary behaviours towards customers and coworkers to help its organisation perform better (Organ, 1988).

There can also be a sort of infectivity effect from relationships with colleagues. For example, positive work attitude from co-workers has a tendency to motivate others to be more productive. Conversely, Staff members who are reluctant to change, or who are unwilling to cooperate others when needed, can "poison" an otherwise productive atmosphere. Considering this affectivity effect, the morale of IQAC functionaries who happen to find others non-responsive are thus sure to be adversely effected. They are less likely to be successful in creating the required degree of group cohesiveness, cooperation and involvement amongst the staff around. Therefore, base on the discussion, the author proposes as:

P6 The IQAC functionaries perceived Coworker Support is positively related to their involvement and consequent effectiveness.

CONCLUSION AND IMPLICATIONS

The most significant implication of this article is that NAAC need to initiate a country wide programme to sensitize all educational mangers about the concept of IQAC supports. The nation' premier assurance agency must regularly communicate to institutions, state governments that desired

IQAC functionaries' behaviours; effectiveness largely depend on their satisfaction with several supports discussed in this paper. Investigations are required whereby, experienced academicians can visit colleges and discuss with IQAC functionaries to have an idea about their problems, required supports and aspirations. In fact, investigating the type and kind of supports that are required by IQAC functionaries will open new areas of research. We can identify the factors that hamper these supports by using questionnaires and can take corrective measures for improving the same. The institutions should encourage students' involvement in IQAC. Further we need to identify the barriers that discourage students from participating in the IQAC activities. The simple conceptual framework proposed in this article is expected not only to help IQAC become more meaningful but also may shape future agendas for research in IQAC-related issues.

References

Eisenberger, R., Fasolo, P. and Davis-LaMastro, V. (1990), "Perceived Organizational Support and Employee Diligence, Commitment, and Innovation", *Journal of Applied Psychology*, Vol. 75, No. 1, pp. 51-9.

Lengnick-Hall, C.A. (1995), ' 'The Patient as the Pivot Point for Quality in Health-care Delivery', *Hospital and Health Service Administration*, Vol. 40, No. 1, pp. 25-39.

Mohr, L. and Bitner, M.J. (1995), "Process Factors in Service Delivery: What Employee Effort means to Customers", in Swartz, T.A., Bowen, D.E. and Brown, S.W. (Eds.), *Advances in Services Marketing and Management*, 4, JAI Press, Greenwich, CT, pp. 91-117.

Organ, D.W. (1988), "Organizational Citizenship Behavior: The Good Soldier Syndrome", *Lexington*, MA: Lexington Books, 1988.

Shore, L.M. and Wayne, S.J. (1993), "Commitment and Employee Behavior: Comparison of Affective Commitment and Continuance Commitment with Perceived Organizational Support", *Journal of Applied Psychology*, Vol. 78, No. 5, pp. 774-80.

Zeithaml, A. Valerie, Berry, L.L. and Parasuraman, A. (1988), "Communication and Control Processes in the Delivery of Service Quality", *Journal of Marketing*, Vol. 52, (April 1988), 35-48.

CHAPTER

14

Drug Abuse among Rural Youth

A Reflection from Field

SHEKHAR RAJPOOT AND NARENDRA PAL SINGH

ABSTRACT

Drug abuse is a complex phenomenon, which has various social, cultural, biological, geographical, historical and economic aspects. The disintegration of the old joint family system, absence of parental love and care in modern families where both parents are working, decline of old religious and moral values, etc. lead to a rise in the number of drug addicts who take drugs to escape hard realities of life. Drug use, misuse or abuse is also primarily due to the nature of the drug abused, the personality of the individual and the addict's immediate environment. The processes of industrialization, urbanization and migration have led to loosening of the traditional methods of social control rendering an individual vulnerable to the stresses and strains of modern life. The fast changing social milieu, among other factors, is mainly contributing to the proliferation of drug abuse, both of traditional and of new psychoactive substances. The present study is a descriptive and partially explorative in nature and centered around males of age group 20-35 years. 100 drug abusers from six villages of Agra district (U.P.) were interviewed. Snowballing sampling technique and information from village elders were used to identify drug abusers. Present study revealed that drug abuse among rural youth is a multifaceted problem. Peer pressure or influence, addiction in family history and exposure to drugs were found to be main instigators for youth to indulge in drug abuse. Factors responsible for continuation of drug abuse were mainly withdrawal symptoms and social labeling of addicts. The main consequences of addiction among youth were found to be negative impact on physical and mental health, loss of social reputation and broken families.

Key words: Drug abuse, Addiction, Rural youth, etc.

INTRODUCTION

Drug use has been an integral part of any culture which affects individual, their families and the society. The epidemic of drug abuse among rural youth has assumed alarming dimensions in India. Changing cultural values, increasing economic stress and dwindling supportive bonds are leading to initiation into substance use. Cannabis, heroin, and Indian-produced pharmaceutical drugs are the most frequently abused drugs in India. Drug use, misuse or abuse is also primarily due to the nature of the drug abused, the personality of the individual and the addict's immediate environment. The processes of industrialization, urbanization and migration have led to loosening of the traditional methods of social control rendering an individual vulnerable to the stresses and strains of modern life.

Incidence of drug abuse among rural areas is getting unexpectedly high. Jaffe (1975) categorized drug addiction as a deviant behavior having medical and psychological components. It is a matter of fact that there is less emphasis on drug abuse as a social problem.

In recent times, U.P. has witnessed a tremendous rise in drug abuse. International narcotics control strategy Report (2004) found that opiates abuse accounted for 43% of Indian drug abuse. Drug users are largely young and predominately male. National survey (2004) on the extent, pattern and trends of drug abuse in India found that opiates are primary drug abused and 49% of inhabitants' families had history of drug abuse. Studies on drug addiction indicated that easy availability of drugs (Hans, 1986) and irrational exaggeration of effects of drugs. Phadke (1989) has resulted in abrupt rise in drug abuse. Jolly (1976) argued that as society cannot fulfil all aspiration of man thus it results in frustration and drug abuse among youth. Randhawa (1991) reported that deviant behavior including drug abuse is learned within primary groups particularily peer group and family.

In Uttar Pradesh, Dube and Handa reported that 22.8 per 1000 were dependent on alcohol and drugs while Thacore from Lucknow gave a figure of 18.55 per 1000. The Important finding of these studies is that alcohol was the commonest substance used (60-98%) followed by cannabis use (4-20%). Epidemiological surveys also revealed that 20-40% of subjects above 15 years are current users of alcohol and 10% of them are regular or excessive users. In a rural population of Uttar Pradesh alcohol was found to be the commonest substance abused (82.5%) followed by cannabis (16.1%). Varma *et. al.* (1980) found that rates of current use of alcohol in Punjab were 45.9% in Jalandhar and 27.7% in Chandigarh whereas it was 28.1% in rural areas of Punjab. Shukla (1979) reported that 38.3% of the rural population in Uttar Pradesh was habitual substance users. In a study conducted in rural community in Bihar prevalence of alcohol/drug use was found to be 28.8% of the study population. Increase in incidences of HIV, hepatitis B and C and tuberculosis due to addiction adds the reservoir of infection in the community burdening the health care system further. The problem of drug abuse among rural youth remains neglected as there is dearth of literature on it.

OBJECTIVES

Present study is designed partially explorative and partially descriptive in nature. Along with the examination of socio-economic profile of inhabitants the present study focuses on the three facets of the problem of drug abuse. First is the examination of precipitating factors for drug abusers (like role of personal, family and non-family factors). Second is examination of factors responsible for communication of drugs (like social labeling, withdrawal symptoms, etc.) and third are to analysis the consequences of addiction on addict, i.e. effect of drugs on health and relationship.

RESEARCH METHODOLOGY

The present study was conducted on males of age group 20-35 years. Interview scheduled was prepared and final interviews were conducted after a pilot study. The help of village elders, medical professionals, chemist was taken to identity drug abuser in these selected villages. A list of 100 drug addicts prepared but only 72 agreed to be part of research study.

FINDINGS AND DISCUSSION

A total of seventy-two drug addicts were interviewed from six different villages. The age group of 20-25 years was selected for the study.

Socio-Economic status of Inhabitants: All inhabitants were male. Majority 96% of inhabitant were Hindu and mostly belongs to scheduled caste while 4% Muslims. The percentage was higher because the study was conducted in dominated areas. Regarding education qualification inhabitant were having educational qualification up to 12th while 40% were illiterate 28 addicts were 8th pass. Only 8% of inhabitants had graduate/post-graduate degree holders. Thus, the sample has inhabitant having lower educational qualification. Majority of inhabitant of agriculture-based occupation, i.e. 41% were small farmers and 31% were agriculture laborers. 9% were unemployed while 8% were students. 7% were doing job and 4% were having their own small business. Majority of addicts 71% had total family monthly income from Rs. 7000 to 11000 while 9% had above 11000 total family incomes. Thus, majority of inhabitant were of lower socio-economic status.

Family Type: Majority (72%) of inhabitants belonged to joint families while 28% belonged to nuclear families. In context of number of family members majority (78%)

inhabitants had more than 6 members in their families while 22% had 1 to 5 family's members. It is evident from the data on socio-economic status that majority of inhabitant hailed from lower strata of society having lower economic and occupational status.

Precipitating Factor for Youth to Indulge in Addiction

TABLE I
Precipitating Factors

Precipitating factor for drug addicts	*Number*	*N=72 (%age)*
A. Personal factors as Precipitating factor		
1. Out of Curiosity	34	47
2. Enjoyment for showing fun/manhood	17	24
3. Frustration	32	45
B. Family factors as Precipitating factor		
1. Imitation of father	43	60
2. Imitation of siblings	23	32
3. Imitation of other relatives	15	21
C. Non-family factors as Precipitating factor		
1. Peer Pressure	50	69
2. Intimacy with drug peddlers	22	31

Table 1 shows the main precipitating factors responsible for induction of youth into drug abuse. Three factors were identified as precipitating factors for addiction, i.e., personal, family and non-family factors. It was observed in the study that more than one factor was responsible as precipitating factors of youth towards drug abuse.

There were 47% of addicts who stated that they had strong curiosity towards drug use and this curiosity acted as propagator for their drug use. 24% drug abusers reported that they had perception that drugs act as sexual vitality enhance. The present study endorses the findings of Ganguly *et. al.* (1993) and Amanpreet (2009) that most of drug abusers initially consumed drugs for fun or to show manhood. 45% addicts stated that they turned to drugs to counter frustration originated from failure in their one or another pursuit of life. With reference to family factors as precipitating factors of drug abuse for youth, 60% of inhabitants reported that they started taking drugs by imitating their fathers who were also addicts while 32% reported that they imitated the habit of addiction among their siblings. 21% drug addicts reported that they copied the habit of drug abuse from their relatives. In non-familial factors, majority (69%) of inhabitants reported peer influence or pressure acted as the main cause of their induction to drugs. The present study endorsed the findings of Henningfield (1991) that influence of peers acted as major precipitating factor for drug abuse among youth. However, 31% of inhabitants reported their intimacy with drug peddlers as one of the reason for their addiction. They reported that this intimacy developed as they were usually sent by their fathers or relatives to purchase drugs from these drug peddlers. There were two cases in which inhabitants reported that local village chemist or quack made them addict. They narrated that initially chemist gave them drug as medicine to kill pain but now they had developed the habit of these pain killers as drugs. Ganguly *et. al.* (1993) and Amanpreet (2009) also reported the similar findings in their studies.

Factors responsible for the Continuation of Drug Abuse among Youth

TABLE 2

Factors Responsible for the Continuation of Drugs

Factors responsible for the continuation of drugs	*Number*	*N=72 (%age)*
1. Avoidance of withdrawal symptoms	48	67
2. To ward off fatigue due to work	34	48
3. Labeling as addict	15	68
4. To forget anxiety due to personal problems	30	42

Above table shows the factors responsible for the continuation of drugs by addicts. There were multiple factors which accounted for the continuation of drugs. Many factors acted collectively for the continuation of drug abuse among addicts. Majority (67%) of inhabitants reported that major precipitating factors for their intake of drug was avoidance of withdrawal symptoms like nausea, vomiting, insomnia, fits and restlessness. Medically withdrawal symptoms of drugs were held responsible for the continuation of drugs by addict. 48% of inhabitants reported that as they do hard physical labour so they use drugs off fatigue. 68% of inhabitants stated that they were socially labeled as addicts. They also reported that they were being identified by different names like 'Nashedi', 'Ganjedi', 'Nashewaj', 'Charsi', Darubaj, etc.

The social labeling of drug abusers not only reinforces their habit of drug abuse but also integrate addiction in their personality. Often drug abuser thinks that they belong to a category of people who abuse drugs and gradually start imitating behavior of hard core drug abuser. They revealed that their social labeling as addicts played a significant role in continuation of their drug abuse. 42% inhabitants reported one of the reasons for their addiction to forget their anxiety while 22% reported that they were continuing drug abuse because they wanted to escape from the reality. They also explained that after taking drugs the feeling of mental satisfaction and escape from their problems were reported by addicts.

Consequences of Drug Abuse

TABLE 3

Effect of Addiction on Drug Abuser

Effect of addiction on drug abuser	*Number*	*N=72 (%age)*
1. Negative impact on health	72	100
2. On social reputation	56	78
3. Decreased work efficiency	22	31
4. Negative effect on their relations with family	47	65

Table 3 indicates consequences of addiction on addict youth. All inhabitants reported negative effect of drugs on their health. Mainly inhabitants suffered from health problems like weight loss, constipation, piles, anxiety, fits and sleep disturbance. 78% inhabitants reported that due to drug abuse they lost their social reputation and credibility. They also revealed that they were first to be scanned by police in any event of crime or other illegal activity in village. 31% addict youth reported decrease in their work efficiency because of addiction. 65% addicts reported that due to addiction their relationship with family suffered. They also reported that their respect among family decreased due to addiction. The present study coincides with the study of Kaur and Gulati (2007) and Amanpreet (2009) as they also reported the implication of drug abuse like damage of health, frustration and negative consequences on family. It was also observed during study that hardened drug abusers did not perform any activity; they only desperately searched for drugs.

CONCLUSION

Present study reveals that drug abuse among rural youth is a multifaceted problem. Influence of peer pressure acted as the major precipitating factor for drug abuse. Among family factors, history of addiction in father, siblings and other relatives also precipitates the habit of drug use among the rural youth. Factors like frustration, curiosity towards drugs also precipitates youth towards drugs.

REFERENCES

Ahmed, Nadeem *et. al.*, Substance abuse...... Pravara, *Med Rev 2009*, 4(4).

Dube, K.C., Handa, S.K., Drug use in health and mental illness in an Indian population. *Br. J. Psychiatry,* 1971; 118:345-6.

Dube, K.C., Kumar, A., Kumar, N., Gupta, S.P., Prevalence and pattern of drug use amongst college students. *Acta Psychiat Scand,* 1978; 57:336-46.

Ganguly, K.K., Sharma, H.K. and Krishnamachari, K.A.V.R. (1995), "An ethnographic account of opium consumers of Rajasthan (In dia): Socio-medical Perspective", *Indian Council of Medical Research and AIIMS,* New Delhi, pp. 9-12.

Hans, Kuljit (1986), "A Psychological Survey of Drug Abuse in a Village of Punjab", Ph.D. Thesis, Psychology, Panjab University, Chandigarh.

Hennigfield, J.E. and Cohen, C., Heishman, S.J. (1991), "Drug Self-ad Ministration Method in Abuse Liability Evaluation", *British Journal of Addiction*, Vol. 86, pp. 1571-77.

International Narcotics Control Strategy Report (2004), cited in www.eld is.org.

Indian Express (2009), "Every Third Male Student in Punjab Drug Addict, HC told", *Indian Express*, Viewed on 18 July 2009, Cited in (http://www.in dianexpress.com/news/every-third-male-stu dent-in-punjab-drug-add ict-hc-told/4 64 04 8/0.) punjab-drug-addict-hc-told/464048/0.)

Jaffe, J.H. (1975), Drug Addiction and Drug Abuse, cited in L.S. Goodman and A. Gilman (Eds.), The pharmacological basis of therapeutics (5 Ed.), New York, Mac Millen, pp. 284-329.

Jena, R., Shukla, T.R., Hemraj, P., Drug Abuse in a Rural Community in Bihar: Some Psychosocial Correlates. *Indian J. Psychiatry*, 1996; 38:43-6.

Jolly, Anu (1976), "Drug Abuse among Panjab University Students—Field Work Monograph", Dissertation Panjab University, Chandigarh.

Kaur Ravneet and Gulati, Jatinder, "Drug abuse: Trends and Issues", cited in http://dspace.iimk. ac.in/bitstream/2259 /34 8/1/387-395

Lal, B., Singh, G., Alcohol consumption in Punjab. *Indian J. Psychiatry*, 1978; 20:212-6.

Lal, B., Singh, G., Drug abuse in Punjab. *Br J Addict*, 1979; 74:441.

Miller, W.R. Sanchez, V.C. Motivating Young Adults for Treatment and Lifestyle Change. In: Howard, G., editor. Issues in alcohol use and misuse in young adults. University of Notre Dame Press; 1993. pp. 55–82.

National Survey (2004), "The Extend Pattern and Trends of Drug Abuse", Indian Ministry of Social Justice and Empowerment and United Nations Office on Drugs and Crime. Cited in www.unodc.prg /ind ia/india_national_Su rvey20 04.h tml

Phadke Anand (1989), Drug Supply and Use, Sage Publication, New Delhi.

Ramachandran, V., The Prevention of Alcohol Related Problems. *Indian J Psychiatry*, 1991; 33:3-10.

Randhawa Meenu (1991). "Drug Addicts in and Around Chandigarh—A Sociological Study", Dissertation Panjab University, Chandigarh.

Ropar, C. (2006). Social use, Abuse and Addiction-site of the Author, University of Texas, Austin.

Sandhu, Ravinder Singh (2006), "Drug Addiction in Punjab: A Sociological Study", Department of Sociology, Guru Nanak Dev University, Amritsar. Viewed on 27 July 2009, Cited in (http://www.tribuneindia.com/2006/20060701/punjab1.htm)

Sharma, Neelam (2008), "Region Drug Abuse Statistics way Ahead of National Average", Viewed on 25 May 2009. Cited in (http://www.expressindia.com/latest-news/Region-drug-abuse-statistics-way-ahead-of-n ational-average/286 653/).

Shukla, B.R., Drinks and Drugs in a North Indian Village—An Anthropological Study. Ethnographic and Folk Culture Society, Lucknow, India, 1979.

Singh, A., Drug Abuse among Rural Youth: A Sociological Study of Punjab, June, 2010, *Sociology*, Vol. 1(9). .

Singh, P. (2005), "Farm Labour, Teenagers Worst hit by Drug Abuse", *The Tribune News Services,* Chandigarh, cited in Kaur and Gulati (2007), Drug Abuse: Trends and Issues International Marketing Conference on Marketing and Society, 8-10 April, 2007, IIMK viewed on 25 June 2009.

Singh, P. (2006). Farm Labour, Teenagers worst hit by drug abuse, *The Tribune News Service.*

Srivastava, A., Pal, H.R., Dwivedi, S.N., *et. al.* National household survey of drug abuse in India. Report submitted to the Indian Ministry of Social Justice and Empowerment and the United Nations Office for Drugs and Crime, 2003.

Thacore, V.R., Drug Abuse in India with Special Reference to Lucknow. *Indian J. Psychiatry,* 1972;14:257-61.

University Students, *Indian Journal of Medical Research* (Kasauli, Punjab, India) 66:627.

Varma, V.K., Singh, A., Singh, S., Malhotra, A.K., Extent and Pattern of Alcohol use in North India. *Indian J. Psychiatry,* 1980; 22:331-7.

WHO, Techn. Res. Ser. No. 886: 1999, p. 48.

CHAPTER

15

Education for Women Empowerment

NIDA SIDDIQUI

INTRODUCTION

To be born a woman means to inhabit, from early infancy to the last day of life, the infant girl will normally grow up to behave, feel and think in ways appropriate to her sex. As the child becomes aware of the world around her, she senses that man and women behave differently. Daddy goes out to work and mommy remains to take care of the home.[1] In addition, much of the women are engaged in household activities leaving no time for their own development. Education has been regarded as an end in itself and as a means of realizing other desirable ends. It develops the personality of the individuals, qualifies them to fulfill, certain economic, political and cultural functions and thereby improves the socio-economic status. Education has been recognized as a major instrument which societies can use to direct the process of change and development towards desired goals.[2]

EMPOWERMENT AND ITS INDICATORS

Women empowerment means that women no matter where they are, are healthy, have enough for their needs, their own survival and that of their family and community, to be able to live with dignity and live and work in a safe and caring environment which allows their growth and holistic development, i.e. physically, socially, emotionally, economically.[3] The national policy in education (1986) is a land mark in this approach to women's education. It has attempted for the first time to address itself to the basic issues of women's inequality.[4]

The programme of action for implementation of national policy of education (POA) spells out the meaning of empowerment:

(a) Building a positive self-image and self-confidence.
(b) Developing ability to think critically.
(c) Building up group cohesion and fostering decision-making and action.
(d) Ensuring equal participation in the process of bringing about social change.
(e) Encouraging group action in order to bring about change in the society.
(f) Providing the wherewithal for economic independence.[5]

For effective participation in the process of development, physical, mental, economic and technological capabilities of women must be developed. But the reality is contrary to it. It is beyond doubt that women were not provided appropriate opportunities for their development. Their position has been of dependent, and they have suffered discrimination on every front, ranging from family, to social, economic, political and legal status. A number of indicators have been evolved for measuring their disadvantages (Rahman, 1996, 425),[6] the indicators generally relate to health, family planning, education, participation, wages, etc. For instance, Morris (1979)[7] produced a physical quality of life index on the basis of female literacy, and female life expectancy and fertility. Sometimes only level of fertility is employed to gauge the status of the women. (Mazay and Lee, 1983)[8]

On global level discussion on status of women got momentum in mid-1960's and efforts were made to identify the determinants of women's status, Villareal (1996, 302)[9] has summarized them. Participation in the labour force and nature of job has been singled out as one of the most important determinant of women's status, for it leads to economic upliftment of women by giving them the independent source of income, access to control over their earning also enhance their domestic autonomy.[10]

Thus, empowerment is a multi-dimensional process which should enable individuals/groups of individuals to realize their full identity and powers in all spheres of life. There is a continued inequality and vulnerability of women in all sectors—economic, social, political, educational, health care, nutrition and legal.[11]

Similarly in India the national policy for the empowerment of women (2001) emphasize on laying down proper judicial legal system, giving women a decision-making power, economic empowerment of women through poverty eradication, micro-crediting, enhancing the participation of women in economic activities, agriculture, industry, social empowerment of women through providing better health, nutrition, drinking water and sanitation, better housing and shelter better environment, by increasing their awareness and participation in science and technology, and protecting and safeguarding minor women, destitute, violence against women, etc. Thus, one can say that empowerment can be categorized in various areas like social, economic, etc. though all these areas are differentiated but are dependent on each other.

EDUCATION

Education is the single most important instrument through which a human resource can be fully developed. It is very well said that knowledge is power. Education's importance has been emphasized by a number of international conventions, including the Universal Declaration of Human Rights and the Programme of Action of the 1994 International Conference on Population and Development. The Fourth World Conference on Women, held in Beijing in 1995, recognized that women's literacy is key to empowering women's participation in decision-making in society and to improving families' well-being. In addition, the United Nations has articulated the Millennium Development Goals (MDGs), which include goals for improved education, gender equality, and women's empowerment. The MDGs emphasize education's essential role in building democratic societies and creating a foundation for sustained economic growth. On the national level the national policy of education (1986) is a landmark in this approach, the national literacy mission is another step towards eradication of illiteracy in the age group of 15-35 years by the year 1995. By educating women of the house, one educates the whole family. As an outcome of the report of the committee on the status of women in India, education was included in the Sixth Plan as a major programme for the development of women.[12]

WOMEN AND EDUCATION

Education is a basic Human Right and is necessary for sustainable social and economic development. Investment in Education is indispensable for human development and proper growth. "The consequences of illiteracy are profound and even potentially life threatening", remarked UNICEF executive director Carl Bellary. At the individual level education opens possibilities that otherwise would be closed, a better chance to lead, healthy and productive lives, to participate fully in civic and political affairs and to defend and protect rights to survival. Education is crucial to poverty reduction, because it is an empowering tool that cannot be restricted to the power building classes.[13]

Mahatma Gandhi believed that a just social order would become possible when women recognized their historic social role, rejected their unequal position and actively involved themselves in working for social transformation.[14] Since the 19th century, women's movement all over the world has always placed the right to education in the forefront of their demand. Within education the entry of women into higher education tended to be viewed as landmarks in social development. During the early years of the international women's decade, governments of both developed and developing nations were very keen to offer indicator of women's status in their countries. Women have miles to go to attain high status and non-discriminatory parity. The Indian dilemma of gender illusions and relations need to be resolved without hypocrisy if the nation is to progress with women taking their rightful place without the corresponding concession of masculine chauvinists.[15]

Women's Education Scenario in the Pre-independence Era

Year	*% of women's literacy*
1881-82	0.2
1901-02	0.69
1911-12	1.05
1921-22	1.81
1931-32	2.93
1946-47	6.0

Source : Various issues of census of India.[16]

Women's Education Scenario in the Post-independence Era[17]

Year	*% of women's literacy*
1951	7.90
1961	12.95
1971	18.69
1981	24.82

Barrier to Women's Education

Swami Vivekananda said, "if you want the nation to prosper include women in every aspect of life". There is several reasons for the low level of literacy in India, not the least of which is the high level of poverty. Although school attendance is free, the cost of books, uniforms, transportation can be too much to keep the girls at home to care for the younger sibling or to work in family enterprises. Female children are given less education and retained at home for help with household tasks. They are married at an early age.[18] If a family has to choose between a son and a daughter because of financial restrictions, typically the son will be chosen, negative parental attitudes towards educating daughter can also be a barrier to girl's education. Many parents view educating son as an investment because the son will be responsible for caring for aging parent. On the other hand, the education of the daughters can be seen as a waste as they will ultimately live with their husband's family and the parents will not get any direct benefit from their education.

Some other factors which act as a hurdle to women education are :

(1) Inadequate school facilities
(2) Lack of qualified female teachers
(3) Lack of transport facilities
(4) Fear of sexual harassment
(5) Lack of toilet facilities
(6) Fixed schooling hours
(7) Lack of hostel facilities

Thus, these factors combine to aggravate the already dismal condition of the female literacy level and there by resulting in high dropout rate among girls.

IMPORTANCE OF WOMEN'S EDUCATION

The curse of male chauvinism will have no place in the new social order and women will have a safe and dignified existence in the society, on equal footing as of man in every sphere of life. Education will make them self-supporting and economically independent thus having freedom and courage of making decision.[19]

Actually Education is capable of molding the entire lifestyle. Women education influences marital and fertility behavior more strongly than husband's education.[20]

Research evidence now shows that mother's level of schooling is highly correlated with infant and child mortality. After analyzing census data for 14 states Sharma and Rutherford concludes that literacy is a basic concomitant of development, for their study showed that literacy is strongly correlated with quality of life indicators such as infant mortality rates, death rate, and %age of married females in the 15-19 age group thereby improving the overall status of women, so that they can also have decision-making power and participate equally in their families. Thus, Education not only improves their present status rather it act as a tool which can have an intergenerational benefit.[21]

Mahmud and Johnston (1994) therefore argued that it would be limiting to see only formal education as providing a positive outcome on fertility control.[22] For various other sources such as adult education Programme, informal education and extension services and every peer and support networks can provide such exposure. This may be especially important for countries like India where these may be more common than formal schooling, particularly in rural india.[23]

Martin (1995), on the basis of data from the demographic and health surveys, also find that there is a decline in fertility rates with an increase in the educational levels of women.[24]

FACTORS RESPONSIBLE FOR SLOW GROWTH OF WOMEN AND WOMEN LITERACY

In the process of development the contribution of women towards the growth of the country is ever increasing. But their social status, educational status, economic status and political status continue to remain below their counterparts. The lower status of women in the society does not give them confidence to come out of their shells. Hence, it is necessary to identify the factors responsible for this serious issue. Our cultural and political history has proved that women are considered as secondary human beings. It is consider that the birth of a son is bliss incarnate, while that of the daughter is the root of family misery. Only the sons are the heirs of their parents and they are eligible to do the final rites of their parents.[25]

According to human development report 2009 India is ranked 114th (.599) in the world gender development index (GDI).

SUGGESTIONS

(1) Trainings, workshops and courses may be organized, so as to raise the self-esteem and self-development of women, irrespective of their literacy.
(2) To reduce the female dropouts, following efforts may be taken.
(3) Girl's education and girls colleges should be promoted.
(4) In all school and colleges, especially which are rural in area toilet facilities for ladies should be provided.
(5) Services like crèches, door delivery of food, mobile health care, etc. should be promoted.
(6) Awareness should be generated among the masses regarding the necessity of educating girls so as to prepare them to effectively contribute to the socio-economic development of the country.
(7) Involvement of local leaders, voluntary agencies and women's group is also necessary. Mahila Mandals need to be revitalized and reoriented to provide an effective forum for the purpose.
(8) School timings should be flexible and fixed to suit the local conditions and needs of the working girls.
(9) The open school system should be expanded extending the facility to all the girls in rural and backward areas.
(10) Girls should be encouraged to do professional courses.
(11) All women working in industries or employed somewhere else should be made literate by the employers by allotting time from the working hours for their education.
(12) Decentralization is the key to the successful implementation of the strategies outlined above.
(13) An overall coordination of health, welfare and educational inputs would be most desirable, this would entail—

(a) Convergent policies in this sector,
(b) Coordination of delivery mechanisms, and
(c) Pooling of allocations.

If the current situation continues, India will have to face a gloomy future. To quote Jawaharlal Nehru," the level of democracy in a country thus can be measured by the level of education of its residents". To conclude a good social environment has to be enabled by the government to promote women to participate in various fields. More efforts should be laid down to bring about good self-development from their childhood. Then only we can have a bright future.

Notes and References

1. Nagendra Shilaja, Issues in Women Education and Empowerment, Publishers, Jaipur, India (2007), p. 38.
2. Nagendra Shilaja, Issues in Women Education and Empowerment, Publishers, Jaipur, India (2007), p. 125.
3. Sharma, Priyanka, Women Empowerment and Working Women, Book Enclave, Jaipur, India (2008), p. 48.
4. Rajwat, Mamta, Women Education and Social Empowerment, Reference Press, New Delhi, (2005), p. 10.
5. Rajwat, Mamta, Women Education and Social Empowerment, Reference Press, New Delhi (2005), p. 11.
6. Rahman, Atiqua, Rural Women and Poverty: The Status and the IFAD Evolving Strategies for Intervention, in U.N, *Ibid.* (1996), p. 425.
7. Morris, M., Measuring The Condition of World's Poor: The PQLT Index, New York, Pergamon (1979).
8. Mazey, M.E. and D.R. Lee, Her Space and Her Place: Geography of Women, Asso, Am, Georges, Resource Publications in Geography, Washington (1983).
9. Villareal Marcela, Women's Economic Activities and Fertility: Overview of the Interactions and Policy Implications, in U.N, *Ibid.*, (1996) p. 302.
10. R.S. Tripathi, R.P. Tiwari, Perspective on Indian Women, APH Publishing Corporation, New Delhi (1999), p. 81.
11. Dr. S. Ram, Encyclopedia of Women and Social Change, Published by Ajay Verma for Commonwealth Publications, New Delhi, Volume 3 (2003), p. 308.
12. Yadav, C.P., Empowerment of Women, Laxmi Shiksha Sansthan, Lucknow and Anmol Publications Pvt. Ltd., New Delhi, Volume 1 (2000), p. 69.

13. Dr. Patanjali, Premcand, Development of Adult education in India, Shree Publishers and Distributors, New Delhi (2005), p. 1.
14. Aggarwal, S.P.; *et. al.* Development of Adult Continuing and Non-formal Education in India, Concept Publication Company, New Delhi (2002), p. 351.
15. Dr. Ram, S., Women and Social Change, Commonwealth Publications, New Delhi (2004), p. 166.
16. Sarkar, I., Women in Changing Society, Serial Publications, New Delhi (2004), p. 204.
17. Nuna, C. Sheela, Women and Development, Published by Registrar, NIEPA, New Delhi (1990), p. 15.
18. Raju Laxmipati, M., Women Empowerment : Challenges and Strategies, Regal Publications, New Delhi (2008), p. 73.
19. Khanna Shashi, Relevance of Distance Education, Mannford Books, New Delhi (2006), p. 237.
20. Tripathi, R.S., Tiwari, R.P., Perspectives of Indian Women, APH Publishing Corporation, New Delhi (1999), p. 91.
21. Patanjali, Premchand, Development of Adult Education in India Shree Publishers and Distributors, New Delhi (2005), p. 153.
22. Mahmud, S. and A.M. Jhonston, 'Women, Status, Employment and Reproductive Outcomes in Gita Sen *et. al.* (eds.) Population Policies, Reconsidered: Health, Employment and Rights, Harvard, Harvard University Press (1994).
23. Martin, T.C., Women's Education and Fertility : Results from 26. Demographic and Health Surveys (1995), 26(4).
24. Savithri, R., Mukhopadhyay Swapna, Poverty Gender and Development—An Analysis of Linkages, Manohar Publication New Delhi (1998), p. 38.
25. Roy Rajarshi, Women Education and Development, Perspectives, Issues and Concerns, Shipra Publications, New Delhi (2009), p. 83.

References

Aggarwal, S.P., *et. al.* (2002), Development of Adult Continuing and Non-formal Education in India Concept Publication Company New Delhi.

Khanna Shashi Relevance of Distance Education, Mannford Books, New Delhi (2006).

Mahmud, S. and A.M. Jhonston, 'Women, Status, Employment and Reproductive Outcomes in Gita Sen *et. al.* (eds.) Population Policies, Reconsidered: Health, Employment and Rights, Harvard: Harvard University Press.

Martin, T.C. (1995), Women's Education and Fertility : Results from 26 Demographic and Health Surveys, 26(4).

Mazey, M.E. and D.R. Lee, Her space and Her Place: A Geography of Women, Asso., Am, Georges. Resource Publications in Geography, Washington (1983).

Morris, Measuring The Condition of World's Poor : The PQLT Index, New York, Pergamon (1979).

Nagendra Shilaja, Issues in Women Education and Empowerment, Publishers, Jaipur, India (2007).

Nuna, C. Sheela, Women and Development, Published by Registrar NIEPA, New Delhi (1990).

Dr Patanjali, Premchand, Development of Adult Education in India, Shree Publishers and Distributors, New Delhi (2005).

Rahman Atiqua, Rural Women and Poverty the Status and the IFAD Evolving Strategies for Intervention, in U.N., *Ibid.* (1996).

Rajwat Mamta, Women Education and Social Empowerment, Reference Press, New Delhi (2005).

Dr. Ram, S., Encyclopedia of Women and Social Change, Published By Ajay Verma For Commonwealth Publications, New Delhi, Volume 3 (2003).

Dr. Ram, S., Women and Social Change, Commonwealth Publications, New Delhi (2004).

Raju Laxmipati, M., Women Empowerment : Challenges and Strategies, Regal Publication, New Delhi (2008).

Roy, Rajarshi, Women Education and Development, Perspectives, Issues and Concerns, Shipra Publications, New Delhi (2009).

Sarkar, I., Women in Changing Society, Serial Publication, New Delhi. (2004).

Savithri, R., Mukhopadhyay, Swapna, Poverty Gender and Development—An Analysis of Linkages, Manohar Publication, New Delhi (1998).

Sharma, Priyanka, Women Empowerment and Working Women, Book Enclave, Jaipur, India (2008).

Tripathi, R.S., Tiwari, R.P., Perspective on Indian Women, APH Publishing Corporation, New Delhi (1999).

Villareal, Marcela, Women's Economic Activities and Fertility: Overview of the Interactions and Policy Implications, in U.N., *Ibid.* (1996).

Yadav, C.P., Empowerment of Women, Laxmi Shiksh Sansthan Lucknow, Anmol Publications Pvt. Ltd., New Delhi, Volume 1 (2000).

CHAPTER

16

Right to Education

Effective Use of ICT for Reaching Out to Socially and Economically Weaker Sections in India

PRABIR PANDA, G.P. SAHU AND FAHEEMA AFZAL

ABSTRACT

Most of the enrolment growth in the coming several decades will be in developing countries and India will contribute a significant proportion of that expansion. India by enacting "Right to Education Act, 2009" has set out on an ambitious path to provide free and compulsory education to all children in the 6 to 14 age group. As a result, the number of students enrolled in elementary schools in far flung villages would most definitely see a quantum jump. Challenges of funding, availability of qualified teachers, and building a sustainable academic culture and school infrastructure are significant and real. Providing access to the free education for the children of downtrodden peoples like tribals, lower castes, and dalits is a complex issue in India wherein the fragmentation in the society along religious, ethnic and linguistic lines is deep rooted. In addition, rampant poverty which is the root cause of child labour leaves no time for the affected children to undertake formal schooling. In this backdrop, in this paper we review various facets of and challenges in providing access to universal elementary education for the children from socially weaker sections in India. We delve into various aspects of this ambitious aim and suggest measures for mitigating the risks and pitfall in India's march towards achievement of 100% literacy of over 1 billion people. We also explore the ways in which the strengths of ICT can be leveraged in achievement of the goal.

Keywords: Right to Education, Use of ICT in education, Compulsory Education, State Policy.

INTRODUCTION

Khan (2001) reported that learning plays central role in sustainable development and it contributes immensely to poverty reduction and income generation, empowerment and consolidation of democracy, disease prevention and sustainable health and to the protection of the environment is by now well known. The close relationship of education, social status and choice of occupation has been underlined by Balasubramanyam and Balasubramanyam (2010). The critical link of education to poverty reduction and human development is depicted in the Figure 1.

The importance of education on affirmative action and upliftment of masses is not lost on Indian policy-makers. In fact, *Altbach (2009)* reported that China and India, which together make up one-third of the world's population and are two of the most rapidly growing economies, are awakening to the significance of education for technological development and for the global knowledge economy. The economic realities of China and India's rapid growth are affecting the world, from increased demand for natural resources to their roles as exporters of products of all kinds, a pattern that will continue regardless of the current economic slowdown. A growing

FIG. 1
Pathways of Education to Poverty Reduction and Human Development

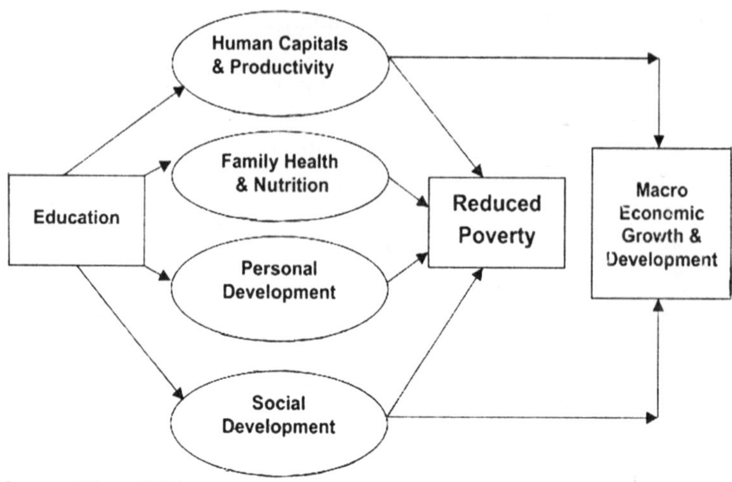

Source : Khan, 2001.

impact of these countries is in higher education; their higher education systems are already among the world's largest, and they are major exporters of students to other countries.

CHALLENGES FOR UNIVERSAL ELEMENTARY EDUCATION IN INDIA

The challenges for India in educating its large population have been reported by *Datta and Mitra (2010)* in their study. They report that about 35% of world's illiterate population is Indian. Despite seemingly optimistic Gross Enrolment Ratios (GER) being recorded and proactive literacy schemes (Sarva Shiksha Abhyan, National Literacy Mission and Mid-day Meal Scheme) being introduced, there is a disparity between these positive indicators and actuality. A high dropout rate of 41.2% is seen at the elementary level. The national literacy rate of girls over seven years is 54% against 75% for boys. In the Northern Hindi-speaking states of India, girls' literacy rates are particularly low, ranging between 33-50%. Quality of instruction and learning is low. Students' understanding and application of written and verbal expression, logic and reasoning, numeric and quantitative knowledge is inadequate. Geographical remoteness and access challenges, regional, gender, and socio-economic inequity, poor infrastructure, amenities and non-conducive learning environments, academically inclined (often in contrast to practical applicability), corporal punishment, apathetic and untrained teachers and theoretical pedagogy, are key causative factors for poor accomplishments in the education sector.

The Sarva Shiksha Abhiyan was launched in 2001-02 to attain universal elementary education in the country for children in the age group of 6 to 14 years. To ensure that all children attend school, several measures were taken under Sarva Shiksha Abhiyan such as mobilization of the community, providing schools within easy reach, and organizing bridge courses for out-of-school children. In order to assess how far these measures have succeeded, a nation-wide independent sample survey of households was conducted in all the States and Union Territories of India in 2009 to provide State-wise estimates of the number and percentage of out-of-school children in the age group 6-13 (http://ssa.nic.in/).

The survey was conducted by *Social and Rural Research Institute-IMRB International (SRI-IMRB).* The findings of the survey indicated that the country had about 19.1 crore children in the age group 6-13 (i.e. below 14 years), of whom 4.3% children were out of school, in 2005 this figure was 6.9%. Amongst the out of school children, 3.2% children had never attended school and 1.1% were dropouts. Among boys 3.9% children were out of school and among girls 4.6% children were out of school. The key statistics for the out of school children (as reported by the study) are appended in Table 1.

The survey brought out that the children belonging to underprivileged and socially backward groups are more likely to dropout of elementary schooling due to one or more of the following reasons acting as a trigger:

(a) Poverty/Economic reason
(b) Child too young to be attending school
(c) Child suffers from some disability or poor health

TABLE I

Comparison of Out of School Children : 2005 v. 2009

Out of School Children (%)		*2005*	*2009*
All (6-13 years)		6.9	4.3
Dropouts		2.2	1.1
Never attended		4.7	3.2
Age group	6-10 years	6.1	3.7
	11-13 years	8.6	5.2
By area	Rural	7.8	4.5
	Urban	4.6	3.2
By Gender	Male	6.2	3.9
	Female	7.9	4.7
By Social groups	SC	8.2	6.0
	ST	9.5	5.6
	Muslim	10.0	7.7
	OBC + Others	5.6	2.7
Percentage of disabled children amongst Out of school children (6-13 years)		38.1	34.8

Source : http://ssa.nic.in/

(d) Child is not interested in studies
(e) Child to supplement household income
(f) Needed to help in domestic work
(g) Education not considered necessary by parents or head of the household
(h) School location not suitable
(j) Needed to take care of siblings

The analysis of the results of the study brought out the flagship educational programmes launched by Government of India, have not been able to make significant inroads in the underprivileged sections of the society. These programmes have not achieved the desired results for the children from weaker sections of the society and children living in remote areas. Under the circumstances it would not be out of place to have a look at the efficacy of affirmative action in India.

Fig. 2

Percentage of Out of School Children in different Social Groups by Location

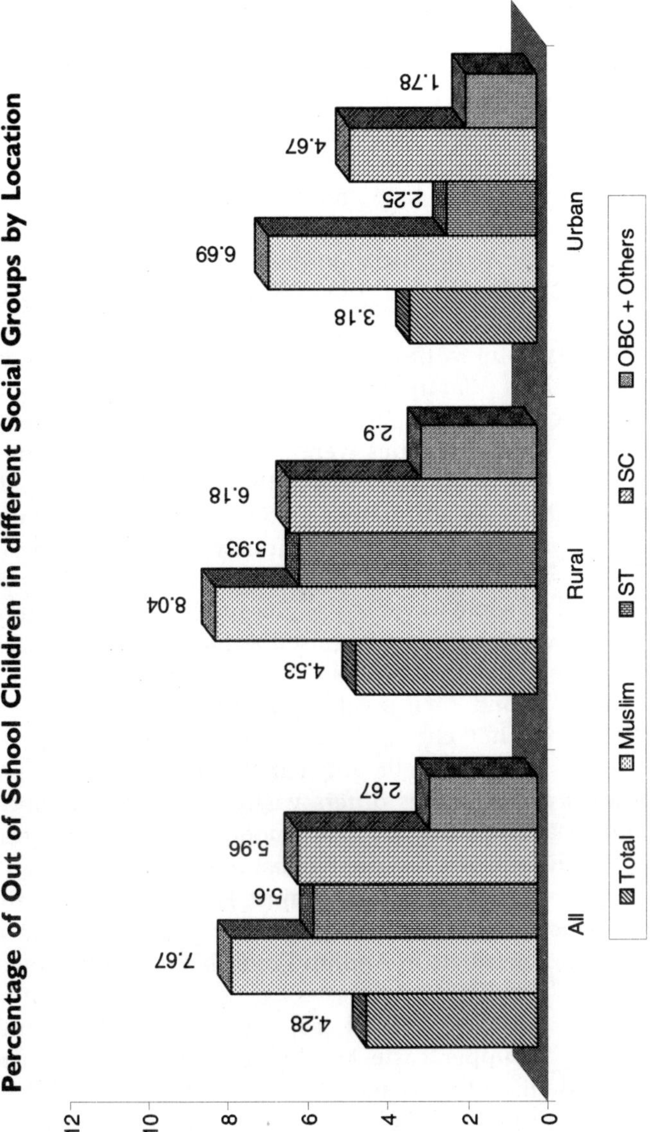

Source : http://ssa.nic.in/

EFFICACY OF AFFIRMATIVE ACTIONS IN INDIA

While positive discrimination has been a policy of the Indian government for decades, a considerable debate is still under way about both the justification for and the effectiveness of the policy. Positive discrimination has been claimed as largely ineffective in raising the status of the downtrodden groups it is intended to help and a mistaken social policy in a meritocratic society *(Mahajan, 2007)*. The studies on affirmative action in India primarily focus on the reservation policy for the scheduled castes/scheduled tribes (SCs/STs), mandated by the Constitution from its inception. Since OBC reservation is comparatively a new issue, few studies have concentrated solely on OBCs. Partly because reservation policy had primarily focused on SC/ST candidates till 1990, separate estimates for these categories were available from government sources. All other castes were put in the "others" category. But inclusion of OBCs for affirmative action since 1999 has resulted in the availability of some data separately for this category as well. Hence, the category of others now includes all upper castes as well as some lower castes close to SCs, and also other lower castes which are not recognised as SCs, STs or OBCs. *Gill (2006)* reported that the same situation prevails in respect of tribals in India and their relative situation (*vis-a-vis* general population) has not changed much over the years. *Sujatha (1999)* in her study brought out that the level of educational development among tribes differs vastly across the provinces. The national average literacy rate among them is 29 per cent. Among the eight provinces, the highest literacy rate among the tribes is 36 per cent, in Gujarat, against 17 per cent in Andhra Pradesh, which is the lowest in the country. Compared to all the provinces, the tribals in Andhra Pradesh stand at the lowest level.

Basant and Sen (2010) reported the educational achievements of upper caste Hindus and other upper castes with that of dalits, adivasis and Muslims during 1983 and 2000. Although the primary school enrolment at all income levels are higher for Hindus and other upper castes over this period, the study shows that there is a narrowing trend in the gap between Hindus and other marginalised groups at the higher income levels. It implies that affirmative action in employment may have contributed to higher primary school enrolment over the years (i.e., more people participating in school education in anticipation of getting jobs through reservation). At the same time, improvement in economic condition has increased the effectiveness of the programme. Households with better economic conditions benefited more from the job reservation as it resulted in higher school enrolment.

RIGHT TO EDUCATION AND ACT THEREOF

In order to achieve universalisation of education in India, the parliament passed Constitution (Eighty-sixth Amendment) Act, 2002 to incorporate right to education as fundamental rights affecting Articles 21A, 45 and 51A of the constitution. Further, the Right of Children to Free and Compulsory Education Act (RTE), 2009 (35 of 2009) received the assent of the President on the 26 August 2009 and was published in the Gazette of India Extraordinary No. 39 on 27 August 2009. On 16 February 2010, Central Government in exercise of the powers conferred by section 1(3) of the Act, stipulated 1 April 2010 as the date on which the provisions of the said Act shall come into force *(Gazette Notification S.O. 428(E))*. In addition, Central Government in exercise of the powers conferred by section 38 of the Act, notified Right of Children to Free and Compulsory Education Rules, 2010 (vide *G.S.R. 301(E), dated 8 April 2010)*.

The salient points of the Act and the rules made thereunder are (http://education.nic.in/):

(a) The Act makes it mandatory for every child between the ages of 6-14 to be provided free education by the State. This means that such child does not have to pay a single penny as regards books, uniforms, etc.

(b) Any time of the academic year, a child can go to a school and demand that this right be respected.

(c) Section 12(1)(c) of the Act provides that private education institutions and specified category schools shall admit (starting 2011) at least 25% of the strength of class I, children belonging to weaker section and children belonging to disadvantaged group from the neighbourhood and provide them free and compulsory education till completion of elementary education.

(d) Strict criteria for the qualification of teachers. There is a requirement of a teacher-student ratio of 1:30 at each of these schools that ought to be met within a given time frame.

(e) The schools need to have certain minimum facilities like adequate teachers, playground and infrastructure. The government will evolve some mechanism to help marginalised schools comply with the provisions of the Act.

(f) There is a new concept of 'neighbourhood schools' that has been devised. This is similar to the model in the United States. This would imply that the state government and local authorities will establish primary schools within walking distance of one km of the neighbourhood. In case of children for Classes VI to VIII, the school should be within a walking distance of three km of the neighbourhood.

(g) Unaided and private schools shall ensure that children from weaker sections and disadvantaged groups shall not be segregated from the other children in the classrooms nor shall their classes be held at places and timings different from the classes held for the other children. Right of Children to Free and Compulsory Education Rules, 2010.

The important government orders/gazette notifications with regards to implementation of the Act are appended in Table 2.

Problem Areas of RTE Act

Jha and Parvati (2010) bring out following problem areas concerning the Act:

(a) Though the act expresses interest in taking necessary steps in providing free pre-school education for children above three years of age, leaving out this critical segment of the child population from the

Table 2
Important Government Orders Pertaining to RTE Act

Notification/G.O. No.	*Details*
(1)	*(2)*
(a) S.O. 749(E) dated 31 March 2010	National Council of Educational Research and Training (NCERT) was authorised to lay down the curriculum and evaluation, procedure for elementary education, and to develop a framework of national curriculum under clause (a) of sub-section (6) of Section 7 of the Act
(b) S.O. 750(E) dated 31 March 2010	National Council for Teacher Education (NCTE) was authorized to lay down the minimum qualifications for a person to be eligible for appointment as a teacher.
(c) F.No. 1-13/2009-EE-4 dated 31 May 2010	National Curriculum Framework 2005 was notified to be the framework for education under the Act till such time as the Central Government decides to develop a new framework.
(d) F.No. 1-4/2010 -EE4 dated 22 Jun. 2010	In consideration of the representations received from State Governments (regarding inability to complete recruitment process to achieve Pupil-Teacher Ratio (PTR) specified in the Schedule to the Act), the following directions were issued: (i) Rationalise the deployment of existing teachers to address the problems of urban-rural and other spatial imbalances in teacher placements; and (ii) Initiate the process of recruitment of new teachers to fill vacant posts as per the PTR stipulated in the Schedule.
(e) S.O 1631(E) dated 8 July 2010	National Advisory Council was constituted (with HRD Minister as chairperson, five Ex-officio Members and nine nominated members) to advice the Central Government on implementation of the provisions of the RTE Act in an effective manner.

(Contd.)

TABLE (*Contd.*)

(1)	(2)
(f) F.No. 61-03/20/ 2010/NCTE (N and S) dated 23 Aug. 2010	NCTE (in pursuance of gazette notification No. S.O. 750 (E) dated 31 Mar. 2010) laid down the minimum qualifications for a person to be eligible for appointment as a teacher in Classes I to VIII in a school referred to Section 2(n) of the RTE Act.
(g) F.No. 1-15/2010-EE-4 dated 23 Nov. 2010	Schools were directed to follow a system of random selection out of the applications received from children belonging to disadvantaged groups and weaker sections for filling the pre-determined number of seats in that class, which should be not less than 25% of the strength of the class. For admission to the remaining 75% of the seats, the schools were directed to formulate a policy under which admissions are to take place. This policy should include criteria for categorization of applicants in terms of the objectives of the school on a rational, reasonable and just basis. Profiling of students, testing and interviews for any child/parent falling within or outside the categories was prohibited. Selection would be on a random basis.
(h) F.No. 1-1S/2010-EE-4 dated 23 Nov. 2010	Directions were issued to state governments for ensuring that the rights of Minority Institutions, guaranteed under Articles 29 and 30 of the Constitution, are protected while implementing the provisions of the RTE Act.
(j) No. 76-4/2010/ NCTE/ Acad. dated 11 Feb. 2011	Guidelines for conducting Teacher Eligibility Test (TET) under RTE Act, 2009 notified.
(k) S.O. 623(E) dated 23 Mar. 2011	Relaxation was granted to the State of Orissa in respect of the minimum teacher qualification norms notified by the National Council for Teacher Education (NCTE) for a period of one year.

definition is worrisome. Not only does the act fail to cover all children, it does not provide definite timelines for many provisions.

(b) The Act fails to tackle the problem of quality of teachers and infrastructure required for undertaking the task involved.

(c) Quality monitoring is attainable only in a culture of accountability. The act does not effectively address issues with regard to quality and disciplinary proceedings against the erring schools. In addition, the unaided schools have been left out of the purview of accountability with regard to the provisions contained in Section 21.1 of the act.

(d) There is no clarity on who will take the lead in financing the Act. Ideally, the central government ought to be shouldering this duty in the light of the poor fiscal situation in most states. Acknowledging this reality, the Act notes that the states may seek a predetermined percentage of expenditure as grants-in-aid from the central government, based on the recommendations of the finance commission on assessment of additional resource requirements for any state.

USE OF ICT IN EDUCATION

Cecchini and Scott (2003) underline that the use of ICT applications can enhance poor people's opportunities by improving their access to markets, health, and education. Furthermore, ICT can empower the poor by expanding the use of government services, and reduce risks by widening access to microfinance. Realizing the poverty-reducing potential of ICT is not guaranteed. It requires attentive public policy formulation and careful project design. Insufficient information and communication infrastructure, high access costs, and illiteracy have bestowed the benefits of ICT on the better-off, urban segments of the population to the detriment of the poor and rural areas.

The specific impact of technology on learning has been reported by *Sharples, Taylor and Vavoula (2005)* in their study.

They brought out that learning is mediated by knowledge and technology as instruments for productive enquiry, in a mutually supportive and dynamically changing relationship. The mediation can be analysed from a technological perspective of human-computer interaction, physical context and digital communication, and from a human perspective of social conventions, community, conversation and division of labour. These two perspectives interact to promote a co-evolution of learning and technology. It describes a cybernetic process of learning through continual exploration of the world and negotiation of meaning, mediated by technology. This can be seen as a challenge to formal schooling, to the autonomy of the classroom and to the curriculum as the means to impart the knowledge and skills needed for adulthood. But it can also be an opportunity to bridge the gulf between formal and experiential learning, opening new possibilities for personal fulfilment and lifelong learning.

The effectiveness of ICT for reaching out to rural masses and delivery of relevant content including education has been recognized by India long back. In fact, India was amongst the first few countries to explore the use of Satcom for carrying education and development-oriented information and services to the rural masses. The applications started with satellite TV broadcasting to schools and rural communities in the mid-seventies. Under the Edusat utilization programme two types of satellite-based VSAT networks i.e., interactive networks consisting of Satellite Interactive Terminals (SITs) and receive-only networks using Receive-Only-Terminals—are being set-up in various states across the country for promoting universal education. Generally, interactive networks are set-up for imparting teacher's training and curriculum-based teaching to students of the arts and science colleges, polytechnics, and management and professional institutes. Similarly, the receive-only networks are being used for imparting curriculum-based education to primary and secondary schools students. To provide these space-based services directly to the rural areas, ISRO has initiated a programme to set-up Village Resource Centres (VRCs) in association with NGOs and trusts and state and central agencies concerned. VRCs are envisaged as single window delivery mechanism for a variety of space-based products and services, such as tele-education; tele-medicine; information on natural resources for planning and development at local level; interactive advisories on agriculture, fisheries, land and water resources management, livestock management, etc.; interactive vocational training towards alternative livelihood; e-governance; weather information, etc. VRCs also address a variety of social aspects locally, and can act as help lines *(Bhaskaranarayana, Bhatia, Bandyopadhyay and Jain, 2007).*

In addition, the Common Services Centers (CSC) is a strategic cornerstone of the National e-Governance Plan (NeGP), as part of its commitment in the National Common Minimum Programme to introduce e-governance on a massive scale. The CSCs would provide high quality and cost-effective video, voice and data content and services, in the areas of e-governance, education, health, tele-medicine, entertainment as well as other private services. A highlight of the CSCs is that it will offer web-enabled e-governance services in rural areas, including application forms, certificates, and utility payments such as electricity, telephone and water bills. The Scheme creates a conducive environment for the private sector and NGOs to play an active role in implementation of the CSC Scheme, thereby becoming a partner of the government in the development of rural India. The PPP model of the CSC scheme envisages a 3-tier structure consisting of the CSC operator (called Village Level Entrepreneur or VLE), the Service Centre Agency (SCA), that will be responsible for a division of 500-1000 CSCs and a State Designated Agency (SDA) identified by the State Government responsible for managing the implementation over the entire State. The CSC Scheme has been approved by Government in September 2006 with an outlay of Rs. 5742 Crores over a period of 4 years. It is expected that 100% CSCs would be rolled by March 2011 *(http://mit.gov.in/).*

The formal inclusion of ICT in education commenced in centrally sponsored Scheme "Information and Communication Technology in School" which was launched in December 2004. The Scheme was meant to be a major catalyst to bridge the digital divide amongst students of various socio-economic and other geographical barriers. The financial assistance (under the scheme), is given to States and other institutions on the basis of the approvals accorded by Project Monitoring and Evaluation Group (PM and EG) headed by Secretary of the Department of School Education and Literacy. The broad objectives of the scheme are *(http://www.indg.in/)*:

(a) To ensure the availability of quality content on-line and through access devices.
(b) Enrichment of existing curriculum and pedagogy by employing ICT tools for teaching and learning.
(c) To enable students to acquire skills needed for the Digital world for higher studies and gainful employment.
(d) To provide an effective learning environment for children with special needs through ICT tools.
(e) Promote critical thinking and analytical skills by developing self-learning. This shall transform the classroom environment from teacher-centric to student-centric learning.
(f) To promote the use of ICT tools in distance education including the employment of audio-visual medium and satellite-based devices.

Datta and Mitra (2010) studied the utilization of technology in education. They reported that national education, especially at the primary and secondary levels, has also failed to adapt the benefits of diverse technologies that are available today for the cause of education.

DISCUSSION AND FINDINGS

Analysis of sources of secondary data from OECD, World Bank, UN and various government portals underline following facts who have bearing on use of ICT in successful implementation of RTE:

(a) The government of India charges Access Deficit charge from the various telecom operators to ensure roll out of telecom services in rural and remote areas which are not profitable. This provides funding for the state owned telecom companies to provide services in rural areas which are not profitable.

(b) The call charges (both local and STD) are one of the lowest in the world which makes mobile calls affordable for the rural populace.

(c) The telecommunication sector in India has been witnessing highest growth rates in the world and the trend continues. The growth in the subscriber base is being caused particularly by the unprecedented growth in mobile telephony. The penetration of mobile phones has been aided by the sharp decline in the cost of mobile instrument with many handset available in the market with longer battery life costing below Rs. 1000. In fact many mobile handsets have facility for solar charging which augers well for remote areas where electricity supply is erratic.

(d) The Government of India has launched many toll free numbers for providing on demand information to the masses.

DIA. 2

Growth of Subscriber-base (in million) from 2000 to 2010

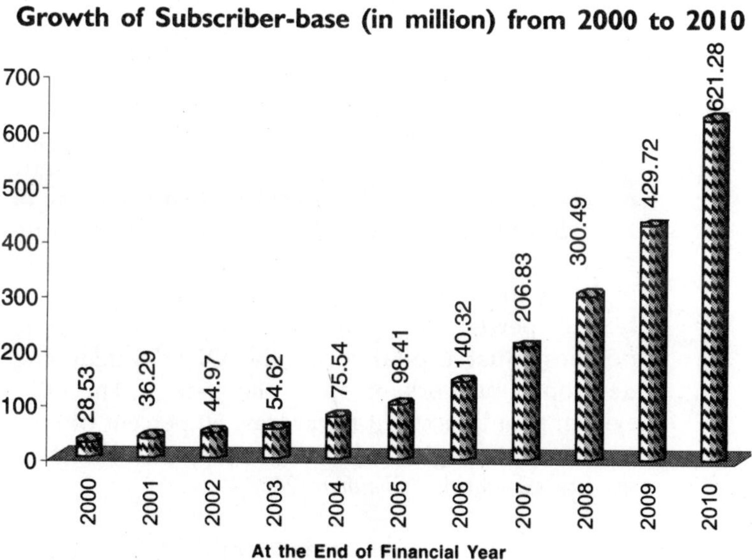

Source: Annual Report, 2009-10, TRAI.

(e) The National e-Government Plan encompasses installation of Citizen Service Centres connecting government to the citizens spread across the length and breadth of the country.

(f) The literacy rate has been increasing over a period of time with corresponding reduction in the poverty levels. The year on year comparison of literacy rates since independence is depicted in Diagram 3.

Dia. 3

Comparison of Literacy Rates in India since Independence

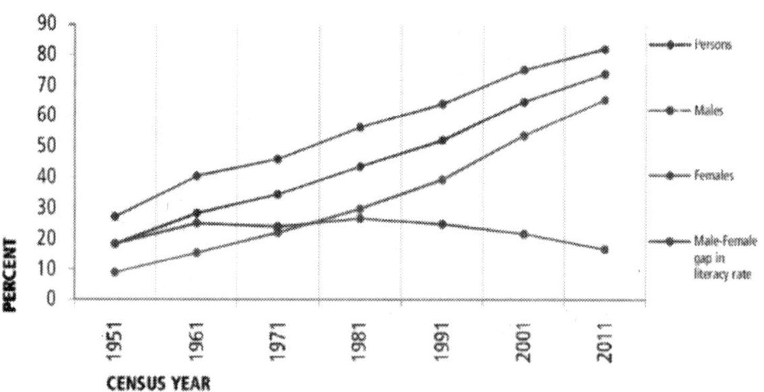

Source : http://www.censusindia.gov.in/

(g) For a country to achieve rapid socio-economic advancement, a 20 to 25 percent participation rate of the relevant age group in higher education is a pre-requisite. Therefore, India must expand its system of higher education further so as to accommodate at least 20 percent of eligible 18 to 24-year-olds. Future policies must capitalize on the ODL system and develop a network of open universities. The ODL system should account for at least 50 percent of total enrolment in higher education and provide a good quality education *(Chauhan, 2008).*

However, a lot remains to be accomplished in order to achieve the mission of 100% literacy envisaged under RTE Act.

We need to increase enrolment of children in the schools, motivate them to complete the schooling, creating an enabling environment for the children from the socially/economically weaker sections to study and at the same time contribute in securing bread and butter for their home. We need to conceive a system whereby education is available on demand and at the convenience of the leaner and not as per the fixed timings of the schooling. This scheme of "education on demand" and "learn while you earn" would enable these children to reap in the benefit accruable through RTE Act and the ICT. Towards this, we could take cue from the bi-modal transmission framework proposed by *Basu and Modak (2010).* Diagram 4 depicts their conceptual framework to establish a

DIA. 4

Bi-modal Transmission Model

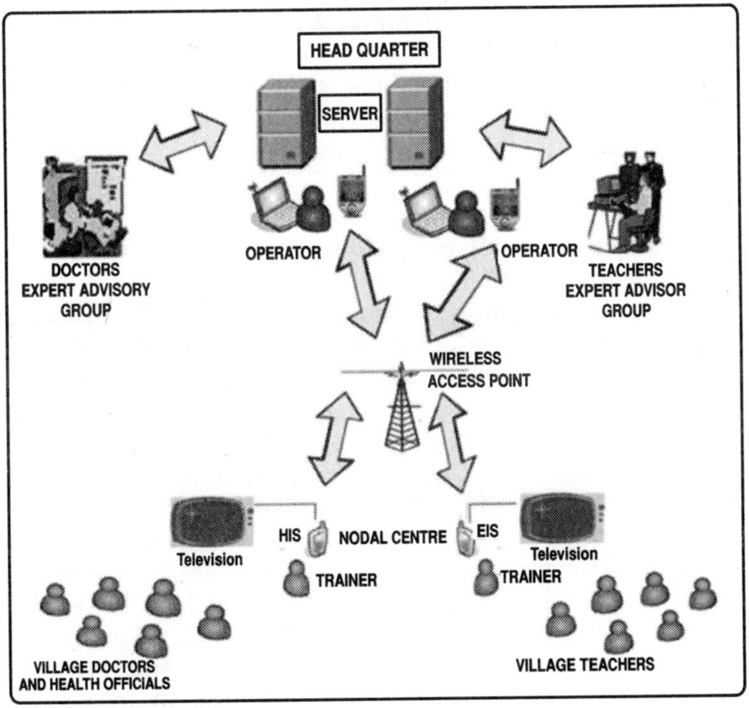

Source : Basu and Modak, 2010.

communication channel between the remote rural areas with inadequate education and health care facility and an expert advisory group consisting of a panel of teachers and doctors respectively, interlinked by a group of operators in order to provide service to rural unprivileged through the servers located in the headquarter. The new mobile technology establishes a new-fangled mobile connectivity layer that allows transportation of all relevant data and information from the service information layer represented by the instructors or group of experts towards the application layer as rural remote schools and health care centers. The communication device being mobile phones, successful information exchange demands a mobile-based information processing system as an Education Information System (EIS) and a Healthcare Information System (HIS) to deliver and receive relevant information back and forth.

RECOMMENDATIONS

In the backdrop of the discussions in preceding paragraphs, we recommend the following measures for ensuring achievement of universal elementary education by effective use of ICT:

(a) Integration of "Formal Education" and "Education on Demand"

The importance Open and Distance Learning environments for developing countries have been underlined by *Dele and Osiki (2008)* in their study. We need to integrate the formal and informal education systems so that a student can switch between both the systems seamlessly at any time, if necessitated due to his/her social/economic compulsions. For this both the systems would need to share the EIS which would also be economically prudent. The bi-modal transmission model may be used for the purpose (refer Para 21 above). The teachers appointed under the RTE Act could form the pool of resources at remote locations for providing education on demand using ICT tools. The framework suggested by *Venkatagiri (2007)* for self-paced learning in networked environments could be used in conjunction with bi-modal telecommunication system for flexibility and content richness in education-on-demand system.

(b) Open Schooling for Higher Education

Bloom and Rosovsky (2001) underlined that higher education is one of the most powerful mechanisms societies have for upward mobility: it has enormous potential to promote prosperity among people with talent and motivation, irrespective of their social origins. Therefore, once a student completes his elementary education, he should be encouraged to study further. This could be achieved by providing him with the opportunity through open/distance learning environments. The institute similar to National Institute of Open Schooling should be opened in each state/UT. The education could be imparted through EIS utilizing VSC/CSC. For higher education, IGNOU already has infrastructure (in the form of Gyandarshan TV channel) and is also actively involved in imparting distance education. In addition, some of the states have opened up state open universities. We need to strengthen these institutions of open/distance learning and improve the quality of education imparted through them.

(c) Adult Literacy Campaign

The need for education of the parents needs no emphasis. Imparting lessons on basic education and financial management to the people of weaker sections (through adult literacy centres in the form of evening classes/EIS) would go a long way in their upliftment. *Cohen and Sebstad (2003)* brought out that financial education can play an important role in contributing to poverty reduction in developing countries by building people's knowledge and skills to optimize the use of resources and take advantage of opportunities. Financial literacy can enhance the ability of people in not so well-off households to interface more effectively with the financial system-not only microfinance institutions, but other formal and informal institutions as well. The attendant awareness from the adult literacy would definitely aid GER.

(d) Involvement of Gram Panchayats and NGOs

Comings and Smith (1995) advocated involvement of

NGOs in various literacy programmes due to their direct connection to the communities they serve. In fact, Gram Panchayats and NGOs can be used for influencing people in enhancing GER and in reducing drop-out rates. In addition, we could enlist support of industry. Recently Ministry of Corporate Affairs, GoI has made it mandatory or the companies to report to their shareholders about the expenditure incurred by them on Corporate Social Responsibility (CSR). We could encourage the corporate houses to adopt divisions/villages for overall upliftment including achievement of 100% literacy. The expenditure incurred towards the welfare could be reported towards CSR. Similarly, leading and reputed private schools could be encouraged to patronize the EIS of a district/village.

(e) PPP in Education

The development of infrastructure of EIS could be undertaken as Public-private partnership project. The investment in this sector could be promoted by giving exemptions on such investments or by allowing tax rebates. In this context, *Prakash (2008)* underlined that with the expected diversification of higher education in the coming years, planners would be more concerned about quality assurance and appropriate institutional planning models for ensuring enough autonomy and an effective accountability framework.

(f) Dealing with Shortage of Teachers in Rural/Remote Areas

The shortage of qualified teachers is a major constraint in remote areas. The problem could be solved by two pronged approach. Firstly, services of retired teachers can be taken to ride over the immediate crisis. Secondly, rural stint may be made mandatory for teachers. The teachers could be encouraged to take up postings in rural/remote areas by improving their working conditions of teachers and giving them suitable compensation.

(g) Emphasize Empiricism

Boswell, Rozelle, Zhang, and Liu (2011) from their study in China emphasize that quantitative, experimental design is the best means to reliably measure success and effectively channel ideas and investments that target the world's most pressing problems. It should be made mandatory for the District Education Officer to carry out survey of population in his/her jurisdiction about the effectiveness of various educational programmes and report the results to state education department and National Literacy Mission. The help of Gram Panchayats should be enlisted for the smooth conduct of survey. These surveys could form the basis for fine-tuning of the education delivery system.

(h) Reduce the Digital Divide

The reduction of digital divide and diffusion of ICT technology to the downtrodden and remote masses is a precursor to universalisation of the education. *Mistry (2005),* underlined the both indirect as well as direct role of the government in bridging the digital divide.

The government needs to take proactive measures and subsidize technology products to bring them within the reach of poor. A right step in this direction is the development of Sakshat (Sanskrit: "Embodiment") tablet PC for bridging the digital divide between the rich and the poor. The Rs. 1,500 ($ 30) Tablet PC is currently not available for sale in the market as government has decided to launch it for students in 2011. The device has been developed as part of the National Mission on Education through Information and Communication Technology that aims to link 25,000 colleges and 504 universities on the subcontinent in an e-learning program via an existing Sakshat portal *(http://sakshattablet.org/).*

CONCLUSION

We conclude by underlining the fact that India is a large developing country. It has many issues to address along its journey to all inclusive growth. We need ensure the benefit of RTE reaches the poorest of the poor living in remote areas by breaking the boundaries of cast, religion and access. We need to address the issue of poverty and stark digital divide before the benefits of ICT could be reaped for dissemination of knowledge. We should direct our efforts towards bringing education and schools at the doorstep of the needy children

Dia. 5

Role of Government in Bridging the Digital Divide

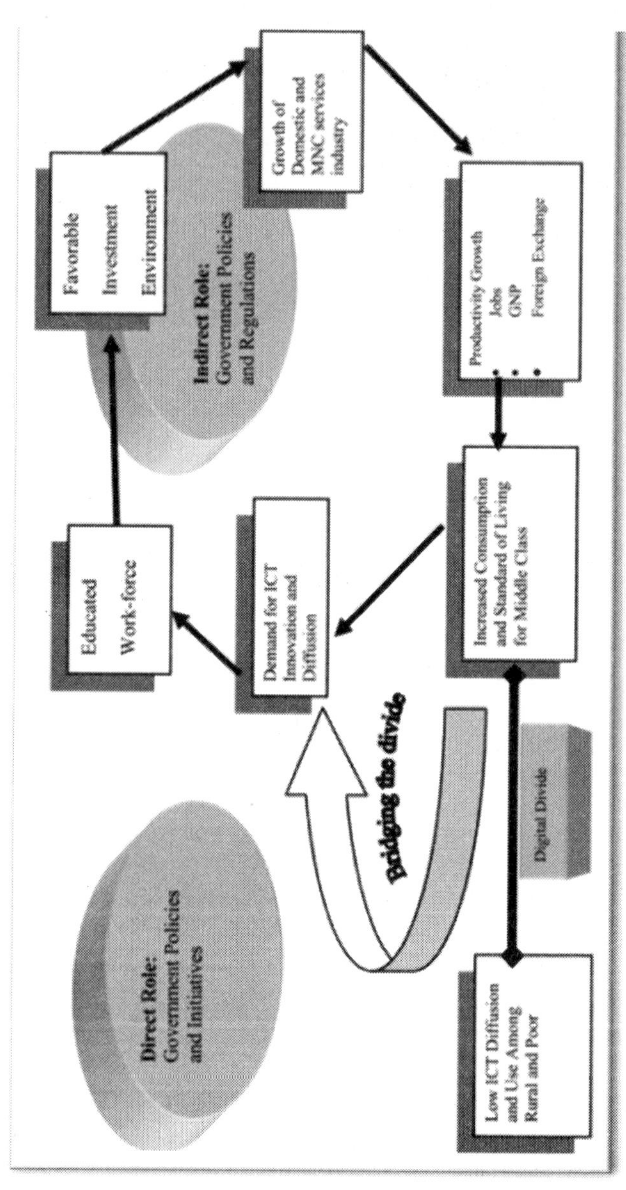

Source : Mistry, 2005.

rather pushing them to schools. Ensuring of 100% literacy of over one billion population is though difficult but not impossible to achieve. All we need is sincerity, commitment and right policy measures.

References

Altbach, P.G. (2009). One-third of the Globe: The Future of Higher Education in China and India. Springer, 39(1), 11-31. doi: 10.1007/s11125-009-9106-1.

Balasubramanyam, V.N., and Balasubramanyam, A. (2010). Human Capital and Development : A Tale of Two Cities; Software Sector in Bangalore and Hyderabad. International Conference on Science, Technology and Economy: Human Capital and Development, Mumbai, India, 11-12 Nov. 2010. Retrieved from www.hss.iitb.ac.in/FGKS_IITB_2010/papers/Balasubramanyam.pdf.

Bhaskaranarayana, A., Bhatia, B.S., Bandyopadhyay, K., and Jain, P.K. (2007). Applications of Space Communication. *Current Science*, 93(12).

Bloom, D.E., and Rosovsky, H. (2001). Higher Education and International Development. *Current Science*, 81(3), 252-256.

Boswell, M., Rozelle, S., Zhang, L., Liu, C., Luo, R., and Shi, Y. (2011). Conducting Influential Impact Evaluations in China: The experience of the Rural Education Action Project. International Initiative for Impact Evaluation, New Delhi. Retrieved from www.3ieimpact.org.

Cecchini, S., and Scott, C. (2003). Can Information and Communications Technology Applications Contribute to Poverty Reduction? Lessons from Rural India. *Information Technology for Development*, 10(2), 73-84. IOS Press. doi: 10.1002/itdj.1590100203.

Chauhan, C.P.S. (2008). Higher Education: Current Status and Future Possibilities in Afghanistan, Bangladesh, Bhutan, India, Maldives, Nepal, Pakistan, and Sri Lanka. *Analytical Reports in International Education*, 2(1), 29-48. doi: 10.3890/arie.2.1.29.

Cohen, M., and Sebstad, J. (2003). Financial Education for the Poor, Working Paper #1. Washington, US. Retrieved from www.global financialed.org/documents/WP1_FinEd4Poor.pdf

Comings, J.P., and Smith, C. (1995). Adult Literacy Programs: Design, Implementation and Evaluation. Center for Human Capacity Development, U.S. Agency for International Development. Retrieved from http://pdf.usaid.gov/pdf_docs/PNABX789.pdf.

Datta, D., and Mitra, S. (2010). M-Learning: Mobile-Enabled Educational Technology. Retrieved from http://www.cks.in/html/cks_pdfs/M-LearningMobile-enabled Educational Technology.pdf.

Dele, B., and Osiki, J.O. (2008). The Impact of Technology on Accessibility and Pedagogy: The Right to Education in Sub-Saharan Africa. *Asian Journal of Distance Education*, 6(1), 53-62. Retrieved from http://www.asianjde.org.

Gazette notification S.O. 428(E). Retrieved from http://education.nic.in/.

Gill, M.S. (2006). Situation of Tribal Population in India. *Demography*, III (540), 91-104.

Govt. Order: F.No.1-13/2009-EE-4, dated 31 May 2010. Retrieved from http://education.nic.in/.

Govt. Order: F.No.1-15/2010-EE-4, dated 23 Nov. 2010. Retrieved from http://education.nic.in/.

Govt. Order: F.No.1-1S/2010-EE-4, dated 23 Nov. 2010. Retrieved from http://education.nic.in/.

Govt. Order: F.No.1-4/2010-EE4, dated 22 Jun 2010. Retrieved from http://education.nic.in/.

Govt. Order:F.No.61-03/20/2010/NCTE(N and S), dated 23 Aug 2010. Retrieved from http://education.nic.in/.

Govt. Order: No.76-4/2010/NCTE/Acad, dated 11 Feb. 2011. Retrieved from http://education.nic.in/.

Govt. Order: S.O 1631(E), dated 8 July 2010. Retrieved from http://education.nic.in/.

Govt. Order: S.O. 623(E), dated 23 Mar. 2011. Retrieved from http://education.nic.in/.

Govt. Order: S.O. 749(E), dated 31 Mar. 2010. Retrieved from http://education.nic.in/.

Govt. Order: S.O. 750(E), dated 31 Mar. 2010. Retrieved from http://education.nic.in/.

Govt. Order: S.R. 301(E), dated 8 April 2010. Retrieved from http://education.nic.in/.

Jha, P. and Parvati, P. (2010). Right to Education Act, 2009: Critical Gaps and Challenges. *Economic and Political Review*, Vol. XLV, No. 13. Retrieved from http://images2.asercentre.org/Contents/RTE_critical.pdf

Khan, A.W. (2001). Learning for a Better Future: Overcoming Disadvantages. 20th ICDE World Conference on Open Learning and Distance Education (pp. 1-5). Düsseldorf, Germany.

Mahajan, N. (2007). The Cream of India's Colleges Turns Sour. *Far Eastern Economic Review*, 170(1), pp. 62-65.

Mistry, J.J. (2005). The Role of E-Governance: A Case Study of India. IADIS International Conference e-Commerce, 2005, pp. 158-66.

Prakash, V. (2008). Directions in Educational Planning: Changing Landscape of Educational Planning in India: Planning and Administration. NUEPA, New Delhi, India.

Right of Children to Free and Compulsory Education Act (RTE), 2009 (35 of 2009). Retrieved from http://education.nic.in/.

Sharples, M., Taylor, J., and Vavoula, G. (2005). Towards a Theory of Mobile Learning Mind. Retrieved from http://www.mlearn.org.za/CD/papers/Sharples-Theory of Mobile.pdf.

Sujatha, K. (1999). Education of India Scheduled Tribes: A Study of Community Schools in the district of Vishakhapatnam, Andhra Pradesh. UNESCO. Retrieved from http://www.unesco.org/iiep.

Telecom Regulatory Authority of India, Annual Report 9-10. Retrieved from http://www.trai.gov.in/.

The Department of Information Technology portal is a single point of availability of all resources pertaining to Information Technology. (http://mit.gov.in/)

The India Development Gateway (In DG) portal is dedicated to empowerment of rural India. In DG initiative is supported by Dept. of Info Tech, MCIT, GoI and executed by Centre for Development of Advanced Computing, Hyderabad. (http://www.indg.in

The Indian Census portal is the most credible source of information on population characterstics, Economic Activity, Literacy and Education, Housing and Household Amenities, Urbanisation, Fertility and Mortality (http://www.censusindia.gov.in/)

The portal of Ministry of HRD contains information on various educational programmes and policies of central government (http://education.nic.in/)

CHAPTER

17

Impact Model of Higher Education for Women's Empowerment

S.K. BHARDWAJ AND PRADEEP KUMAR SINGH

ABSTRACT

Empowerment as delegation of power to someone has been a mechanism to increase personal and work life quality of women in recent decades. Higher education and occupation is effective instrument to empowerment of women but culture role can't be denied in this relation. Social norms can directly or indirectly limited women empowerment. In this article the role of higher education and occupation in psychological empowerment of women in India has been quested. Current research is a descriptive-practical research. Education and occupation were independent variable and empowerment was dependent variable. Random sampling was used and 600 questioners were completed by women in India. To determine validity of scale we took advantages of construct validity and factor analysis.

The reliability index of Cronbach's alpha was 0.8945 and spearman correlation and structural equations model was used for statistical analysis. Results of research indicate that higher education and organizational occupation determine the level of to empowerment for women in India.

INTRODUCTION

The concept of power has a long history in social sciences and its derivatives like empowerment is one of the controversial topics among social science and management researchers. Since early years of the 20th century, feminism has built a body of theory and in recent decades women empowerment has been suggested as a mechanism to improve the quality of women's work as well as their personal lives. The empowerment of women is an essential precondition for the elimination of world poverty and the upholding of human rights. This concept is accompanied with, freedom, self-determination and power, which are necessary for the women all over the world. Empowerment gives rights to women which enables them to be independent of men. Since education and employment are key factors in empowerment of women in western societies, theorists believe that there may be the same connection between these factors in non-western societies. There is much theoretical and practical studies that stress educational and employment opportunities as critical means for women to attain control over their lives (United Nations, 1994). Although education and employment can empower women, the role of culture can't be denied. Namely, powerful patriarchal norms can hold back women's empowerment plans. Some studies show that, in some cultures, better access to education and the jobs for women in the preceding decades have not significantly changed power relationships within families. In these cases, educated and employed women are as deprived as uneducated and unemployed women. Social norms determine the level of women's empowerment. Social norms can restrict women's empowerment directly or indirectly. Social norms may limit women's willingness to empowerment directly or they may influence the access of women to education and income. Sometimes, these norms permit women to earn money without retaining control over it or gaining any position in the family or society, in these situations men are the ultimate beneficiaries of women empowerment. In some cases even if women can control their earnings within the family, the outcome may not be completely positive for them, or their family then the women fell happy because of achieving a better financial status, and being able to keep it and save it, but earning money doesn't mean more money for the whole family, because their husbands or fathers might deprive the women from their money, the money of the husband or father, once they became aware of the women's financial position. It might also lead to marital problems, as earning money would mean they threatened the power balance in the family. Education and revenue don't cause to empowerment if necessary base for presence of women are not facilitated by social institutions. Based on some researches, educated and job-holder women even have worse condition than none educated and housekeeper women in some countries (Mason, 2002); namely in this ground cultural expectation and prescription are strong determinant. There is probability that with existent institutions Iranian educated and job-holder women could not gain necessary freedom and empowerment (Shafiq, 1991).

FORMAL EDUCATION AND EMPLOYMENT IN INDIAN CULTURE

In a preliminary society (protohistory), the most economical promotion had happened by women. In matriarchy age, women had had authority of rule, judge, and family and society administration. For long, when men were hunting, women were farming around their tent, and were creating many domestic arts; each of them now, is base of many important industries. Early women innovated first cord and after that textile from cotton; and in highly probability, cause progression of loom, pottery, carpentry and mason arts. She often commerce and aroused domestic club and gently involved man, then taught him decorum and society art. But when agriculture and industry progressed and developed, the stronger gender extended his ascendancy upon it little by little.

Agriculture, which was thought ordinary in the eyes of hunters of the old age, completely attracted men, therefore man grabbed economical predominance which was the outcome, from woman; specially because plough, which needed more muscular force, supervision shifted from woman to man. Increasing the tangible assets helped men to make women more obedient because then the man asked her to be loyal so the born children were the real children of the man. Man's paternal right had been recognized in family, hence inheriting which up until that time was through woman, was authorized by man. Maternal right surrendered to paternal right, and in society, instead of matriarchy, patriarchy had been recognized as legal, political and economical unit. God, which until that time was embodied in women, changed to men, wearing beard which indeed were symbols of fathers and tribe chiefs. Around these gods "Harems" were built like what men had dreamt in their solitude (Durant, 20-60-2001). Durant argued that Iranian women had lofty status in Zoroaster time like it was common in the past. They came among people with complete liberty and could become landlords and estate owners. After Darius (Medes king), women's dignity, especially among plutocracy, decreased (Durant, 432-434, 2001); poor women retained their liberty since they have to came among people for work. Iranian culture was mixed with Islamic culture after Moslems overthrew Sassanid Dynasty. According to Islamic men and women are equal concerning juridical laws and financial independence. Woman is allowed to do any lawful jobs. She can possess her gain and spend it as she wishes (Durant, 231, 2001). Since the beginning of Islam in Iran until Safavie period, Iranian women always had right of possessing tangible and intangible assets. At this age, many buildings were constructed by women everywhere in Iran (Hejazi, 230-232, 1997). Besides housework, women were engaged in productive activities such as carpet weaving and sewing; although these activities were mainly done for meeting the needs of the family, they were also sort of jobs and money making activities (Hejazi, 1997, 243-244). During Safavid period, Iranian women were interested in speech and sermons; they enthusiastically pursued social issues, there isn't any community report which hasn't mentioned the presence of women. Based on available documents at this age, women were literate and interested in science; great men taught their wives and relatives at their home. These women not only contributed at speech and sermons but also held gatherings in their home. Some of them wrote some books about literature, jurisprudence, astronomy and Islamic laws; taught them and became famous (Hejazi, 1997: 175-180).

METHODOLOGY

Regarding the purpose the present research is a practical one and regarding the data collection method it is a descriptive one which is a branch of field study, therefore the connection between the variables is causative. The method of performing the research has been observing method that its greatest advantage is that you can generalize the results. 4.1 Research variables: formal education and organizational employment are the independent variables and empowerment was the dependent variable. 4.2 Society and statistic sample: the statistic sample includes women in Tehran. The samples were provided randomly. The number of participants based on Morgan Table is estimated 600 people. 27 out of 621 which is 4.3% were not having a diploma, 190 people that is 30.6% were holding diploma, 5 people that is 0.8% had post-diploma degree, 330 people that is 53.1% were holding B.Sc., 56 people that is .09% were holding M.S degree and 13 people that is 2.1% were Ph.D. holders. 454 people that is 73.1% didn't have any management experience and 167 people that is 26.9% had management experiences. 4.3 Data collection means and its clarity and stability: In this study we used a questionnaire survey to collect data. For this purpose, a scale was designed for empowerment variable by means of discovery component analysis with 13 version of SPSS software. Necessary accuracy was made when questions of questionnaire were designed so that they are simple and clear enough. The first Questionnaire was made up of 34 questions 4 of which were eliminated because of low factor loading. Likert scale with a five-point scoring format was used for items [Strongly disagree (1), Disagree (2), Neutral (3), Agree (4), Strongly agree (5)]. Education and occupation are independent variables and empowerment is the dependent variable. Random sampling was used in current and 600 questionnaires were completed by women in Tehran city. Based on Morgan table statistics sample size contained 621 persons as 4.3% (27 persons) under diploma, 30.6 (190 persons) diploma, 0.8% (5 persons) post diploma, 53.1% (330 person) B.S., 0.9% (56 persons) M.S. and 2.1% (13 persons) had doctorate. 73.1% (454 persons) have not had any management precedent but 26.9% (167 persons) have had it. From 800 questionnaires which were distributed, 630 questionnaires were restored, 9 questionnaires were discarded to defect and 621 questionnaires have been used on analysis. The rate of the questionnaires which were fully completed was 78% which is a satisfactory rate. The 30 questionnaires were distributed for determination of reliability. Coefficient of Chronbakh's Alpha of the women empowerment scale is 0.8945 which is a proof of instrument reliability. Also content and factor validity were utilized to examine the validity of the questions. We utilized experts' opinions to evaluate the questionnaires' content validity. At this step, several interviews were performed and necessary reformations were made; hence we confined the questionnaire evaluates same trait which we wanted to evaluate Test of the questionnaire factor validity were made with confirmatory factor analysis and utilization of 8.53 LISREL software package. The LAZEL output of the model to measure empowerment is a good one because the K2 value, RMSEA value and the proportion of K2 to its free degree was little and also the values of GFI and AGFI were above 90%. Ale T values are meaningful. The results, on the whole expresses that this questionnaire is creditable and clear to a high extent. Findings: Evaluation of correlation between variables was tested by Spearman rating correlation test using SPSS software. Causal relationship between independent and dependent variable of research was tested by structural equation model using LISREL 8.53 software. In this research we utilized Spearman test because the variables are qualitative. It is perceived that relationship between income, education and empowerment of women in Tehran is positive and meaningful; it means whatever women's income and education increase, they feel more empowered. Structural equation model is used for evaluation of casual relation which is mentioned in the hypothesizes; this is the final step of confirmatory factor analysis, which already is performed on the evaluating research scale, and also by means of fit indexes of the model shows validity of the conceptual model which is purposed. As it is seen, firstly, hypotheses of the research are confirmed because t-values are meaningful which means formal education and income have significant effect on women's empowerment. Second, validity and appropriate fitness of the model is confirmed because its χ^2 value, RMSEA and χ^2 ratio into degree of freedom, are low and its GFI and AGFA are more than 90%. As χ^2 value and χ^2 ratio into degree of freedom in the attachment shows model has appropriate fit, and RMSE (Note 1) is less than 0.05 and GFI (Note 2) and AGFA (Note 3) are more than 90% and also all the t-values are meaningful in 99% confidence level. These outcomes demonstrate the questionnaire of the research has high validity and reliability.

MENTAL HEALTH AND WOMEN IN INDIA

Depressed women in India often present with somatic rather than emotional symptoms [4, 5]. Consequently, when they attend busy primary care settings with somatic complaints, the diagnosis of depression is often overlooked [6] and families incur unnecessary costs for healthcare consultations, investigations and treatments, and psychosocial interventions are not initiated. Depressed women in India attribute their condition to a range of factors including poverty, traditional expectations of women's role, lack of affection and conflict with their husbands, widowhood and divorce, and difficulties providing dowries for their daughters [5, 7]. Post-natal depression in India affects 11–23% of women, and is linked to poverty, antenatal psychiatric morbidity, poor marital and family relationships, lack of support, marital violence and birth of a girl child [8-10]. Women subjected to violence have a higher risk of mental illness including depression, anxiety and psychosomatic symptoms [11]. Violence against women in India is a common social problem. A household survey of 500 women in rural Maharashtra reported 23% had been beaten in the last six months. The husbands of 12% of these women had explicitly threatened to pour kerosene on them and set those alight [12].

MENTAL HEALTH CARE IN INDIA

The National Mental Health Program, launched in 1982 and reviewed in 1995, sought to integrate mental health care with PHC [13]. It has had mixed success in achieving this goal and 90% of the rural population remain without access to mental health services [4, 13, 14]. Most care for people with mental illness is provided by the family. Many people remain untreated, and those families who do seek treatment will often turn to non-allopathic providers including practitioners of traditional medicine, religious healers, faith healers and astrologers.

MENTAL HEALTH PROMOTION

Mental health is more than the absence of mental illness and is defined by the World Health Organisation (WHO) as a state of well-being in which the individual realises his or her own abilities, can cope with the normal stresses of life, can work productively and fruitfully, and is able to make a contribution to his or her community [15]. A mental health promotion framework that represents a public health approach to mental illness prevention identifies the following as key social and economic determinants of community and individual mental health [16]:

1. *Social inclusion*: social relationships, involvement in group activities, civic engagement.
2. *Freedom from discrimination and violence*: valuing diversity, physical security, self-determination and control over one's life.
3. *Access to economic resources*: work, education, housing and money promoting mental health by addressing these determinants is a strategy for preventing mental illness, just as promoting exercise and a healthy diet prevents heart disease and diabetes.

References

Chandran, M., Tharyan, P., Muliyil, J., Abraham, S.: Post-partum Depression in a Cohort of Women from a Rural Area of Tamil Nadu, India: Incidence and Risk Factors. *British Journal of Psychiatry,* 2002, 181:499-504.

Jain, D., Sanon, S., Sadowski, L., Hunter, W.: Violence against Women in India: Evidence from Rural Maharashtra, India. Rural Remote Health, 2004, 4:304.

Khandelwal, S.K., Jhingan, H.P., Ramesh, S., Gupta, R.K., Srivastava, V.K.: India Mental Health Country Profile. *International Review of Psychiatry,* 2004, 16:126-41. Krug, E.G., Dahlberg, L.L., Mercy, J.A., Zwi, A.B., Lozano, R.: World Report on Violence and Health Geneva: WHO; 2002.

Patel, V., Kirkwood, B., Pednekar, *et. al.*: Gender Disadvantage and Reproductive Health Risk Factors for Common Mental Disorders in Women. *Archives of General Psychiatry,* 2006, 63:404-413.

Patel, V., Rodrigues, M., DeSouza, N.: Gender, Poverty, and Postnatal Depression: A Study of Mothers in Goa, India. *American Journal of Psychiatry,* 2002, 159:43.

Patel, V., Saraceno, B., Kleinman, A.: The Moral Case for International Mental Health. *American Journal of Psychiatry,* 2006, 163:1312-1315.

Pereira, B., Andre, G., Pednekar, S., Pai, R., Pelto, P., Patel, V.: The Explanatory Models of Depression in Low Income Countries: Listening to Women in India. *Journal of Affective Disorders in Press.*

Raguram, R., Weiss, M.G., Keval, H., Channabasavanna, S.M.: Cultural Dimensions of Clinical Depression in Bangalore, India. Anthropology and Medicine, 2001, 8:31-46.

Rodrigues, M., Patel, V., Jaswal, S., De Souza, N.: Listening to Mothers: Qualitative Studies on Motherhood and Depression from Goa, India. *Social Science and Medicine,* 2003, 57:1797-1806.

Simon, G.E., Vonkorff, M., Piccinelli, M., Fullerton, C., Ormel, J.: An International Study of the Relation between Somatic Symptoms and Depression, NEJM, 1999, 341:1329-1335.

Thara, R., Padmavati, R., Srinivasan, T.: Focus on Psychiatry in India. *British Journal of Psychiatry,* 2004, 184:366-373.

World Health Organization: The World Health Report 2001: Mental Health—New Understanding, New hope Geneva: WHO; 2001.

CHAPTER

18

RTE—An Universal Elementary Education System in India

G. PRASAD BABU, TALATA C. RATNAYAKE
AND ASHRAF IMAM

INTRODUCTION

Education is a process of bringing desirable changes in human behaviours. It is a lifelong process which helps an individual : (a) adopt himself to the real world through participation and reciprocal interactions (Transactions) with the environment, and (b) enhances the quality of social professional and national life. Education is a process of character-building, strengthening mind and expansion of intellect. The purpose of education according to Mahatma Gandhi is to establish a non-violent, non-exploitative social and economic order. Different children at the same biological age respond to the same environmental situation differently depending on the development of their perceptive and cognitive skills such as seeing, hearing, smiling, touching and mentally processing that information to diagnose the patterns. So we need for a better education policy for all around development of a child. The Indian government lays emphasis to primary education up to the age of fourteen years (referred to as Elementary Education in India) The Indian government has also banned child labour in order to ensure that the children do not enter unsafe working conditions. However, both free education and the ban on child labour are difficult to enforce due to economic disparity and social conditions. 80% of all recognized schools at the Elementary Stage are government run or supported, making it the largest provider of education in the Country. However, due to shortage of resources and lack of political will, this system suffers from massive gaps including high pupil to teacher ratios, shortage of infrastructure and poor levels of teacher training. There have been several efforts to enhance quality made by the government. The District Education Revitalization Programme (DERP) was launched in 1994 with an aim to universalize primary education in India by reforming and vitalizing the existing primary education system. 85% of the DERP was funded by the central government and the remaining 15 percent was funded by the states.

INITIATIVES TO IMPROVE PRIMARY EDUCATION IN INDIA

1. National educational policy was started in 1986 with special emphasis on the removal of disparities and to equalise educational opportunity, especially for Indian women, Scheduled Tribes (ST) and the Scheduled Caste (SC) communities to achieve these, the policy called for expanding scholarships, adult education, recruiting more teachers from the SCs, incentives for poor families to send their children to school regularly, development of new institutions and providing housing and services.
2. Operation Blackboard was started in 1987 aimed to improve the human and physical resources available in primary school.

3. Restructuring and reorganization of teacher education (1987) created a resource for continuous upgrading of teacher's knowledge and competence.
4. Minimum level of learning (1991) laid down levels of achievement at various stages and revised textbooks.
5. National programme for nutritional support to primary education was started in 1995 to provide cooked meal every day for children in Class I-V of all Government, Government-aided, and local body schools.
6. District Primary Education Programme (DPEP) was started in 1993 emphasizing planning and management, improved teaching and learning materials, and school effectiveness.
7. Sarva Shiksha Abhiyan (SSA) was launched in 2001 aiming at universalizing elementary education of satisfactory quality in the country.
8. The Rashtriya Madhyamik Shiksha Abhiyan (RMSA) on the liner of SSA, is expected to bring in the desired investments in secondary education and facilitate the process of universalizing secondary education in the country.

India has the largest education system in the world after the China. However, an issue of quality education and access remains as challenges in some parts of the country. Accordingly 86th Amendment Act (2002) has been made elementary education a fundamental right and as a part of this new Article 21-A has been inserted declaring that "the state shall provide free and compulsory education to all children of age of six to fourteen years in such a manner as the state may determine." The year 2009 is a landmark year in the development history of elementary education, when the government finally managed to pass the 86th Amendment to the constitution that made Right to Education (RTE) constitutional provision for education. Now RTE is a fundamental right for all children in the age group of 6-14 years. In simple words, it means that the government will be responsible for providing free education to every child up to the eighth standard irrespective of class, caste, religion, race, sex, etc. It has thus found the way to building a strong, literate and empowered youth of the country.

Important Features of the Act

(1) Free and compulsory education to all children of India in 6-14 age group.
(2) Calls for fixed student-teacher ratio.

Student-teacher ratio	*Class*
30:1	1-V class
35:1	VI-VIII class

(3) Under this act no child shall be liable to pay any kind of fee or charges or expenses which may prevent him or her from pursuing and completing the elementary educaiton.
(4) No child shall be held back, expelled or required to pass a board examination until completion of elementary education.
(5) No child shall be subjected to physical punishment of mental harassment.
(6) Norms and standards for a school have been laid down.
   - No of teachers—At least 3 subject teachers for class VI-VIII
   - Building—one class room for teachers
   - One office-cum-store for headmaster
   - Separate toilets, Drinking water, playground, boundary wall
   - Minimum no. of working hours—200 for (I-V class)
   - Minimum no. of working hours—220 for (VI-VIII class)
   - Minimum no. of working hours/weak/teacher— 45 hours including preparation hours
   - Teaching and learning equipment provided to each class
   - Library
   - Play material, games, sports equipments

(7) It is a right to—Admission, participation and completion of elementary education.
   - No corporal punishment
   - Stress-free school experience
   - No detention
   - No expulsion

(8) A child friendly curriculum having the following features :
   - It should be inconformity with the values enshrined in the constitution
   - It should ensure all round development of the child
   - It should make sure building up childs' knowledge, potentiality and talent
   - There should be development of physical and mental abilities to the fullest extent
   - Learning through activities, discovery and exploration in a child-friendly and child-centred manner
   - Medium of instruction shall be in child's mother tongue
   - It should make child free of fear, trauma and anxiety and helping the child to express views freely
   - There must be comprehensive and continuous evaluation of childs' understanding of knowledge and his/her ability to apply the same
   - Every child completing his elementary education shall be awarded a certificate.

(9) School teachers will need adequate professional degree within five years or else will lose job.

(10) Provide 25% reservation for economically disadvantaged communities for admission to Class I in all private schools.

(11) Mandates improvement on quality of education.

(12) Financial burden will be shared between state and central governments.

(13) Screening procedure shall be punishable with fine.

(14) No teacher shall be deployed for any non-educational purposes.
(15) No teacher shall be engage himself/herself in private tuition.
(16) The schools have to train all its teachers within 5 years.
(17) Seventy-five percent (75%) members of the school management committee will comprise parents of the students who will monitor the functioning of the schools and utilization of grants.
(18) The school management committee or the local authorities will identify the out of school children and admit them to standards appropriate to their age, after giving them proper training.
(19) When a child is required to move from one school to another, either within a state or outside, for any reason whatsoever, such child shall have a right to seek transfer to any other school.
(20) National commission for protection of child rights constituted for protection of child rights act, 2005.

Thus the act envisages providing quality and compulsory education to all children and equips them with knowledge, skill and values to make them enlightened citizens in India.

CHALLENGES

Though this act has vibrant and outstanding features, it has many challenges to be addressed, which includes that there are over 12.6 lakh vacancies of teachers across the country. There are 7.72 lakh untrained teachers constitutes 40% of the total number of teachers in 1.29 million recognized elementary schools. 46% schools do not have toilets for girls which has been an important reason to parents for not sending children to the schools. Over 53% schools have the student-teacher ratio of well above 1:30, prescribed under the act. Existances of inadequate infrastructure facilities have been noticed widely in almost all parts of India. As far as the finances are concerned, the act provides for sharing it with the states, with centre contributing 55% of the total expenditure. It has been estimated the implementation of the act will require 1.71 lakh crores in the next five years. Low income groups send their children to work for adding to the family income, lack of awareness, early marriages, migration of the people for sustenance, absence of well-defined grievance redressal mechanism are some other challenges need to be addressed for successful implementation of the act.

CONCLUSION

RTE is a landmark initiative of the government to strengthen the education system in India. The realization of this goal: therefore call for a united effort by all stakeholders—The parents, the teachers, the schools, the NGOs, the society at large, the state and central governments. India has thus embarked upon a massive programme to lay foundations of a strong country with a statutory support. It has joined the small group of countries which have such statutory provision. It is indeed a path breaking step towards universalization of education. Minorities, girl students, poor, downtrodden will be the focus of the effort to provide education to all. It is for us to use this goal through. The education is in the concurrent list undertaken the need to better cooperation at all levels.

References

Anil Kumar Biswas (2011). Universalization of Education. *Kurukshetra*, May issue, pp. 7-12.

Ashok Handoo (2010). The Right to Education now a Fundamental Right. *Kurukshetra*, September issue, p. 19.

http://www.cbgaindia.org/files/featured_articles/Right%20to%20Education%20Act%202009%20-%20Critical%20Gaps%20and%20Challenges.pdf

http://education.nic.in/Elementary/elementaryRTE.asp

http://education.nic.in/Elementary/RTI1.pdf

CHAPTER

19

Migrant Women and HIV/AIDS

A Study of their Vulnerability

QURRATUL AEIN ALI

INTRODUCTION

Millions of people move around the world or within their countries for many reasons—for livelihood, to survive, to create better lives for themselves, to escape conditions of poverty, drought, conflict or war-like situations. All theories of migration concede that migration occurs when the region of origin lacks the opportunities which the destination promises. It is inherently a combination of pull and push factors. Variation in economic development across regions is a primary motive for migration to greener pastures. The International Organisation for Migration (IOM) reports that there are over 200 million migrants in the world (not counting the estimated 20-30 million who are unauthorised migrants). The IOM states: "Migration is one of the defining issues of the twenty-first century. It is now an essential, inevitable and potentially beneficial component of the economic and social life of every country and region. The question is no longer whether to have migration, but rather how to manage migration effectively so as to enhance its positive and reduce its negative impacts.

At the start of the new millennium, spatial movement of the human population has become more pronounced. Migratory movements characterized by increased quantitative growth and qualitative differentiation along the lines of migratory patterns, nature of migrants, their quality and final destination have facilitated a differentiated development pattern creating spaces of vulnerability. The unfolding of the socio-political dynamics of different countries and the persistent economic growth along the individual and introduced instability at all levels. This has increased the migration of populations within and across the geographical contours of the nation-state. In the globalization debate, movement of people received scant attention. Yet the sheer magnitude of migration-forced and voluntary, regular and irregular, clearly suggests that migration has the potential to pose a potential public health challenge. *Migration can expose individuals and groups in many settings at health risks.* Many individuals and groups, in certain kinds of settings, remain excluded from the benefits of health and healthcare.

Migration has occurred throughout human history, but globalisation has led to a new phase in its history with unprecedented movement of people. While HIV/AIDS (especially for migrant men) and trafficking (especially for migrant women) dominate the discourse around migrant health, it is increasingly imperative today to see the broader connections between migration and health or the implications of migration on health patterns of migrants themselves. Diseases such as HIV/AIDS and the current swine flu pandemic have highlighted the connection between the large scale movement of people and health.

WOMEN MIGRATION AND THEIR HEALTH

Gender disparity and discrimination shown to women emerged as a major issue in 21st Century, and the case of migrant women even worse than others. According to IOM

Deputy Director General Ndioro Ndiaye to mark International Women's Day, "Women and girls, especially when forced to migrate or when in an irregular situation, are disproportionately affected by the risks of migration because of their vulnerability to exploitation and violence".

The health of the women in India, as anywhere else is dependent in their social status, their capacity to meet basic needs, their working and living conditions and the health of their family and community. (Mudunuri, Lakshmipathi, Raju, (2007). In the case of migrant women, they are usually not familiar with the surroundings, so, they cannot avail many of the government facilities. Pregnancy outcomes and prenatal health indicators suffer as well, and crude death rates of migrant women are higher than baseline rates in their areas of origin (PIP). Rape and prostitution among migrant women become key factors in transmission of HIV/AIDS and sexually transmitted diseases. Among women, the stress of migration and resulting cultural shock has also led to unexplained health problems (psychosocial) and the health profile clearly demonstrates that the situation is far from satisfactory.

Disaggregated information on the types of migrants in India, their magnitude and their vulnerabilities impacting their health and access to healthcare has been presented. The migrants are vulnerable at the source, throughout the migratory process and at the destination areas.

The objective of this paper is to shed light on the working condition, vulnerability, and the factors which supports HIV/AIDS among the migrant women, in-depth interview as well as Focus Group Discussion (FGD) would be followed. The universe of the study is the different construction site of the Aligarh suburbs.

VULNERABILITIES WITH MIGRATION

Vulnerability is a relative term. Similarly, factors leading to vulnerability are varied and relative. In the case of migrants, the common factor that justifies their vulnerability is perhaps the fact that their origin differs from their present residence. The difference is not merely limited to the experience of change of space but extends to other experiences of differences of culture, language and people. The vulnerability which is primarily premised on the alien status of the migrant gets complicated by the combination of factors at the area of destination. Limited choice and reduced capacity to negotiate results in increased discrimination in life chances. The migrant is considered an 'outsider'. Various survey and studies have shown that migrants are disadvantaged relative to the native population regarding employment, education and health. These circumstances are not formally separable into causes such as deficient education and health, initial prejudice, and effects such as poor wages, inferior healthcare provision and sustained discrimination. But they mutually reinforce each other.

Following are the some vulnerability usually they encountered:

- Migrants are disadvantaged relative to the native population.
- They often have a low socio-economic status with no access to either healthcare or social services. They suffer from mental and emotional vulnerability and low self-esteem.
- Lack of provision of social goods, education and health, impedes the integration of migrants into the local population.
- Refugees and illegal migrants often get caught up in the internal geopolitics of the host countries and have no legitimate right that can protect them. They are denied basic rights.
- Delay in health-seeking is also due to associated costs, inability to miss work, problems of transportation. Many are unfamiliar with the local health-care systems and have linguistic or cultural difficulties Communicating their problem.
  Source : Census India, 2001.

Degrees of Vulnerability along Types of Migrants affecting Health—An Exploration of their health impact vulnerability can be understood as a state of being exposed to or susceptibility to danger or abuse. It comprises of weakness of physical and mental strength, defencelessness, unprotectedness, fragility and exposure to undesirable conditions/factors. In addition to the health environment in the place of origin, transit and destination (including disease prevalence), they include patterns of mobility (regular, circular, seasonal, etc.) that define the conditions of journey and their impact on health; the status of migrants in destination areas that determines their access to health and social services; and familiarity with the culture and language of the host community. They have no legitimate right that can protect them. They are denied basic rights.

Delay in health-seeking is also due to associated costs, inability to miss work, problems of transportation.

National health-care plans often discriminate against temporary migrants. This forces migrants to delay health-seeking till the condition is sufficiently hazardous to justify going to emergency clinics. Another factor which prevents irregular international migrants from seeking healthcare and treatment is the fear of their illegal status being discovered (WHO, 2003). Few list of the reasons of their poor health and hygenic condition are economic affordability, quality of available services and the prior conditions of health like right to safe and healthy working conditions, right to adequate food, physical accessibility of health services, culturally sensitive and good quality health services, and the right to seek and receive health-related information. *Local bias stigmatizes* migrants and may be used as an excuse by host communities to supply inferior care, impede integration, restrict the migrant's career and educational mobility and ultimately act as a socially and culturally indenturing force. Bias also acts as a self-perpetuating force, sustaining the migrant's negative conditions and thus major reasons for migration.

MIGRANT WOMEN'S VULNERABILITIES AND HIV/AIDS

A defining feature of migration this decade has been the "feminization of migration", a term that refers to the phenomenal number of female migrants moving in search of livelihoods. Although discussed within the framework of marriage in the past, and later in the context of trafficking, more and more women are migrating independently. Statistics from the IOM show that women constitute 49.6% of global migrants

For women, unsafe migration and the vulnerabilities associated with it, including the dependency on possibly unreliable male escorts, can put them at additional risk of sexual abuse and exploitation. This makes them vulnerable to STDs and HIV in a specific way. Other vulnerabilities arise when they have low levels of information and poor knowledge about contraception, abortion and other reproductive health issues, and when they have low negotiation power to ensure the use of condoms.

In a country where poverty, illiteracy and poor health are life, the spread of HIV presents a daunting challenge. Previously it was thought that around 5 million people were living with HIV in India—more than in any other country. Better data, including the results of a national household survey conducted in 2005-06, led to a major revision of the prevalence estimate in July 2007. It is now thought that around 2.3 million people in India are living with HIV. (UNAIDS and NACO agreed on a new estimate—(between 2 million and 3.1 million people living with HIV). Of these, an estimated 39% are female; their heightened vulnerability has both biological and socio-economic reasons. Early marriage, violence and sexual abuse against women are the major socio-economic reasons of their vulnerability to HIV infection. Their biological construct makes them more susceptible to HIV infection in any given heterosexual encounter. Since migrants are towards the higher side of such vulnerabilities, which need to address on apriority basis as well as with special consideration and programs.

Why Prone to HIV/AIDS?

Because of some interrelated problems :

- Illiteracy
- Poverty
- Unawareness
- Inaccessibility to the health settings

- Low availability and awareness for condoms
- Low immunity
- Low health status
- Risky maternal practices
- High rate of STDs
- Exposed situation,
- Sexual abuse
- High prevalence of trafficking
- Risky behaviours
- More adulteration
- Low bargaining power for the safe sex
- More uncertainty
- Limitation of the recreational activities
- Lack of morals and values for relationships and life
- Less religious practices, so less social control
- High prevalence rate of alcohol and drug abuse

Abstinence and condom use are usually not the options available to women since social norms are that women are not 'supposed' to be sexually knowledgeable. This is compounded in respect of illiterate, rural, poor, sex workers as well as migrant women who are doubly stigmatised and marginalised.

Prevalent notions of masculinity and femininity generally mean that women have little control or negotiating power in their sexual relationships, including marriage.

Women have poor access to information and education, which is critical in the context of HIV since behaviour change is the key to controlling the epidemic. This is further accentuated among poverty-stricken communities, like migrants.

Violence against women and HIV/AIDS continue to be inextricably linked: rape, incest, assault by family members or friends, violence in the course of trafficking or at workplace expose them to HIV infection. (Women are at the receiving end of the HIV/AIDS)

Women have poor access to health services as a result of lower priority given to their health and their lack of decision-making powers within the family. Also, women usually have poor mobility, which inhibits access to information and services. In the case migration some time they are not familiar with the surroundings, as well as they cannot avail many of the government facilities.

Migration further alleviates the problems of the women in general and to their health condition in particular, in present scenario (from the last one and half decades) HIV/AIDS became the centre of all the health concern as it is a social disease, (with lots of myths and panics).

According to the latest (2008) WHO and UNAIDS global estimates, women comprise 50% of people living with HIV. Proportion of women living with HIV has been increasing in the last 10 years. Norms related to femininity can prevent women—especially young women—from accessing HIV information and services. Only 38% of young women have accurate, comprehensive knowledge of HIV/AIDS according to the 2008 UNAIDS global figures.

According to the primary data collected during the survey, conducted in the different construction site of the Aligarh suburbs of Uttar Pradesh with the migrant women involved in the construction activities, 97.1% migrant women were illiterate against 59.1% of national average (NFHS-3) similarly, awareness regarding the HIV/AIDS was only 2.8%, even this two percent comprises of those migrant women workers who were settled in Aligarh from years, and 30% Hindu respondents out of this 2.8%, were aware about the HIV/AIDS.

These HIV infections are higher in eastern UP, possibly due to its higher migrant population and is spreading westward, migrant population is a major reason for high prevalence of HIV/AIDS in U.P. so in Aligarh. This small study reflects the gravity of the problem, and migrant women's vulnerability towards their poor health and HIV/AIDS.

SUGGESTIONS

The reasons which make the women vulnerable and cause the health problems are more aggravated and threatening in the lives of migrant women. Even have access to health care; it is not always "migrant friendly". Cultural differences, language barriers and xenophobic attitudes can and do impact on a migrant's ability to get the necessary care she needs. Unaware of their right to access health services, and health personnel unaware of their obligation to provide these services, can stop displaced women getting the help they need.

Migrant hosting communities the world over need to provide accessible, acceptable and affordable maternal health services for all migrants, irrespective of their legal status, region, religion and caste, in order to lessen the vulnerability of women to migration, says the International Organization For Migration (IOFM).

The situation demands for :

- Very effective and rigorous awareness programme, (like of pulse polio programme) once migrant women become aware, they would definitely ask for the services, and realise their health importance.
- Specially designed awareness programme on HIV/ AIDS, for the temporary migrant population.
- Awareness regarding proper use of condoms.
- Social marketing of the contraceptive devices.
- Behaviour modification of the couples, through Family Life Education (FLE).
- Sensitization of employers towards the responsibilities for their workers.
- Integrated, decentralized policy and programmes.

With more than 200 million migrants in the world, migration-internal and across borders—is here to stay. New programme and strategies has to initiated (inclusive migrant women) by the central and state governments under the NRHM, such as Janani Suraksha Yojana, Chiranjeevi Yojana, etc. More importantly, it is crucial to integrate migrants' rights and their needs in health policies of a nation to arrive at more holistic results and, in public health terms, a healthy population.

References

Bhat Mari, P.N., K. Navaneetham and S. Irudaya Rajan, 1995. Maternal Mortality in India: Estimates from a Regression Model, Studies in Family Planning.

Koblinsky, M.A., Oona, M.R. Campbell and S.D. Harlow, 1993. Mother and More: A Broad Perspective on Women's Health. In Marjorie A., Koblinsky, J. Timyan and J. Gay (eds.). The Health of Women: A Global Perspective, Boulder, Co: West-view Press.

Pandit, R.D., 1987. Changing Trends in Maternal Mortality in Developing Countries. *Asia Oceania Journal of Obstetrics and Gynaecology,* 13, 4: 385-94.

Registrar General, India, 2006. Maternal Mortality in India: 1997-2003, Trends Causes and Risk Factors, Sample Registration System, New Delhi.

UNFPA, 1997. India Towards Population and Development Goals, Oxford University Press, Delhi.

World Health Organisation (WHO), 1977. International Classification of Diseases. Manual of International Classification of Diseases, Injuries and Causes of Death, Geneva, WHO.

CHAPTER

20

Conceptual and Policy Issues in India's Higher Education System

RAJESH KUMAR, SURENDRA SINGH
AND HIMMAT SINGH DEORA

INTRODUCTION

This paper analyzes interrelated facets of Higher Education policy in India: the key distortions in higher education policies and what explains them. It first sets the stage by laying out the principal conceptual issues that need to be considered when thinking about an appropriate policy framework for higher education in India. It examines Indian higher education with regards to markets, the state and civil society (philanthropy). The paper examines the political economy of Indian higher (tertiary) education and seeks to explain the ideological and political underpinnings of these distortions and how they work in practice. Higher education in India is being *de facto* privatized on a massive scale. But this privatization is not a result of changing preferences of the key actors—the state, the judiciary or India's propertied classes. Rather, this privatization has resulted from a breakdown of the state system. As a result, it is a form of privatization in which ideological and institutional underpinnings remain very weak. Instead of being part of a comprehensive program of education reform, much of the private initiative remains hostage to the discretionary actions of the state. Consequently, the education system remains suspended between over-regulation by the state.

Conceptual and policy issues relating to higher education in general (and not just in India) face an analytical conundrum: any discussion of these issues has to begin by acknowledging that from a policy point of view it is not easy conceptualizing what "good" higher education means, and therefore what kind of regulatory framework is appropriate. India is not unique in experiencing a crisis in the higher education system, and the debate on optimal regulatory frameworks across the world is quite indeterminate in its conclusions.

"The real difficulty is that people have no idea of what education truly is. We assess the value of education in the same manner as we assess the value of land or of shares in the stock-exchange market. We want to provide only such education as would enable the student to earn more. We hardly give any thought to the improvement of the character of the educated. The girls, we say, do not have to earn; so why should they be educated? As long as such ideas persist there is no hope of our ever knowing the true value of education." (M.K. Gandhi)

Literacy is not an end of education or even the beginning. All literate men may not be truly educated while the 'illiterate rural masses' at time may cultivate refined sensitivity and progressiveness that 'true education' is supposed to bring out. "Rural areas are less literate but have a better more balanced gender ratio than urban areas. The harsh truth is that modern education has increased social discrimination instead of eradicating it. It is generally believed that the gender ratio is adverse (in favor of men) in those states where the literacy rate is lower and the gender ratio is more balanced where the literacy rates are higher. This is a completely false interpretation. Beginning with a ratio of 972 females per 1000 males in 1901 the proportion was, on the whole, moving down consistently through the decades (except for slight increases in the year 1951 and 1981) and arrived the lowest figure of 927 females in 1991, while the literacy rate has been steadily up from a low of 5.39 per cent in 1901 to a high of 64.66 per cent in 2001 and 76 percent in 2011 proposed census data.

STRUCTURE AND SCALE OF INDIAN HIGHER EDUCATION

In 1950-51 India had 27 universities, which included 370 colleges for general education and 208 colleges for professional education (engineering, medicine, and education). By 2007 India had 361 Universities (comprising 219 State Universities, 21 Central Universities, 110 Deemed Universities, 11 Private Universities, 18 Institutions of National Importance (5 established under state legislations and 13 Institutes by Central Legislation). In addition, there are 18,064 colleges. The total number of students enrolled in the universities and colleges was 14 million. While we don't have data for the distribution of students by discipline, in 2003 of the 2 million-odd graduates, engineering and medicine graduates accounted for 7 percent and 0.7 percent respectively. Nearly two-thirds of the colleges in 2005 were classified by the University Grants Commission (UGC—the apex government regulatory body for higher education) as "Arts, Science, and Commerce Colleges". Recent growth is much greater in professional colleges (especially engineering, management and medicine), as well as in private vocational courses catering especially to the IT sector.

There has been a rapid expansion in higher education, with student enrolment growing at about 5 percent annually over the past two decades. This growth is about two-and-half times the population growth rate, and results from both a population bulge in lower age cohorts as well as increased demand for higher education. However, even today's gross enrolment ratio of Indians in institutions of higher education is approximately 11 percent of the age cohort, which is considerably higher than developing country averages, but lower than the average for Asia as a whole and much lower than OECD countries. Enrolment ratios vary across Indian states, with the southern and western states faring better than their eastern counterparts. Women now constitute about 40 percent of all student enrolments, varying from a low of 20 percent in Orissa to a high of 58.8 percent in Kerala. The bulk of students (nearly two-thirds) are enrolled in arts and science, with another 18 percent in commerce/management. This is of some importance because most "private investment" in higher education is concentrated in engineering, medicine and management, and consequently does little for the majority of students. Notwithstanding the great hopes reposed by a spate of committee reports on alternative sources of funding for higher education, the state will continue to have to occupy the commanding heights of at least this sector of the economy. Although total expenditure on higher education has risen since independence, from 483 crores to 2418.3 crores between 1980 and 1995, spending per pupil in real terms declined for nearly two decades (Tilak, 1997). Higher education occupies a low priority in public expenditure real public expenditure per student in higher education declined by 21 percent between 1993-94 and 2003-04. Its share of GNP was nearly 1 percent during the 1970s, just 0.35 percent in the mid-1990s, before increasing modestly to 0.6 by the end of the decade. After the formulation of the New Policy of Education (NPE) in 1986, the central government gradually increased its contribution to the funding of elementary education, and this trend continued in the 1990s. As a result, in total expenditure on education, the share of higher education spending declined from 12.2 percent during 1982-92 to 11.4 percent for the states, and more dramatically, from 36.2 to 23.3 percent for the center. Notwithstanding the high growth rate after economic liberalization, the real rate of growth of public expenditure on higher education declined from 4 about 5.5 percent during 1982-92 to 5.3 percent between 1993-2004, largely because of deceleration in spending by the states. The average real expenditure on higher education per enrolled student declined at 2.4 percent annually during this period—from Rs. 8,322 in the period 1981-82 to 1991-92, to Rs. 6,790 in the period 1992-93 to 2003-04 (at 1993-94 prices). Until very recently, most state governments had virtually ceased to expand the list of government aided institutions, thereby increasing the percentage of "self-financed" or "private unaided institutions," most noticeably in professional and technical education. In contrast to cash-strapped state governments, in June 2007 the Center announced plans to set-up and fund 30 new central universities across the country. India has 20 central universities (18 funded by the UGC), spread over just 9 states, Delhi and Puducherry. The remaining 19 states of India would receive first priority in getting central universities. In addition, the central government announced that it would work with the states to support the expansion of colleges to the 340 districts that have extremely low college enrolments. To increase the likelihood of enrolment from these districts it also announced plans to set one high-quality school in every block of the country (6000) which would also establish benchmarks for excellence in public schooling.

CONCEPTUAL AND POLICY ISSUES

Conceptual and policy issues relating to higher education in general (and not just in India) face an analytical conundrum: any discussion of these issues has to begin by acknowledging that from a policy point of view it is not easy conceptualizing what "good" higher education means, and therefore what kind of regulatory framework is appropriate (Kapur and Crowley, 2007). India is not unique in experiencing a crisis in the higher education system, and the debate on optimal regulatory frameworks across the world is quite indeterminate in its conclusions. Appropriate policy frameworks for Higher Education are difficult to design for several reasons. First, there is considerable disagreement over the social rates of return in Higher Education. This confusion over this issue is reflected in World Bank reports on this issue (Higher Education: The Lessons of Experience, 1994 and Priorities and Strategies for Education: A World Bank Review, 1995). The confusion and obfuscation in the 1994 report is evident, it is contradictory claims. To quote: Indeed, it is arguable that higher education should not have highest priority claim on incremental public resources available for education in many developing countries, especially those that have not yet achieved adequate access, equity and quality at the primary and secondary levels.

This is because of the priority these countries attach to achieving universal literacy; because the social rates of return in investments in primary and secondary education usually exceed the rates of return on higher education and because investment in basic education can improve equity because it tends to reduce inequalities. (World Bank, 1994, p. 3) Ironically, the executive summary of the same document reads: Higher education is of paramount importance for social and economic development. Institutions of higher education have the main responsibility for equipping individuals with advanced knowledge and skills required for positions of responsibility . . . estimated social rates of return of ten percent or more in many developing countries also indicates that investments in higher education contributed to increase in labor productivity and to higher long-term economic growth essential for poverty alleviation. (World Bank, 1994, p. 1) There is a substantial technical literature on the social rates of return on investment in higher education, which is not our concern here. But there is a judgment call governments have to take in making the appropriate allocative decisions. All we would like stress here is that allocative decisions in India have, by and large, not been governed by any serious debate over this question. They are rather determined, as we shall see later, by political economy considerations. While recognizing the difficulty of this question, any sensible public policy ought to be able to publicly justify its allocative priorities on rational grounds. The Eleventh Plan draft, for instance, envisages doubling public investment in Higher Education. But much of this has been driven by the need to defuse the political backlash caused by India's affirmative action policies, rather than by a rigorous examination of allocative priorities.

The second issue concerns the distribution of investments within an education system. In any optimum system of regulation this question will have two aspects. First, how are private investment decisions made? Second, given (as we explain below) significant market failures in higher education, public investments will be required. But on what informational basis are public investments made? We first address the question of private investment decisions in higher education. In the Indian context it is important to emphasize that while there is considerable private investment (detailed later), it would an exaggeration to describe this as entirely market driven. Most private investment requires regulatory approval, and its character will be determined by the character of regulatory regime. Regulatory bottlenecks distort the character and degree of private investment in higher education in several important ways. A. Distorted Markets First, the process of regulatory approvals diminishes the capacity of private investment to respond to market needs. In some areas like management and IT diplomas, institutions have managed to skirt the regulatory process by running "unrecognized" institutions, but in most areas severe distortions remain. Two examples illustrate this point. There has been an explosion in the demand for nursing. Yet setting up nursing colleges, or even increasing seats in existing ones requires regulatory approval that can frequently take years. So paradoxically, India remains a country that produces more doctors than nurses. India's civil aviation sector experienced phenomenal growth from 2001 onwards; yet approvals for aviation engineering schools were not forthcoming. As a result, India is a net importer of aviation engineers and pilots. Second, if the regulatory process is perceived to be corrupt and opaque, it produces an adverse selection in the kind of entrepreneurs that invest since the success of a project depends less upon the pedagogic design of the project but rather the ability to manipulate the regulatory system. The cumulative effect is to deter entrepreneurs who are interested in education rather than expending their energies in manipulating state functionaries. Third, there are significant market failures in acquiring physical assets that are necessary for institutions. Land is one such key asset. But the land market in India is severely distorted, and this has ramifications for the ability of educational entrepreneurs to set-up institutions. Fourth, the templates under which approvals are given to institutions are extremely rigid on two dimensions. They stipulate infrastructure requirements irrespective of costs or location. And regulatory agencies insist that new institutions instead of innovating academically conform to centrally mandated course outlines, degree structures and admissions policies. Fifth, a key element of a well functioning market-competition—is often severely distorted. For instance, foreign universities are not allowed to set-up campuses in India, and this arguably prevents benchmarking to global standards. There are other micro rules, about institutions not being allowed to operate outside the state they are registered, high entry barriers for universities, the ability of the state to withhold operating licenses on the grounds that there are already enough institutions in a particular area, all of which impede competition. Sixth, the central element of a well functioning market, informational transparency, is woefully inadequate. The state's view is that accountability is best imposed through two instruments. The first is direct state inspection. The second is bringing these institutions under an accreditation process. Both mechanisms are deeply flawed. It is literally not possible for the state to physically inspect thousands of colleges; and the inspector raj is subject to abuse and corruption. The accreditation process is deeply flawed because one single accreditation agency does not have the capacity to fairly, rigorously and transparently accredit a large number of institutions. Instead, the state might be better of creating some competition in the accreditation process by licensing a number of agencies. The state would also be better of focusing on enforcing transparency: requiring institutions to share basic information that empowers students to make more informed choices. Although the regulatory agencies have made attempts in this direction, output-related information that is critically lacking: namely, what has been the performance of an institution in terms of where its students end up after graduation. Few institutions are even required to track their own performance, let alone share this information publicly. Another significant lacunae on the issue of transparency is that while the state has a plethora of laws to regulate institutions (and if need be even close them down), there are no laws specifically pertaining to fraud or misrepresentation in the education sector. Under current law, the regulatory institutions may close down fraudulent institutions, but they do not have the legal instruments for prosecuting those who have engaged in outright fraud. For instance, some institutions admit students, and grossly misrepresent their legal status. In the middle of the degree course, the institution simply "vanishes" leaving the students with a number of "wasted" years and large financial losses. There are no laws specifically to prosecute such cases of fraud. So the irony is that the one piece of legislation that could make strengthen student protection in relation to private institutions, without curtailing their autonomy is missing. But a whole series of other restrictions are selectively enforced by regulatory agencies. Finally, the private sector will for some time to come, free ride on years of accumulated scarcity. This scarcity is of two kinds. On the supply side, it is not easy to overnight tap into the kind of human capital that might be required to run good institutions; on the demand side, the scarcity is such that even weak institutions that would not have otherwise survived a competitive environment do so. There is an important analytical point here. Even if a system is formally competitive, in that there is a choice of institutions available and no institution (or a small number) commands a large market share, competition alone may not ensure accountability if aggregate demand remains high. The cautionary tale is that the accountability effects of competition will not kick in until demand is met. In the short-run measures like regulating fees seem to create access, but in the long-run they diminish the supply of the education system as a whole. At least with regard to private investment, the distortions can be removed by crafting regulatory regimes that address the aforementioned concerns.

State Distortions : We takes it to be the case that public investment will play a major role in higher education. There will be significant market failures in education. For instance, it is not clear that even under the best of conditions the market will create an environment conducive to research that has long time horizons or which responds to important social needs. These will have to be met through public funding. If higher education has significant public good aspects it will be under supplied. If it is a private good there could be significant credit market failures that impede access. The important policy questions are who should be making the allocative decisions on behalf of the state and what principles should guide them? The question of who should be making allocation decisions is particularly significant in the Indian context. At the moment, it is fair to say that these decisions are centralized to an extreme degree. The Planning Commission and the Ministry of Human Resource Development not only determine aggregate Higher Education Budgets, but the forms in which they will be spent (this includes everything from the kinds of institutions, subject areas and so forth). The University Grants Commission, the premier funding body for public institutions has also greatly centralized allocation decisions. The quality of these allocation decisions will depend entirely upon the informational resources a very small group of decision-makers have access to. In our view such extraordinary centralization of allocations is bound to produce significant distortions, because it presupposes an omniscience that few decision-makers can have. For instance, in the 11th Plan draft, the Planning Commission envisages thirty new central universities.

EDUCATION OF MARGINALIZED GROUPS

All the evidence from studies of primary and secondary education suggests that the place where parents discriminate most against a female child is in the preference for public *versus* private expenditure. Parents are more likely to incur private expenditure for sons than daughters. If this is the case, it is difficult to imagine these ratios dropping in the absence of public subsidies. Another piece of evidence against the proposition that education subsidies go largely to the privileged is the increase in enrolment of India's most marginalized social groups, namely, Scheduled Castes (SC) and Scheduled Tribes (ST). The ratio of general to SC/ST students has dropped from almost 12:1 in the late 1950s to 8:1 during the late 80s to just above 6:1 in 2004. There is no reliable study on this, but there is strong suggestive evidence to show that the proportion of first generation graduates in universities has been rising dramatically in both state and, to a somewhat lesser degree, Central Universities. If one uses the fact that at least one parent was a graduate as a proxy for privilege, then the dramatic increase in the proportion of first generation graduates belies the claim that state expenditure only subsidies the privileged.

Global patterns of funding clearly show that higher education remains very much a state-dominated sector. In

OECD countries such as Denmark and Holland, public funding provides 98 percent of the resources for higher education; the figure is almost 90 percent for Canada. Even in the United States, the figure is as high as 78 percent. There is absolutely no doubt that the public sector has a preeminent role to play in higher education (Kapur and Crowley, forthcoming). The need for subsidies is not at issue. What is at issue is their form and structure. Historically in India there have been few moves by the government to remove subsidies and recovering user costs. The recovery of user costs (or costs recovered from students) remained at roughly 5 percent during the entire decade, substantially less than the Punayya Committee's recommendation that the government aim at recovering 25 percent of costs from students. The general principle has been more widely accepted both by the 11th Plan and the National Knowledge Commission. But there are risks in the way in which this might be implemented for public universities. While this proposal is a good aggregate target, the outcome will be sub-optimal, if this is converted into a simple formula applicable to each university. For the ability of institutions to raise fees and resources will vary considerably. The risk of rigidly imposing this formula may be to weaken weak institutions even more. The second issue with subsidies is that the cost of education bears no relationship to the earning potential of degrees. In other words, the issue is whether fees structures are rationalized in relation to markets for individual students based on their potential earning capacity, background and so forth. There is a sense in which a lot of middle class students are beneficiaries of subsidies in that the fees they pay has no relation to their earning potential. But the emphasis on uniformity in the area of fees and of course meant uniformly low fees. Indeed it is an astonishing application of the uniformity principle that even in areas of fees, the requisite degree of variation is not allowed adding to the impression that subsidies go to the rich. Thus even as Indian students are going abroad in droves, spending nearly two orders of magnitude per capita than the Indian state spends per student in India, even elite public educational institutions are constrained from raising fees that correlates with the earning potential of graduates. Creative fee structures that all higher education institutions (at least the elite ones) to charge fees based not on costs but instead on initial earnings of students after graduation. This is equivalent to a risk-sharing contract or a "claw-back" mechanism based on real future stream of student earnings rather than costs of a monopolist, which is also more fairness to both parties. Public universities in India need radical reform on every single dimension imaginable. Detailing those reforms would take a paper in its own right. These institutions are run on an endless series of perverse incentives that militate against productivity and excellence, much of the investment is not matched to the objectives and educationists have little control over pedagogical and evaluation decisions. To take a few examples: one of the striking features of university expenditure is that most of it goes to salaries; in some instances as much as 95 percent of total expenditure. The result is, to put it mildly, very poor infrastructure and intense competition for scarce resources resulting in higher politicization. The second feature leading to a dramatic politicization of university life was the introduction of the so called "promotion schemes" during the late seventies. Under this scheme university promotions were considered analogous to civil-service promotions, in that one ought to be entitled to promotion if one had demonstrated minimal competence. In principle, this scheme had all kinds of review mechanisms built into it, but it essentially resulted in two things. It enabled many mediocre academic professionals to rise to top positions of responsibility, and decreased the mobility of individuals who were seeking promotions across universities. In some ways, this scheme did most damage not by removing incentives for performance (it could, in principle have attracted more talent to universities), but by ensuring that non-academically oriented administrators got the upper hand in university administration. There is some argument over whether this scheme was a response to real pressure from the teaching community or a preemptive attempt by the state to buy them off. But the net result is that the clout of the teaching community is considerable. It does not take the form of policy formation (teachers' unions do not have that sense of corporate identity), but as a powerful lobby that has resisted attempts at change and reform in the education system. One striking feature is that of the ten universities we surveyed, it was almost always teachers who went on strike rather than students during the past decade. The point is that a nexus of state power and the entrenched educational establishment more or less governs policy in the area of education. One area we would like to highlight that cuts across the public and private divide is the issue of "quality" At one level there is a great concern with quality. But the credibility of institutions depends largely on selection mechanism for students. In fact, part of the ideological evolution of the system has been the displacement of debates over pedagogy to debates over selection mechanisms. But even this focus on selection mechanism is largely at the top institutions. There is a potentially radical conclusion that could be drawn from the Indian experience. Rather than worry about the quality of higher education institutions *per se,* India should simply replicate the success of IIT or IIM selection mechanisms on a larger scale and across different domains across the country.

The provision of the Higher Education services would also be subject to regulations already in place or to be prescribed by an appropriate regulatory authority (MHRD, 2006-07)— hardly the most welcoming policies to attract the world's best universities, especially when so many countries are vying for their attention. Whose Interests Does this System Serve? Three key variables help understand the political economy of India's higher education: the structure of inequality in India; the principal cleavages in Indian politics; and the nature of the Indian state. While India is not exceptional by conventional measures of income inequality, it is an outlier when measured by educational inequality. Indeed, India is to educational inequality what Brazil is income inequality (Kapur, 2007). Such extreme inequalities inevitably result in populist redistributive backlash. However, the specific redistributive mechanisms are conditioned by the principal cleavages in Indian politics and the nature of the Indian state. The growth of identity politics has sharply enhanced political mobilization around two key cleavages in Indian society: caste and religion. Consequently, redistributive measures follow these two cleavages rather than other possibilities such as income and class, region (urban-rural), or gender.

CONCLUSION

Despite impressive reforms elsewhere, Indian higher education sector remains the most tightly controlled and least reformed sector. Deep ideological and vested interests have made reform in India's Higher Education sector all but impossible. Indeed, for the next generation of reforms in India, this is the central puzzle. The rapid rise in skill premiums in India in the last few years has exposed an important paradox about India's labor markets. Despite its enormous size, the pool of skilled labor is relatively shallow, the result of a deep crisis in higher education despite the success of a few professional schools. The veneer of the few institutions of excellence masks the reality that the median higher education institutions in India have become incapable of producing students with skills and knowledge. The process neither serves a screening or signaling function for the vast bulk of students, nor prepares students to be productive and responsible citizens. Consequently, students are forced to spend more years (and, increasingly, larger resources) to acquire some sort of post-graduate professional qualification, as they desperately seek ways to signal their qualities to potential employers. It would not be an exaggeration to say that India's current system of higher education is centralized, politicized and militates against the production of general intellectual virtues. The fact that the system nonetheless produces a noticeable number of high-quality students is due to the sheer number of students and the Darwinian struggle at the high school level to gain admission into the few good institutions. The most acute weakness plaguing India's higher education system is a crisis of governance, both of the system and of individual institutions. We have argued that precisely because there are few clear analytical criteria to the central question of what is "good" higher education, a regulatory system than emphasizes diversity, flexibility and experimentation is in the long-run most likely to succeed. Such a system will also need a different conception of accountability than the one currently prevailing in the Indian system, which can be characterized as a vertical command and control system, with state authorities empowered to enforce accountability from the top. Instead

India needs to move to a regulatory system which has more horizontal accountability that empowers students to take better informed decisions. The crisis of governance in Indian higher education is most visibly manifest in the acute shortage of qualified faculty. The generation that was inspired by a broad commitment to the public good has retired or will do so soon.

There is little likelihood of sufficient replenishment, given entrenched mediocrity in institutions with lifetime appointments, few competitive pressures and abysmal governance. The result has been the academic equivalent of Gresham's law—the bad drives out the good. The prevailing political ideological climate in which elite institutions are seen as anti-democratic, finds its natural response in political control to influence admissions policies, internal organization, and the structure of courses and funding. As quality deteriorates, students are less and less willing to pay the very resources without which quality cannot be improved. In India's case, the answer has been the growth of private sector higher education institutions and increasingly the consumption of education abroad. However, as our analysis suggests, private sector investment has been confined to professional streams, bypassing the majority of students.

Furthermore, private institutions are also plagued by severe governance weaknesses, raising doubts as to their ability to addresses the huge latent demand for quality higher education in the country. This crisis of governance is not going to be amenable to merely technical solutions. The burden of this paper has been to argue that higher education is so deeply implicated in politics, so deeply inflected by large ideological objectives that have little to do with pedagogy that it would be the height of optimism indeed to think that there is a technocratic solution to this crisis. But we hope that when the appropriate opportunity arises there will be serious and more rigorous reflection on all the aspects of education that need to be regulated: entry, access, quality, accreditation, institution formation. Fundamentally, Indian policy-makers have to recognize two things. First, the competition for talent is now genuinely global. If the design of institutions is not commensurate with this reality; if the freedoms, incentives and quality benchmarks on offer do not allow you to compete on a global scale, building quality institutions will remain a chimera. There is, in principle, no reason why India could not become a global education hub, if it got its regulatory system in order. Second, a vibrant system requires enlisting the energies of a whole range of actors. It also requires responding to a diversity of challenges and unexpected opportunities. Only a system that draws on the competitive energies of the market on the one hand, a flexible and supple state system on the other, and a genuinely committed non-profit sector as a third leg will be able to meet India's challenges. The scale of demand in India is such that it needs to draw resources and energies from all sources rather that engage in a politics that benefits incumbents, constrains supply and rewards mediocrity with regard to quality.

References

Agarwal, Pawan, 2007. "Higher Education in India: Growth, Concerns and the Change Agenda," *Higher Education Quarterly,* 61 (2): 197-207.

Ashok Sanjay, Guha, Mukul Majumdar, Dilip Mookherjee and Debraj Ray, 2002. "Strategy for Economic Reform in West Bengal", *Economic and Political Weekly,* October 12.

Bhagavan, Manu, 2003. Sovereign Spheres: Princes, Education and Empire in Colonial India, Oxford University Press, New Delhi.

Dam, Shubhankar, 2006. "Unburdening the Constitution: What Has the Indian Constitution Got to Do With Private Universities, Modernity and Nation-States". *Singapore Journal of Legal Studies,* pp. 108-47. Available at SSRN: http://ssrn.com/abstract=952211.

Kapur, Devesh, 2007. "Globalization and the Paradox of Indian Democracy," draft.

Kapur, Devesh and Megan Crowley, 2008. "Higher Education and Developing Countries".

C. Kapur, Devesh, Ajay, S. Mehta, R. Moon Dutt, 2004. "Indian Diasporic Philanthropy," in Peter Geithner, Lincoln Chen, and Paula D. Johnson, eds., Diaspora Philanthropy and Equitable Development: Perspectives on China and India. Cambridge, MA: Harvard University Press.

Mani, Anandi and Sharun Mukand, 2007. "Democracy and Visibility", *Journal of Development Economics,* 83 (2): 506-29.

Mitta, Manoj, 2004. "AIIMS is now free to Appoint its Profs", *Indian Express,* April 4.

Modi, H. and Mukhopadhyay A., 2000. An Analysis of Tax Concessions of Charitable Organizations. NIFP, Delhi.

Mukherjee, Mita. 2004. "Slash prelude to funds full stop." *The Telegraph*, March 17.

Srivastava, Ravi, 2007. "National Knowledge Commission: Meeting Social Goals or Neoliberal Reform," *Economic and Political Weekly*, March 10, pp. 812-15.

Sundar, Pushpa, 2000. Beyond Business: From Merchant Charity to Corporate Citizenship, New Delhi: Tata McGraw Hill.

Sundar, Pushpa, 2002. For God's Sake: Religious Charity and Social Development in India (Sampradaan: Indian Center for Philanthropy).

Tilak, J.B.G., 1983. Voluntary Contributions to Education in India, *Punjab School of Economics and Business*, Vol. 4, No. 2.

Tilak, J.B.G., 1997. "The Dilemma of Reforms in Financing Higher Education in India", *Higher Education Policy*, 10 (1): 7-21.

Tilak, J.B.G., 2000. "Higher Education in Developing Countries," Minerva, Vol. 38, pp. 233-40.

Tilak, J.B.G., 2003. "Public Expenditure on Education in India", in Financing Education in India (New Delhi: NIEPA: Ravi Books).

Vishwanathan, S. 2003. "The Seats Market", *Frontline*, March 15, 2003. Wolf, Alison. 2002. Does Education Matter? London: Penguin.

World Bank, 1994. Higher Education: The Lessons of Experience. Washington, DC: The World Bank. Reports: Government of India, Department of School Education and Literacy, 2007. Annual Report 2004-05, URL: http://www.education.nic.in/AR/AR0607-en.pdf. Government of India, 2007.

CHAPTER

21

Social Security in Technocratic Era

A Study of Special Economic Zone (SEZ) in India

MOHAMMAD RAUF

MEANING AND DEFINITION OF SOCIAL SECURITY

India, being a welfare State, has taken upon itself the responsibilities of extending various benefits of Social Security and Social Assistance to its citizens. The social security legislations in India derive their strength and spirit from the Directive Principles of State Policy as contained in the Constitution of India enforcement of Social Security Acts through institutional mechanisms would impact on the level of trust and confidence of the working class.[1] Social Security is both a concept as well as a system. It represents basically a system of protection of individuals who are in need of such protection by the State as an agent of the society. The Social Security Laws in India at present can be broadly divided into two categories, namely, the contributory and the non-contributory. The contributory laws are those which provide for financing of the social security programmes by contributions paid by workers and employers and in some cases supplemented by contributions/grants from the Government.[2] The important contributory schemes include the Employees' State Insurance Act, 1948 and the Provident Fund, Pension and Deposit Linked Insurance Schemes framed under the Employees' Provident Funds and Miscellaneous Provisions Act, 1948. The three major non-contributory laws are the Workmen's Compensation Act, 1923, the Maternity Benefit Act, 1961 and the Payment of Gratuity Act, 1972. The concept of social security is now generally understood as meaning protection provided by the society to its members through a series of public measures against the economic and social distress.[3] The fundamental objective of minimum wage fixation is to improve the standard of living of those sections of the working population in the sweated sector whose wages are very low and who's living and working conditions leave much scope for improvement. In fact, the original SEZ Bill, introduced for debate in Parliament in May 2005, had a number of provisions that denied workers social security even their basic human rights. For instance, Section 50 of the Bill said: 'Directing that any of the provisions of any state Act relating to trade unions, industrial and labour disputes, welfare of labour including condition of work invalidity, old-age pensions, and maternity benefits or any other activity relating to the SEZ shall not apply.

Definition of Special Economic Zone (SEZ)

A Special Economic Zone (SEZ) is a geographical region that has economic laws more liberal than a country's typical economic laws.[4] The SEZs are expected to have hi-tech industries suitable to the process of globalisation. This means for the local population, which is not skilled enough for such high tech jobs, will not find any employment in the new economic activities; rather the locals will find employment as unskilled labour.[5] Since the social security laws of India, as they stand today in statute books, are not going to be made applicable in the SEZs, the protections under existing labour laws will not be available to these workers. That will mean that unskilled labour in the SEZs will be working as daily wagers at the mercy of the contractors who hire them. This will cause the self-reliant farming community to be converted into a dependent community of bonded laborers. When the local population, dependent on agriculture, loses their mother land, they will lose their livelihoods too. Article 21 of the Constitution of India guarantees the fundamental right to life and livelihood.[6] The development of India is in violation of the Indian Constitution.

SOCIAL SECURITY LABOUR LAW AND SPECIAL ECONOMIC ZONE

The concept of social security is based on ideals of human dignity and socio-economic justice[7]. In other words, ensures a person (worker) against economic duties resulting from various contingencies and ensures him a minimum level of living consistent with the nation's capacity to pay. Labour rights are enshrined in the Universal Declaration of Human Rights (UNDHR),[8] the International Covenant on Economic, Social and Cultural Rights (ICESCR), the International Covenant on Civil and Political Rights (ICCPR) and Conventions of the International Labour Organisation (ILO) such as Convention 87—freedom of association; Convention 98—the right to collective bargaining; Conventions 29 and 105—the prohibition of forced labour; Conventions 100 and 111—covering non-discrimination in employment and remuneration; and Convention 138—minimum age for employment to eliminate child labour. Virtually all nation-states have ratified these conventions and have committed to enforce such standards accordingly. Several researches have pointed out that core labour standards are frequently violated in SEZs and that national legal frameworks which safeguard the rights of the workers are commonly circumscribed.[9] The tendency of SEZs to ignore the rights of workers is often encouraged by the government as part of providing investors a friendly environment in the host countries. International labour rights guarantee, among others, a minimum wage, defined working hours, a safe working environment, freedom of association, freedom to form and join labour unions, the right to strike and the rights of female workers, and the abolition of child labour.[10] Almost all of these rights are constantly being violated in SEZs all over India. The health standards in these zones were often very poor. Workers were forced to live mostly in dormitories close to the enclaves. Safety regulations were not followed properly and factory fires were quite common in Indian SEZs.

Exploitation of Women Workers in SEZs

Women dominate the workforce in EPZs in most developing countries like India. For instance in the Noida Special Economic Zone (NSEZ) the share of women workers in total EPZ employment was 64% in 2000.[11] That woman is paid less than men for similar jobs and is subjected to gender violence in these zones. Majority of women are engaged in low-paying, low-productive jobs with insecure contracts and without any social/health/maternal benefits. Over time, as the SEZs evolve with higher technological inputs, female workers are simply replaced by more skilled male workers. Country experiences illustrate the exploitation of women in SEZs.

THE PRESENT TECNOCRATIC ERA : INDIAN LABOUR SECURITY

The Trade Union Act has been so amended that the entry of central trade unions into SEZs has been barred. The consequence is that employer-sponsored trade unions will hold the monopoly and will act as the agents of employers to suppress any genuine labour struggle. The total number of office bearers of the registered trade union in an unorganized sector, 50 per cent can be the persons not employed in the industry.[12] Thus, trade union leaders not employed in any industry can be become office-bearers of the registered trade union, a proviso has been added to Section 22 of the Trade Union Act. In view of the matter, national trade unions cannot form their unions within SEZ.[13] The Act is silent on the question of the applicability of the Minimum Wages and fact that minimum wages are generally not paid by employers, gives the latter complete freedom to give wages that are less than the rate prescribed under Minimum Wages Act.[14] The most serious problem in an SEZ is the self-certification of compliance with the Minimum Wages Act. The Supreme Court held in the case of *PUDR* v. *Union of India*,[15] that Under the Minimum Wages Act, wages are notified by the state government periodically; non-payment of Minimum Wages or payment of wages less than the rate prescribed under Minimum Wages Act is not only a criminal offence but also violative of Article 23 of the constitution. The zones are exempted from the Contract Labour (Regulation and Abolition) Act, 1970. This has resulted in the companies in the zones going in for casual/contract labourers than for permanent employees. In many zones, these labourers are provided by middlemen/recruiting agencies and these workers do not even find a place in the companies' work register and are also forced to surrender a part of their wages as commission. Despite being the victims of an exploitative work culture, the workers have no real avenues to air their grievances. The powers and obligations of the labour officer have been conferred on the Development Commissioners of the zones. Being the person responsible for maintaining a production-oriented milieu in the zone and attracting investors, the Commissioner invariably tends to go for image-building rather than address the grievances of the workers, who are after all, 'disposable' any time. The Supreme Court of India in the *Standard Vacuum Refinery Company* v. *Their Workmen*[16] observed that contract labour should not be employed where (i) the work is perennial and must go on from day-to-day; (ii) the work is incidental to and necessary for the work of the factory; (iii) the work is sufficient to employ a considerable number of full-time workmen; and (iv) the work is done in most concerns through regular workmen. The CLA was created with the objective of gradual abolition of casual labour hiring, and to regulate the working conditions of casual labour, wherever permitted. The Supreme Court in *Steel Authority of India Ltd.* v. *National Union of Waterfront Workers and Others*[17] held that the contract workers would have no right to automatic absorption. They would only have a right to a preference in employment if permanent workers were to be employed to fill in the vacancies created by the removal of the contract workers. The court added that on issuance of a notification by the appropriate government under Section 10 prohibiting employment of contract labour in a given establishment, it is for the contractor to provide work to his labour in other establishments, where the contract labour system is not prohibited. The increase in the number of special economic zones (SEZs) and foreign companies in India has led to a fresh stipulation for the relaxation of labour laws in SEZs areas. There is also a debate about having a new set of labour and employment laws for the SEZs. In tone with this demand, the Ministry of Commerce and Industries, this briefly sets out some of the factors for the success of SEZs and advocates a flexible labour policy for the zones.[18] The only concern is that the free market argument with no level playing field puts workers at the mercy of developers and, therefore, all labour laws are now applicable to SEZs as well.[19] So far there has been a concession on economic aspects, now providing concession on social cost of doing business would make doing business in SEZ more profitable. The support from the Federation and consideration to this effect of the Ministry would help in the grant of concessions in retrenchment laws.

CONCLUSION

In fact, the original SEZ Bill, introduced for debate in Parliament in May 2005, had a number of provisions that denied workers even their basic human rights. For instance, Section 50 of the Bill said: 'Directing that any of the provisions of any state Act relating to trade unions, industrial and labour disputes, welfare of labour including condition of work . . . invalidity, old-age pensions, and maternity benefits or any other activity relating to the SEZ shall not apply. . . . Though this section was later deleted, under pressure from the left parties, the fact that it was even drafted shows that the UPA government actually wanted to keep SEZs out of the purview of the country's labour laws. The present SEZ Act, 2005, SEZ Rules 2006, and subsequent State policies grossly negate the ideals of a socialist, democratic republic proclaimed in the Indian Constitution. We demand that issues raised by the author must be kept in mind. "Social Security" has been recognised as an instrument for social transformation and progress and must be preserved, supported and developed .as such. Social security organized on a firm and sound basis will promote progress, since once men and women benefit from increased security and are free from anxiety, will become more productive. SEZs create workplaces in one country often at the cost of the livelihoods of workers in another country. Therefore, it is obvious that the large figure on employment-creation in SEZs in India is misleading. No real analysis is even available regarding the destruction of livelihoods resulting from the expansion of SEZs into new areas. The next chapter will focus on this unsaid part of SEZ-development in India. The critical appraisal of the impact of SEZ on the poor's access to land and livelihoods reveals that the existing structural inequalities would be further intensified with the continued expansion of SEZs in India.

Notes and References

1. The Encyclopadedia American; Vol. 26, 186, 14 (1983).
2. Sri William Beveridge, Report on Social Insurance and Allied Services, (1982).
3. Saxena, R.C., Labour Problems and Social Welfare, 386, (1974).
4. Section of SEZ Act, 2005.
5. Aggarwal (2007).
6. The Constitution of India.
7. Human Rights Committee, General Comment No. 6 adopted at the Sixteenth session (1982). on Art. 6 of ICCPR. available at ttp://193.194.138.190/tbs/doc.nsf/099b725fe87555ec8025670c004fc803
8. Universal Declaration of Human Rights (UNDHR) 1948.
9. Anant, T.C. *et. al.* (2006). "Labour Markets in India: Issues and Perspectives", in Jesus Felipe and Rana Hasan (edited): *Labour Markets in Asia: Issues and Perspectives*, Palgrave Macmillan, for Asian Development Bank, Manila.
10. Agarwala, A. (2005). *"Performance of Export Processing Zones: A Comparative Analysis of India, Sri Lanka and Bangladesh"*, Working Paper 148, Indian Council for Research on International Economic Relations, New Delhi.
11. Singh, Jaivir (2007). 'Labour Laws' in Kaushik Basu ed. *Oxford Companion to Economics in India*, New Delhi: Oxford University Press.
12. Under Section 22 of the Trade Union Act, 1926.

13. In Schedule-II of the SEZ Act, 2005.
14. Sivaramakrishnan, K.C. (2009). "Special Economic Zones: Issues of Urban Growth and Management", Occasional Paper No. 19, *Centre for Policy Research*, New Delhi.
15. 1982(3) SCC-235.
16. (1960-II-ILJ page 233).
17. 2001 (4) LLN 135.
18. Federation of Indian Chambers of Commerce and Industry, 2001.
19. Aggarwal, Aradhna (2005): Performance of Export Processing Zones.

CHAPTER

22

Education and Problem of Unemployment

RESHU AGARWAL

ABSTRACT

The Problem of unemployment means the problem of giving work to those who are willing to work. A large number of educated and uneducated people wander here and they are without any job. So the problem of unemployment is unwilling joblessness. People who are either out of job or not having a regular job suffer great hardships. Unemployment has given rise to other problems also. Unemployment is on the increase. It is one of the greatest problems of our society. After the students come out of the schools and colleges, what should they do? This is a big question before them. There are no jobs for millions of youth that are pouring out of educational institutions every year. India is basically an agricultural country. Agriculture is the backbone of our economy. Agriculture in India is not developed enough to accommodate all the unemployed youth. The developed countries like the

U.S., England, France, Germany, Italy, etc. also suffer from this problem, but it is more pronounced in India. There are millions of young men and women waiting and waiting for job opportunities. This chronic problem of unemployment is not confirmed to any particular class, segment or society. It is all pervading. There is massive unemployment among educated, well-trained and skilled people, and it is also there among semi-skilled and unskilled laborers, small and marginal farmers and workers. Then there is underemployment. The jobs being created have miserably failed to keep pace with the ever increasing number of job-seekers. It is a problem which presents a great challenge to leaders, thinkers, planners, economists, industrialists and educationists. This research paper throws the light on the major challenges facing by educated unemployed also what we have to change in our education system to that people can get employment after completion of their studies in their area of interest. So that they perform better for their own as well as for overall society devolvement.

INTRODUCTION

Education in the largest sense is any act or experience that has a formative effect on the mind, character or physical ability of an individual. In its technical sense, education is the process by which society deliberately transmits its accumulated knowledge, skill, and values from one generation to another.

Our education system should be reviewed and changed according to our present needs. Like factories our universities, colleges and schools are still producing on a large scale, a rich crop of graduates fit only for white collar jobs in these offices. These graduates are fit only for such jobs as those of clerks, assistants, officers and bureaucrats sitting at tables in the offices. These educated but unemployed youths numbering millions and millions are a source of great anxiety and concern. Our education should be work-oriented. It should be such as enables a person to stand on his own feet instead of depending on others. It is really an irony that our highly educated and trained personnel like engineers, doctors, scientists, etc. run after the government jobs. It is perhaps because of the education system started by the Britishers long ago, which has totally lost its relevance and still prevails. They depend too much on the government and lack the courage and inspiration to stand on their own feet. There should be more and more emphasis on vocational education. There should be more and more technical institutions and training centers. Indiscriminate and unplanned admissions in colleges and universities should also be checked. Higher education should be reserved only for those who really deserved it.

To alleviate this problem of unemployment and under-employment in villages a progressive employment scheme called Jawahar Rozgar Yojana was introduced in 1989. Over 440 lakh families living under the poverty-line are likely to benefit from it. More such schemes are need to create gainful employment opportunities for scheduled tribes, scheduled castes and other backward classes and communities in the rural areas of the country. The rural unemployment has been a major contributory factor of this highest incidence of poverty in spite of our efforts towards development and industrialization.

India is basically an agricultural country. Agriculture is the backbone of our economy. Agriculture in India is not developed enough to accommodate all the unemployed youth. Our agriculture is still dependent on old and traditional ways of farming. The use of technology is not very popular in India. Unless agriculture is modernized with latest scientific methods it cannot provide bread and butter to all the rural youth. They will continue to seek employment outside the bounds of their hereditary profession.

Unemployment is closely related to the increase in population. The population of this country is increasing by leaps and bounds. All the steps to control growing population will help in solving the problem of unemployment. Problem of educated unemployed is all the more serious. When the educated youth fail to get employment as per their capability, they turn hostile. They fall prey to anti-social elements. They exploit them to serve their ends. They become a challenge for the society. They create law and order problem. The country has not become so industrialized that it can accommodate the unemployed youth. This situation has led to migration. There is a lot of pressure on big cities like Delhi, Mumbai, Kolkata, Chennai, etc. Every day thousands of youth reach these cities in search of employment. They create pressure on the civic amenities of these cities.

The problem of unemployment is a world-wide reality. The developed countries like the U.S., England, France, Germany, Italy, etc. also suffer from this problem, but it is more pronounced in India. With the passage of time it has become worse. It has become a threat to India's economic well-being and social development. It is one of the major causes of our poverty, backwardness, crimes and frustration among the people. India is the second largest country after China in terms of populations and man-power. But because of large scale unemployment there is no suitable employment for them. They are forced to remain idle.

There are millions of young men and women waiting and waiting for job opportunities. This chronic problem of unemployment is not confirmed to any particular class, segment or society. It is all pervading. There is massive unemployment among educated, well-trained and skilled people, and it is also there among semi-skilled and unskilled laborers, small and marginal farmers and workers. Then there is underemployment. The jobs being created have miserably failed to keep pace with the ever increasing number of job-seekers. It is a problem which presents a great challenge to leaders, thinkers, planners, economists, industrialists and educationists. India's educated youths are facing some serious issues like educated unemployment and underemployment. Currently, in India, we have fairly low inflation but unemployment is high. In particular, educated unemployment is very high. It is around 20% among graduates. One suspects that political instability in the country, lack of entrepreneurship, lack of quality education and quality students, for instance is the result of excessive unemployment.

Bad education is hurting the economy. Recently, Mr. Kapil Sibal has tried to de-affiliate some of the colleges. Colleges play a very vital role in making students. If colleges provide quality education, the scenario would be better. There are many private and old government colleges which fail to do this and hence provide a less skilled graduate. Opening of more private engineering colleges are fuel to the unemployment problem.

Education has just become a profession. Colleges are being set-up not to give quality education but to earn money. I highly appreciate the step taken by our education minister to modernize our present education system but still lot needs to be done. I also appreciate the removal of board examinations of Xth standard. Many of us may feel this hard harmed the competency among the students. Yes, that was the idea! Children of 16 years are unable to take such high pressures mounted over them.

Another factor for increased unemployment is the pressure from parents. Educated unemployment is due to a mismatch between the aspirations of graduates and employment opportunities available to them. It is seen in Indian community that parents put his son after getting 95% in science stream in view to make him an Engineer or a Doctor. Parents hardly think what his child wants to study, what are his wishes.

Now-a-day craze of Engineering has gone sky high. Students move to any private colleges and take admission. They feel Engineering is the way to earn quick money. Colleges need to be selected in a proper way. An affiliation by AICTE is must for engineering colleges. NBA accreditation which is given by AICTE board is an added advantage and gives a chance for the student to choose a branch from the Engineering College.

According to latest report by NASSCOM only 25% engineering graduates in India are employable, this is because of poor quality of education in engineering colleges. Government should take some steps to improve the quality of education in Indian colleges. Also the syllabus should be made par to the industry standards. The unemployment, and much more so, the underemployment of graduates, are devastating phenomena in the lives of graduates. However, the incidence of underemployment among the graduates is much higher. Maximum students in this country are from middle class. Parents spend lakhs of rupees on them in a view that he will get a job after completing his graduation. But when the student fails to get a job, his mental position detoriates and gets depressed.

After 10+2 comes a very crucial period where we almost get puzzled to what stream to go into. This is the time we should sit down and think what will be best for us. What is the career that we should pursue that will help us grow. Students of today are very much afraid to take up unconventional courses as a part of their study. The whole INDIA has become saturated by producing doctors, engineers and MBA's. Now other professions are really climbing the ladder and it is very important for each student to identify his capabilities, his interest before taking up any course. Because it is better to think before, rather than roaming here and there for getting a job.

Problem of unemployment is unwilling joblessness. People who are either out of job or not having a regular job suffer great hardships. Unemployment has given rise to other problems also. Unemployment is on the increase. It is one of the greatest problems of our society. After the students come out of the schools and colleges, what should they do? This is a big question before them. There are no jobs for millions of youth that are pouring out of educational institutions every year. India is basically an agricultural country. Agriculture is the backbone of our economy. Agriculture in India is not developed enough to accommodate all the unemployed youth. The developed countries like the U.S., England, France, Germany, Italy, etc. also suffer from this problem, but it is more pronounced in India. There are millions of young men and women waiting and waiting for job opportunities. This chronic problem of unemployment is not confirmed to any particular class, segment or society. It is all pervading. There is massive unemployment among educated, well-trained and skilled people, and it is also there among semi-skilled and unskilled laborers, small and marginal farmers and workers. Then there is underemployment. The jobs being created have miserably failed to keep pace with the ever increasing number of job-seekers. It is a problem which presents a great challenge to leaders, thinkers, planners, economists, industrialists and educationists. This research paper throws the light on the major challenges facing by educated unemployed also what we have to change in our education system to that people can get employment after completion of their studies in their area of interest, so that they perform better for their own as well as for overall society devolvement.

CHAPTER

23

Use of IT in Promoting Education

RIZWAN ALAM

ABSTRACT

The future of India will be fashioned in the classroom. While India has made great strides in improving the education system but much still remains to be done. If you see the current scenario then you will find that there is a flood of advanced technology all over the globe but our education system is not benefiting due to the lack of information and knowledge of teachers, students and the administration. The students have their own restrictions, teachers have their own and the administration is also admitting the fact that the education system is really in a poor shape today. The goal of this paper is to outline how information technology can help to create an education system that is based on the principles of helping teachers, students and administration to be effective in what they do, improving the quality and relevance of teaching-learning process.

INTRODUCTION

Information Technology in Education, effects of the continuing developments in information technology (IT) on education. The pace of change brought about by new technologies has had a significant effect on the way people live, work, and play worldwide. New and emerging technologies challenge the traditional process of teaching and learning, and the way education is managed. Information technology, while an important area of study in its own right, is having a major impact across all curriculum areas. Easy worldwide communication provides instant access to a vast array of data, challenging assimilation and assessment skills. Rapid communication, plus increased access to IT in the home, at work, and in educational establishments, could mean that learning becomes a truly lifelong activity—an activity in which the pace of technological change forces constant evaluation of the learning process itself.

SIGNIFICANCE OF IT IN EDUCATION

Access to Variety of Learning Resources

In the era of technology. IT aids plenty of resources to enhance the teaching skills and learning ability. With the help of IT now it is easy to provide audio visual education. The learning resources are being widens and widen. Now with this vivid and vast technique as part of the IT curriculum, learners are encouraged to regard computers as tools to be used in all aspects of their studies. In particular, they need to make use of the new multimedia technologies to communicate ideas, describe projects, and order information in their work.

Immediacy to Information

IT has provided immediacy to education. Now in the year of computers and web networks the pace of imparting knowledge is very fast and one can be educated anywhere at any time. New IT has often been introduced into well-established patterns of working and living without radically altering them. For example, the traditional office, with secretaries working at keyboards and notes being written on paper and manually exchanged, has remained remarkably stable, even if personal computers have replaced typewriters.

Any Time Learning

Now in the year of computers and web networks the pace of imparting knowledge is very very fast and one can be educated. One can study whenever he will irrespective of whether it is day or night and irrespective of being in India or in US because of the boom in IT.

Collaborative Learning

Now IT has made it easy to study as well as teach in groups or in clusters. With online we can be unite together to do the desired task. Efficient postal systems, the telephone (fixed and mobile), and various recording and playback systems based on computer technology all have a part to play in educational broadcasting in the new millennium. The Internet and its Web sites are now familiar to many children in developed countries and among educational elites elsewhere, but it remains of little significance to very many more, who lack the most basic means for subsistence.

Multimedia Approach to Education

Audio-Visual Education, planning, preparation, and use of devices and materials that involve sight, sound, or both, for educational purposes. Among the devices used are still and motion pictures, filmstrips, television, transparencies, audiotapes, records, teaching machines, computers, and videodiscs. The growth of audio-visual education has reflected developments in both technology and learning theory.

Studies in the psychology of learning suggest that the use of audio-visuals in education has several advantages. All learning is based on perception, the process by which the senses gain information from the environment. The higher processes of memory and concept formation cannot occur without prior perception. People can attend to only a limited amount of information at a time; their selection and perception of information is influenced by past experiences. Researchers have found that, other conditions being equal, more information is taken in if it is received simultaneously in two modalities (vision and hearing, for example) rather than in a single modality. Furthermore, learning is enhanced when material is organized and that organization is evident to the student.

These findings suggest the value of audio-visuals in the educational process. They can facilitate perception of the most important features, can be carefully organized, and can require the student to use more than one modality.

Authentic and up-to-date Information

The information and data which are available on the net is purely correct and up-to-date.

Internet, a collection of computer networks that operate to common standards and enable the computers and the programs they run to communicate directly provides true and correct information.

Online Library

Internets support thousands of different kinds of operational and experimental services one of which is online library. We can get plenty of data on this online library.

As part of the IT curriculum, learners are encouraged to regard computers as tools to be used in all aspects of their studies. In particular, they need to make use of the new multimedia technologies to communicate ideas, describe projects, and order information in their work. This requires them to select the medium best suited to conveying their message, to structure information in a hierarchical manner, and to link together information to produce a multidimensional document.

Distance Learning

Distance Learning, method of learning at a distance rather than in a classroom. Late 20th-century communications technologies, in their most recent phases-multimedia and interactive, open up new possibilities, both individual and institutional, for an unprecedented expansion of home-based learning, much of it part-time. The term distance learning was coined within the context of a continuing communications revolution, largely replacing a hitherto confusing mixed nomenclature—home study, independent study, external study, and, most common, though restricted in pedagogic means, correspondence study. The convergence of increased demand for access to educational facilities and innovative communications technology has been increasingly exploited in face of criticisms that distance learning is an inadequate substitute for learning alongside others in formal institutions. A powerful incentive has been reduced costs per student. At the same time, students studying at home themselves save on travel time and other costs.

Whatever the reasoning, distance learning widens access for students unable for whatever reason (course availability, geographical remoteness, family circumstances, individual disability) to study alongside others. At the same time, it appeals to students who prefer learning at home. In addition, it appeals to organizers of professional and business education, providing an incentive to rethink the most effective way of communicating vital information.

Better Accesses to Children with Disabilities

Information technology has brought drastic changes in the life of disabled children. IT provides various software and technique to educate these poor peoples. Unless provided early with special training, people profoundly deaf from birth are incapable of learning to speak. Deafness from birth causes severe sensory deprivation, which can seriously affect a person's intellectual capacity or ability to learn. A child who sustains a hearing loss early in life may lack the language stimulation experienced by children who can hear. The critical period for neurological plasticity is up to age seven. Failure of acoustic sensory input during this period results in failure of formation of synaptic connections and, possibly, an irremediable situation for the child. A delay in learning language may cause a deaf child's academic progress to be slower than that of hearing children. The academic lag tends to be cumulative, so that a deaf adolescent may be four or more academic years behind his or her hearing peers. Deaf children who receive early language stimulation through sign language, however, generally achieve academically alongside their hearing peers.

The integration of information technology in teaching is a central matter in ensuring quality in the educational system. There are two equally important reasons for integrating information technology in teaching. Pupils must become familiar with the use of information technology, since all jobs in the society of the future will be dependent on it, and information technology must be used in teaching in order to improve its quality and make it more effective.

CONCLUSION

Instructors still need to direct student learning activities, but they must also put responsibility for learning on the students. It is going to be an uncomfortable, but worthwhile transition. The measure of success should not simply be test scores, but instead, increased attendance, attention and participation.

Once teachers see their students engaged and excited about learning and producing thoughtful work, they will find it easier to make the transition from actor to director.

In order to educate students to be life-long learners and successful contributors to the new global market, educators must change the way they teach and the way students learn. We need to remember that if we want to help students achieve a high level of competency and competitiveness, we have no choice but to make technology an integrated tool in the field of education. As being a student of computer science and information technology my vision is that youth should not develop the attitude of just swallowing the things and availing the benefits commercially developed inventions but they should involve themselves into the research and development and come up with some unexplored and undiscovered pinnacles of information technology. This will open the new dimensions for IT in the academic scenario.

CHAPTER

24

Impact of Prime Time Soap Operas on Rural Children

A Study in Maharashtra with Special Reference to Pune District

ROHIT C. PAWAR AND R. MADHAVI

INTRODUCTION

Hum Log was the first TV program aired in India; it was a story of a family comprising of three generations. It was urban, it was middle-class, and it was new, and till today, it, along with Buniyaad, is considered among the best-made Indian serials to be seen by an Indian audience. After the liberation of Indian markets, many TV channels enter into the Indian market and sole goal of these channels was profit. All the channels in order to capture the maximum eye balls (audience) stated producing the content which was mediocre in nature. It had faster and greater impact on society. In a democratic, secular and linguistically diverse country like India, television plays a significant role. But, Indian television is going through a mediocre phase as a majority of the shows, music videos and desi family dramas are showing regressive content. The majority of the income for a channel is generated through family dramas (Sass-bahoo programs). The content focuses on conflict between two women, extra marital affairs, violence with respect to property, etc. These programs are aired during prime time, i.e 7 p.m. to 9 p.m. target towards urban Indian middle class women.

Most of the Indians have a single TV set and TV viewing becomes a family activity. Small children are also exposed to such type of programs. Few research work say that on an average an Indian child is exposed to 18 hours of TV per week, i.e. almost 2.5 hours per day. In fact some parents use TV as a baby sitter. TV is used to keep small children engage. Children—who do not have the emotional or cognitive tools to evaluate what's being shown. Children start perusing the TV world as a real world or in other words we can say that they develop a wrong perception about real world. Hence, TV leads to developing wrong values for economic, social and cultural ends of the Rural Community. This also leads to some of the ill-effects like aggressive behavior, desensitize children to the effects of violence, and give the impression that the world is more dangerous than it really is. 70% of Indian population lives in rural areas but TV content never show rural life, all the content depicts urban life.

Rural India has been always deprived by government in terms of overall development. According to latest Reports by Ministry of Rural Development the people below poverty line have increased from 32% to 47% over the period of last five years. The prime reason for maximum poverty in rural India is high rate of Inflation. Lots of research is being done in the countries like USA and Europe, but very few such type of studies are being made in Indian context. The said Research will comment on the type of programs shown during the prime time and its impact on rural children with reference to wrong development of economic and social values. Also the policies adopted by the government and channels for such programs.

OBJECTIVES

- To know what type of programmes are telecasted during the prime time.
- To understand, what sort of world (Images, Language, Lifestyle) is created for children by these television programmers.
- To study the impact of TV programs on children in understanding the real world around them.
- To what extent is policy-makers and programme producers in Indian Television Industry are aware of rural children as their audience.

HYPOTHESES

- There is direct negative impact on children, they compare real world around them with TV world.
- There is a huge difference between lifestyle depicted on TV and real lifestyle in India.

CONSTRUCT

(1) Impact—Perception of children about the real world.
(2) Daily Soap—The family programs aired by the Marathi General Entertainment channels.
(3) Children—from the age group of 6 to 12.
(4) Rural Maharashtra—Making there living on or characteristic of farming.
(5) Prime time—6 to 10 p.m.

BRIEF BACKGROUND

In 1992, the government liberated its markets, opening them up to cable television. Five new channels belonging to the Hong Kong-based STAR TV gave Indians a fresh breath of life. MTV, STAR Plus, BBC, Prime Sports and STAR Chinese Channel were the 5 channels. Zee TV was the first private owned Indian channel to broadcast over cable. A few years later CNN, Discovery Channel, National Geographic Channel made its foray into India. Star expanded its bouquet introducing STAR World, STAR Sports, ESPN and STAR Gold. Regional channels flourished along with a multitude of Hindi channels and a few English channels. By 2001 HBO and History Channel were the other international channels to enter India. By 2001-03, other international channels such as Nickelodeon, Cartoon Network, VH1, Disney and Toon Disney came into foray. In 2003 news channels started to boom—NDTV, IBN, India TV, etc.

The Indian television business has some 70 million television homes, giving a viewing population of close to 400 million individuals. We have more 100 plus channels to choose from, it is a large market which has attracted many a channel from overseas. But the channels that attract eyeballs are—state owned broadcaster Doordrashan, Zee TV, Sony Entertainment, Star Plus, ESPN Star Sports, Sun TV, Raj TV, Eenadu TV, the local cable TV operator run pirated movie channel. The English and foreign language channels are niche players struggling to stay on their feet. English language channels dubbed in local languages are faring much better.

Television has been the most dynamic medium of the 21st century, because of so many channels, coming in there are lots of pressures and completion among the channels. The main two problems first is the contain or the software's that has to be developed for 24 hrs. and second one is to get the maximum TRPs (television rating points) to get maximum advertisement. Because of such pressures the quality of the programs has become bad; most of the softwares/programs are copy of the western program and to suit the advertising interest of the advertisers.

SIGNIFICANCE OF STUDY/RELEVANCE

On an average every Indian spends one and the half hour watching the television, if this is the case the content of this medium must be studied to understand its impact on its audience. Amongst the audience small children develop their perception about the real world by watching visuals on the TV, most of the women are housewifes, the only way to spend their time is TV and unfortunately children are also bombarded with same content.

Statement of Problem (Cements the Study is Going to make)

In India the most popular/the maximum watched program is "Sas Bhi Kabhi Bahoo thi" and "Kusum", such type of programs are biased on conflict between women for men and violence for the property. The characters, costume, make-up and location used in such programs are not real, they are more exaggerated and larger than life. Same is the case with advertisements, they are far from real people, i.e. all the characters, location, costume are urban-based and highlight western culture. 60% of the population live in rural India and agriculture is the main occupation but media always show western culture and larger than life visuals, rural India are almost absent

In most Asian countries, children under the age of 15 comprise around 30 per cent of the population. In these countries where the economies are growing rapidly, rampant commercialism has entered childrens media programming.

Some of the Relevant Facts about India

According to Census of India 2001, India had a population of 1,027 million, which is estimated to cross 1,600 million by 2050. During 1991-2001, India's population recorded a decadal growth rate of 21.3 per cent, slightly lower than the 23.9 percent recorded during 1981-91.

- About 30 per cent Indians live in urban areas.
- More than 15 per cent are 0-6 years of age.
- Children below 15 years of age constitute 36 per cent and those below age five about 12 per cent of the sample population.
- 38 per cent of rural and 31 per cent of urban population are below age 15.
- Those 60 years or older, account for eight per cent.

Above mentioned facts shows that more than 30% of the total population are children. Childhood days are considered important and crucial for the development of the child. On an average an Indian child is exposed to one and half hours of TV contain every day.

Children make perception about the real world from the kind of visuals he is exposed to. Soap operas are the major part of software used in general entertainment channels.

Hence, it's important to study the impact of such soap operas on small children, because they are going to be the future of India.

There are lots of studies conducted with respect to television but all the studies are related to following issues—Woman in TV, Children in TV, Sex on TV and Violence in TV. But rarely any studies are done in Indian context.

The issue has become more important with new kind of TV programs like reality show, etc. Hence the issue is of contempory importance and relevant.

SOME OF THE FACTS ABOUT DEPRIVED RURAL INDIA

In order to understand rural children it's important to understand rural India. Rural India has been constantly ignored by the government. Politics in India is more urban centric, because government is more interested to protect the interest of rich industrialist. Indian media has always been urban centric has never highlighted the issued which are of concern to rural India, media is also owned and dominated by politicians. With the 9% annual growth rate India is fastest growing nation of the world. But this is only one side of the coin, the fact is rich are getting richer and poor are getting poorer. There no balance growth. Urban bourgeois have no concerns about rural India because they are enjoying all the facilities of development and are ignorant about the facts of rural India. Majority of the population of India is rural. Moreever 40% of the children in India belong to rural India. About 75% of the Indian population lives in rural areas and about 80% of this population is dependent on agriculture for its livelihood. Agriculture accounts for about 37% of the national income. Since our research is mainly focused on rural children, it's important to understand rural India. Following are the key features or highlights of rural India, which are being brought forward by studying following reports produced by credible organization.

(1) World Development Report, 2010,
(2) Unisef child development Report, 2009,
(3) Rural Development Report, 2010 (by Govt. of India),
(4) Sexsena Rural Development Repor 2011 (by Govt. of India), and
(5) Report of Ministry of Rural Development, 2009.

Illiteracy

Schooling is made compulsory till the age of 14 by Indian government Bill of Right to education was passed in the year 2010 by Congress government. According to one the UNISEF reports in the year 2008, 20 per cent of rural children aged 6 to 14 are still not in school. Several problems persist; issues of 'social distance' arising out of caste, class and gender differences deny children equal opportunities. Schools available are mostly Government schools. These schools lack in infrastructural facilities like toilets, benches, roofs, drinking water facilities, etc. Teachers are poorly paid hence it doesn't become an attractive career. Student to teacher ratio is 1:60 which is very high as compare to all the countries. This affects the quality of teaching. Hence, many poor children prefer to work, then go to school. Education has been made free and compulsory by passing 'Right to Education Act, 2010', but facilities are not provided to implement the law.

Malnutrition

Between the year 2004 and 2008 due to high inflation cost of cost of all necessary goods went up by 62%. Wheat and rice became unaffordable to many of the rural Indians. 50% of the childhoods deaths are attributed to malnutrition. 47% of the rural children are under weight. Similar kind of facts is also applicable to female. People below poverty line are having increased. Aid provided by the government is not able reach to poor because of high corruption in the democratic Indian government.

Issue of Child Labour

Extreme poverty and bad school education of rural India leaves poor children no option but to work. This unique feature of rural India makes our country, the country with highest number of child laborers in the world. With an estimated 12.6 million rural children engaged in hazardous occupations.With the heavy pressures from international community and UNICEF, Indian government has passed the law of banning child labor, but law remains only on paper.

Caste System

Untouchables and higher and lower caste system still remains in rural India. 99% of bonded laborers belong to backward caste. 60% of the rural population constitutes of backward cast people. Lower caste people are deprived to have access of developmental facilities. Places in the rural village where backward class people stay, lack in the facilities of schools, roads, electricity, etc. Most of the upper caste people have migrated to urban cities of India, as rural India is less developed. This caste system has hampered the growth of rural India. Villages of Maharashtra are formed on the basic of caste system called "Balutedar" people from different caste and community and caste get the place to stay and participate in the administration on the basics of his caste system.

Burden of Indebtedness Leading to Suicide

Though agriculture is the main occupation of India. And it contributes to 23% of national GDP. But the fact is 90% of the farmers in debt with heavy borrowings. On an average 16500 farmers commit suicide every year. Maharashtra state rank 1st for maximum farmers committing suicide. Majority of farmers are surveying only because of subsidies provided by the government on bank borrowings. Hence, farmers committing suicide is very common in the state of Maharashtra. The burden of indebtedness in rural India is great, and falls mainly on the households of rural working people. The exploitation of this group in the credit market is one of the most pervasive and persistent features of rural life in India, and despite major structural changes in credit institutions and forms of rural credit in the post-Independence period, Darling's statement (1925), that "the Indian peasant is born in debt, lives in debt and bequeaths debt," still remains true for the great majority of working households in the countryside.

Unemployment

90% of Indian agriculture depends on monsoon rains. From the past 15 years irregularities and delay in Monsoon rains is observed and reasons are associated with deforestation and global warming. This makes farming activity possible only for 4 to 6 months, rest of month farmers have nothing to do. Lack of industries and extreme poverty in rural India leads to lower payment capacity of the employers, which lead to maximum encouragement of child labor. 72% of rural youth are unemployed which is the prime reason for malnutrition of rural India.

The list drawbacks in rural India could be endless, there has been no development since Independence. The fact is people below poverty line are increasing and people are dying with hunger. The basic infrastructural facilities like roads, schools, hospitals, etc. are missing. The spend by the government doesn't reach to the rural Indians because of heavy corruption

Indeed majority of the children who grow with above mentioned features are extremely poor and week. Considering these children as future of India it important to know there perception of reality which are unknowingly manipulated by TV daily soap opera.

THE FUNCTIONING OF TV CHANNELS/ PROGRAM PRODUCERS IN INDIA

The major problem of broadcasting companies in India is red tape and corruption involved in getting a broadcast licenses. Deals regarding broadcasting rights are never transparent and open to public. The broadcasting companies are forced for under table deals, which ads on to the cost of functioning of the channels. Because of heavy investments channels have to archive huge turnover targets.

These TV channels depend on TRP (TV Rating point) data, for the kind of programs they produce.TRP fingers determine the popularity of a program, higher the TRP ratings more the popularity of the program and lower the TRP ratings less is the popularity of the program. Popularity means more eye balls are watching the programs, this helps is getting more advertisements and also could charge more for the same. Major revenue contribution to the TV Channels is through advertisements. Hence, advertisement rates and the decision to advertise depend upon the TRP ratings. TAM India is the company in India who provides TRP data. This company not only provides the TRP data but they also provide other detailed information like Who watch the programs?, Which geographical areas your programs popular, etc.

PRIVATE TV RATING SYSTEM OF PRIVATE BROADCASTERS

Television Rating Points—TRP is the criterion that indicates the popularity of a channel or programme and this data is very useful for the advertisers. In a highly clustered market targeting audiences it is very problematic because in the market there are numerous channels with a variety of programmes catering round the clock to a vast and scattered population. Television ratings provide information about the viewers' TV watching habits and the socio-economic background of the audience. This helps advertisers and corporate media planners in selecting the right media at the right time.

Presently, TAM India (Television Audience Measurement) is the only electronic rating agency functioning in India. TAM uses two methodologies for calculating TRP. First is frequency monitoring, in which 'people meters' are installed in sample homes and these electronic gadgets continuously record data about the channel watched by the family members. 'People meter' is costly equipment, which is imported from abroad. It reads the frequencies of channels, which are later, decoded into the name of the channels and the agency prepares a national data on the basis of its sample homes readings.

DRAWBACK IN THE TAM TECHNIQUE

(1) As cable operators frequently change the frequencies of the different channels before sending signals to the

homes. It may be very misleading to read a channel according to a particular frequency even if the down linking frequency is same all over India.

(2) It is the company's policy to maintained secrecy about the installation of people meters. Some sources say that there are only 5000 approx. people meters are installed in India to judge more than a billion populations with 90% of them having access to TV.

(3) It's the policy decision of the company that towns which have population of more than 1 lakh will be only considered for installation of people meter and data collection. 80% of the Indian villages have the population of less than 1000, moreover there are very few villages don't have population of more than 3000. Considering this we can conclude that TAM rating system does not consider rural India as the target audience and data collected is more urban centric.

TRPS IMPACT ON DEVELOPING TV CONTENT

(1) Since the popularity of the program is judged by collecting data only from urban cities ignoring the 60% of the rural population.

(2) The scripts, language and culture of the programs is more urban centric. Even if the program has rural content it is depicted in more stereotypical way to suit urban requirements.

(3) Children as an audience are entirely ignored by the general entertainment channels.

(4) Prime time programs of general entertainment channels are more focused on women. Because most of the product advertisements are targeted towards women.

(5) In Prime time TV programs content revolves more around issue of Love, disputes over property and conflict between women. Because such content captures more interest of women.

STUDY AREA : MAHARASHTRA, PUNE DISTRICT

About Maharashtra

The state is highly urbanized—40 per cent of the population lives in cities and majority stay in rural areas. Mumbai, the capital of Maharashtra is also called as the Business Capital of India is the industrial hub of the state. Major industries of Maharashtra are textiles, automobiles and chemicals, etc.

According to the census 2001, the population of Maharashtra was 96,752,247 in the 12th hour of March. The population of the state is the second in the country after Uttar Pradesh and ranks 12th in the worldwide rankings of most populated states of the world. In the census 2001, it was seen that there was an improvement in the literacy rate from 64.87% to 77.27%. Maximum number of the population in Maharashtra is Marathi speaking, which amounts to a whopping 62,481,681 according to the census. Marathi is the state language, and the most commonly used language also. The other languages used by the people are Hindi, Gujarati and English. Ahirani language is spoken by a minor population.

Maharashtra is a state with Hindu majority who form 80.2% of the population. Muslims, Buddhists, Jains and Christians are the other religion who constitute 10.6%, 6% and 1% respectively.

Population Demographics

- Population Density: 322.5 inhabitants per square km
- Male Population: 50.3 million
- Female Population: 46.4 million
- Urban Population: 42.4%
- Sex Ratio: 922 females to 1000 males
- Literacy Rate: 77.27%
- Male Literacy Rate: 86.2%
- Female Literacy Rate: 67.5%
- Decadal Growth Rate: 22.57%

Pune District

Pune is well known as the 'Queen of Deccan' due to its

scenic beauty and rich natural resources. Besides, it is famous for its religious and historical places. Pune city is known on the world map beacuase of its educational, research and development institutions. The district also has an importance as an important military base. Pune is the most industrialized district in western Maharashtra and a famous IT hub in the country.

Pune is a developed city and is a well known IT hub but only three Talukas are developed, i.e except Haveli, Mulshi, and Khed rest of all the 10 Talukas are rural and underdeveloped. Hence, for the said research a sample of 180 childern was selected from Bhor Taluka. The data has been collected from three schools from village called Velu, Shinde Wadi, Kalevde in response to the questioner was prepared to satisfy the objectives of our research. The questionnaire was prepared and got filled from the children for the age group 6 to 14.

RESEARCH METHODOLOGY

Many research in India and abroad have shown that children undergo negative impact of viewing violent programs and the programs made with commercial intent. The issue was highlighted in 1987 with a book by Mira Aghi and Binod Agrawal. 'Television and the Indian Child' which was published by UNICEF. In this book clearly indicated that Children television viewing remained a "family activity" under the parents shadow.

With reference to this we conducted a convenient sample survey with the sample of 180 participants from Bhor taluka. The data was collected from three schools from village called Velu, Shinde Wadi, Kalevde in response to the questioner which was prepared to satisfy the objectives of our research. The questionnaire was prepared and got filled from the children for the age group 6 to 14.

Following are the key features of the sample analysed:

(1) The average annual income of families is Rs. 1 lakh approx.

(2) The source of their family income is only through Agriculture.
(3) All have a TV sets or access to TV.
(4) All the schools are Zilla Parishad Schools (Govt. Schools) because these are the only schools available in the rural India. Schools are available in the village is till 7th standard. Hence all the participants are below age of 15.

DATA ANALYZED

Following are the key findings of the data analyzed with reference to each question asked in the questionnaire. The data has been analysed with the help of SPSS computer based software programme. The data may vary 2% to 3% in producing the conclusions because of the missing data. (which will be rounded-off using statistical technique)

(1) Percentage of Male to Female

		Percent	*Valid Percent*	*Cumulative Percent*
Valid	Male	50.0	51.2	51.2
	Female	47.6	48.8	100.0
	Total	97.6	100.0	
Missing	System	2.4		
Total		100.0		

To avoid gender bias in our findings, we have tried to keep male to female ratio in the sample of equal proportion. Hence 51% of male and 48% of females are considered.

(2) What Kind of Age Group was Analysed?

The maximum respondents are from the age group of 10 to 12, this age group has a better capacity to read, understand and fill the questionnaire. Children belonging to the age group from 13 to 15 were poor in the attendance to schools. Male

		Percent	*Valid Percent*	*Cumulative Percent*
Valid	9	6.0	6.0	6.0
	10	27.4	27.7	33.7
	11	27.4	27.7	61.4
	12	21.4	21.7	83.1
	13	8.3	8.4	91.6
	14	6.0	6.0	97.6
	15	2.4	2.4	100.0
	Total	98.8	100.0	
Missing	System	1.2		
Total		100.0		

children prefer to work in fields and hotels, while female children prefer to do household work. Moreover in rural schools teachers are insufficient in number to teach. Yet we have managed to get 18% of questionnaires filed from the age group of 13 to 15.

Children below the age 9 find difficulty in understanding and answering the questionnaire. Hence, different method of data collection like focused group discussion could be applied to study this age group.

(3) Which Kind of TV Connection do you have?

		Percent	*Valid Percent*	*Cumulative Percent*
Valid	DD	32.1	34.2	34.2
	Cable	13.1	13.9	48.1
	DTH	48.8	51.9	100.0
	Total	94.0	100.0	
Missing	System	6.0		
Total		100.0		

(a) The above mentioned data clearly reflects that rural people of Pune prefer DTH connection to receive the satellite signals for TV. Cable networks have poor distribution network in rural Pune, because of less population and poor accountability of customers; the cable network owners are unable to provide good service. Hence, DTH wins over cable connection.

(b) Majority of the families in village are joint families, the families which are big can afford a DTH connection. But 32% of families have only DD connection i.e. free to air government channels. This significant percentage also indicates either of the two: (i) rural families don't want to pay extra for entertainment, and (ii) rural families cannot afford a cable or DTH connection, hence they have only DD connection.

(4) Which Channel do you Like?

Preference I

		Percent	*Valid Percent*	*Cumulative Percent*
Valid	DD	13.1	14.5	14.5
	Zee Takies	10.7	11.8	26.3
	Star Pravaha	15.5	17.1	43.4
	Zee Marathi	3.6	3.9	47.4
	Zee Tv	3.6	3.9	51.3
	Nick	2.4	2.6	53.9
	Hungama	7.1	7.9	61.8
	Pogo	3.6	3.9	65.8
	Cartoon Network	3.6	3.9	69.7
	Max	4.8	5.3	75.0
	Star Plus	4.8	5.3	80.3
	Sony	11.9	13.2	93.4
	Star Cricket	4.8	5.3	98.7
	Dicovery	1.2	1.3	100.0
	Total	90.5	100.0	
Missing	System	9.5		
Total		100.0		

(a) Findings clearly revel that children like to see General entertainment channel more over children Channels like Cartoon Network, Hangama, Nick, etc.
(b) Children like regional channel (Marathi) more than national channels (Hindi).
(c) Significant number of children like to watch movie channels over other channels, 11% of children like Zee Takies which a movie channel, which broadcasts old Marathi family drama movies.
(d) Star Pravaha is the most liked TV channel, which is famous for family drama during the prime time.

(5) Which Channel do you Like? (Gender-based Classification)

7 * 3 Gender Cross-tabulation

	Channels	*3 Gender*		*Total (%)*
		Male (%)	*Female (%)*	
7	DD	6	5	11
	Zee Takies	2	7	9
	Star Pravaha	3	11	14
	Zee Marathi	0	3	3
	Zee Tv	2	1	3
	Nick	1	1	2
	Hungama	6	0	6
	Pogo	3	0	3
	Cartoon Network	2	1	3
	Max	3	1	4
	Star Plus	0	4	4
	Sony	5	5	10
	Star Cricket	4	0	4
	Dicovery	1	0	1
Total (%)		37	39	76

The figures clearly indicate the difference in likings of the two genders.

Boys like DD, Cricket, Hungama, Pogo and Sony. Likings of boys is spared over variety of channels. They like sports and Adventure orientated channels.

Girls like DD, Star Pravaha, and StarPlus. Star television is known for its tearful family drama programs; hence we could say that little girls of this country like to see tears on TV.

Significant number of sample has only DD connection to receive satellite signals, so they don't have anything to watch other than DD. Hence DD seems to be popular in both genders.

(6) Which Program Children Like to Watch?

Prefrence I

		Percent	*Valid Percent*	*Cumulative Percent*
Valid	mere desh ki baiti	1.2	1.3	1.3
	Maan Udhan warria che	15.5	16.7	
	Olakh	1.2	1.3	19.2
	Jhasiki Ki Rani	9.5	10.3	29.5
	Dum dama dum	4.8	5.1	34.6
	Nanhi si beti meri ladli	7.1	7.7	42.3
	Pavitra Rista	6.0	6.4	48.7
	Char divas sasu che	3.6	3.8	52.6
	Pratidnya	1.2	1.3	53.8
	Comedy Express	1.2	1.3	55.1
	Pokeman	1.2	1.3	56.4
	Tujbin Sakhyare	1.2	1.3	57.7
	Ware ware	2.4	2.6	60.3
	Tere liye	2.4	2.6	62.8
	Bhagyalaximi	1.2	1.3	64.1
	Pinjara	1.2	1.3	65.4
	Krishnabehan Khakra wale	1.2	1.3	66.7
	Bidaai	1.2	1.3	67.9
	CID	17.9	19.2	87.2

	Power Ranjers	1.2	1.3	88.5
	Gita	1.2	1.3	89.7
	Chota Bhim	7.1	7.7	97.4
	Amchi mati amchi mansa	1.2	1.3	98.7
	Per man	1.2	1.3	100.0
	Total	92.9	100.0	
Missing	System	7.1		
Total		100.0		

Mana Udhan Wariache (love Ttringle/Family Darama) and CID (Crime) are the most popular programess. Though significant number of children have only DD connections children like the programs on other channels, they watch those programes at their friends and relatives place. Nahani si beti mare ladly is the 4th ranked popular programme of Doodarshan.

(7) Which Programme do You Like? (Gernder-based analysis)

Cross-tabulation Gender-based

Channels		*4 Gender*		*Total*
		Male	*Female*	
(1)	*(2)*	*(3)*	*(4)*	*(5)*
12 which evening programms. do.u.like	Mere desh ki baiti	1	0	1
	Maan Udhan warria che	7	6	13
	Olakh	1	0	1
	Jhasi ki Rani	5	3	8
	Dum dama dum	0	4	4
	Nanhi si beti meri ladli	2	4	6
	Pavitra Rista	1	4	5

(Contd.)

TABLE (*Contd.*)

(1)	(2)	(3)	(4)	(5)
	Char divas sasu che	1	2	3
	Pratidnya	0	1	1
	Comedy Express	0	1	1
	Pokeman	1	0	1
	Tujbin Sakhyare	1	0	1
	Ware ware	2	0	2
	Tere liye	0	2	2
	Bhagyalaximi	0	1	1
	Pinjara	0	1	1
	Krishnabehan Khakra wale	0	1	1
	Bidaai	0	1	1
	CID	10	5	15
	Power Ranjers	1	0	1
	Gita	0	1	1
	Chota Bhim	4	2	6
	Amchi mati amchi mansa	1	0	1
	Per man	1	0	1
Total		39	39	78

Data clearly reflects the contrast in likings of two Genders.

Boys like adventure and crime-based programmes and most like once are CID, Chota Bhim, etc.

Girls hate adventures and stick to family Drama and most like once are CID, Pavitra Rista, Chadivas sasu che, etc.

Surprisingly for the programme Man Udhan Waria Che (love tringle and family drama) both boys and girls have expressed almost equal likings.

(8) With Whom do you Watch TV for Maximum Time? (In General)

Data clearly shows that in general childen watch TV with their family members.

		Percent	Valid Percent	Cumulative Percent
Valid	Family	82.1	85.2	85.2
	Friends	7.1	7.4	92.6
	Alone	7.1	7.4	100.0
	Total	96.4	100.0	
Missing	System	3.6		
Total		100.0		

(9) Which Programme Children Watch during the Prime Time 7.30 to 9.30 ?

Which evening prime time programs do you like?

		Frequency	*Percent*	*Valid Percent*	*Cumulative Percent*
(1)	*(2)*	*(3)*	*(4)*	*(5)*	*(6)*
Valid	Maan Udhan warria che	12	14.3	16.7	16.7
	Olakh	7	8.3	9.7	26.4
	Jhasiki Ki Rani	5	6.0	6.9	33.3
	Dum dama dum	5	6.0	6.9	40.3
	Nanhi si beti meri ladli	6	7.1	8.3	48.6
	Kyo ki jina esi ka nam hai	1	1.2	1.4	50.0
	Dhina din Dha	3	3.6	4.2	54.2
	Pavitra Rista	2	2.4	2.8	56.9
	Char divas sasu che	7	8.3	9.7	66.7
	Ye dil ke riste	1	1.2	1.4	68.1
	Swapna chya Palikade	1	1.2	1.4	69.4
	Tujbin Sakhyare	2	2.4	2.8	72.2
	Ware ware	2	2.4	2.8	75.0
	Khel mandla	2	2.4	2.8	77.8
	Tere liye	1	1.2	1.4	79.2
	Geet	1	1.2	1.4	80.6

(*Contd.*)

TABLE (*Contd.*)

(1)	*(2)*	*(3)*	*(4)*	*(5)*	*(6)*
	Bhagyalaximi	2	2.4	2.8	83.3
	Krishnabehan Khakra wale	1	1.2	1.4	84.7
	Zunjj	1	1.2	1.4	86.1
	CID	7	8.3	9.7	95.8
	Power Ranjers	1	1.2	1.4	97.2
	Amchi mati amchi mansa	1	1.2	1.4	98.6
	Kunku	1	1.2	1.4	100.0
	Total	72	85.7	100.0	
Missing	System	12	14.3		
Total		84	100.0		

Prime time is the only time when entire family comes together. Parents after hard work on the fields return home in the evening time. TV remains the only source of entertainment which is cheap and easily available. Generally families have their dinner while watching TV, in other words, children consume TV while consuming food. The discipline and timings for dinner are followed because of TV, children and parents arrive in time not only for dinner but to watch their favourite programes. For mothers TV acts as a baby sitter, children get engage in the TV programme and unconsciously consumes food. It is an ironical fact that members of the family are not connected by face to face conversation, but they are connected by TV. These connections are strongly established during the prime time. Since maximum families are glued to TV during prime time, advertising to be made during this prime time is expensive and maximum. This time generates maximum revenue for general entertainment channels, hence, makers of the prime time programme also take extra efforts to get maximum eyeballs. With reference to this explanation and in the light of our objectives, it's extremely important to know what kind of programmes are specifically liked by the children to understand the impact.

The data analysed clearly says that the programmes liked by the children and prime time programmes which they watch are same. The most like and most watched programme during the prime time is Mana Udhan Waria Che. Other Programms like Nahanisi Bayti Meiri Ladly (DD) and CID (Sony) are ranked after this.

(10) With Whom do you Watch Prime Time Programmes?

		Percent	*Valid Percent*	*Cumulative Percent*
Valid	Family	84.5	88.8	88.8
	Friends	6.0	6.2	95.0
	Alone	4.8	5.0	100.0
	Total	95.2	100.0	
Missing	System	4.8		
Total		100.0		

In rural India we still have the culture of joint families. Agriculture being the main occupation joint family system had its own benefits. TV when started in India it started as community TV, i.e. one TV was enough for one community, community people weather from a colony or village used to sit around the TV sets to view the programmes. Doordarshan was the only channel available and it used to broadcast programme only for 2 hours, morning and evening. Later on by the late 90s because of globalization and Industrialization there was a significant gowth in per capita income of the country and TV became a household product. Unlike western countries consumption of TV still remains a family activity if not a community activity. In western countries a single family may have multiple TV sets. But in India both in rural and urban places one TV in one house is a common practice.

With reference to previous data and this data we could concluded that maximum times children watch TV programme during prime time along with their families.

(11) Who Takes the Decision of which Program to see during the Prime-time?

		Percent	*Valid Percent*	*Cumulative Percent*
Valid	Mother	21.4	24.0	24.0
	Father	17.9	20.0	44.0
	Big brother	19.0	21.3	65.3
	Big sister	15.5	17.3	82.7
	Young sister	4.8	5.3	88.0
	Young brother	6.0	6.7	94.7
	Grand mother	1.2	1.2	1.3
	Your Self	1.3	96.0	
	Grand father	3.6	4.0	100.0
	Total	89.3	100.0	
Missing	System	10.7		
Total		100.0		

Majority of time children watch TV with their parents/ Family members and the above mentioned data clearly show that spouses dominate TV. Surprisingly Mothers have maximum share in dominance than Fathers. This observation contrasts with the male dominated rural society. May its true that women are the Boss in the home. Big brother and big sisters also exercise substantial dominance for the Programme to be watched during the prime time.

We could easily conclude that children have no control over the TV programme they watch.

Programmes which they watch and like are essentially the programme which elder members of the family like and see. Children are constantly exposed to the programmes which are not made for them, these programmes are made for elders and requires mature cognitive abilities. Hence, there could be a chance of negative impact.

(12) Who Controls the Remote while Watching Prime-time Programs?

		Percent	*Valid Percent*	*Cumulative Percent*
Valid	Mother	21.4	24.0	24.0
	Father	17.9	20.0	44.0
	Big brother	19.0	21.3	65.3
	Big sister	15.5	17.3	82.7
	Young sister	4.8	5.3	88.0
	Young brother	6.0	6.7	94.7
	Grand mother	1.2	1.3	96.0
	Grand father	3.6	4.0	100.0
	Total	89.3	100.0	
Missing	System	10.7		
Total		100.0		

While watching the programme also children don't have any chance to change the programme during the commercial brake. Control on remote means control on programme viewing pattern. The above mentioned data shows maximum control of mothers followed by fathers. Hence, we can conclude that child has no option but to see the programes which elder members of the family want them to see. This lives children with no choice.

(13) Do You Like Watching Prime-time Programmes?

		Percent	*Valid Percent*	*Cumulative Percent*
Valid	Yes	88.1	97.4	97.4
	No	2.4	2.6	100.0
	Total	90.5	100.0	
Missing	System	9.5		
Total		100.0		

In the previous observation we have concluded that programmes are bombarded to them and they have no choice but to watch that program. Hence, there was a need to ask specifically whether they like those prime time programmes and undoubtedly majority of them have said Yes.

(14) Which Prime-time Programme do you like?

24 Which Evening Programmes do you like?

		Frequency	*Percent*	*Valid Percent*	*Cumulative Percent*
Valid	Mere desh ki baiti	1	1.2	1.4	1.4
	Maan Udhan warria che	12	14.3	16.9	18.3
	Olakh	4	4.8	5.6	23.9
	Jhasiki Ki Rani	1	1.2	1.4	25.4
	Dum dama dum	5	6.0	7.0	32.4
	Nanhi si beti meri ladli	7	8.3	9.9	42.3
	Dhina din Dha	1	1.2	1.4	43.7
	Pavitra Rista	4	4.8	5.6	49.3
	Char divas sasu che	6	7.1	8.5	57.7
	Pratidnya	1	1.2	1.4	59.2
	Haya Gogirvanya Gharat	1	1.2	1.4	60.6
	Rab Ne Milai Jodi	1	1.2	1.4	62.0
	Veha Mai Ghar Ghar	1	1.2	1.4	63.4
	Tujbin Sakhyare	7	8.3	9.9	73.2
	Ware Ware	2	2.4	2.8	76.1
	Jina esi ka nam hai	1	1.2	1.4	77.5
	Tere liye	1	1.2	1.4	78.9
	Geet	1	1.2	1.4	80.3
	Krishnabehan Khakra wale	1	1.2	1.4	81.7
	CID	8	9.5	11.3	93.0
	Power Ranjers	1	1.2	1.4	94.4
	Chota Bhim	2	2.4	2.8	97.2
	Amchi mati amchi mansa	1	1.2	1.4	98.6
	Kunku	1	1.2	1.4	100.0
	Total	71	84.5	100.0	
Missing	System	13	15.5		
Total		84	100.0		

We specifically we need to ask this question because there is huge difference in programme watching and liking. If there is a difference in their likings and actual programmes they watch we could conclude that children forced to watch certain programes. But the observations show that programmes they watch and like are same. The most liked programme is Man Udhan Waria Che of the channel Star Pravaha, second most liked programme is CID of Sony TV, third most like programme is Nahanni Se Beati Mari ladly. Char Divas Sasu Che of ETV Marathi is also liked substantially. Out of the four programmes liked three are family drama and one is crime thriller. The most liked programme is Man Udhan Waria Che, is a combination of love triangle and has intense family drama. With this feedback we can say that children like to see family conflict and love drama during the prime time.

(15) What do you like to see in the Evening?

		Percent	*Valid Percent*	*Cumulative Percent*
Valid	Dance	6.0	11.1	11.1
	Comedy	31.0	57.8	68.9
	Action/fight	16.7	1	31.1
	Family Drama	2.5	100.0	
	Total	53.6	100.0	
Missing	System	46.4		
Total		100.0		

In the earlier observations though the genre of programme which children have claim to be liked maximum is Family Drama. Family drama programs are supposed to be based on internal conflict of family. Generally, a conflict is set-up between two women or a woman against a family. The simple formula is the conflict between two families. A strong attempt is made to make programs more tearful by introducing strong verbal and physical violence. Considering the features of family drama its surprising to know that maximum children like to see comic elements in the programme

Children are not able to make distension between the genres. Actually children like to see comedy genre but viewing and TV set is entirely controlled by parents, they have to see what their parents want to. This data bring out the fact that children view the programs simply because their parents see it, moreever prime time is a dinner time and entire family comes together to consume TV and food. Children have no way to escape, unknowingly they are exposed to the programmes which are not made for them. Children watch the TV programmes as a ritual or custom. Small children don't have ability to understand complex human relations and larger than life visuals bombarded by TV on them.

Further research questions help us to understand the impact of TV on children.

(15a) What do you like to see on TV? (Cross-tabulation with Gender)

29 What.do.u.like.in.evening programes*
3 Gender Cross-tabulation

What do u like to see?		*3 Gender*		*Total*
		Male	*Female*	
	Dance	3	2	5
	Comedy	16	10	26
	Action/fight	11	3	14
Total		30	15	45

Cross-tabulation clearly shows that boys like action and girls stick comedy, Although boys have reflected their likings to both action and comedy.

We are not sure the relevance of the said cross-tabulation, because we have already discovered that children don't like to see programs which have family drama. They see and remember only the part which has comedy and action.

(16) Can You Recall the Story of Evening Programes ?

		Percent	*Valid Percent*	*Cumulative Percent*
Valid	Yes	19.0	21.1	21.1
	No	71.4	78.9	100.0
	Total	90.5	100.0	
Missing	System	9.5		
Total		100.0		

With the previous findings we have made it is being discovered that children want to see different genre of programme, but because the TV is entirely controlled by the elder members of the family. Nether children have a clear understanding and maturity about different types of programmes for them watching certain programmes has become a routine or a custom. Since children watch prime time programmes unwillingly, majority of children are not able to recall the story.

(17) Which Characters do you like?

34 which.Ch.do.u.like

		Frequency	*Percent*	*Valid Percent*	*Cumulative Percent*
(1)	*(2)*	*(3)*	*(4)*	*(5)*	*(6)*
Valid	Salman Khan	13	15.5	21.7	21.7
	Guddi	1	1.2	1.7	23.3
	Ashwarya	4	4.8	6.7	30.0
	Rishab	1	1.2	1.7	31.7
	Chendari	1	1.2	1.7	33.3
	Hritik	1	1.2	1.7	35.0
	Surya	5	6.0	8.3	43.3

(Contd.)

TABLE (Contd.)

(1)	(2)	(3)	(4)	(5)	(6)
	Jhon shinha	3	3.6	5.0	48.3
	Khali	6	7.1	10.0	58.3
	Madhuri Dikshit	1	1.2	1.7	60.0
	Rani Mukherjee	8	9.5	13.3	73.3
	Radhika	1	1.2	1.7	75.0
	Gauri	1	1.2	1.7	76.7
	Abhijeet	1	1.2	1.7	78.3
	Muskan	1	1.2	1.7	80.0
	Sharuk Khan	4	4.8	6.7	86.7
	Akshay Kumar	2	2.4	3.3	90.0
	Prinyanka	1	1.2	1.7	91.7
	Anurag	1	1.2	1.7	93.3
	Daya	4	4.8	6.7	100.0
	Total	60	71.4	100.0	
Missing	System	24	28.6		
Total		84	100.0		

The findings of this data endorse our previous findings that children watch prime time soap operas as a custom. They are not actually involved with the programme to recall the name of the Characters they like. Majority of the children have given the names of Popular Bollywood actors and actresses, very few of them could recall the names of the TV actor.

Children

(18) Why do you like a Character?

Majority of children have recalled only the comic nature and situation of the character. Very few could recall the characters to the actual situation. Children also like action and magic.

		Percent	*Valid Percent*	*Cumulative Percent*
Valid		71.4	71.4	71.4
	A girl from poor family is married to a rich family.	1.2	1.2	72.6
	because she likes nikhil and chlenges her love	1.2	1.2	73.8
	because she want to be a CID	1.2	1.2	75.0
	Bhenji is the ch I like	1.2	1.2	76.2
	Comedy	1.2	1.2	77.4
	Comedy and fighting	3.6	3.6	81.0
	he does comedy	1.2	1.2	82.1
	In tuj bin sakhya re the intence love between Radhika and Rishab	1.2	1.2	83.3
	Kirshnabhen	1.2	1.2	84.5
	Krishnabhen teaches good moral	6.0	6.0	90.5
	like forgiving	1.2	1.2	91.7
	Like omega rengers and red rengers	1.2	1.2	92.9
	like to see Akshay Kumar fighting	2.4	2.4	95.2
	like to to see body of Salman	1.2	1.2	96.4
	likes magic fairy of giigily appa.	1.2	1.2	97.6
	likes niraja, because she talks a lot and wares good cloths, she dances and shouts	1.2	1.2	98.8
	Mithun	1.2	1.2	100.0
Total		100.0	100.0	

Surprisingly the reasons and situation given by the children for liking a particular character does not resemble to prime time soap operas they watch.

(18) Which Incidence of the Programme do you Remember Now?

		Percent	*Valid Percent*	*Cumulative Percent*
Valid		73.8	73.8	73.8
	CID	1.2	1.2	75.0
	I recall a song dupatta tere lal rang ka.	1.2	1.2	76.2
	Like Daya of CID and like to See amitab bachan.	1.2	1.2	77.4
	like nannhi si bate	1.2	1.2	78.6
	Mahacinema	1.2	1.2	79.8
	Man udhan	1.2	1.2	81.0
	Man udhan wari che when famili is haveing food, gauri is told to have food but niraja comes.	1.2	1.2	82.1
	Nana and Nani have came to visit Guddi and request her to ware sari, but she cannot ware it	7.1	7.1	89.3
	Poor mother struggles to keep their children happy	1.2	1.2	90.5
	Remembers the song, Duppata tere no rang ka, has re tera dil magta	1.2	1.2	91.7
	Songs	1.2	1.2	92.9
	Thuj ben shakhay re	1.2	1.2	94.0
	Vivek go up on big building, and get into a well having no steps	2.4	2.4	96.4
	What to be police/remebers amitab bachan	2.4	2.4	98.8
	when nikhil is going to office, nirija call him on the taress and tell not to marry gauri	1.2	1.2	100.0
Total		100.0	100.0	

Children recalled the situation which have comic or adventure situation.

The results clearly say that they are not able to recall family-drama situations from the programe they watch. They can recall only comic situations from the prime-time programes they watch maximum. Hence we could say that children remember the situations they like. Prime time programmes they watch as ritual only.

(19) Which Incidence you will like to see again and again?

		Percent	*Valid Percent*	*Cumulative Percent*
Valid		64.3	64.3	64.3
	Awards functions	1.2	1.2	65.5
	Ajay atul tom an jerry	6.0	6.0	71.4
	Cant remember	1.2	1.2	72.6
	CID Gilli Appa	1.2	1.2	73.8
	Comedy	1.2	1.2	75.0
	Family members disguised themself, guddi who has lost his memory bits them up	2.4	2.4	77.4
	Guddi is unable to ware Sari	2.4	2.4	79.8
	I will like to see gauri and nikhil marring Happily	1.2	1.2	81.0
	Krishnabhen lots order and she completes with in given time	1.2	1.2	82.1
	I	1.2	1.2	83.3
	Like hero	2.4	2.4	85.7
	Like the fight with aliance	4.8	4.8	90.5
	like to see magic	1.2	1.2	91.7
	Marathi paul padthi pude. where in various artist perform.	1.2	1.2	92.9
	meri jang	1.2	1.2	94.0
	mother taking care of child	1.2	1.2	95.2
	Munni badnam Hui	2.4	2.4	97.6
	The incidences between Surya and Guddi in Nanhi si Pari mari ladli	1.2	1.2	98.8
	Will like to be police/tiger	1.2	1.2	100.0
Total		100.0	100.0	

The channels which aimed at children, follow the policy of repeating the programmes. Because children like to see the programmes they like again and again. Children have expressed their desire to watch the comic, action or magic situation again and again. Similar to the previous findings they don't want to see watch intense family daram. Hence, the situation they want to see again and again are from the genre of comedy and action programes.

(20) What do you like to see in the Evening Programes?

		Percent	*Valid Percent*	*Cumulative Percent*
	Cloths and Jewelry	3.6	4.2	4.2
	Decorative Items of the house	15.5	18.1	22.2
	the lead Actress and Actor	32.1	37.5	59.7
	Childartist	6.0	6.9	66.7
	background music and Title song	7.1	8.3	75.0
	food and other drinks	7.1	8.3	83.3
	vehicles	14.3	16.7	100.0
	Total	85.7	100.0	
Missing	System	14.3		
Total		100.0		

Children like to see lead Actors and Actresses of the programme. They don't remember their names but they like to see them. The cast chosen for lead characters for this prime time programme are young and beautiful. They are always dressed in attractive and latest fashioned cloths. Many of TV channels get their cloths designed and made-up from famous dress designers. The people who play lead rolls in the prime-time soap-operas are usually chosen from fashion and modelling Industry, hence they are all essentially experienced models with attractive body figures and skin tones. Moreover, apply heavy make-up to look beautiful and attractive. Hair-styles are also well done, accoding to trends of fashion. Rural children don't see such attractive people in their real life and are highly enfluenced. Naturally for rural children these models become a piece of attraction and glamour. A models job is to attract people and look beautiful, results of this survey shows that they are successful.

(21) Which World do you like? (the surrounding in which they live in)

		Percent	*Valid Percent*	*Cumulative Percent*
Valid	of TV	48.8	52.6	52.6
	real world around u	44.0	47.4	100.0
	Total	92.9	100.0	
Missing	System	7.1		
Total		100.0		

More the 23% of the Indian population is surviving below poverty line, and majority of them belong to rural India. Rural India being poor cannot afford to have properly build houses. The houses which are developed in rural India are popularly known as "Kacha House", i.e. the houses are made up of mud, cow-dung, stone and dry leafs available or tin roofs. The prime reason for such kind of housing is that they can't afford cement and RCC constructions. Because of small landholdings and joint family systems the space in the house is small and congested. In contrast to this the houses and the settings shown in the TV are extremely big and setting have urban orientation. The fact is even in urban cities don't have hug houses which TV shows. These houses are known as "Pakka houses" which are made out of cement and steel. Construction of such houses is costly and cannot be afforded by majority of Indians.

Moreover the interiors developed in the house are very expensive. Rural children who are constantly bombarded with such visuals feel inferior about the house they stay in, there is an inherent feeling that has developed over a period of time that world apart from their village is rich and wealthy where in they are suffering from poverty. Children don't have cognitive senses developed to understand that the visuals shown on the TV are all fake and untrue.

Children indeed become the victim glamorous world setting shown on the TV and like TV world then their actual world they stay in.

(22) If you like the TV world the pls specify the reason?

		Percent	*Valid Percent*	*Cumulative Percent*
Valid		52.4	52.4	52.4
	actors and comedy	6.0	6.0	58.3
	Actors who do comedy	1.2	1.2	59.5
	I don't like to write I like to watch	1.2	1.2	60.7
	In nanhici baiti, she does not know how to cook.	1.2	1.2	61.9
	learn good things	1.2	1.2	63.1
	like comedy and actors	1.2	1.2	64.3
	like nirija, the cloths, make up, jewellery, and the nature, attitude	1.2	1.2	65.5
	Like son and hero	2.4	2.4	67.9
	like song, acor actress and dance	7.1	7.1	75.0
	Like the food	1.2	1.2	76.2
	like to get info about HIV	2.4	2.4	78.6
	like to see songs and lead actors	1.2	1.2	79.8
	like to see the actors and the actress	3.6	3.6	83.3
	Likes krishnabhen and her helping nature	2.4	2.4	85.7
	likes to see food	3.6	3.6	89.3
	likes TV world very much	2.4	2.4	91.7
	love by mothers	3.6	3.6	95.2
	TV image look green and clean	2.4	2.4	97.6
	want to work and leave life like TV	1.2	1.2	98.8
	we learn good things from TV	1.2	1.2	100.0
Total		100.0	100.0	

By these open ended question it is clear that children like to see comic and action events. Other answers also indicate that children are highly influenced by larger than life Images of TV. To make TV visual look larger than life and attractive TV channels use huge settings, expensive Interior Design, young models as actors, make-up and costumes. All this adds to additional glamour and TV world becomes more attractive than real world around rural children.

The ambience in which the characters are set is usually urban depicting exaggerated reality. Rural children unable to understand that TV images are fake and artificial. Rural children believe that urban world of TV is beautiful and the real world in which they survive. The data shows that rural children are highly influenced by the glamour on the TV.

(23) Which Food do you like?

		Percent	*Valid Percent*	*Cumulative Percent*
Valid	Food of TV	21.4	22.5	22.5
	Food from real world around u	73.8	77.5	100.0
	Total	95.2	100.0	
Missing	System	4.8		
Total		100.0		

There are many occasions shown on the TV where characters are shown having food involved especially certain occasions like weeding, holi, diwali or any other festival is shown as celebrated in a grand way. We usually see a lot of variety during the festivals. Kitchens where food is cooked are big in size and where always special food is being cooked. Food consumption habits are normally western in nature for example people are shown consuming toast and butter for the breakfast, in contrast to this Indians usually will never have bread and butter, he will prefer Roti or Chapati.

The data shows that majority of children don't like TV food, still significant number of children like TV food.

(24) Which Cloths do you Like?

		Percent	*Valid Percent*	*Cumulative Percent*
Valid	of TV	25.0	26.2	26.2
	of real world around u	70.2	73.8	100.0
	Total	95.2	100.0	
Missing	System	4.8		
Total		100.0		

The costumes are always the major and special attraction of prime time soap operas. Considering the huge female audience of prime-time soap operas, the channels takes extra efforts to make costumes attractive and glamorous to the maximum extent as possible. TV channels invest heavy Budget for costume glamour; a lot of time is spend at shooting sets to get costume and make-up right. The lead characters are usually professional models who are trained to carry the costume in the most effective way.

Majority of children have said that they like the cloths of the real world, but if we apply the two way chi square test of significance and compare the data with the question. Which world do like? The answer is significant; hence in other words, we can say that there is an impact to some extent which is significant.

(25) Which Jewellery and Make-up do you like?

		Percent	*Valid Percent*	*Cumulative Percent*
Valid	of TV	32.1	34.2	34.2
	of real world around u	61.9	65.8	100.0
	Total	94.0	100.0	
Missing	System	6.0		
Total		100.0		

Jewellery and ornaments of gold are sign of wellness in Indian culture. Gold is considered as purest form of metal and ornaments of gold are consider holy. Gold is precious and costly. The cost of gold is almost Rs. 23000 Rupees per 10 gms. Rural India where 23% of population is below poverty line can never afford to buy gold. TV channels irrespective of economic condition of their characters in soap operas make them where jewellery which looks extremely precious and costly. Needlees to say that such jewellery is not real, if an artificial jewellery made up for the purpose of TV soap operas only. Children unable to understand this fact, and wonder that how come people livening in some part of India are rich enough to afford new jewellery in every episode?

Make up is an TV production requirement. In order to hide sweat and defects of the skin make-up is needed. Make-up is also important to make people look like certain charecters. As per the lighting requirements make-up is made because skin might reflect light. Moreover make-up makes people look beautiful and young. Heavy make-up is always applied to the Characters of soap-operas for the said reasons. In rural India make-up is uncommonly used. Most of the rural people being poor can't afford cosmetics. In contrast to this visuals of soap-operas show each and every character with heavy make-up. The make-up is so heavily done the one could feel the layer of foundation cream and lipstick. Such heavy make-up also hides original skin texture and skin colour of every character looks the same. Most of the times hairs of the characters are not original, they all use artificial hairs to over-come their age or to glorify beauty. For women long hairs is considered as sign of beauty and health, hence TV women generally are shown with long hairs. If we want to put in a nut shell we can say that each and every human aspect of the TV character is manipulated to produce larger than life experience. Poor rural children become the victims unknowingly, they develop a perception that people apart from their village or town use heavy make-up to look beautiful. Children also might envy the TV world. Hence, they like to see make-up and jewellery.

(26) Which family do you like?

		Percent	Valid Percent	Cumulative Percent
Valid	of TV	6.0	6.2	6.2
	of real world around u	89.3	93.8	100.0
	Total	95.2	100.0	
Missing	System	4.8		
Total		100.0		

Indeed small children have to strong bonding with their family. One of the strong reasons is rural India still have joint family system, which daily soap have failed to on TV.

(27) Which mother do you like?

		Percent	Valid Percent	Cumulative Percent
Valid	of TV	16.7	17.5	17.5
	of real world around u	78.6	82.5	100.0
	Total	95.2	100.0	
Missing	System	4.8		
Total		100.0		

Assuming that rural children are heavily dependent on their mother for both survival and emotional needs we had posed this question. If at all the first person they like in the world is their mother. Indeed the data also show that children like there mother. But still 17% of children like television mother more than the real mother, the said figures are quite significant.

Rural children on an average spend 1 and ½ to 2 hours watching daily soaps. Rural India is extremely underdeveloped as compare to urban areas and cities. The basic infrastructural facilities are like electricity, drinking water and roads are missing. In contrast to this because of industrialization all the infrastructural facilities are available to urban areas. The life-style and standard of living of rural and urban areas is completely different. Daily soap majorly developed with urban-based content. The visuals, characters and ambiance are majorly urban centric and larger than life. Due to this constant exposer of such visuals rural children fill insecure and backward. Because children are not aware and exposed to the realities of the world they presume TV world as the real world and better world. Hence, they also like the mother charecters in the film.

(28) If you like the mother on the TV please specify the reason?

		Percent	*Valid Percent*	*Cumulative Percent*
Valid	she takes good care of children	3.6	60.0	60.0
	of real world around u	2.4	40.0	100.0
	Total	6.0	100.0	
Missing	System	94.0		
Total		100.0		

If we apply two way chi-square test and compare the said data with TV likings, 17% result of liking towards TV mother is quite significant. Small children with their minimum cognitive abilities and because of less exposer to the realities of life. Children who are watching without any control are constantly exposed to the TV as result of this they start believing the TV. The larger than life visuals. Attractive make-up and settings of TV are in contrast of their poor life standards indeed they develop a felling of backwardness as compare to the ureal world of TV. As TV channels generally hires beautiful fashion models who are at times too young to suit the role of mother's character. These young mothers are perfect with their dialect, moreover, their characters are always

		Percent	Valid Percent	Cumulative Percent
Valid		76.2	76.2	76.2
	I just don't like	3.6	3.6	79.8
	I just don't like it	8.3	8.3	88.1
	Just not like	3.6	3.6	91.7
	mother takes extra care and never let her child in trouble	1.2	1.2	92.9
	my mother forces me to go to school	1.2	1.2	94.0
	She takes extra care and never get angry	1.2	1.2	95.2
	They have shown the ill effects if child is without mother, TV mother takes good care.	1.2	1.2	96.4
	TV mother does not get angry even after fighting	1.2	1.2	97.6
	TV mother never gets angry	2.4	2.4	100.0
Total		100.0	100.0	

victims of wrong doings of bad characters, hence they are outstandingly soft spoken and humble to other charecters. Real rural mothers are poor, short heighted and have to struggle to satisfy their daily needs. Children unconsciously compare their real life with TV life and get the feeling that TV life is better than real life.

Children who like TV mother have said that TV mothers are extra careing and never gets angry on their children.

(29) Do you feel that programes on TV are unreal and made-up?

Significant number of children believe that TV depicts real life. A similar kind of observation is being found in the research done in various parts of the world. Children do get influenced by TV and try to ape TV in real life. Because of less exposer of the world they presume TV world as a better world, which have good standard of living than their real life.

		Percent	*Valid Percent*	*Cumulative Percent*
Valid	Yes	56.0	58.0	58.0
	No	40.5	42.0	100.0
	Total	96.4	100.0	
Missing	System	3.6		
Total		100.0		

Children want their life to be like TV. But somewhere this children don't understand that their life can never be like TV because TV life is fake and made-up just for entertainment. Children often intent to cross the line entertainment and presume TV as real life.

(30) Do you think that your Life is Poor and Miserable than the TV?

		Percent	*Valid Percent*	*Cumulative Percent*
Valid	Yes	41.7	43.8	43.8
	No	53.6	56.2	100.0
	Total	95.2	100.0	
Missing	System	4.8		
Total		100.0		

As significant children already believe that TV is real so. Because of regular bombarding of snobbish and larger than life images children tent of believe their own life as is poor and miserable. This kind of wrong perception boots fellings of low self-esteem in the children. Such low feeling hampers the overall development of the children. Children always feel underdeveloped and backward leading to constant decay of positive felling towards life. While children are watching TV, subconsciously they compare real life with life of the characters in the TV. The result is obliviously lower self-esteem and confidence which hampers overall development of the children.

(31) What Changes you would like to make in Your Real Life with the Inspiration from TV?

		Percent	*Valid Percent*	*Cumulative Percent*
Valid		40.5	40.5	40.5
	Change home, do make up, would decorate house	1.2	1.2	41.7
	Change house and cloths	2.4	2.4	44.0
	changes in life	2.4	2.4	46.4
	House	4.8	4.8	51.2
	House and new vehical	1.2	1.2	52.4
	like new sari	1.2	1.2	53.6
	like to chance curent life	1.2	1.2	54.8
	like to do many changes	1.2	1.2	56.0
	like to get new house and moter car	2.4	2.4	58.3
	No changes	4.8	4.8	63.1
	want to change house	4.8	4.8	67.9
	want to change house, cloths,	6.0	6.0	73.8
	want to drive good motor car	1.2	1.2	75.0
	We are poor and would like to improve my life	1.2	1.2	76.2
	we feel happy to watch and learn new things	1.2	1.2	77.4
	when grow up I will build new house, and become kavri and ware new cloths	1.2	1.2	78.6
	when I will grow you I will behave like TV	1.2	1.2	79.8
	will like to get new cloths, decorate house, like to behave good	1.2	1.2	81.0
	Will study more	8.3	8.3	89.3

would change the house	1.2	1.2	90.5
would like to be rich and don't poor	1.2	1.2	91.7
would like to change my home	1.2	1.2	92.9
Would like to change my house, need more jewellery to my mother, want new choths	1.2	1.2	94.0
would like to have new cloths	4.8	4.8	98.8
would like to ware new dress and sari	1.2	1.2	100.0
Total	100.0	100.0	

We have already discussed that the gap between TV life and rural life is different. There is a huge economic gap, being majority of the rural population poor and underdeveloped they can never afford the luxuries or the leaving standards shown in the TV. But rural children dream of life in TV. Dreams of these little children are clearly reflected while answering this open-ended questions. Most of the children dream about getting good cloths, jewellery, choths, and better home to live. Children are not able to understand that life in the TV is fiction, the cloths, house and the decorative things we see on TV are all artificial and not real. Children fail to distinguish between entertainment and reality. There is need to highlight the plus points of rural style of living how they could living a better and happy life with the existing reality. TV through soap operas always depict urban and unreal lifestyle which is blown to larger than life situations. We can conclude that poor rural children have became the victim of TV soap-operas.

(32) Which of the following you would like to change in real life?

Majority of children want to change their house and decorative items in the house. Such a kind of desires clearly is an impact of constant and uncontrolled impact of daily soap opera.

Constant bombarding of unreal visuals with huge urban settings and unreal decorative items results in such

		Percent	Valid Percent	Cumulative Percent
Valid	Big brother	1.2	1.5	1.5
	Home	20.2	25.4	26.9
	Corridors of home	4.8	6.0	32.8
	Other decorative things	44.0	55.2	88.1
	Other things	9.5	11.9	100.0
	Total	79.8	100.0	
Missing	System	20.2		
Total		100.0		

unsatisfiable desire. Mahatma Gandhi believed that real India is rural India and had adopted his lifestyle according to the life existed in rural India. He had also started the "Swadeshi Movement" for banning western goods and services in India. Morden TV Industry seems to be forgotten about 70% rural India and are depicting only unreal urban lifestyle. At least the soap-operas which are major part of their TV programme content relevant to rural india. Current TV contain make them feel bad and poor about their house and location they stay.

Briefly the findings of my research could be as follows:

(1) Maximum children watch TV during the prime time along with their parents. They have no control over the viewing as the remote of the TV is controlled by the Parents in the house.
(2) Children like to see comedy and action programs but they are forced to see the programs of family drama. These programs are targeted for adults. The content is based more on love and relationship. Children are not mature enough to understand the same and indeed have negative impact
(3) Children feel they are more poor and backward than the TV world. Sense of backwardness is Developed.
(4) They like the house and settings shown on the TV more than the real house they stay in.

(5) Children are highly influence by the cloths and Jewellery which in their real life they can never dream of.
(6) Children like to watch private TV channels than Doordarshan.
(7) Children like mother in the TV programs more then their real mother, because she gives good food to eat and take extra care.

Indeed prime time soap operas have negative impact on small children and is the serious issue which India is ignoring for a longer period of time..

Are the Rules and Regulations of Law followed ?

Rule 6(1)(a), (d), (k), (o) and 6(5) of Cable Television Networks Rules, 1994, says, "The visuals, which were found to be obscene, denigrated women and were not suitable for children and unrestricted public exhibition."

Moreover the rule in the said law also says that "Programmes unsuitable for children must not be carried in the cable service at times when the largest numbers of children are viewing."

If we consider the above mention rules/laws are been violated very often over a large period of time.

RESPONSIBILITY OF THE GOVERNMENT

It is understood that private channels have to mold the content of their programs according to TRP ratings because the aim of this company is profit maximization. This private broadcasting company may not bother about the social and long-term impact of the content they are producing. Because the aim of private broadcasting channels is profit.

The Prasar Bharati (Broadcasting Corporation of India) Act, 1990 rule no. 12 talks about the Functions and powers of Corporation. Some of the important Functions are highlighted by the act are as follows:

(1) The primary duty of the Corporation to organise and conduct public broadcasting services to inform,

educate and entertain the public and to ensure a balanced development of broadcasting on radio and television.

(2) Providing appropriate programmes keeping in view the special needs of the youth.

(3) The Corporation shall be paying special attention to the fields of education and spread of literacy, agriculture, rural development, environment, health and family welfare and science and technology :

Providing adequate coverage to the diverse cultures and languages of the various regions of the country by broadcasting appropriate programmes.

Doordarshan, the public broadcasting company which come directly under Prasar Bharati have forgotten the important functions which they are supposed to do. Even if some attempts are made, the program quality is so poor that no body watches.

SUGGESTIONS

(1) Government should make the law more concrete and efficient. Eg. The definition of Children channel should be piscribed by law.

(2) Doordarshan should work to improve its quality of programs. New programs should made which are more regional centric.

(3) 36% of Indian population is young, Government should make an extra efforts to reach out to the young population. They should make programs which will help in developing quality of life of children. They should be considered as an asset of India.

(4) Private channels are constantly producing mediocre content, most of the channels are aping western channels and producing the content. These contents are lacking in regional appeal.

(5) There is strong need to again repeat the experiments like SITE. Programs should be made with participation of regional people according to their requirements.

(6) TRP rating system should be made more transparent and consider rural audience in collection of data.
(7) Private channels should consider their role and responsibility and improve the content, which will lead to the better citizens of India.
(8) Media education should be made compulsory in the school syllabus. Children should be made aware about media right from the school days.

References

Agrawal, Binod C., 1978, Television Comes to Village : An Evaluation of SITE. Bangalore : Indian Space Research Organisation.

Agrawal, Binod C., 1987, Television Expansion and the Indian Child: A Historical Perspective. In Television and the Indian Child: eds.; Binod C. Agrawal and Mira B. Aghi; pp. 3-10. New Delhi : UNICEF.

———, 1998, Viewing Under Parents' Shadows. Paper presented during the "Second World Summit on Television for Children". London, U.K., March 9 to 13, 1998.

———, 2000, Children Media Use in India : A Current Scenario. Newsletter from the UNESCO International Clearinghouse on Children and Violence on Screen, Volume 4, No 1.

Agrawal, Binod C. and Shalini Raghaviah, 2006, Child Right and Television in India, A Country Report. Singapore: AMIC.

Anonymous, 2004, Spanning the Digital Divide—An Assessment Study. Ahmedabad: TALEEM Research Foundation (unpublished report).

———, 2009, Changing Viewers' Preferences of Channels and Programmes: A Comparative Analysis of ZEE TV and Colors. Ahmedabad : TALEEM Research Foundation. (unpublished report)

Arora, U.K., (Editor), 2007, Gyan Darshan, Gyan Vani, November 2007. New Delhi : Electronic Media Production Centre, IGNOU.

Bhaskara Rao, N., 2009, Whither Children's Television in India. www.consindia.org /cms/events/children:/20 television.doc

Desai, Mira K., Binod C. Agrawal, Cry for Cultural Crisis: Transnational Television in India. New Delhi: Concept Publishing Company.

D'Silva, Marget U.A. Futrell and G.V. Reyes, 2007, Children's Consumer Behaviour in the Age of Globalization: Examples from India and Mexico. *Intercultural Communication Studies*, XVI (2), pp. 253-59.

Ekstrom, Karin M. and Birgitte, Tufte, 2007, Introduction. In Children Media and Consumption; pp. 11-30; eds., Karin, M. Ekstrom and Birgitte Tufte. Goteborg: Goteborg University and International Clearinghouse on Children, Youth and Media.

Khurana, B.K., C. Krishnaswamy and Saroj Malik, 1987, Impact of Television on Children. In Television and the Indian Child eds., Binod C. Agrawal and Mira B. Aghi, UNICEF

Mathiyalagan, N., 1995, Television and Children : A Study of Factors Related to the Uses of Television Among School Children. Coimbatore: Development of Communication, PSG College of Arts and Sscience (Unpublished Ph.D. Thesis).

Shah, Sona and Shastri, Jigisha, 1997, Television Viewing Pattern of Pre-school Children and Their Home—Television Environment. *Perspectives in Education,* 13(1) : 21-41.

Shastri, Jigisha and Mohite, Prerana, 1997, Television Viewing Pattern of Primary School Children and its Relationship to Academic Performance and Cognitive Skills. *International Journal of Early Years Education,* 5(2) : 153-60.

Unnikrishnan Namita and Shailaja Bajpai, 1996, The Impact of Television Advertising on Children. New Delhi, Sage Publications India Pvt. Ltd.

von Feilitizen, Cecllea, 1999, Electronic Games Pornography, Perceptions. In Children in the New Media Landscape—Games Pornography Perceptions; eds., Cecillia von Feilitizen and Ulla Carlsson; pp. 13-23. Goteborg: The UNESCO International Clearinghouse on Children and Violence on the Screen.

Wartella, Ellen, Ronda Scantlin, Jennifer Kotler, Aletha C. Huston and Edward Donnerstein 2000, Sexual Messages on Entertainment TV in the USA. In Children in the New Media Landscape—Games Pornography Perceptions. Cecilia von Feilitzen and Ulla Carlsson, eds., pp.141-54. Nordicom: The UNESCO International Clearinghouse on Children and Violence on the Screen.

O' Guinn Allen, Semenik, "Advertising 2", South-western College Publishing, 2000.

Sharon Beder, "Marketing to children", New College Institute for Values Research, Sydney http://www.uow.edu.au/arts/sts/sbeder/children.html

James, U. McNea, 'Kids as Customers: A Handbook of Marketing to Children', New York: Lexington Books, 1992, p. 91.

Childhood Obesity, Food advertising in context—Children food choices, Parents understanding and influence,and the role of food promotions, http://www.ofcom.org.uk/research/tv/reports/food_ads/

Sharon Beder, "Marketing to children", New College Institute for Values Research, Sydney, http://www.uow.edu.au/arts/sts/sbeder/children.html

Bandyopadhyay, S., Kindra, G., Sharp, L. (2001), "Is television advertising good for children? Areas of concern and policy implications", *International Journal of Advertising*, Vol. 20, pp. 89-116.

Mass Media and Child Obesity—The advertising impact on increased weight gain—Column published by 'Dr. Richard Visser' in http://www.lafamily.com/display_article.php?id=1433

———, Mindy Bilgery, Advertising's Impact on Kids, Health A to Z available at http://www.healthatoz.com/healthatoz/Atoz/common/standard/transform.jsp?requestURI=/healthatoz/Atoz/hc/chi/kids/alert10102002.jsp

Books Referred

Mass Media Research, Roger Wimmer and Joseph Domnic.

Mass Communication In India, Keval Kumar.

Intoduction to Mass Communication, Puja Narula.

An Introduction to TV studies, Jonathan Bignell.

Mass Communication theory, Stanley Baran and Dennis Davis.

Mass Communication Theory, Jone Ficks.

Mass Communication Research Methods, Hsia H.J.

The Practice of Social Research, Babbie, E.R.

Methods in Social Research, Kothari, C.R.

Basics of Qualitative Research? Strauss Anselm, Corbin Juliet.

How to Publish Communication Research, Edt., Alison Alexander *et. al.*

Qualitative Research Methods in Public Relations and Marketing Communication, Daymon Christine and Holloway Immy.

Broadcast Journalism, Techniques of Radio and TV News, Andrew Boyd.

Ethics for Media, William Reeves and Cleave Mathews.

Ethics in Journalism, Jeffrey Olen.

CHAPTER

25

A Distributed Model for Distance Learning

SACHIN GARG AND SANDEEP JAIN

ABSTRACT

Distance education via the Internet has been greatly developed during recent years. Large number of educational institutions use the Web to develop programs that lead to academic degrees. Furthermore, a considerable number of companies use the Internet and Intranet in order to develop educational programs within the company. The use of the Internet for educational purposes has increased the number of educational programs offered in the framework of distance learning. However, it should be noted that this new educational setting (and the educational programs offered through it), may function as an alternative educational form for those who cannot take part in traditional educational forms for various reasons. Usual common characteristic of these programs is that are products of a single institution. Education via the Internet allows for the development of flexible educational programs, which could be developed by more institutions. The success of an educational program either in its traditional setting or its virtual setting is determined by a number of factors. The comparative advantages of the Web-based learning are the way of delivery of the courseware material, the development of effective communication (in the new electronic environment) among all partners involved in the educational process (tutors, students, technicians, etc.), the use of modern pedagogical methods based on the constructivist approach (problem-based learning, collaborative learning) and the possibility of access in on-line digital libraries and other multimedia educational resources.

This paper presents a flexible distributed model of providing education via the Internet, adjusted to the needs of lifelong learning. This educational model is designed for users who want to continue their studies either for carrier development or to maintain their current job position or to redefine their position in the labor market.

INTRODUCTION

There is an increasing demand for education from companies and the individuals due to the new technologies and the new economy's characteristics. The use of these new technologies enables enterprises and organizations to function with networks, geographically distributed nationally and internationally. These changes require acquisition of new specialized knowledge and skills. This is the reason why during the last years has opened in all the developed economically countries a dialogue with regard to the importance of education for the dynamic employability of the human capital and the competitiveness for the companies and organizations.

The cost of traditional form of education and training is particularly high for companies seeking to train their personnel. Gathering workers or employees in a classroom for corporate seeking to train their personnel. Gathering workers or employees in a classroom for corporate training and education or for follow-up academic courses is difficult and exceptionally costly. Networked Open Learning (NOL) in the near future will be a very important alternative for providing educational programs to companies and individuals. Networked Open Learning (NOL) or simply Networked Learning (NL) is the educational form that covers all forms of delivery of educational programs in which the following features are crucial:

- People ('tutors' and 'learners') communicate using computers linked to networks.
- People access resources stored on computers linked to networks.

The geographical dimension in Networked Learning is not an important one because more important from the distance is the way the educational material is distributed, regardless if the participants are at the same place or not. The success of educational programs offered through the WWW requires a detailed design of all the components of the programs and especially those concerning the characteristics of the new media (such as interactivity, adaptability, development of multimedia applications for educational purposes, development of educational applications with the use of virtual reality, allowing access to larger audiences.

The target group for the model in this paper is working adult learners. These learners have special educational objectives resulting from their working environment or individual career objectives. These learners want to have the control over the time, the place and sometimes the content (according to their needs and personal perspectives) of their learning activity. A NL course should be adapted to each user's learning needs and should be connected to each user's personal objectives in a logical time framework.

The most common and cost-effective platform for the provision of distant education is the World Wide Web. The Internet/WWW tends to replace every other medium of providing distance education, due to its low cost and the effectiveness. The Internet/WWW and its technologies can accommodate the development of an institute for distance educational programs, which is functionally designed as a distributed system.

DISTRIBUTED NETWORKED OPEN LEARNING

For the provision of a distant educational program via the WWW, the involved parts are:

- The tutors and other supporters of education,
- The courseware material (interface and databases),
- The technological infrastructure (server), and
- The trainees.

Training via the Internet allows us to redesign the traditional models of providing education. In a distributed educational system, all of the above parts must be decentralized. The advantages of such a design are many, including:

- The participation of more tutors and other specialists from different institutions and with different backgrounds.
- The courseware material developed by the co-operating educators is enhanced because it is based on the specialized knowledge of many. Such an approach also improves the timeliness of a course, especially if it is in areas where the subject matter changes rapidly.
- The workload for producing and the responsibility for supporting the educational process may be distributed into several parts.
- Ability to develop flexible educational programs based on the characteristics and needs of the user. The material can be retrieved from different distributed databases. An example can be the various educational consortia where different institutions contribute different learning units of a course.
- Ability to design several kinds of programs which can lead to certification and cover needs for lifelong learning.

DISTRIBUTED DEVELOPMENT OF COURSEWARE MATERIAL

The term—distributed development of courseware material "refers to the process during which tutors and other specialists from different geographical locations, and educational organizations, cooperate in order to produce a NOL course.

In a distributed model (a consortia of institutions) there is a better chance of producing courseware in areas where the subject matter changes rapidly, if you have a large group of experts. They can contribute important and diverse views in a particular scientific area enhanced with experiences from the real world. Thereby your chances of including the cutting edge, state-of-the-art materials are improved. This is especially so, when communications are carried on via the computer. The computer can act as a medium for talent and resources.

DISTRIBUTED DELIVERY OF THE COURSE

The term—distributed delivery of educational programs refers to the process during which, education is not provided by only one provider but by more. It also means being able to instruct over broad geographical areas asynchronously. In one interpretation, every tutor may offer the part of the courseware material which developed. Another way of employing a distributed delivery model is to have some teachers contribute in the process of developing the courseware material and others to facilitate the course.

Networked Open Learning courses help trainees to be more active since they have to communicate with the instructor and peers for various reasons. Trainees are encouraged to exchange knowledge gained either from ongoing course units and from their experiences or from material (information) they can get on the net (i.e. digital libraries).

In the distributed model of education via the Internet, a number of institutions could cooperate. For the development of such a system, the existence of a main server, which will process trainee profiles, as well as all of the administrative work described above, is required. The courses reside in the

Institution's servers. In each server the interface (common to all courses) is installed, as well as the relevant databases for courseware material. These databases are accessed and coordinated in order to create customized programs. For the development of the courseware material and the delivery of the training program, tutors and other specialists cooperate, as mentioned above.

A model of institutional cooperation is shown in Figure:

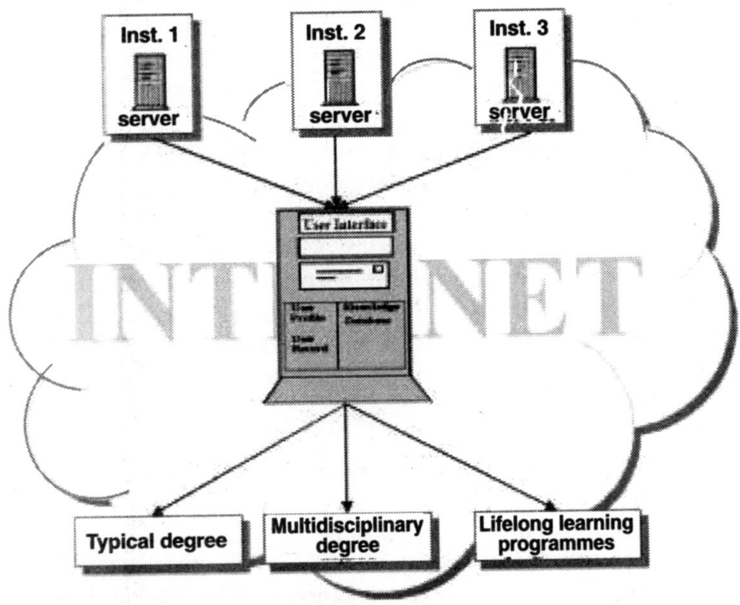

CONCLUSION

Now-a-days, because of the Internet distance education has been transformed drastically. Employees and companies can satisfy their needs for lifelong learning, through programs offered by Institutions that provide NOL education (Universities, etc.). These programs are parts of the typical educational curricula that lead to academic degrees or training programs that lead to a certification.

The success of educational programs offered through the WWW requires a detailed design of all the components of the program and especially those concerning the characteristics of the new media. These issues are more crucial when educational programs are offered in a distributed manner, as a result of collaboration between institutions. This form of collaboration presents some advantages such as:

- the possibility to bring together tutors and other specialists (from the different institutions and other organizations) for all the learning activities,
- the ability to offer custom made learning programs which lead to degrees or certification,
- the possibility to reduce the total cost of the educational programs, and
- the possibility to meet more markets (which means important economies of scale), etc.

The World Wide Web allows the development of new forms of education based on modern pedagogical methods, i.e. constructivism and collaborative learning (where the trainee has a significant control on how he/she learns) by using attractive and effective technologies in terms of capabilities and involved cost

References

Bouras, Ch., Destounis, P., Garofalakis, J., Gkamas, A., Sakalis, G., Sakopoulos, E., Tsaknakis, J. and Tsiatsos, Th. (2000), Efficient web-based open and distance learning services, *Telematics and Informatics*, 17, pp. 213-37.

Cresson, E. (1995), European Commission White Paper Teaching and Learning: Towards the Learning Society. Memo 95/162.

Dede, C. (1996a), Emerging technologies and distributed learning.

European Commission White Paper (2000). Teaching and Learning: The eLearning Action Plan Designing tomorrow's education. Available online:

http://europa.eu.int/comm/education/elearning/doc_en.html

Harasim, L. (1999), A Framework for Online Learning: The Virtual-U. *IEEE Computer*, 32(9), pp. 44-49.

IEEE Learning Technology Standardization Committee: Draft Standard for Learning Objects Metadata (LOM), Feb. 2001.

IMS (2001), Instructional management systems global learning, http://imsproject.org

Kirkpatrick, D. and Mclaughlan, R. (2000), Flexible Lifelong Learning in Professional Education. *Educational Technology and Society*, 3(1), pp. 24-31.

Lytle, R. (1999), Asynchronous Learning Networks for Knowledge Workforce Learning, *Journal of Asynchronous Learning Networks*, 3(1), pp. 67-76.

Stamatis, D., Kefalas, P., Kargidis, Th. (1999), A Multi-Agent Framework to Assist Networked Learning, *Journal of Computer Assisted Learning*, 15(3), pp. 201-10.

CHAPTER

26

Education

The Comprehensive Strategy for the Social and Economical Growth of India

Sadaf Khan

ABSTRACT

The role of education as a contributor to economic growth and its impact on population control, life expectancy, infant mortality, improving nutritional status and strengthening civil institutions is well recognized. The creation of world-class skills is assumed to be a route to economic prosperity, reduced income inequalities and social cohesion.

Keeping in view the growing demand of education, the article focuses on the role played by it for the social and economical development. The article focuses at the global skills race and that is why stress is given to push ahead faster with our knowledge and education. The article examines the role of education on both economic growth and social development with particular reference to India. It emphasis on the fact that the development of education is an important aspect of our plan priorities. The article also tells that the access to basic education lies at the heart of development. It also talks about the education system of India and the role played by the government for the upliftment of the society by promoting the education.

Key words: Education, Society, Economic, Upliftment, Social, Development.

INTRODUCTION

Education is universally recognized as a central component of human capital. The role of education as a contributor to economic growth and its impact on population control, life expectancy, infant mortality, improving nutritional status and strengthening civil institutions is well recognized. Moreover, the social rates of return on investments in all levels of education much exceed the long-term opportunity cost of capital. Its role of in facilitating social and economic progress is well recognized. Education empowers the poor to participate in the growth process. It opens up opportunities leading to both individual and group entitlements. Education, in its broadest sense of development of youth, is the most crucial input for empowering people with skills and knowledge and giving them access to productive employment in future. Improvements in education are not only expected to enhance efficiency but also augment the overall quality of life. It is the process whereby society passes on the accumulated knowledge and experience of past generations to its youth in a systematic and abridged form, so that the next generation can start off where past generations have ended and move on from there. Today, through education we have access not only to the knowledge of our own direct ancestors but to the accumulated experience and wisdom of people the world over. In this globalized era, knowledge and skills assume ever-greater importance. The challenge is to outsmart other national economies—whether established or emerging—in the 'knowledge wars' of the future.

India's performance in the field of education has been among the most disappointing aspects of its post-independence scenario as the country currently houses the largest number of illiterates and has the dubious distinction that every third illiterate in the world is an Indian. Out of approximately 200 million children in the age group 6-14 years, only 120 million are enrolled and the net attendance figure is just over 60 percent (which may be an overestimate) of enrolment. In short, the prospects of even minimal literacy appear to be bleak.

EDUCATION SYSTEM IN INDIA

Education in India is provided by the public sector as well as the private sector. The whole management and fund comes from three levels: federal state, and local. For the upliftment of the society government has made child education compulsory. Though Nalanda University was the oldest university-system of education in the world but with the establishment of the British Raj western education became ingrained into Indian society. Education in India falls under the control of both the Union Government and the state, with some responsibilities lying with the Union and the states having autonomy for others. The various articles of the Indian Constitution provide for education as a fundamental right. Most universities in India are Union or State Government controlled.

The National Council of Educational Research and Training (NCERT) is the apex body for curriculum-related matters for school education in India. The NCERT provides support and technical assistance to a number of schools in India and oversees many aspects of enforcement of education policies. In India, the various curriculum bodies governing school education system are:

- The state government boards, in which the majority of Indian children are enrolled.
- The Central Board of Secondary Education (CBSE) board.
- The Council for the Indian School Certificate Examination (ICSE) board.
- The National Institute of Open Schooling (NIOS) board.

- International schools affiliated to the International Baccalaureate Programme and/or the Cambridge International Examinations.
- Islamic Madarsah schools, whose boards are controlled by local state governments, or autonomous, or affiliated with Darul Uloom Doeband.
- Autonomous schools like Woodstock School, Auroville, Patha Bhavan and Ananda Marga Gurukula.

In addition, NUEPA (National University of Educational Planning and Administration) and NCTE (National Council for Teacher Education) are responsible for the management of the education system and teacher accreditation.

India has made progress in terms of increasing attendance rate and expanding literacy to approximately two-thirds of the population. India's improved education system is often cited as one of the main contributors to the economic rise of India. Much of the progress especially in Higher education, Scientific research has been credited to various public institutions. The private education market in India is merely 5% although in terms of value is estimated to be worth $ 40 billion in 2008 and will increase to $ 68 billion by 2012.

India continues to face stern challenges. Despite growing investment in education, 25% of its population is still illiterate; only 15% of Indian students reach high school, and just 7% graduate. As of 2008, India's post-secondary high schools offer only enough seats for 7% of India's college-age population, 25% of teaching positions nationwide are vacant, and 57% of college professors lack either a master's or Ph.D. degree. As of 2007, there are 1522 degree-granting engineering colleges in India with an annual student intake of 582,000 plus 1,244 polytechnics with an annual intake of 265,000. However, these institutions face shortage of faculty and concerns have been raised over the quality of education. Literacy rate, which is an indicator of status of primary education in any country, is 61 percent in India and is far below in comparison to several developing countries (like China, South Korea, and Sri Lanka) and developed countries.

EDUCATION AND DEVELOPMENT

"There is in our time no well educated literate population that is poor; there is no illiterate population that is other than poor."
—(John Kenneth Galbraith)

This simple but forceful message stresses that education alone can be the salvation for poverty, and upliftment of the socially discriminated. In a poverty stricken country like India where even with education life is difficult, there can be little hope without it. Poor as well as middle-income group, rural as well as urban all are willing to send their children to school. There is solid evidence from all over the country for this increasing appetite for education across all social groups and across all income groups. Professor Amartya Sen recently emphasized education as an important parameter for any inclusive growth in an economy. Access to basic education lies at the heart of development. Lack of educational access, and securely acquired knowledge and skill, is both a part of the definition of poverty, and a means for its diminution. Sustained access to meaningful earning that has value is critical to long-term improvements in productivity, the reduction of inter-generational cycles of poverty, demographic transition, preventive health care, the empowerment of women, and reductions in inequality. The unemployment rates fall faster for workers with higher levels of education, since their skills are more transferable, than for workers with less education.

Investment in education yields a higher rate of return than investment in physical capital. Empirical studies in the literature on education and economic growth also find compelling evidence for the hypothesis that a substantial proportion of the growth of the economies is attributable to the rise in the educational levels of the workforce. There is always positive association exists between stocks of human capital and economic development and that the association becomes stronger at higher levels of education. In agriculture, that primary schooling affects productivity positively, particularly in times of rapid technological change. This brief survey examines the returns to education in India, and then examines the role of education on both economic and social growth.

The Scheduled Castes (SCs) and Scheduled Tribes (STs) are among the most socially and educationally disadvantaged groups in India. The histories of exploitation and marginalization of Scheduled Caste and Scheduled Tribe communities have produced different engagements with education as a path to social mobility. For Scheduled Castes, access to education has been a focal point in their struggle for equity and social justice. It has special significance for the SCs and STs who are facing a new situation in the development process to admit themselves properly in the changing circumstances. It not only helps them to promote their economic development but also helps to build their self-confidence and inner strength to face new challenges. They have been the targets of economic exploitation, harassment, atrocities, injustice, etc. due to their illiteracy linked to their poverty. To eliminate these social problems, Government of India has made special provisions in the Constitution through its Articles 29(1), 46, 15(4), 350-A to promote education among SCs and STs. Investing in education plays a key role in meeting the World Bank's social development objectives, which support inclusive growth, social cohesion, and accountability in development.

World over economist believed that education as an important parameter for any inclusive growth in an economy. Access to quality basic education is imperative not only to reduce social and regional disparities, but also to achieve balanced growth and development. Availability of resources alone does not guarantee faster social sector. Quality education has different connotation for various communities throughout the world. Education increases equality as well. The poor countries get much higher rates of return than the rich countries from investing in education. It is, undoubtedly, a basic component of human development (Planning Commission, 2001). It is not only a means to enhance human capital, productivity and, hence, the compensation to labor, but it is equally important for enabling the process of acquisition, assimilation and communication of information and knowledge, all of which augments a person's quality of life.

Employability : The more educated you are the less likely you are to be out of work.

Unemployment rates by level of education*

Rate	Level of education
5.0%	**Bachelor's degree and higher**
8.0%	**Some college or associate's degree**
10.5%	**High school diploma, no college**
15.6%	**Less than a high school diploma**

***As of February 2010, seasonally adjusted**
Data : Bureau of Labour Statistics

A Plan panel meeting chaired by deputy chairman Montek Singh Ahluwalia adopted the Suresh Tendulkar Committee report which had suggested inclusion of expenditure on health and education besides food to compute poverty. Argued by several researchers, such developments have contributed to the increases in overall economy.

GOVERNMENTS' ROLE IN SPREADING EDUCATION AWARENESS IN INDIA

Governments all over the world want their countries to have high-value, high-skill economies, and they realize that the first step towards this aim is to have a well-educated workforce. Indian government is also spending money for social upliftment of the society through proper education. While there has been a manifest inability to meet the expenditure levels recommended by previous commissions set-up by the Indian government there has been an increase in the expenditure allocations for elementary education in recent plans: the 8th Plan (1992-97) allocated 406,00 (Rs. Million), there was 147,500 (Rs. Million) in the 9th Plan (1997-2002) and an allocation of 287,500 (Rs. Million) for the 10th Plan (2002-07) and 275,000 (Rs. Million) in the 11th Plan (2007-13). The expenditure on education by both central and state education departments was 2.81 per cent of GDP in 2005-06, with half the amount going in elementary education (Tilak, 2009). Additionally, while the revenue collected by the levy of the 2 per cent cess was Rs. 7,036 crores the budget outlay for elementary education was only over half that amount.

India's Public Expenditure on Education : 2009-10

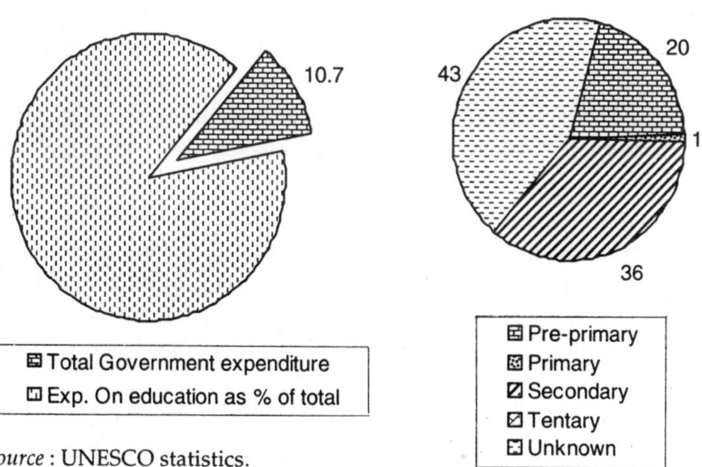

Source : UNESCO statistics.

The Tenth Plan laid emphasis on Universalization of Elementary Education (UEE) guided by five parameters: (i) Universal Access, (ii) Universal Enrolment, (iii) Universal Retention, (iv) Universal Achievement, and (v) Equity. The major schemes of elementary education sector during the Tenth Plan included SSA, District Primary Education Programme (DPEP), National Programme of Nutritional Support to Primary Education, commonly known as Mid-Day Meal Scheme (MDMS), Teacher Education Scheme, and Kasturba Gandhi Balika Vidyalaya Scheme (KGBVS). The schemes of Lok Jumbish and Shiksha Karmi were completed but DPEP will extend up to November 2008. KGBV has now been subsumed within SSA.

The Eleventh Plan places the highest priority on education as a central instrument for achieving rapid and inclusive growth. It presents a comprehensive strategy for strengthening the education sector covering all segments of the education pyramid. The 11th Plan proposes 19.9% share for education. Roughly Rs. 2.85 lakh crore is proposed to be set aside for Elementary, Adult, Secondary and Higher Education. Top Planning Commission sources have said that in terms of percentage, this is almost 2.7 times the allocation in the last plan. For elementary education, Rs. 1.25 lakh crore is being earmarked, which is a major hike from the Rs. 30,000 crore allocated in the last Plan. Likewise the share of adult and secondary education is being increased to Rs. 6,000 crore and Rs. 53,000 crore, respectively. The major increase in the budget for education is an attempt to achieve 'Inclusive Growth'. Apart from increased financial allocations, the 11th Plan also envisages major reforms in education like introducing credit and semester systems along with exam reforms. There are proposals for reforms in Sarva Shiksha Abhiyan as well, in particular improving quality of learning, teachers' recruitment and performance. The Eleventh Plan also addressed major challenges including bridging regional, social, and gender gaps at all levels of education.

Sarva Shiksha Abhiyan (SSA) is a flagship programme of Government of India for achievement of universalization of elementary education in a time bound manner, as mandated by the 86th Amendment to the Constitution of India making free and compulsory education to children of ages 6-14 (estimated to be 205 million in number in 2001) a fundamental right. The programme aims to achieve the goal of universalization of elementary education of satisfactory quality.

Right to Education in India : In India the right to free and compulsory education was retained in Article 45 of Part IV of the Constitution that incorporates the Directive Principles of the State Policy, thus making a distinction from the Fundamental Rights. The most relevant interpretation of Article 21 from education point of view was the Supreme Court's Unnikrishnan Judgement (1993). The Court ruled that Article 45 of the Directive Principles of State Policy must be read in harmonious conjunction with Article 21 since right to life and personal liberty loses its meaning if a child is deprived of elementary education. However, though this Article 21A has provided renewed opportunity to reduce the increasing inequality in education at the elementary level and achieve the goals of justice—social, economic and political, it has yet to acquire the stature of other fundamental rights. The recent report of the CABE (Central Advisory Board of Education) Committee (2005) advocated Free and Compulsory Education Bill. In Articles 45 and 46 there is provision of Early Childhood Care and Education to children below the age of six years. The State shall endeavor to provide early childhood care and education for all children until they complete the age of six years.

The Right to Education Bill : The Bill states that private schools have to provide 25% seats for weaker sections until Grade VIII. There is no obligation for continuation of education of such children in higher grades. The Bill ignores the 0-6 age group—commonly referred to as Early Childhood Care and Education (ECCE). While a child of this age obviously doesn't go to school, documented and research studies by Mina Swaminathan, Venita Kaul and others show that ECCE has a positive impact on emotional and intellectual growth. Most importantly, ECCE also addresses the needs of women and older siblings (especially girls) that have to leave work and school respectively to look after toddlers. This is tantamount to a selective withdrawal of rights available to children through the Unnikrishnan judgement of 1993, which declared education a fundamental right for all children up to 14 years.

When India signed the UN sponsored Child Rights Convention in 1991, there was a conscious introduction of a rights-based framework to educational access and children's participation in education. From mid-1990s, many International Non-government Organizations in collaboration with domestic NGOs turned their attention to schools and adopted a holistic approach. They focused on improvement in infrastructure, facilities, teachers and supplies coupled with individual incentives like uniforms and books to children—addressing both schools as well as children's issues. The National Policy on Education (NPE), 1986 and its Programme of Action (POA), as reviewed in 1992, envisage improvement and expansion of education in all sectors, elimination of disparities in access, a stress on improvement in quality and relevance of education at all levels, along with technical and professional education.

CONCLUSION

From the above one can conclude that some concerted efforts is all that is required in particular in rural areas where the problem is at large to improve the quality of education for the weaker sections. Community elders with their positive participation and involvement can help solve many existing problems both financial and physical. Thus, what is required is a systematic, accountable and transparent approach without piecemeal inputs. This would help to meet the challenges of universal access to quality education and betterment of our downtrodden still existing in our society. With the development of modern media that brings sound and video images into every household, and with the advent of the Internet that enables us to reach out to sources of knowledge around the world, education offers both unprecedented richness of content and the capacity to deliver it. If only we could break free from the limitations of out-dated curriculum and out-moded delivery systems, we could utilize the opportunity to close the education gap that separates the world's most prosperous communities from their poorer cousins. Greater coverage and better quality education at all levels from basic literacy to hi-tech science and technology is the essential prerequisite for raising agricultural productivity and industrial quality; spurring growth of India's budding IT and biotechnology sectors, stimulating growth of manufactured and service exports, improving health and nutrition, domestic stability and quality of governance.

We may also note that in any case, in terms of resource allocations, almost throughout the post-independence period, the governments at the centre treated the Social Sectors—like health, education, housing, and water and sanitation as being inferior to the Economic Sectors. Despite various efforts made by the government to give a boost to education, every third illiterate person in the world is an Indian. Rising budgetary allocations have increased the number of schools but the quality of education offered is still sub-standard mainly because of supply side constraints. The introduction of schemes, such as MDMS and SSA has helped in increasing enrolment but drop-out rates before completion of primary education are still high, implying wastage of public money which often runs into crores. Therefore, continuous effort is always needed from the goverment side.

References

Fennell, Shailaja, 2010. "Educational Exclusion and Inclusive Development in India." RECOUP Working Paper No. 35. University of Cambridge.

Gupta, S.P., 2002. Report of on India Vision 2020. Planning Commission Government of India. New Delhi.

NESSE, "Gender and Education—Lessons from Research for Policy-makers Report."

Seshadri, C., 2008. "Philosophy of Education as a Knowledge Field." National University of Educational Planning and Administration. New Delhi.

Smawfield, David; Poulsen, Helen, 2000. "Mainstreaming Gender through Sector Wide Approaches in Education: India Case Study." London. DFID.

Srivastava, R.S. (2002), 'The Right to Education in India', Preliminary Paper for Discussion, CSRD, JNU, New Delhi.

http://www.education.nic.in

http://www.nesse.fr/nesse/activities/reports

UNDP, "Human Development Report, 2006".

Country Strategy Paper 2007-13

http://www.planningcommission.nic.in

World Bank (1997), India: Achievements and Challenges in Reducing Poverty.

CHAPTER

27

Education for All

A Theoretical Perspective

SALIHA KHATOON

ABSTRACT

Education for all is a global movement lead by UNESCO, aiming to meet the learning needs of all children, youth and adults by 2015. The world conference held in Jomtein in 1990 for education for all was a successful movement. It had six goals and there was a world education forum also held in Dakar 2000, it aims to meet the needs of children, youth, adults by 2015. According to Kothari Commission report the destiny of India is being shaped in the classroom education is very important and essential for the development of human beings objectives of education for all according to the constitution of India is to provide educational opportunities to all the people of the country. There are number of problems also to achieve education for all such as lack of funds urban-rural imbalance, lack of woman education, backwardness of communities. Educationally according to NPE envisages that there should be

universal elementary education for all. There should be equalization of educational opportunities to all. There should by free 7 compulsory education for all children up to the age of 14 years is the constitution commitment in India.
India's progress in literacy has been tremendous during the last five decades. There is an equality of educational opportunities at the primary stage and secondary stage and hence Indian constitution has promoted equality of educational opportunities to all. There is an equal opportunity of education to women. In the Indian content education for all includes expansion of early childhood care and development authority including family and communities universal elementary education viewed as a composite program for all children up to 14 years of age universal participation till they complete the elementary stage through formal 7 non-formal education program, Sarva Shiksha Abhiyaan is a historic stride towards achieving the long cherished goal of universalization of elementary education through a time bound integrated approach. The objectives of Sarva Shiksha Abhiyaan are:

(1) Focus on elementary education.
(2) Bridge all gender and social category gaps.
(3) Universal retention by 2011.

The resources and aid for the universalization of elementary education was given by national and international investments in education. There has been a program for the nutritional support that is mid-day meal program was launched in 1995 with the main aim to provide education for all and universalization of elementary education up to the age of 14 there is a global commitment to provide quality and basic education for all children, youth and it affirmed to be successful till 2015.

INTRODUCTION

Education for all is a global movement led by UNESCO, aiming to meet the learning needs of all children, youth and adults by 2015. UNESCO has been mandated to led the movement and coordinate the international efforts to coach education for all government departments, agencies, civil society, non-government organizations and the media are but some of the partners working towards reaching these goals.

The EFA goals also contribute to the global pursuit of the eight millennium development goals, especially MDG2 on universal primary education and MDG3 on gender equality in education by 2015.

The fast track initiative was set-up to implement the EFA movement aiming at "accelerating progress towards quality universal primary education".

WORLD CONFERENCE ON EDUCATION FOR ALL (JUNCTION, 1990)

The movement was launched in 1990 at the world conference on education for all in Jomtain and Thailand. There responsibilities of the international community (155 countries) as well as responsibilities from some 150 organizations agreed to universalize primary education and massively reduce illiteracy by the end declaration of education for all was adopted which stated that education is a fundamental human right and pushed countries to strengthen their efforts to improve education in order to ensure that basic learning need for all were met the framework for action to meet the basic learning needs established six goals for the year 2000.

- Universal access to learning
- Focus on equality
- Emphasis on learning outcomes
- Broadening the mean scope of basic education
- Enhancing the environment for learning
- Strengthening partnership by 2000

WORLD EDUCATION FORUM (DAKAR, 2000)

In 2000 ten years later, the international community met again at the world education forum in Dakar, Senegal an event which drew 1100 participants, the forum took of the fact that many countries were far from having reached the goals established at the world conference on education for all the participants agreed on the Dakar framework for action which reaffirmed their commitment to achieve education for all by the year 2015 and identified six measurable education goals which aims to meet the learning needs of all children, youth and adults by 2015.

- expand early childhood care and education,
- provide free and compulsory primary education for all,
- promote learning and life skills for young people and adults,
- increase adult literacy by 50 percent,
- achieve gender parity by 2005 gender equality by 2015, and
- improve the quality of education.

Education for All in India

Authority to Kothari Commission report "the destiny of India is being shaped its classrooms", education is very important and essential for the developments of human beings it inculcate social and civil responsibilities among the pupil. Education is the basic needs of the human being. Through education we achieve peace, freedom, equality, justice. The 2 aspects of human being it inculcate social and civil responsibility among the pupil education is the basic needs of the human being through education we achieve peace, freedom, equality, justice, the 2 aspects of human being that is biological and social is maintained and transmitted from generation to generation and helps for the enrichment of culture.

Objectives of Education for All

The Article 45 of the Indian constitution encourages that the state should endeavors to provide within a period of ten years from the commencement of this constitution free and compulsory education to all children will they complete the age of fourteen years. Therefore, to achieve this goal efforts have been made by the government. The constitution of India also has the provision for educational opportunities to all the people of the country, most of the developing and backward countries are realizing the importance of education fro all their people according to S.S. Mathur All other reforms and progress in other field will sceraly follow it, adult literacy is made universal and not only universal but persistent and not only persistent but a motivating force creating favor and zeal among the people for social reform. The emergence of India as a powerful world nation has clearly depicted the importance of education for all.

Problems in Education for All

In India there are number of problems to achieve the goals of universaliasation of education or education for all such as host there are luck of funds, urban, rural, imbalance, lack of woman's education and conditions of backwardness of communities economically.

ACCORDING TO NATIONAL POLICY OF EDUCATION, 1986

The national policy document encourages that there should be universal elementary education of "education for all". This target will be completed till 2000 A.D. but these targets could not be achieve for several reasons.

Equalization of Educational Opportunities for All

Equality of opportunity has become important in education. A.H. Halseys says that the role of education is to mention in the society as equal. The sociologist the politician the writers the educationist opines that every citizen should and must have equal opportunities. Sargents report (1944) suggested the equality of opportunity could be provided primary stage through free schooling like mid day meals, books, scholarship, etc. after independence India formulated the goal of equality of opportunity in education and employment.

Historical Development Towards "Education for All"

Free and compulsory education for all children up to the age of 14 years is the constitutional commitment in India (Article 45) at the time of the adoption of the constitution in 1950, the aim was to achieve the goal of universalisetion of elementary education within the next 10 years that is by 1960 keeping in view the educational facilities available in the country at that time the goal was far too ambitious to achieve within a short span of ten years to facilitate the achievement of UEE goal. The National Council of Educational Research and Training (NCERT) the National Institute of Educational Planning and Administration (NSEPA) and many other institutes were set-up in 1960's as resource research and training centers in order to give access to elementary education for all children up to 14 years of age and for universal participation till they complete the elementary stage of educational programs the national policy on education.

NPE in 1968, the NPE in 1986, the program of action elaborated in the NPE of 1986 and the updated form of the NPE in 1992 gave an unqualified priority to the universalization of elementary education program. At the time of independence in the year 1947 India inherited a system of education which was not only quantitatively small but also characterized by the persistence of large intra and inter-regional as well as structural imbalance. Only 14 percent of population was literate and one child out of three had been enrolled in the primary school. The need for a literate population and universal education for all in the age group of 6-14 was recognized as a critical input for nation building and was given due consideration in successive five year planes. At the same time it was decided that the various parameters of implementation of new policy must be review after 5 years, this would ascertain the progress of implementation of the policy and focus on the emerging trends in the area of education.

The NPE, 1986 which was modified in 1992 as a program of action made certain modification in the earlier policy. The POA, 1992 emphasized three aspects, universal access and environment universal retention of children up to age of 14 years and a substation improvement in the quality of education to enable all children to achieve essential levels of learning at the primary educational levels.

LITERACY

India's progress in literacy has been tremendous during the last five decades, however a feature that remains consistent in the literacy situations in India is the existence of large disparities in literacy achievements between different factions of populations based on genders and residence.

TABLE I

Growth of Literacy in India : 1951-2001

Year	*Total*	*Male*	*Female*	*Sex Disparity*
1951	16.67	24.95	7.93	0.54
1961	24.02	34.44	12.95	0.48
1971	29.45	39.45	18.69	0.38
1981	36.23	46.89	24.82	0.33
1991	42.49	52.68	32.52	0.27
2001	65.38	75.85	54.16	0.22

Source : Census of India, 2001, Provisional population totals.

Since 1990 the gross enrolment ratios at the primary stage in the country as a whole and in most of its states exceed 100 percent free are quite a few states where the ratio is considerably lower during this line the GER in some cases exceed more than 100 percent, this happened because the counts of over and under aged children in the schools were not objected which calculating the GER, this problem till continues to be present in the system. The problem gets more complicated as the drop-out rates inspite of a detaining trend continue to be high.

EQUALITY OF EDUCATIONAL OPPORTUNITIES AT THE PRIMARY STAGE

Basic education of primary education for the student. The Article 45 of the constitution declares the state shall endeavour

TABLE 2

Gross Enrolment Ratio at Primary and Upper Primary Levels

Year	Primary Grades IV			Upper-primary Grades V-VIII			Elementation Grades		
	Boys	Girls	Total	Boys	Girls	Total	Boys	Girls	Total
(1)	(2)	(3)	(4)	(5)	(6)	(7)	(8)	(9)	(10)
1950-51	60.6	24.8	42.6	20.6	4.6	12.7	46.4	17.7	32.1
1960-61	2.6	41.4	62.4	33.2	11.3	22.5	65.2	30.9	48.7
1970-71	92.6	59.1	76.4	46.5	20.8	34.2	75.5	49.4	61.9
1990-2000	104.1	85.2	94.9	67.2	49.7	58.8	90.1	72.0	81.3
2000-01	107.3	85.8	96.8	76.2	53.3	65.3	97.3	75.5	86.8
2001-02	103.1	82.3	93.0	80.3	57.7	69.6	95.7	74.6	85.6
2002-03	101.4	89.4	95.6	63.2	48.6	56.3	87.1	74.4	81.1
2003-04	100.8	95.7	98.3	66.9	57.7	62.5	88.0	81.5	84.9
2004	111.4	105.5	108.6	74.8	65.8	70.5	97.6	90.6	94.2

Source : SES MHRD.

to provide free compulsory and universal education without any disecrimmation of caste, creed and sex.

Equality of Educational Opportunities at the Secondary Stage

Education at the secondary stage is as important as primary education but here provision should be there for the diversified curriculum to suit the needs and interest of the pupils.

Promoting Equality of Educational Opportunities to All

Provision of educational opportunity is the needs of the hour in the modern world. People believe that they can improve their economic status only through education.

Equal Opportunities of Education to Women

There should be equal educational opportunities given to women for the improvement of women's and to provide equal Job opportunities. There are many provisions made for the equal education to women's if a single woman in a house is educated then the whole house is educated if the women's are given the equal opportunity of education then the whole nation will be developed according to Shakshartha Mission in India.

Article Related to Education for All

Article 16 equality of opportunity, "No citizen shall on any grounds like caste, creed, sex, etc. be ineligible for or discriminate against in respect of any employment of office under the state there shall be equality.

Education for All in the Indian Content

(1) Expansion of early childhood care and development activities including family and communities especially for poor, disadvantage and children.
(2) Universal elementary education viewed as a composite program of access to elementary education for all children up to 14 years of age, universal participation till they complete the elementary stage

through formal and non-formal education program and universal achievement of at least the minimum levels of learning.

(3) Drastic reduction in illiteracy particularly in the 15-35 age group bringing the literacy level in this age group at least to 80 percent in each gender and for every identified disadvantage group ensuring that the levels of three RS are relevant to the living and working condition of the people.

(4) Provision of opportunities to maintain use and upgrade their education and provision for the facilities for development of skill to all persons who have reviewed primary education through the formal and non-formal channels.

(5) Creation of necessary structure and setting in motion processor which would empower and make education an instrument of woman's equality.

(6) Improving the content and process of education people's culture and their living and working conditions thereby enhancing their ability to learn and cope with problems of livelihood and environment.

SARVA SHIKSHA ABHIYAN (SSA)

The Sarva Shiksha Abhiyan is a historic stride towards achieving the long cherished goal of universalizaion of elementary education through a time bound integrated approach in partnership with states which promises to change the face of elementary education sector of the country aims to provide useful and quality elementary education to all children in the age group of 6-14 by 2010.

The objectives of Sarva Shiksha Abhiyan are:

(1) All children in school education grantee center alternative school or back to school camp by 2003.

(2) All children complete eight years of schooling by 2010.

(3) All children complete five years of primary schooling by 2007.

(4) Focus on elementary education of satisfactory quality with emphasis on education for life.
(5) Bridge all gender and social category gaps at primary stage by 2007 and at elementary education level by 2010.
(6) Universal retention by 2010.

RESOURCES AND AID

National Investment in Education

Improving access to and the quality of basic education depends partly on increasing public explanative in GNP was above 3% in year 2004. Between 1999 and 2004 the share feed in India national public spending on ECCE is very low. The share of pre-primary education in total public expenditure on education in 2004 was less than 5%.

International Investment in Education

Fast track initiative designed primarily by the World Bank the FTZ was launched in April 2002 as a process that would provide quick and incremental technical and financial support to countries that have policies but are not on track to alto in universal primary education by 2015. The FTI has raised high expectations that significant new funding would be mobilized for achieving this goal but has yet to receive substantial and specific international support for its activities, educational sector plans were evaluated using criteria from the indicative framework developed by the World Bank and arrived from the Banks analysis of a group of developing countries that have either attained UPE or made considerable process towards this goals.

National Program for Nutritional Support (Mid-day Meal)

The national program for nutritional support to primary education (launched in 1995) provides food grains cooked meals to children in primary classes. 100 grams of food grains per day for children attending schools for at least 80 percent of the total school days a month Annual Report MHRD in 1999-2000 states that 9.90 million children were covered under the scheme and allocated 2.71 million metric tones of food grains in that year along with teachers the local community is also given responsibility in the distribution of food grains.

Global Commitment

The education for all movement is a global commitment to provide quality basic education for all children, youth and adults. The movement was launched at the world conference on education for all in 1990 in Jontain, Thailand when responsibilities of the international community agreed to universalized primary education and massively reduce illiteracy by the end of the ten years later with many countries far from having reached this goal, the international community met again in 2000 in Dakar, Senegal and affirmed their commitment to achieving education for all by the year 2015.

Implication for Education for All

(1) "Education for all" means to achieve minimum level of learning.
(2) It also means universalisation of elementary education.
(3) It also implies education for all up to the age of 14.
(4) It lays equal emphasis for girl education.
(5) It envisages bringing improvement in building school facilities, etc.
(6) The sixth implication is to provide equal privileges to all.
(7) Education for all in rural areas can be articulated which is essential for making a success.

CONCLUSION

Education should be universal for the all round development of material and spiritual attainments of children. There should be equal opportunity must be given for the over all development of the child education is a unique investment in the present and future, it is the main aim according to national policy of education (NPE). 10+2+3 structure of education is common to all, for all leads to national vs. international understanding, hence education to all is a dynamic process which is a must for the development of the nation.

References

Report Education for All : Reaching the unreached EFA mid-decade assessment meeting report.

Report EFA—Global monitoring report, 2003-04, UNESCO.

Report EFA—Global monitoring report, 2007, regional overview.

Report gender and education for all—the lap of equality in regional overview—EFA Global monitoring report, 2003-04, UNESCO.

Mehta, Arun C., Elementary Education in India—where do we stand state report card, 2005-06, national university of educational planning and administration.

Mehta, Arun, C., Education for all in India with focus on elementary education current status, recent initiatives and future prospectus.

R. Govinda, "Lok Fumbish : An innovation in grassroots levels management of primary education" in Change Inaction, UNESCO, Paris, 1995.

CHAPTER

28

Teaching Mindfulness

SHABNAM

ABSTRACT

Teaching Mindfulness emphasizes how the teacher's personal familiarity with mindfulness plants the seed for an education infused with attention, awareness, kindness, empathy, compassion, and gratitude. In the process of understanding oneself as a teacher of mindfulness, one considers the authenticity, authority, and friendship that are taken into the practice. The role of the teacher is not one of lecturing or direct instruction but of balancing the authority of being a leader with specialized information with meeting the group as a friend and equal in the moment. Mindfulness, which features focused awareness training, is increasing in popularity among mental health professionals and focused attention to internal and external experiences in the present moment of time, without judgment. While mindfulness interventions have been used in treatments for clinical problems, researchers suggest that this type of training also can be beneficial in everyday life. This theoretical paper is an attempt to propose that training in mindfulness has the potential to enhance attention and focus, and improve memory, self-acceptance, self-management skills, and self-understanding. Finally, mindfulness meditation exercises the feature attending to cognitive processes.

INTRODUCTION

Children can be taught to begin to pay attention to those things in the present moment that they never noticed before through a process called mindfulness. Mindfulness is defined as "the awareness that emerges through paying attention on purpose, in the present moment, and non-judgmentally to the unfolding of experiences moment by moment" (Kabat-Zinn, 2003). The first part of this definition expresses the idea that mindfulness is an active process; it involves active attention which leads to awareness. The second part of the definition highlights that it regards the present, rather than the past or future. The third part emphasizes that the attention is non-judgmental and accepting, without thinking that the experience of the present moment is good or bad, right or wrong, important or not. It involves attending to the external environment such as sights, sounds, and smells, as well as to internal bodily sensations, thoughts, and feelings. In practicing mindfulness, one becomes aware of the current internal and external experiences, observes them carefully, accepts them, and allows them to be let go of in order to attend to another present moment experience (Hooker and Fodor, 2008).

Mindfulness has its origins in the Buddhist tradition, through Eastern practices of meditation. It is often learned and practiced through meditation exercises. However, mindfulness should not be confused with meditation. The goal is not to achieve a higher state of consciousness or to distance oneself from the present experience, but rather to have an increased awareness of the present moment. To highlight with an example, one form of meditation is meditation using a mantra, in which the focus is to be aware of the chanting of a syllable or phrase, and only on the chanting (LeShan, 1974). In contrast, the focus of a mindfulness meditation is to be aware of and observe the constantly changing internal and external stimuli (Baer, 2003). Mindfulness also should not be confused with relaxation (Dimidjian and Linehan, 2003). Again, they are related in that mindfulness may result in a more relaxed physical and mental state. However, the goal of mindfulness is not to become more relaxed, but to be aware of and accepting of whatever state the body and mind are in. Mindfulness can be practiced through meditation, but unlike these other techniques, mindfulness can be practiced through mindful eating, mindful driving, mindful walking, or any experience in our lives (Dimidjian and Linehan, 2003).

Mindfulness is simply paying attention to life, here and now, with kindness and curiosity. One of the primary ironies of modern education is that we ask students to "pay attention" dozens of times a day, yet we never teach them how. The practice of mindfulness teaches students how to pay attention, and this way of paying attention enhances both academic and social-emotional learning. As human beings we have the unique capacity to pay attention to/be aware of our internal and external worlds and the interactions between the two. We can attend to the breath, the body, thoughts, emotions, tastes, smells, sights, sounds, and our impulses and actions and their effects on others and our environment. This ability to pay attention is a natural, innate human capacity (Hooker and Fodor, 2008).

WHY IS MINDFULNESS IMPORTANT?

Stress and Learning

As a classroom teacher, a person already knows that many of your students are stressed. For some, the stress is simply living in our fast-paced, media-saturated, multi-tasking world. For others, the stress is performing, "succeeding," and getting into a "good" college. For still others the stress is surviving in extremely challenging, even traumatic, home environments and life circumstances. One also most likely realized that student stress frequently inhibits their ability to learn, and that the emphasis on academics is neglecting the development of the social-emotional qualities essential for skillful world.

Students are being diagnosed with depression, anxiety, ADHD, eating disorders, cutting, addictions and other self-destructive behaviors at epidemic rates. Cruelty, bullying and violence are on the rise. Most, if not all, children could benefit from learning to focus their attention, to become less reactive, and to be more compassionate with themselves and others. Fortunately, science is now documenting the negative impact that stress is having on learning every day, in classrooms across the country. Related studies have shown that self-compassion has academic benefits, especially when dealing with perceived failure.

MINDFULNESS AS A FOUNDATION FOR LEARNING

The newly emerging discipline of Mindfulness in education is actively investigating whether offering mindfulness to children and adolescence enhances attention, executive function, and learning, and promotes pro-social behavior and general well-being. The preliminary data are encouraging; below are summaries of four recent studies that demonstrate the benefits of offering mindfulness across the age spectrum. Integrative program of mindfulness and relaxation showed significant increases in attention and social skills and decreases in test anxiety and ADHD behaviors. In studying second and third graders who did Mindfulness Awareness Practices for 30 minutes twice a week for 8 weeks, Flook, and her colleagues at the Mindfulness Awareness Research Center at UCLA documented that children who began the study with poor executive function had gains in behavioral regulation, meta-cognition, and overall global executive control. These results indicate Mindfulness Awareness Practice training benefits children with executive function difficulties.

Mindfulness is being used to treat many physical and psychological problems, including stress, anxiety, depression, borderline personality disorder, chronic pain, addiction, and eating disorders (Hooker and Fodor, 2008). See Baer (2003) for a superb review of the literature on the use of mindfulness as a clinical intervention and a description of the applications of mindfulness to mental health problems.

STRESS AND CHRONIC PAIN

One of the earlier and most frequently cited uses for mindfulness is stress reduction, through Jon Kabat-Zinn's program, Mindfulness-Based Stress Reduction (MBSR). This program is for people referred for stress-related disorders and chronic pain. It involves an eight-week course conducted in groups, focused on practicing mindfulness skills and mindfulness meditations, as well as discussion of stress and coping strategies. Researchers have adapted Kabat-Zinn's MBSR methodology for treating a variety of emotional problems, among which are borderline personality disorder, anxiety and depressions, eating disorders, and substance abuse (Hooker and Fodor, 2008).

BORDERLINE PERSONALITY DISORDER

Mindfulness training is a central component of Marsha Linehan's Dialectical Behavior Therapy (DBT) for borderline personality disorders. (Linehan, 1993a; 1993b). Mindfulness training is one of the core components taught first in this program, honing the issue of shifting mood and affect modulation to promote acceptance and change. In DBT, "clients are encouraged to accept themselves, their histories, and their current situations exactly as they are" (Baer, 2003, p. 127). Linehan (1993), in adapting the program from Kabat-Zinn to her borderline populations, elaborates on the three "what" skills of mindfulness as observing, describing, and participating, and the "how" skills of mindfulness which stress being non-judgmental and developing effective coping skills (Hooker and Fodor, 2008).

ANXIETY

Mindfulness training also has been used successfully to treat anxiety disorders. Moving beyond mindfulness as stress reduction training, Roemer and Orsillo (2002) posit a conceptual connection between anxiety and the utility of mindfulness to alleviate such symptoms. They view anxiety symptoms as forms of experiential avoidance in that the person is not in contact with bodily sensations, thoughts, emotions, and memories. The first way in which mindfulness can help is by reducing this experiential avoidance. The way most people think about anxiety is as a chronic focus on worries about the future, without acknowledging the reality of the present. An anxious person worries about what might happen in the future, rather than focusing on what is happening in the present. Even a non-anxious person, during the process of worrying, is engaged in future-oriented thinking, talking to self, and focuses on anticipated events (Borkovec, 2002). Mindfulness provides an alternative focus as attention is drawn to the present moment, thus breaking the maladaptive cycle of worrying (Mennin *et. al.*, 2002; Roemer and Orsillo, 2002). Mindfulness also may be useful for other characteristics of anxiety. In addition to the focus on the future, individuals with anxiety by self-report were found to have reported higher levels of intensity of emotional experience than control individuals, thus identifying a marked need to regulate and control their negative emotional experiences—a task that mindfulness practice can help them achieve (Mennin *et. al.*, 2002). Anxiety also is marked by displayed difficulties in the ability to identify, describe, and accept emotional experience and deficits in ability to pacify them while experiencing negative emotions (Mennin *et. al.*, 2002). Through mindfulness, the anxious person learns to identify emotions, be aware of them, and accept them, whether they are positive or negative (Hooker and Fodor, 2008).

It should be said that no universal agreement exists regarding the utility of mindfulness practice as an intervention for anxiety, and thus it should be used with some caution. Wells (2002) argues that "mindfulness meditation does not contain information that can lead to unambiguous disconfirmation of erroneous beliefs about worry". Thus, he cautions that rather than using mindfulness alone, mindfulness might be better used in conjunction with cognitive-behavioral techniques to address the irrational thoughts. Roemer and Orsillo (2002) in further studies, integrate mindfulness training in acceptance-based treatment with cognitive-behavioral treatments for anxiety (Hooker and Fodor, 2008).

DEPRESSION

Mindfulness has also been used in the treatment of depression and the prevention of depression relapse (Segal, Williams, and Teasdale, 2002). Two characteristics of depression discussed in the literature can be addressed through mindfulness: despairing thoughts and lack of focus on the self (Baer, 2003). Mindfulness training may enable depressed individuals to notice their despairing, hopeless thoughts and redirect attention to other aspects of the present moment, such as breathing, walking, or environmental stimuli. Mindfulness also has been shown to increase depressed patients' recall of autobiographical information, including memories of past experiences, thoughts, and feelings—which can be greatly lacking in depressed individuals—by drawing attention to the self and surroundings. Clinical research studies by Segal, Williams, and Teasdale (2002) stress the importance of the therapist actively engaging in mindfulness practice himself/herself while conducting mindfulness training with groups of depressed clients (Hooker and Fodor, 2008).

EATING DISORDERS AND ADDICTION

Eating disorders and addiction are similar to each other in that the individual is focused on a persistent thought of future actions: when he or she will eat or not eat in the future, fear of gaining weight, or when there will be an opportunity for the next high. There are also similarities in the experiences of self-criticism: in individuals feeling terrible about themselves for binging and purging or for using the drug, hating their bodies, hating their life circumstances, and experiencing a strong sense of shame (Hooker and Fodor, 2008). Mindfulness can be useful for relapse prevention by shifting the focus to the present moment rather than to future actions, and through self-acceptance of whatever the present feeling or thought is without judgment and criticism (Baer, 2003). The individual can learn to note the urge, accept it, and let it go without acting on it. In addition, in the case of eating disorders, the "self-observation skills developed through mindfulness training might lead to improved recognition of satiety cues in binge eaters, as well as increased ability to observe urges to binge without yielding to them" (Baer, 2003).

How does mindfulness have a beneficial effect on these clinical problems? It appears that the mediator, by engaging in a process of enhancing awareness, is undergoing a self-management, self-acceptance, exposure, and cognitive therapy rolled into one experience (Hooker and Fodor, 2008).

COGNITIVE CHANGE

Mindfulness actually may lead to changes in thought patterns and the attitude of one's thoughts: cognitive change. Kabat-Zinn (1990) suggests that this occurs through the practice of non-judgmental thinking as well as the understanding that thoughts are not necessarily the reality or the truth. For example, "feeling afraid does not necessarily mean that danger is imminent, and thinking 'I am a failure' does not make it true" (Baer, 2003). Thinking get changes when this is realized and accepted.

SELF-MANAGEMENT

Mindfulness practice, sitting and attending to one's thought, is in itself a self-management intervention. Again, the first stage in change is self-awareness of a problem or pattern. For example, the anxious person can sit and become aware of what they are worrying about, without the pressure to change. The bulimic person or substance abuser becomes aware of their urges, as well as the desire for the food, substance, or fix that will facilitate avoidance. By sitting and using focused awareness on what's happening at the moment the urges emerge; the triggers and stressors may also come into awareness and facilitate more active problem-solving (Hooker and Fodor, 2008).

RELAXATION

As stated earlier, mindfulness is not the equivalent of relaxation, nor is relaxation the goal. However, by meditating, a person may become more relaxed. Through mindfulness practice, there is a slowing of the racing thoughts simply by practicing to take time and note and observe each thought. There is often a decrease in muscle tension, a slowing of the breathing, and a slowing of heart rate (Hooker and Fodor, 2008).

ACCEPTANCE

A component of mindfulness training is acceptance of where one is. Gestalt therapy, which has many features in common with mindfulness training, posits a paradoxical theory of change (Hooker and Fodor, 2008). By fully owning and accepting where one is, change does occur (Beisser, 1970). In work with medical and clinical populations, mindfulness training includes an acceptance of pain, worries, thoughts, and emotions without trying to escape, avoid, or change them. By being willing to stay with the pain and negative emotions, researchers suggest, individuals may benefit through a greater sense of self-acceptance (Baer, 2003).

MINDFULNESS PRACTICE TO CHILDREN

Mindfulness practice for children is not dramatically different from that for adults. Exercises can be adapted to fit different ages and abilities. One should be aware of what the experience of a child is like. Children's thinking is more concrete; therefore, activities should be clear, concrete, and descriptive in their instructions. But children are also imaginative and are able to use their creativity and imagination. They enjoy movies, cartoons, and fantasy books. The use of humor also helps (Hooker and Fodor, 2008).

In teaching mindfulness to children, it is important to start with success, so starting simply is better. For example, while an adult might start trying to meditate for 15 minutes, it would be more appropriate for a child to start with five minutes. The exercises presented herein will likely be helpful to most children: beginning with the more concrete attention to the external environment, then moving to the experience of the body, and finally, introducing attention to the mind and meditation exercises (Hooker and Fodor, 2008).

Another important note about teaching mindfulness to children is that the person teaching should be comfortable with the exercises prior to the teaching, and have practiced mindfulness in general. We must practice what we teach. As Kabat-Zinn (2003) states, mindfulness "cannot be taught to others in an authentic way without the instructor's practicing it in his or her own life" (p. 149). It is not something you learn about at a seminar or read about and then pass along. Some children may have difficulty with meditation and not take to it at first, but they should be encouraged to try, perhaps with different forms of meditation or shorter lengths of time (Hooker and Fodor, 2008).

To begin, meditation should be discussed with the children. They may have questions about it, or misperceptions. Gunaratana (1991) presents a list of myths about meditation, discussing the truth about each one. One myth that children may believe about meditation is that it is for saints and holy men. While saints and holy men, particularly in some religions, practice meditation, a lot of people meditate. They may believe that meditation means going into a trance. Rather than going into a trance, mindfulness meditation actually involves being highly aware of the present sensations, thoughts, and feelings. Children may also have the misperception that meditation is just used for relaxation. It is true that meditation produces a physiological state of deep relaxation, with slower metabolic rate and heartbeat (LeShan, 1974). But meditation is much more than relaxation, as it involves focus and awareness.

One specific caution in teaching mindfulness to children is that for some, there may be a heightened experience of anxiety as a result of the exercises. Some individuals report feeling more anxious after practicing meditation. This may happen because people are uncomfortable paying attention to themselves. Additionally, if the thoughts and sensations they are observing are related to worries and fears, they may feel increased anxiety by recognizing them (Kabat-Zinn, 1990). For a child who has this sort of negative response to mindfulness, encourage him or her to keep trying and, at the same time, try to determine what part of the experience is causing the anxiety. It may be that the child does not like observing negative thoughts. In this case, it will help to practice letting go (Hooker and Fodor, 2008). Another possibility is that the child feels he or she cannot let go and has a feeling of being tightly wound to "hold it together," and a fear that letting go would increase anxiety. In this case, it will be helpful to encourage using mindfulness to increase focus and control on the present moment. If, after practice, the child still has a very negative experience, exercises such as meditation may not be right for that child. However, the activities such as awareness of the environment and the raisin meditation may still be appropriate. As in many interventions, customizing the right techniques and applications for each individual is important (Hooker and Fodor, 2008).

CONCLUSION

Given the recent interest and popularity of mindfulness training with adults and its demonstrated usefulness to medical and clinical populations, it is believed that children could benefit from this focused awareness training as well. Schools seem to be ideal settings for introducing mindfulness techniques. Mindfulness training could be introduced in schools using the progression of exercises and techniques. The school psychologist or counselor also could consult with teachers to design or adapt mindfulness training to be appropriate for each classroom, level, and school setting. Over time, mindfulness training could be incorporated into the curriculum and used throughout the school day. There are ideal times to use these mindfulness techniques. The beginning of the day (e.g., homeroom) may be a useful time to practice bringing awareness to the present, perhaps using a visual meditation, in order to focus attention on beginning the school day, and to begin the day freshly. Similarly, mindfulness might be used at other transition points during the school day, such as before or after recess, after lunch, and the end of the day. Mindfulness practice can also be used before important events such as tests, sporting events, and competitions. The goal is for children to learn to use mindfulness techniques whenever they need to calm themselves and refocus their energy and attention. Such a refocusing could enhance concentration, memory, and learning, as well as facilitate a more productive and relaxed—less anxious and stressful—school environment. Through bringing increased awareness to the external environment and to the internal experience of the body and the mind, children will likely benefit psychologically and emotionally, as well as through gaining a general sense of well being.

References

Baer, R.A. (2003). Mindfulness Training as a Clinical Intervention: A Conceptual and Empirical Review. *Clinical Psychology: Science and Practice,* 10(2) 125-43.

Beisser, A.R. (1970). The Paradoxical Theory of Change. In: Gestalt Therapy Now, J. Fagan and I.L. Shepard (eds.) Palo Alto, California: Science and Behavior Books.

Borkovec, T.D. (2002). Life in the Future *versus* Life in the Present. *Clinical Psychology: Science and Practice,* 9(1):76-80.

Dimidjian, S. and Linehan, M.M. (2003). Defining an Agenda for Future Research on the Clinical Application of Mindfulness Practice. *Clinical Psychology: Science and Practice,* 10(2) : 166-78.

Gunaratana, V.H. (1991). Mindfulness in Plain English. Boston: Wisdom Publications.

Hooker, Karen E. and Fodor, Iris E. (2008). Teaching Mindfulness to Children. *Gestalt Review,* 12(1) 75-91.

Kabat-Zinn, J. (1990). Full Catastrophe Living: Using the Wisdom of Your Body and Mind to Face Stress, Pain, and Illness. New York: Delacorte.

Kabat-Zinn, J. (2003). Mindfulness-based Interventions in Context: Past, Present, and Future. *Clinical Psychology: Science and Practice,* 10(2): 144-56.

LeShan, L. (1974). How to Meditate: A Guide to Self-discovery. New York: Bantam Books.

Linehan, M.M. (1993a). Cognitive-Behavioral Treatment of Borderline Personality Disorder. New York: Guildford Press.

Linehan, M.M. (1993b). Skills Training Manual for Treating Borderline Personality Disorder. New York: Guildford Press.

Mennin, D.S., Heimberg, R.G., Turk, C.L. and Fresco, D.M. (2002). Applying an Emotion Regulation Framework to Integrative Approaches to Generalized Anxiety Disorder. *Clinical Psychology: Science and Practice,* 9(1): 85-90.

Roemer, L. and Orsillo, S.M. (2002). Expanding Our Conceptualization of and Treatment for Generalized Anxiety Disorder: Integrating Mindfulness/Acceptance-based Approaches with Existing Cognitive-behavioral Models. *Clinical Psychology: Science and Practice,* 9(1): 4-68.

Sangpo, T. (1999). The Thirty-seven Practices of Bodhisattvas. Dalai Lama, Teaching, The Beacon Theatre.

Segal, Z., Williams, J. and Teasdale, J. (2002). Mindfulness-based Cognitive Therapy for Depression: A New Approach to Preventing Relapse. New York: Guilford Press.

Wells, A. (2002). GAD, Metacognition, and Mindfulness: An Information Processing Analysis. *Clinical Psychology: Science and Practice,* 9(1): 95-100.

CHAPTER

29

Public-Private Partnership in Education in Uttar Pradesh

A.P. PANDEY AND SHAILENDRA KUMAR SINGH

1. INTRODUCTION

India's recent economic growth rates have generated much optimism about its general social and economic development. But has there been accompanying progress in indicators of educational outcomes? How good are Indian educational achievements in relation to China's, the country with which it is increasingly compared? What are the most significant developments in Indian school education and what has been the impact of various education policy initiatives? This paper presents a critical overview of the school education sector in India using newly released data and a survey of existing studies with new model of PPP. The story of India's educational achievements is one of mixed success. On the down side, India has 22 per cent of the world's population but 46 per cent of the world's illiterates, and is home to a high proportion of the world out of school children and youth. On the positive side, it has made encouraging recent progress in raising schooling participation. While the base of India's education pyramid may be weak, it has emerged as an important player in the worldwide information technology revolution on the back of substantial (absolute) number of well educated computing and other graduates. This paper provides an assessment of the current situation and recent progress of school education.

2. INDIAN EDUCATIONAL ACHIEVEMENTS IN INTERNATIONAL PERSPECTIVE

Presents India's adult and youth literacy rates alongside equivalent figures for its regional neighbors, as well as for countries in the BRIC grouping (Brazil, Russian Federation, India and China). While India does well compare to Bangladesh and Pakistan, it lags substantially behind all the other BRIC countries and Sri Lanka. Indeed it is striking that its overall adult literacy rate is similar to and female adult literacy rate lower than that of Sub-Saharan Africa. The comparison with China is of particular interest and it shows India to be at a considerable educational disadvantage: India's adult literacy in the early 2000s was wholly 30 percentage points below China's. Even focusing more narrowly at only the youth literacy rates, India's disadvantage with respect to China is a large 22.5 percentage points. India's disadvantage *vis-a-vis* other countries in primary school participation rates is much smaller compared to that for youth literacy rates, since 93.4% of Indian elementary school age children were enrolled in school in 2006 according to ASER survey (Pratham, 2007). However, at the secondary school level, India is again at a large disadvantage with respect to all three other BRIC countries where secondary enrolment rates are far above those predicted for countries at their levels of per capita GDP. Brazilian and Russian secondary school net enrolment rates are 27 percentage points higher than India's that India is more than 30 years behind China in terms of the proportion of the population with completed secondary and post-secondary schooling.

Educational Attainment, India and China

Comparable data on learning achievement of students are not available for most of the countries with which India is commonly compared. For instance, none of the South Asian countries nor China participated in the international studies of learning achievement such as the Trends in International Mathematics and Science. Study (TIMSS, 2003) in which 46 countries participated, or in the Progress in International Reading Literacy Study (PIRLS, 2001) in which 35 countries participated. Moreover, South Asia does not have the equivalent of the SACMEQ study, which is a regional inter-country comparative study of achievement levels in 14 African countries. However, World Bank (2006) applied the TIMSS questions to secondary school students in the Indian states of Rajasthan and Orissa, with permission of the Indian Ministry of Human Resource Development. The findings show that international mean achievement in maths test was 52 percent for grade 8 students but the average scores of Rajasthan and Orissa students on the same test were 34 and 37 percent respectively. Similarly, the international mean of achievement was 57 percent for Grade 12 students but the corresponding scores for Indian students were 44 and 38 percent in Rajasthan and Orissa respectively. However, the high international average percentage mark from the 46 TIMSS countries included both high and low income countries. When India did participate in international studies of learning achievement in early 1970s, the performance of Indian children was poor relative to most participating developing countries, according to the International Association for the Evaluation of Educational Achievement (IEA).

3. SCHOOLING ACCESS AND QUALITY

At Independence, India inherited a legacy of large-scale illiteracy and lack of proper provision for education. At the first post-Independence Census of 1951, only 9 per cent of women and 27 percent of men were literate. It was resolved by the framers of the constitution that the new Indian state would endeavor to provide free and compulsory education to all children up to age 14 by 1960. This goal turned out to be elusive and the deadline for its achievement has been put back repeatedly in the past 55 years. While even today this goal remains unfulfilled, there has been very encouraging progress in schooling participation and other educational outcome indicators in recent times. We consider several educational access and quality indicators next.

Primary and Secondary Enrolment Rates

The ASER 2006 survey provides the latest picture of schooling participation in India. It finds that 93.4 per cent of all elementary school age children (6-14 year olds) were enrolled in school, an encouraging statistic, reflecting a good deal of progress compared to enrolments in the early 1990s. Among children 11-14 years old enrol was lower: 10.3% of girls and 7.7% of boys were out of school (either never enrolled in school or dropped out). Among 15-16 years olds, the corresponding out-of-school figures rose steeply to 22.7% and 20.2% respectively for girls and boys. The gross enrolment rate in secondary education of 47%, which we noted was below the level predicted for a country of India's per capita income level. Schooling participation depends on both the extent of demand for and the availability of supply of schooling. According to Seventh All India Education Survey (NCERT, 2006), in 2002, there were only one-fifth as many secondary schools (those with grade 10 classes) as the number of primary schools.

Thus, it seems likely that secondary school enrolment rates are low partly because of the lack of supply of nearby secondary schools. However, despite supply constraints, demand for secondary education has risen and is likely to rise (partly via increase in private schooling) because it is lucrative level of education to acquire. Kingdon (1998) and Kingdon and Unni (2001) find that the education-wage relationship is convex in India, i.e. returns to secondary and higher education are significantly greater than to primary and middle levels of education, using National Sample Survey data, also shows that the economic returns to education increase with education level, i.e. since the coefficient on the quadratic term in years of education is large, positive and statistically significant in almost every state for both genders. That for men and women, the returns to higher secondary and tertiary education has risen consistently over time. For women, the return to primary education has fallen but for men, it has remained static. These findings are based on National Sample Survey data analysed by Duraisamy (2002), Vasudeva-Datta (2006), and World Bank (2006). Using National Sample Survey data for 1999-2000, there is a good deal of interstate variation in the extent of inequality in access to secondary schooling. The inequality (measured as the difference in access to secondary education among those in the top and bottom quintiles of the distribution of household per capita income) is greatest in Haryana, Andhra Pradesh and the so-called BIMARU (Sick) states. Bihar, Madhya Pradesh, Rajasthan and Uttar Pradesh which lag behind in many other indicators of social development. The inequality is lowest in the left leaning states of Kerala and West Bengal.

Great inter-state variation in gender-disparity in secondary school enrolment rates. The gender parity index here is the male to female secondary school enrolment ratio. A ratio of 1 represents gender equality. States such as Bihar and Rajasthan have grotesque gender inequality: girls are only half as likely to enrol in secondary school as boys. Other BIMARU states, Uttar Pradesh and Madhya Pradesh, together with their split-offs (Jharkhand and Chhattisgarh) also have appalling gender inequality, but on the bright side, many states have gender parity or even slightly pro-female secondary enrolment rates, e.g. Kerala and Tamil Nadu. Kingdon (2005) finds that an important part of the reason for gender inequality is to be found within the household, as opposed to institutional explanations (indeed, policy promotes girls, enrolment by instituting tuition free schooling for girls). Using household fixed effects equations, she finds strong within-household bias against daughters in terms of enrolment and household educational expenditure.

School attendance rates, Current attendance rates are a more reliable indicator of schooling participation than enrolment rates, since large enrolment rates measured at the start of the school year can mask non-attendance and/or drop-out later in the school year. Current school attendance rates from the National Family Health Surveys (NFHS), 1993 and 1999. In this short 6-year period, school attendance among rural 6-10 year old girls and boys increased by 20 and 12 percentage points respectively; these are very substantial increases. In the rural 11-14 year age group, increases were more modest but still large, especially for girls, at 13.7 per cent. Urban increases were smaller. Andhra Pradesh, Madhya Pradesh, Rajasthan, and Uttar Pradesh made very large improvements in their current school attendance rates, particularly in rural areas where, in each of these four states, attendance rates rose by over 25 percentage points in the six-year period. Overall, nearly 80 per cent of all 6-14 year olds were attending school in 1999. As Kingdon *et. al.* (2004) notes, while attendance rates then are not a guarantee of grade completion or of achieving minimum levels of learning; these are nevertheless highly encouraging trends.

Data from the 1991 and 2001 Indian censuses in the population aged 7 years and older, literacy rates rose substantially in the 1990s from 52 per cent to 65 per cent, an increase of 13 points. This is the highest absolute increase in any decade since records began in 1881. Over this 10 year period, the gender gap also began to close noticeably. Some states experienced particularly rapid literacy increases, e.g. in Madhya Pradesh and Rajasthan, literacy rates rose by 20 and 22 percentage points respectively. The increase in female literacy was also large in these states as well as in Uttar Pradesh and Andhra Pradesh. However, Bihar and Gujarat made poor progress.

Unfortunately, age-specific literacy data were not available from the 2001 Indian census even in early 2007. However, such data from the National Family Health Survey (NFHS) of 1993 and 1999 show encouraging trends shows that during the short 6 year period between 1993 to 1999, literacy rates in the young age groups rose rapidly for girls: taking rural and urban areas together, female literacy in the youngest age group 6-10 rose by nearly 14 percentage points. For rural girls aged 6-19, literacy rates rose by about 15 points. Overall, the national literacy rate for males and females aged 6-19 years increased by about 10 percentage points. Any major improvement in national literacy in the future will depend crucially on its progress among young persons in the four large north Indian states of Bihar, Madhya Pradesh, Rajasthan, and Uttar Pradesh (the so-called BIMARU or sick states) which have lagged behind particularly seriously in the past. Examining recent progress in these states is perhaps the most informative statistic when attempting to foresee the future of literacy in India. marked acceleration over time in literacy rates among 10-14 year olds in these states. Whereas the literacy rate among the young increased by only 6 percentage points in each of the two decades of the 1960s and 1970s, it increased by 14 points in the 1980s and by 18 points in the 1990s.

Learning achievement levels in primary education : A large body of evidence suggests that workers' Productivity and earnings depend not only on years of education acquired but also on what is learnt at school. This literature is summarised in Hanushek (2005). He cites 3 US studies as showing quite consistently that a one standard deviation increase in mathematics test performance at the end of high school in the US translates into 12 per cent higher annual earnings. He also cites three studies from the UK and Canada showing strong productivity returns to both numeracy and literacy skills. Substantial returns to cognitive skills also hold across the developing countries for which studies have been carried out, i.e. in Ghana, Kenya, Tanzania, Morocco, Pakistan and South Africa. Hanushek and Zhang (2006) confirm significant economic returns to literacy for 13 countries on which literacy data were available. This evidence underlines the importance of ensuring that what schools do leads to learning achievement. Unfortunately, no national data on learning achievement levels were available in India until 2006. India's largest educational NGO, Pratham, carried out a survey of learning achievement in 2005 and repeated the survey with a bigger sample of about 330,000 households in 2006. It visited 20 homes each in 30 randomly selected villages in each one of 549 Indian districts, and interacted with all children aged 6 to 16 years old in the sample homes. The ASER 2005 and 2006 reports are published by Pratham (2006; 2007). The findings make grim reading. In 2006, nearly 47% of children who were in school and studying in grade 5 could not read the story text at grade 2 level of difficulty. In arithmetic, 55% of grade 5 and 25% of grade 8 children could not solve a simple division problem (3 digits divided by 1 digit). In both reading and arithmetic, there was significant inter-state variation in student performance. For example, in 2005 based on the sample of grade 5 children, in West Bengal, Haryana, Bihar, Uttaranchal and Chhattisgarh less than 50% children were unable to do the simple division problems. In the bottom five states, 62-75% of grade 5 children could not solve the same division problems. Mathematics and environmental science were administered and each student's marks were recorded in percentage terms. These tests were administered by the National Council of Educational Research and Training (NCERT) in 2002 and the results published in 2006, soon after the release of the ASER survey. The average percentage mark for India as a whole is 50.3 per cent in science, 46.5 per cent in maths and 58.6% in language. While it is not clear how to interpret these, they appear to confirm ASER's findings of low learning levels.

Learning achievement levels in secondary education

Given the weak base of learning at the primary level, it is expected that learning levels at the secondary level of education will also be poor. We already saw that in cross-country comparison, achievement levels of Indian students appear to be well below the international average, though the latter does include developed countries. While each Indian state examination board sets its own curricula and examinations and there are no national level data based on a common standardized achievement test in India, the Council of Boards of Secondary Education (COBSE, 2004) provides pass rates in the High School and Intermediate (senior secondary) examinations in different states. 2004 pass rates in the High School exam varied from 37% in Manipur to 80% in Andhra Pradesh but such inter-state comparison is meaningless since curricula, exam papers, passing requirements, etc. all differ from state to state. In any case, the high school pass rates cannot be taken at face value as they are much inflated due to the phenomenon of wide-spread cheating, if the experience of Uttar Pradesh can be generalized. While the true levels of learning achievements in secondary education are generally hidden, fortuitously they became visible one year in Uttar Pradesh, that when the Kalyan Singh government brought in an anti-cheating rule and installed police at all examination centres in 1992 to prevent the mass-cheating that routinely takes place at board examinations in Uttar Pradesh, the pass rate in the High School exam fell from 57% in 1991 to a pitiful 14.7% in 1992 (17% among regular candidates and 9% among candidates who appear for exams privately, i.e. through self-study, without attending any school). This is when the bar for passing is set very low, i.e. a student only needs on average 33% marks in their various subjects in order to pass High School. This suggests the true extent of the problem of low achievement levels in secondary education, though it is possible that achievement levels in Uttar Pradesh are lower than those in other states. Moreover, students rely on guess papers, which are prepared and sold a few weeks before the exams. These attempt to anticipate exam questions and are often remarkably close to them. There is frequent leaking of papers in advance of examinations.

4. ROLE OF PRIVATE SCHOOLING

Poorly resourced public schools which suffer from high rates of teacher absenteeism can have encouraged the rapid growth of private (unaided) schooling in India, particularly in urban areas. Private schools divide into two types: recognised schools and unrecognised schools. Government recognition is an official stamp of approval and for this a private school is required to fulfil a number of conditions, though hardly any private schools that get recognition actually fulfil all the conditions of recognition. The emergence of large number of unrecognized primary schools suggests that schools and parents do not take government recognition as a stamp of quality. Private schooling share according to official and household data. Despite data deficiencies, it is clear that there is a substantial fee-charging private schooling sector in India. The enrolment share of private schools in rural and urban India, according to both official school returns data from 1993 and 2002 and household survey data from 1993 and 2006. The bottom half of the table shows corresponding figures for Uttar Pradesh, a state with high levels of private school participation.

The latest official data on enrolment by school-type are for 2002 from the Seventh All India Education Survey, though only the national figures are available (in early 2007). The true size of the private sector in India is more than three times that shown in official statistics. For example, according to official statistics for 1993, only 2.8 per cent of all rural primary school students were attending private schools but according to household survey data for the same year, 10.1 per cent were in rural Uttar Pradesh the corresponding figures were 8.8 per cent and 30.7%, again the survey estimate being more than three times the official estimate. By the time of the PROBE survey in 1996, 36 per cent of all primary-age students (6-11 year olds) in rural UP attended private schools (Probe Team, 1999). The official enrolment share of private schools at primary level rose from 2.8% in 1993 to 5.8% in 2002. If the extent of under-estimation in 2002 is the same as in 1993, then the true private school share of total primary enrolments in rural India in 2002 was three times as high as 5.8%, i.e. 17.4%. This is close to the only recent national estimate available, as seen in the last column of ASER 2006 (Pratham, 2007, p. 32) national sample survey of about 330,000 households across 16,500 villages finds that 18.6 percent of all (and 19.5% of school-going) rural primary age children (7-10 year olds) attended private schools in 2006. The urban India private schools share of total enrolment in 2002 was between about 30 and 40 percent at different levels of education.

The reasons for the large discrepancy between household survey estimates and official estimates of the size of the private schooling sector in India are two-fold (Kingdon, 1996a; Drèze and Kingdon, 1998). First, government and aided school teachers have incentives to over-report their enrolments when there is low demand for their services (since a school with falling rolls would lose teachers), and this reduces the apparent enrolment share of private schools. Second, all official school censuses are carried out only in the government-recognized schools and in most Indian states, there is no requirement on private primary schools to be even registered, let alone be government recognized. Evidence suggests that the true size of the private schooling sector is greatly underestimated in official data due to enumerating only the recognized schools. Household survey data give a picture far closer to the truth than official statistics since parents have no incentives to over-report enrolment in publicly funded schools or to report enrolment in recognized schools only. Household survey data in the indication of the extent to which the enrolment share of private schools in primary education is underestimated in official data namely by about 67% in rural areas. Muralidharan and Kremer (2006) find that in their national survey of 20 states, 51% of all private rural primary schools were unrecognized. This accords with evidence from individual states in other studies.

Private schooling is utilized even among the poor in India. Findings from the MIMAP survey show that, of all enrolled children aged 5-10 years old living below the poverty line, 14.8% attended private schools (8% in rural and 36% in urban India). The corresponding figures for ages 11-14 (junior school age) and 15-17 (secondary school age) were 13.8% and 7.0% respectively (Pradhan and Subramaniam, 2000). That private schools are used by poor families is also found in 5 north Indian states (PROBE Team, 1999) and by Tooley and Dixon (2005) in Delhi.

Growth in Private Schooling

The most telling statistic, however, is not the share of private schooling in the stock of total school enrolment but, rather, the share of private schooling in the total recent increase in school enrolment at different levels. This shows the relative growth of private schooling in India (i.e. relative to the growth of government and aided schooling). The proportion of the total enrolment increase (over time) that is absorbed by private schools. It is constructed from underlying numbers. Even though information on enrolment by school management-type can only be gleaned from official statistics (i.e. it excludes unrecognized schools), even recognized private school growth numbers are felling.

We learn two things: firstly, that growth of private schooling has accelerated over time; secondly, that in urban areas, the growth of private schooling has consistently been the greatest at the primary level and progressively smaller at the middle and secondary school levels, something perverse from the equity point of view since children of the poor are most well represented at the primary schooling level. 60.5% and for the period 1993-2002 was 95.7%. Clearly, the pace of privatisation increased greatly in the 1993-2002 period. In these nine year period, government and aided primary schools together absorbed only 4.3% of the total increase in primary school enrolments, i.e. their numbers or enrolments grew very slowly. Nearly 96% of the total increase in urban primary enrolment was due to the growth of private schooling! It bears emphasising that even this dramatic statistic is likely to be an underestimate since it takes no account of enrolment growth in the numerous unrecognized private schools that are excluded from the official statistics. The recent growth of private primary schooling in urban India has been nothing short of massive. In rural India the rate of expansion of private primary schooling has been much slower but even here the pace of privatisation picked up over time: only 2.8% of total rural growth in primary enrolment in the 1978-86 period was absorbed by private schools, but the corresponding figure for the 1986-93 period was 18.5% and for the 1993-02 period 24.4%. The ASER survey (Pratham, 2007) shows that among the major Indian states, in Punjab, Haryana and Kerala the percentage of children attending private school increased by more than 10 percentage points between 2005 and 2006. It bears emphasising that these figures are all underestimates since they do not include growth in enrolments in the unrecognized private primary schools (Kingdon, 1996a). It is also worth stating that any increase in aided school enrolments—(if it comes from the establishment of new aided schools rather than merely from expansion in enrolment size in existing aided schools) represents in fact an increase in private schools since aided schools are private schools that start receiving government grants-in-aid. In some states, acceleration in the growth of private schooling was spectacular even in the 1986-93 periods. For instance, in urban Uttar Pradesh, 94 per cent of all new primary schools enrolment over the period 1986-93 occurred in private schools. Data by state for 2002 are not yet available. The growth of private schooling, particularly at primary and middle levels of education, signals growing inequality of educational opportunity. The growth of private schooling offers a possible explanation for why, despite falling or virtually static per capita public education expenditure in several Indian states and falling share of basic education expenditure in state domestic product (Drèze and Sen, 2002, Chapter 5), these states have improved their educational outcome indicators in the 1990s (Kingdon, *et. al.*, 2004).

Relative effectiveness of private and public schools why has private schooling been growing rapidly in recent times? Muralidharan and Kremer (2006) present an OLS regression of the presence of a private school (in a village) on village level predictors. Controlling for village population, village per capita income, pupil-teacher ratio in public schools in the village, and state fixed effects, they find that private schools are significantly more likely to exist in villages with high mean level of teacher absence in the public schools. Their finding that private schools are disproportionately located in areas with poorly performing public schools supports the qualitative reflections of the PROBE Report which believes that in explaining the increased popularity of private education, the breakdown of government schools is often more decisive than parental ability to pay. In rural Himachal Pradesh, for instance, there is a good deal of purchasing power but the government schools function well, so that there are few private schools. In central Bihar, by contrast, poverty is endemic, yet private schools can be found in many villages due to the dysfunctional state of government schools. (PROBE Team, 1999, p. 102).

National data on learning achievement levels in ASER 2005 (Pratham, 2006) found that private school students of grades 2 to 5 were 37.4% more likely than government school students to be able to read a text of grade 2 standard. They were also 50% more likely to be able to solve a division problem (3 digits divided by 1 digit). Of course, these are raw figures and private school students typically come from more privileged homes. There is a small literature examining the relative effectiveness of private and public schooling after controlling for the differing student intakes of private and government schools. Due to the lack of achievement data linked to school and teacher characteristics, studies of the relative effectiveness of public and private schools in India have had to rely on achievement tests carried out by the researchers themselves, typically in small samples of schools (Bashir, 1994, 1997; Govinda and Varghese, 1993; Kingdon, 1994, 1996b). These studies have been carried out in different parts of India (Tamil Nadu, Madhya Pradesh and Uttar

Pradesh respectively) and differ in several respects but they share the common conclusion that private school students generally outperform their public school counterparts in learning achievement even after controlling for schools student intakes. Muralidharan and Kremer (2006) corroborate the findings of earlier studies but with nationally representative data on rural primary schools in their study private school students. Achievement was 0.41 standard deviation higher than that of government school students in the same village (i.e. using a village fixed effects achievement production function), after controlling for observed school characteristics and pupils, home background. While most of these studies did not test the possibility that the private school effect may be driven by unobserved heterogeneity (more able or more motivated students systematically selecting into private schools), Kingdom's study for Uttar Pradesh did correct for sample selectivity bias and while this correction greatly reduced the private school advantage, there remained a substantial private school advantage over government and aided schools in the teaching of numeracy skills.

Relative costs of private and public schools : Available evidence suggests not only that private schools are more effective than public schools in imparting cognitive skills in India but also that they have much lower unit costs than publicly funded (i.e. government and aided) schools. This is due largely to teacher salaries in private schools being only a fraction of those in publicly funded schools. Findings from five different states summarised in Kingdon (2006) show that in the early to mid-1990s, private school teachers. pay was about 40-50% of government teachers pay but that by 2002, this had fallen to only about 20%. Muralidharan and Kremer (2006), based on their 2003 national survey of rural schools in 20 Indian states conclude: even conservatively, rural private school teacher salaries are typically around one fifth that of regular government teacher salaries and they are often as low as one-tenth the salaries of regular government teachers.. Such massive private-public segmentation in the teacher labour market can exist because of excess supply of educated individuals and because while the private sector pays market wages, government and aided school salaries are bureaucratically set minimum wages. Clearly there are huge economic rents in the salaries of government school teachers. Kingdom and Muzammil (2003, Chapter 13) estimate that the impact of the Government of India, Fifth Pay Commission. In Uttar Pradesh in the late 1990s was to hike, overnight, a high school Principal's monthly pay by 43% and assistant teachers'. pay by between 26% and 55% depending on teacher category. The authors show the central role of teacher unions in securing these salary increases.

5. GOVERNMENT AND NGO EDUCATION INITIATIVES

While the data presented above on student learning levels, teacher absenteeism and school facilities paints quite a grim picture of the state of schooling quality in India, there are several reasons for more optimism about progress of school education in the future. Firstly, a number of recent fiscally-demanding public education initiatives suggest that India has begun in earnest to give greater priority to improving school education. Secondly, a number of educational NGOs have emerged such as Pratham, Digantar, Azim Premji, MV Foundation and others and some have acquired substantial stature both in terms of their contributions to educational improvements in a number of dimensions, as well as in terms of their influence, advocacy voice, public/media profile, research capacity and ability to mobilize funds for education both from individual donors in India and abroad and from the Indian corporate sector. Below we consider some of the important initiatives and their impact on educational outcomes.

Sarva Shiksha Abhiyan

The Sarva Shiksha Abhiyan (SSA). Literally Campaign for Universal Education in India literally to universalize elementary education (grades 1 to 8) by the year 2010. It is a scheme sponsored by the Central government that is funded out of revenues from a new cess, equal to 2 percent of all taxes, which was introduced in 2004 (increased to 3% in March 2007). SSA provides additional funding to states to enrol out-of-school children and to improve school quality. SSA funds civil works (capped at 33 percent of total cost); salaries of additional teachers to reduce pupil-teacher ratio to 40:1; establishment of alternative schools and education guarantee scheme (EGS) schools in small habitations; establishment of block or cluster level resource centers; establishment of bridge courses for dropouts; in-service training for teachers; and grants for teaching-learning materials. As well as these supply-side interventions, SSA includes demand side measures to close caste and gender gaps in education. These include free textbooks to all female and low caste students, special facilities for girls and grants to districts to support students with disabilities.

SSA also funds a national component covering capacity building, technical support, financial management, monitoring and evaluation, etc. To this authors knowledge, there is no rigorous evaluation of the impact of this massive intervention or its individual components so far. Two recent impact evaluations of the District Primary Education Project the predecessor to SSA and quite similar to it are by Schmid (2006) who uses a treatment intensity approach, and Jalan and Glinskaya (1999) who use a propensity score matching approach. The treatment intensity of a certain age group in a specific district depended on the years DPEP was in place and on the number of years that the group was in school-going age during this time period. While both studies find substantial programme impacts and find that impacts were greater for low caste children, Schmid finds that effects were stronger for girls but Jalan and Glinskaya find they were negligible, although the latter evaluated the impact of only the first phase of the DPEP while Schmid evaluated the impact of all three phases.

Mid-day Meal Scheme

In late 2001, the Indian Supreme Court directed all states to implement the Mid-Day Meal Scheme by providing every child in every government and government assisted primary school with a prepared mid-day meal with a minimum content of 300 calories and 8-12 grams of protein each day of school for a minimum of 200 days. By 2006, the MDM scheme was near universal in all states, following public mobilization efforts to encourage states to act. This is a centrally funded scheme in that the central government provides grains, funds transportation and also pays food preparation costs, though the state government is responsible for providing the physical infrastructure for cooking the meals. Though it is not yet free of problems of quality and corruption, the fact that mid-day meals have become a part of the daily routine in most primary schools across the country is a major achievement. (Khera, 2006). The scheme provides lunch to about 120 million children every school day and, as such, is the largest school meal scheme in the world. Certain states have gone beyond the mandated scope of the scheme, for instance in Kerala and Tamil Nadu the destitute and the aged are allowed to take the MDM and in Gujarat the scheme covers children from Grades 1 to 7 rather than only in the primary grades (1 to 5).

Although there are no rigorous evaluations (e.g. randomized experiment studies) of the impact of this scheme on children's school enrolment and attendance and on nutritional and health status, several micro-studies suggest major increases in enrolment immediately after the introduction of mid-day meals, e.g., 23% in Barmer district of Rajasthan, 36% in Madhya Pradesh, and other large increases in Karnataka. However, Deaton and Drèze (2006) note that the consumption of mid-day meals in primary schools appears to be heavily under-recorded in the National Sample Survey (NSS) data, making it hard to verify the impact of MDMs on school attendance from NSS surveys.

Para Teacher Schemes

From the mid-1990s, several states began using low-cost untrained teachers known variously as Shiksha Karmis, Shiksha Mitras, Vidya Volunteers, etc. By 2002, about 220,000 such para-teachers had been appointed and by 2004, their number had risen to about 500,000 (Govinda and Josephine, 2004). The schemes have been expanding rapidly since 2002 because from that year states could appoint contract teachers with central government grants. Under these schemes, persons with educational qualification requirements below those of government primary school regular teachers are employed on salaries that are one-fifth to one-half of government teacher salaries, in order to : (i) expand schooling in a low cost way to small hamlets which are unserved by regular government schools, (ii) to increase the number of instructors in single-teacher schools, and (iii) to reduce high pupil-teacher ratios. Although the model varies from state to state, the para-teacher jobs are typically tenable for ten months per year, but are annually renewable. Para teacher schemes have raised a number of concerns about the ethical, legal, and political difficulties of sustaining two different standards of employment between regular teachers and contract teachers. Some authors have also raised concerns about the quality of teaching provided by these less qualified instructors. Others have pointed that para-teachers may exhibit greater accountability due to closer community involvement in their recruitment and dismissal and because of the impermanence of their job-contracts. Drèze and Sen (2002) believe that the contribution of these low-cost schemes so far is uncertain and that it is premature either to applaud or dismiss them. We are not aware of any serious evaluations of these schemes though several micro-studies find that learning achievements of children taught by para-teachers and regular teachers are no different (Leclercq, 2005; Govinda and Josephine, 2004; Pratichi Trust, 2003).

Public-Private Partnerships in Education

A substantial public-private partnership (PPP) system does operate in India, at least at the secondary and higher levels of education. This is the system of government grant-in-aid to privately managed schools known as aided schools. In 1995-96 the percentage share of aided schools in total schools was 34.0% and 44.3% respectively at the secondary and higher secondary levels, though at the primary and middle levels, it was only 3.4% and 10.1% respectively (Bashir, 2005). However, over time, largely due to successive governments conceding teacher union demands, aided schools have become more and more like government schools: their teachers are now paid directly by the state government treasury at the same uniform salary rates as for government school teachers, and are recruited by a government-appointed selection committee rather than by the school. Aided schools also have the same fee policy as in government schools. Perhaps not surprisingly, learning achievements in aided schools are similar to those in government schools and significantly lower than in private schools after controlling for student intake and selection bias (Kingdon, 1996b). The current draft, Right to Education Bill under consideration at the Indian Parliament proposes to establish a new form of PPP in education, requiring all private schools to give 25% of their places to government-paid students from disadvantaged homes. This measure does not propose to give money to the disadvantaged students to attend a school of their choice but rather proposes to give money directly to the private schools that accept the students. In recent years, increased advocacy in favour of PPPs in education in various countries has been associated with introduction of school choice by parents, typically by means of school vouchers. The recommendations for decentralising reform in India, including the current draft, Right to Education Bill, have never seriously included consideration of the possibility of providing school vouchers, as a way of empowering (especially poor) students/parents and improving accountability of schools and teachers towards students and parents. This is unlike the situation in Chile, Colombia, New Zealand, US, UK and some other countries where there has been vigorous debate about and experimentation with alternatives to public schools, such as school choice and other forms of PPPs. There are several potential explanations for this difference and also some concerns about school vouchers schemes (Kingdon, 2006). Vouchers would be a radical reform of teacher and school incentives, and one reason why they have not been debated in India could be because of their perceived political infeasibility as they would be resisted by powerful vested interest groups.

NGO Education Work

Widespread education-related work by a large number of NGOs in India is a relatively new phenomenon but one which has grown rapidly. Their important contribution has been not only in grassroots educational work but also in terms of successful advocacy for education at the macro-level by contributing to national educational debates and helping to make education access and quality prominent public issues. For instance, the role of the NGO Right to Food Campaign at both the micro and macro-levels was critical in mobilizing public opinion and building pressure for the rapid implementation of the school Mid-Day-Meal scheme in Indian states. Similarly, Pratham whose aim is to have every child in school and learning well did pioneering work in testing the learning achievements of elementary school age children in 509 Indian districts in 2005 and producing a public report in February 2006. This brought the whole issue of low learning levels and low schooling quality to the fore in public and media discussion in India and also encouraged greater openness in the government's premier educational research institution (National Council for Educational Research and Training, NCERT), which immediately put its own report of learning tests in the public domain tests which had been carried out in 2002. Finally field experiments in education are typically more readily facilitated by educational NGOs on a small scale rather than by governments and, as such, provide invaluable opportunities to test the cost-effectiveness of particular educational interventions. They can thus inform education policy as to what types of educational innovations and policies give the greatest impacts at lowest costs (Duflo, 2006). NGOs other education activities are far too numerous to summarise but include delivering bridge courses that prepare children who dropped-out of schooling earlier to re-join school; arranging for street children to settle with foster parents and attend schools; organising learning camps for girl children and for working children; and many other educational innovations.

Some of the latter have received prominent attention in recent times. For instance, Pratham runs a large scale Bal Sakhi programme which provides an assistant teacher for remedial teaching of weak children in government schools. A randomised evaluation of this scheme in Gujarat and Mumbai by MITs Poverty Action Lab (Banerjee *et. al.*, 2003) showed that it dramatically increased learning by focusing on improving basic literacy and numeracy skills and that it was very costpara-teachers. Another NGO, Seva Mandir, runs primary single-teacher non-formal education centres in tribal villages in Rajasthan and faces the problem of high teacher absenteeism. Seva Mandir tried to incentivize teachers by introducing an attendance-contingent bonus which was a function of the number of days the teacher was present in school. It selected

120 schools to participate in an experiment where teachers in 60 schools were given a camera with a tamper-proof date and time function and instructed him• to take pictures of himself with his students every day at school opening and closing time, to provide proof of presence. Duflo and Hanna (2005) found that the intervention resulted in an immediate and long-lasting improvement in teacher attendance: the absence rate was cut from 42 to 22 percent. Due to fewer absences, treatment schools taught the equivalent of 88 childdays more per month than comparator schools, resulting in a 0.17 standard deviation increase in test scores after one year.

6. CONCLUSION

This paper has sought to build a picture of school education in India. Lastly, looked at some public education initiatives. The Sarva Shiksha Abhiyan, mid-day meal scheme and the para-teacher scheme were each discussed briefly. Unfortunately, the impacts of these massive interventions (or of their sub-components) on children's school attendance and learning outcomes have not been rigorously evaluated. This is necessary if decision-makers are to hone future education policy-making in light of knowledge about the cost-effectiveness of alternative interventions. Moreover, radical measures to improve teacher and school incentives have not been considered in India, perhaps because they stand to upset powerful vested interest. While the existence of fiscally-demanding education initiatives and the introduction of the two percent education cess to fund them testifies to the Indian government's increased commitment to school education and gives grounds for optimism about the future, serious challenges remain.

References

Barro, Robert J., and Lee, Jong-Wha (2004), International Data on Educational Attainment: Updates and Implications, CID Working Paper, No. 42, Harvard University.

Deaton, Angus and Jean Drèze (2006), Tracking Mid-Day Meals in Indian Schools, Draft notes, March, cited in Khera (2006).

Drèze, Jean and Geeta Kingdon (1998), Biases in Education Statistics. *The Hindu*, 6 March, 1998.

Drèze, Jean and Amartya Sen (2002), India: Development and Participation, Clarendon Press, Oxford and Delhi.

Duflo, Esther and Rema Hanna (2005), Improving Teacher Attendance in Rural India, mimeo, Poverty Action Lab, MIT.

Duraisamy, P. (2002), Changes in Returns to Education in India, 1983-94: by gender, age-cohort and location. *Economics of Education Review*, 21: 609-22.

Hanushek, Eric (2005), The Economics of School Quality, *German Economic Review*, 6(3), 269-86.

Hanushek, E. and L. Zhang (2006), Quality-consistent Estimates of International Returns to Skill, NBER Working Paper 12664 http://www.nber.org/papers/w12664.

CHAPTER

30

Academic Problems and Remedial Measures

A Study of Aligarh Muslim University, Aligarh

MOHAMMAD PARVEZ AND MOHD. SHAKIR

ABSTRACT

Aligarh Muslim University, Aligarh is prestigious world fame Central University of India, it occupies a distinct position among Indian Universities and its contribution to nation building is very significant. It attracts students from all over the world especially Africa, West Asia and South East Asia. In this Investigation, an attempt has been made to find out the opinion of teachers and the students of the A.M.U., Aligarh towards the Academic problems of AMU, and to suggest various remedial measures. A sample of 65 teachers and 177 students was taken randomly from almost all faculties of AMU; the opinionnaires used are developed by the investigators to collect information regarding the academic problems of the A.M.U., Aligarh. In this study, investigators made an effort to draw certain findings on the basis of interpretation and analysis of data.

Keywords: Academic, Bunking tradition, Refresher courses, Board of studies, Orientation Programmes, Examinations and Teaching Methodologies.

INTRODUCTION

The Aligarh Muslim University is one of the old, big prestigious Central Universities of India. It owes its existence to the selfless and untiring efforts of the great visionary Sir Syed Ahmad Khan. Deeply moved by the socio-economic and educational plight of his community after the First War of Independence of 1857, he was quick to realize that the panacea for these ills lay in inculcating the spirit of free enquiry and modernism in the community. His exposure to the British Universities, particularly those at Oxford and Cambridge, and their public schools, inspired him with a new vision of a harmonious pattern of culture, combining the best elements in the cultures of the East with the arts and sciences of the West. Due to its specific, historical, secular, residential, cultural and educational features, it is known, not only in India but also in the world. Aligarh Muslim University is not merely a university. It is a movement. This revolutionary movement was started by Sir Syed Ahmad Khan. This university is a living symbol of the composite culture of India and bulwark of its secular principles.

The present study is an attempt to find out the mind set of teachers and the students of the Aligarh Muslim University, Aligarh towards the academic problems of Aligarh Muslim University, Aligarh and to suggest various means and ways to find out a solution to the existing academic problems of Aligarh Muslim University, Aligarh.

OBJECTIVES

1. To identify various aspects of academic management of the university.
2. To make an analysis of the functioning of academic management.

3. To find out academic problems of the Aligarh Muslim University, Aligarh.
4. To suggest remedial measures to overcome academic problems of Aligarh Muslim University, Aligarh.

DESIGN AND METHODOLOGY

Population and Sample

In the present study, the target population is the teachers and the students from almost all faculties of AMU randomly. The sample consists of 65 teachers and 177 students of AMU.

Research Tools Used

In the present study, the opinionnaires used (One for Teachers and One for Students) are developed by the investigators. The main purpose of both the opinionnaires was to collect information regarding the academic problems of the Aligarh Muslim University, Aligarh. The respondents were requested to respond on the opinionnaires so that general trends and academic problems of Aligarh Muslim University could be studied and an analysis may be possible to understand the loopholes in the management process to overcome the academic problems. The statements were to be rated on a 3 point scale viz., Agree (A) is used, undecided (U) and disagree (D). The respondents were required to tick mark (Ö) on the response that was most appropriate to indicate their opinion.

To make the opinionnaires valid and reliable for the study, they were given to the experts of Education and the Experts of Psychology. Finally, 16 out of 26 statements were selected for the opinionnaires meant for the teachers. 18 Out of 30 statements were selected for the opinionnaires meant for the students.

DATA COLLECTION

In order to collect data for the present study, the investigator himself approached the respondents to collect relevant data about academic problems of Aligarh Muslim University, Aligarh. The respondents were asked to go through the general instructions given on the front page before filling up the opinionnaires. After that the opinionnaires were collected from the respondents.

STATISTICAL TECHNIQUES USED

Item-wise Analysis on the Basis of Average (Mean) and Percentages.

Findings and Suggestions (on the basis of Analysis of Data and its interpretations).

Major findings based on the item analysis of the responses given by teachers (Table 1).

TABLE I
Item-wise Responses of Teachers in Terms of Percentage

No. of Items	*(%)*		
	Agree	*Undecided*	*Disagree*
1	55.39	7.69	36.92
2	46.15	4.62	49.23
3	86.15	1.54	12.31
4	66.15	12.31	21.54
5	15.39	18.46	66.15
6	95.38	4.62	00.00
7	70.77	9.23	20.00
8	24.62	6.15	69.23
9	52.31	30.77	33.85
10	35.38	30.77	33.85
11	50.77	18.46	30.77
12	73.84	12.35	13.85
13	47.69	35.39	16.92
14	66.16	16.92	16.92
15	69.23	9.23	21.54
16	61.54	15.38	23.08

Item 1: E-Learning Facilities are Available for the Teachers

Since 55.39% respondents say that e-learning facilities are available for the teachers and 36.92% say that e-learning facilities are not available for the teachers. 7.69% are undecided. It shows that e-learning facilities are available for the teachers. But, the investigators have observed that e-learning facilities for the teachers are not sufficient. Teachers should be provided better e-learning facilities so that they may update their knowledge.

Item 2. The Course Content of the Subjects is Regularly Updated to Meet the Emerging Needs of Students/Society

Since 46.15% respondents say that the course content is regularly updated to meet the emerging needs of students/ society and 49.23% respondents disagree, only 4.62% respondents are undecided. Therefore, nothing can be said confidently about the regular updating of the course content of the subjects to meet the emerging needs of student/society. But, investigators have observed that in Aligarh Muslim University, the updating of the course content is the need of the hour. Course content should be regularly updated to meet the individual as well as social needs.

Item 3: Regular Refresher Courses are Organized in the University

86.15% respondents are of the opinion that regular refresher courses are organized in the university and only 12.31% respondents say that regular refresher courses are not organized in the university only 1.54% respondents are undecided. It shows that the regular refresher courses are organized in the university.

Item 4: The Teacher Should not be Appointed as Guest Faculty

66.10% respondents say that the teachers should not be appointed as guest faculty and 21.54% respondents say that the teachers can be appointed as guest faculty, 12.31% respondents are undecided. It shows that the teachers should not be appointed as guest faculty as far as possible. The investigators' opinion is that the teachers should be appointed through a selection committee on regular pay scales.

Item 5: Pay/Honorarium to Guest Faculty is Adequate

15.39% respondents say that pay to guest faculty is enough and 66.15% respondents say that pay to guest faculty is not enough and 18.46% respondents are undecided. It shows that, pay of guest faculties is not adequate. It is therefore, suggested that the practice of appointing guest faculty should be discontinued and regular appointment of teachers should be made on approve pay-scales.

Item 6: Selection Committee for the Teachers Should be Held in Time

Almost all (95.38%) respondents say that selection committee for the teachers should be held in time. Only 4.62% are undecided. The investigators have also observed that selection committees are not held in time, which is one of the major reasons for the shortage of teachers. Therefore, it should be given due attention by the university administration.

Item 7: The Students Attend the Classes Regularly

70.77% respondents say that the students attend the classes regularly and 20% say that the students do not attend the classes regularly. 9.23% are undecided. The percentage of Agreed responses 70.77% clearly highlighted the fact that the students attend the classes regularly. But the investigators have observed that some students attend the classes for the sake of attendance only and not for the sake of getting knowledge. Since teachers are the reservoirs of knowledge, therefore, the students should attend the classes regularly so that they can benefit from the vast experiences of the teachers.

Item 8: There is no Bunking Tradition in the University

24.62% respondents say that there is no bunking tradition in the university whereas 69.23% say that there is a bunking tradition in the university. 6.15% are undecided. It shows that there is a bunking tradition in the university. But, the investigators have observed that the bunking tradition is not in all the departments of the university. In Education Department there is no bunking tradition. The university must develop remedial measures to stop bunking which severely affects the teaching-learning atmosphere.

Item 9: The Faculty as Well the Committee for Advanced Studies and Research Meetings are Held as Per Ordinances

52.31% respondents say that the Faculty as well as the Committee for Advance Studies and Research meetings are held as per ordinances and 16.92% says that the Faculty as well as Committee for Advance Studies and Research meetings are not held as per ordinances, and 30.77% are undecided.

Item 10: Proposals Made by the Departments are given due Consideration by the University Administration

35.38% respondents say that proposals made by the departments are given due consideration by the university administration and 33.85% say that proposals made by the departments are not given due consideration by the university administration. 30.77% are undecided. As the percentage on three points scale, i.e. agree, disagree and undecided is more or less same, nothing can be said confidently.

Item 11: Funds are Available to Participate in National/ International Seminars/Conferences

50.77% respondents say that funds are available to participate in national/international seminars/conferences and 30.77% say that funds are not available to participate in national/international seminars. 18.46% are undecided. It clearly shows that funds are available in the university to participate in national/international seminars. But the investigators have observed that the fund given to teachers for the purpose is not sufficient and the process of getting fund is much time-consuming. University administration should provide sufficient funds to teachers in time to participate in national/international seminar/conferences.

Item 12: Meetings of Board of Studies are held to make Development Plans for the Department

Since the majority (73.84%) of respondents says that meetings of Board of Studies are held to make developmental plans for the department and 13.85% say that meetings of Board of Studies are not held to make developmental plans. 12.31% are undecided. It shows that the meetings of Board of Studies are held to make departmental plans for the department.

Item 13: Meetings of the Academic Council are held Regularly

47.69% respondents say that meetings of the Academic Council are held regularly and only 16.92% say that meetings of the Academic Council are not held regularly. 35.39% are undecided. It shows that meetings of the academic council are held regularly.

Item 14: There is a Lack of Coordination among Various Administrative Machineries

66.16% respondents say that there is a lack of coordination among various administrative machineries and 16.92% say that there is no problem as such 16.92% are undecided. It shows that there is a lack of coordination among various administrative machineries. It is one of the major problems and this problem leads to many other problems. It is suggested that the university administration should pay due consideration to overcome this problem.

Item 15: Orientation Programmes and Refresher Courses, Organized by Academic Staff College, are Helpful in Improving the Quality of Education

69.23% respondents say that orientation programmes and refresher courses, organized by Academic Staff College are helpful in improving the quality of education and 21.54% say that these orientation programmes are not helpful in improving the quality of education, 9.23% are undecided. It shows that orientation programmes and refresher courses, organized by ASCs are helpful in improving the quality of education.

Item 16: Academic Council is Helpful in Improving the Academic Standard of the University

61.54% respondents say that Academic Council is helpful in improving the academic standard of the university and

23.08% say that academic Council is not helpful in improving the academic standard of the university and 15.38% are undecided. Therefore, it can be concluded that Academic council is helpful in improving the academic standard of the university.

Major findings based on the item analysis of the responses given by Students (Table 2).

TABLE 2
Item-wise Responses of Students in Terms of Percentage

No. of Items	*(%)*		
	Agree	*Undecided*	*Disagree*
1	71.43	15.58	12.99
2	64.94	16.88	18.18
3	48.05	18.18	33.77
4	63.64	14.29	22.07
5	70.13	10.39	19.48
6	20.78	16.88	62.34
7	36.36	15.58	48.06
8	27.27	10.39	62.34
9	77.93	5.19	16.88
10	64.94	10.39	24.67
11	36.36	18.18	45.46
12	59.74	10.39	29.87
13	50.65	22.08	27.27
14	84.42	9.09	6.49
15	48.05	14.29	37.66
16	59.74	23.38	16.88
17	40.26	22.08	37.66
18	66.23	12.99	20.78

Item 1: The Teachers Generate Interest in the Concerned Subject

71.43% respondents say that the teachers generate interest in the concerned subject, while 12.99% say that the teachers do not generate interest in the concerned subject. 15.58% are undecided. It can be concluded that the teachers generate interest in the concerned subjects.

Item 2: Teacher is Accessible out of the Class for Students' Guidance and Help

64.94% respondents say that teacher is accessible out of the class for students' guidance and help and 18.18% say that teacher is not accessible out of the class for students' guidance and help. 16.88% are undecided. It shows that teachers are accessible for students' guidance and help.

Item 3: Total Syllabus is Taught in the Class Properly

54.55% respondents say that the total syllabus is taught in the class properly, and 27.27% say that the total syllabus is not taught in the class properly 18.18% are undecided. It shows that total syllabus is taught in the class properly.

Item 4: Reference Books are Available to the Students

63.64% of respondents say that reference books are available to students and 22.07% say that reference books are not available to students. 14.29% are undecided. It shows that reference books are available to students in the central library as well as in the seminar libraries of the different departments of the University. It is suggested that the latest standard reference books should be made available in the seminar libraries of the universities where they are not available.

Item 5: The Teacher Regularly Takes the Assigned Classes

70.13% respondents say that the teacher regularly takes the assigned classes, while 19.48% say that the teacher does not regularly take the assigned classes 10.39% are undecided. It shows that the teachers regularly take the assigned classes.

Item 6: Students Visit the Industries, Laboratories, Banks, Colleges and Universities, etc. for Practical Knowledge and First Hand Experience

20.78% respondents say that students visit the industries, laboratories, banks, colleges and universities for practical knowledge and 62.34% say that students do not visit these working places for practical knowledge. 16.88% are undecided. It shows that students do not visit the industries, laboratories, banks, colleges, and other universities, etc. for practical knowledge. It is therefore suggested that university should provide the opportunities and facilities for visiting working places to supplement the theoretical knowledge of the students.

Item 7: The Course Content is Relevant to the Real Life Situation

36.36% respondents say that the course content is relevant to the real life situation while 48.06% say that the course content is not relevant to the real life situation. 15.58% are undecided. It shows that the course content is not relevant to the real life situation. It is suggested that the syllabi should be revised from time to time to make it need-based.

Item 8: Examinations are the True Test of Knowledge

27.27% respondents say that examinations are the true test of knowledge while 62.34% say that examinations are not the true test of knowledge. 10.39% are undecided. It clearly shows that examinations are not the true test of knowledge. Therefore, it is the demand of the situation that university should ponder over it seriously.

Item 9: The Pattern of Examination Needs Change

77.93% respondents say that the examination system needs change and 16.88% say that the pattern of Examination does not need change. 5.19% are undecided. Therefore, it can be concluded that the system of examination needs change.

Item 10: The Central Library is Sufficient Enough for Students

64.94% respondents say that the central library is sufficient enough for the students while 24.67% disagree. 10.39% are undecided. It shows that the central library is sufficient enough for the students. But the investigators have observed that there is a need of building more reading-rooms.

Item 11: A Proper Coaching and Guidance Centre is Available in the University

36.36% respondents say that a proper Coaching and Guidance Centre is available in the university and 45.46% say that a proper Coaching and Guidance Centre is not available in the university. 18.18% respondents are undecided. It shows that a proper Coaching and Guidance Centre is not available in the university. But, the investigators have observed that university has a well-equipped Coaching and Guidance Centre. But, the services of more trained counselors are required.

Item 12: Proper Medical Facilities are Available for University Students

59.74% respondents say that proper medical facilities are available for the students and 29.87% say that proper medical facilities are not available for the students. 10.39% are undecided. It shows that proper medical facilities are available for the students. But the investigators have observed that there is a need of better medical facilities. It is suggested that monthly medical camp for medical check-up of the students should be organized in halls of residences.

Item 13: The Students Work Mostly Remain Pending in the University Offices

50.65% respondents say that the students work mostly remain pending in the university offices and 27.27% say that the students work does not remain pending in the university offices. 22.08% are undecided. On the basis of, responses it can be concluded that the students work, mostly; remain pending in the university offices.

Item 14: Teachers Need Training in Teaching Methodologies

84.42% respondents say that teachers need training in teaching methodology while 6.49% say that teachers do not need training in teaching methodologies. 9.09% are undecided. It shows that teachers need training in teaching methodologies.

Item 15: Students are Encouraged to Participate in the Co-Curricular Activities

48.05% respondents say that students are encouraged to

participate in the co-curricular activities. 37.66% say that students are not encouraged to participate in the co-curricular activates. 14.29% are undecided. It shows that students are encouraged to participate in the co-curricular activities. But the investigators have observed that students are not encouraged in all the departments to participate in co-curricular activities. Therefore, it is suggested that all the departments should encourage their students to participate in the co-curricular activities which is the integral part of holistic-education.

Item 16: The Chairpersons of the Departments are Available in the Offices to Solve the Students' Grievances

59.74% respondents say that the Chairpersons of the department are available in the office to solve the students' grievances and 16.88% say that the Chairpersons are not available. 23.38% are undecided. It shows that the Chairpersons of the department are available in the office to solve the students' grievances.

Item 17: The Provosts of the Halls Provide Good Reading Room Facilities

40.26% respondents say that the provosts of the halls provide good Reading Room facilities and are undecided. Respondents are not very clear in giving responses to the Problem. But the investigators have observed that there is a dearth of good books in the reading rooms. During the period of the examination, the reading rooms are insufficient to accommodate all the students. Provosts of the halls should try to solve this problem with the help of university administration.

Item 18: Students Face Problems in Meeting University Officers to Deal with their Problems

66.23% respondents say that students face problem in meeting university officers to deal with their problems and 20.78% say that students do not face problems in meeting university officers to deal with their problems. 12.99% are undecided. It shows that students face problems in meeting university officers to deal with their problems. Investigators have observed that there is not a proper mechanism for solving the problems. Therefore, it is suggested that there should be a proper mechanism.

References

Best, J.W. (1970), Research In Education, New Jersey, Prentice Hall.

Buch, M.B. (1991), Fourth Survey of Research in Education, 1983-88, New Delhi, NCERT.

Buch, M.B., (1997), Fifth Survey of Research in Education, 1988-92, New Delhi, NCERT.

Dash, M., (2004), Education in India, Problems and Perspective", New Delhi, Atlantic Publishers and Distributors.

Maheshwari, A. (2001), Aligarh Muslim University, Aligarh—Perfect past Precarious present, New Delhi, UBS Publishers and Distributor Ltd.

Mohammad, S. (1978), The Aligarh movement (Basic Documents, 1864-98), Meerut, Minakshi Prakashan, Vols. 1, 2 and 3.

Nizami, K.A. (1995), History of the Aligarh Muslim University (1920-45), Ida rah-i-Adbiyat-I-Delhi, Vol. 1.

Qureshi, I.A. (1992), The Aligarh Muslim University, Past and Present, Published by A.M.U.

Siddiqui, M.A. (1995), Management of Education in Muslim Institution, New Delhi, Ashish Publishing House.

Singh, A.K. (2008), Tests Measurement and Research Methods in Behavioral Sciences, New Delhi, Tata McGraw Hill.

CHAPTER

31

Excellent Higher Education through IQAC in India

MOHD. SHAMIM AND FOZIA CHOWDHARY

INTRODUCTION

The meaning of quality and effective higher education has changed a lot with the era of globalization. To match with the global standards of higher education, India has a long way to go. The number of initiatives and efforts has been made by the Government of India through different bodies and institutions. The National Assessment and Accreditation Council was established as an autonomous institution under the UGC in September 1994. The NAAC has been playing important role for Higher Educational Institutions (HEIs) leading to continuous institutional improvement. The institutions of higher learning across the country have since come to know the benefits of NAAC appraisal and validation.

There are different apex institutions to make reforms in their specialized area like SEBI is for the reforms in capital market, RBI for the banking industry, IRDA for insurance, etc. More than 100 universities and thousands of colleges in the country have been successfully assessed and accredited by NAAC in the past last few years. Gone are the days when education was only confined to class rooms, where teachers used to deliver lectures and students had to listen. The era has changed tremendously. The effective and meaningful education is need of the hour. We have to bring our higher education level at par with the global standard. At global level lot of technology is used with innovative methods of providing education to make the quality of education excellent. Many educational institutions are relying on Internal Quality Assurance Cell (IQAC) in India. The cell meets frequently to plan out and evaluate the progress of every activity like:

1. Development and application of quality benchmarks/parameters for the various academic and administrative activities of the institution.
2. Organisation of workshops, seminars and staff development programmes on quality-related themes to enhance the teaching efficiency of the teachers and promotion of quality education.
3. Giving incentives to the staff for taking part in seminars, conferences, presenting papers, publishing papers, attending UGC Refresher courses and Orientation courses. Initiating counseling cell for the betterment of the students.
4. Preparation of the Annual Quality Assurance Report (AQAR) which has to be submitted to NAAC based on the quality parameters.
5. Yearly planning of various activities for each department so that their evaluations in regard to set targets could be made. IQAC is involved in preparing proposals to get financial assistance under UGC XI Plan.
6. Initiating different literary and cultural activities, motivating students to participate, monitoring of students' attendance and follow-up.

CONTRIBUTIONS OF IQAC

IQAC facilitates in the following manner to the educational institutions:

1. IQAC helps in Identifying constraints, problems and challenges relating to curriculum, teaching, infrastructure, administration, and recommend changes and reforms to address the problems and challenges relating to curriculum, teaching, infrastructure, administration, and access.
2. Explore possibilities for innovation in teaching methods, curriculum development and research opportunities and suggest means of raising standards and promoting excellence in undergraduate education.
3. Conference and seminars are mostly attended by faculty members of the colleges' universities of the country, researchers, Principals, academics and intellectuals and the outcomes of their research-oriented papers may suggest the solution easily to the challenges and problems in higher education.
4. On the basis of the outcomes in seminars and conferences the Government has prioritized education sector and comprehensive plans are on anvil to equip all the institutions with the required infrastructure besides teaching staff. Even foreign educational institutions may have 100% FDI in education industry.
5. To a heightened level of clarity and focus in institutional functioning towards quality enhancement and facilitate internalization of the quality culture.
6. Endowment prizes for recognition of merit of students, financial Aid to economically backward but meritorious students, Audio Visual Aids in teaching, Telephone and Fax facilities, Stationary Bookshop, Co-operative Store, Parent-Teacher Association, Language Laboratory, Career Guidance and Placement Services, arranging alumni meet,

arranging periodic exhibitions, other co-curricular activities, etc. are organized and encouraged by IQAC.

7. It makes educational institutions also to achieve the set targets at different level as well as for the different segments like administration, teachers/faculties, students and other non-teaching staff. It also helps in creating health and competitive environment for the betterment of the institution.

MAJOR PROBLEMS OF HIGHER EDUCATION IN INDIA

The policy-makers should keep themselves aware of the challenges in the field of Higher Education. We should have an introspection of the challenges which higher education has in India. The reason for deterioration in schools and colleges is that teachers are not well paid. They form a vital section of society and must be offered various incentives and concessions. Some of the basic problems of our higher education are as follows:

1. India boasts of having the third largest higher education system in the world and has more than 20,000 colleges. But unemployment is on rise, which shows that qualitative education is not being imparted. The crises confronting higher education nowadays is that most of the graduates coming out of Universities and Colleges are unfortunately found to be unemployable.
2. Lack of discipline in the institutions and accountability of faculty members are the vital issues which higher education is faced with.
3. The education is a dynamic process and changes with the time. Most of the Universities have not updated their curriculum for years. As a result of this, the educated students are struggling in the market to get the job. Even if they get jobs, their acquired knowledge is not matching with the actual corporate work.

4. The primary problem encountered is that of resistance—to change. It has been experienced that if there is a change in the education system than it is resistance by the seniors first as they are not ready to adjust themselves with the changes made even for the betterment of the institution. A lot of convincing and persistent measures to alter strategies wherever needed has resulted in a lot of time being lost.
5. Establishing IQAC in the educational institutions may have another road lock in the form of financial commitment. No doubt, a full-fledged requires staff, separate department to arrange all the programs on regular basis.
6. Lack of Coordination from different segment of the institution is another problem in establishing IQAC in the educational institutions, as all are target bound whether teachers, administration students or other non-teaching staff.
7. Infrastructure development, educational and physical, is necessary for access and excellence. Inadequate and uneven infrastructure, both physical and educational, poses impediments for the teaching-learning process.
8. Many colleges lack basic facilities such as adequate classrooms, examination halls, libraries, laboratories, computer centers, auditorium, play grounds, health centers, common rooms and canteens, etc. Lack of adequate funds and proper planning inhibits proper infrastructural development in most colleges and lack of qualified and competent office staff and technical personnel leads to improper use of resources.
9. Staff members quite often show resentment due targets they have to achieve and even with extra hours of working in the institutions.
10. Students and teachers have to go for training which practically not much feasible due to time constraints. The implementation and monitoring of the IQAC may be costly affairs.

During last few years, a number of universities have accredited by the NAAC in regard to its IQAC in the educational institutions in India. As a result, most of the educational institutions have experienced qualitative as well as quantitative changes in the overall efficiency. Staff members have become more productive as more emphasis they are giving on publications, getting different projects from the UGC and other bodies to fulfil their infrastructural requirements. So and so, they are delivering better education as a result of addition in their knowledge after doing some projects.

STRATEGIES FOR EFFECTIVE IMPLEMENTATION OF IQAC

1. Most of the Universities have not updated their curriculum for years. The reason for deterioration in our schools and colleges is that teachers are not well paid. They form a vital section of society and must be offered various incentives and concessions. We are bound to keep global needs in mind while designing new curriculum, and vocational courses must be introduced by all premier institutes. The wide gap in existing infrastructure facilities in different colleges should be minimized. Minimum basic infrastructure must be provided particularly in colleges located in rural and suburban areas. Colleges must get adequate financial grant from the government for developing their infrastructure.
2. Public-private partnership should also be developed beyond the financial level: sharing a laboratory, or human expertise. The state cannot abdicate its responsibility with regard to providing access to higher education to larger numbers. However, education has to be part of larger societal concerns which need to be expressed and encouraged through public-private partnerships within the framework of transparency and accountability.
3. The Government needs to improve the basic infrastructure in all the educational institutions for

achieving quality education which could enable the students of this State to compete at the national level.

4. We are bound to keep global needs in mind while designing new curriculum, and vocational courses must be introduced by all premier institutes. New methods of teaching and participative learning programs must be enforced.
5. "The considerable increase in the allocation of funds to education sector in the current five-year plans shows that the Government is interested in improving the system of education. It is the responsibility of every stakeholder to contribute in making higher education qualitative keeping in mind the paradigm shift in the national and global educational system".
6. We need to provide education in a free and fair atmosphere. For this basic education in mother-tongue is essential. Unless the learner is not encouraged to think critically and question the age-old dogmas, the real purpose of education will be a distant dream.
7. Class load of teachers will be regularly evaluated in context of taking classes and in terms of the course covered. Attendance of the students will be reviewed on monthly basis and the irregular ones will be notified and proper action will be taken. Grievances of the students will be regularly monitored, by the IQAC so that IQAC can place it before the concerned authority for urgent attendance.
8. The grievances of the students should be heard in the line of availability of textbooks and reference books in the library, feasibility of the class routine, laboratory inconveniences, career counseling, etc.
9. IQAC should continue to conduct special talks on modern approaches to pure and applied subjects (as we are to basically clinched with the already existing framework).
10. IQAC will continue to suggest every department to

conduct talks to highlight scopes and relevance of the subjects they may have taken as their major subject.

11. IQAC with the help of the students' union and the authority will continue to find out students who can excel in sports, music, theatre, literary activities specially debating and quiz and to impart them proper training with the help of the alumni of the college, expert in the respective field/event (so that they may be sent to participate in competitions and represent the College and the State).
12. Encouragement should be made and dedication and commitment on the part of the staff is to be appreciated. It will make conducive to the academic environment. Employees should have easy access to the administration, Principal and the Management and satisfied with the working conditions.
13. Research collaboration, Extension centers in the college of distance education programs of University, Online availability of journals, Digitalization facility in the library, Residential accommodation to both the teaching as well as non-teaching staff, Transport facility, Students' motivation to make them appear in Civil Services Examinations and other National Competitive Examinations, organizing career seminars, Periodic feedback, Anti-harassment Cell (Women), Women's Hostel, etc. be initiated.
14. Regular feedback from the students will be taken about their class teachers and should be circulated back to the concerned teachers individually so that he or she may have an insight into ones own performance.

CONCLUSION

Higher Education in India is expected to play a significant role in imparting quality education to provide competent manpower to the nation and offering relevant education for the development of the local community. These expectations have become challenges in the present scenario and they are new and very specific for two reasons: (1) Fast changing profile of the nation, and (2) Global academic change. Hence, it is necessary to bring about constant qualitative improvement in the system of higher education to make teaching and learning more learner and skill centric; to promote institution and industry interface; to assure quality in examination system, to keep abreast of other institutions through ICT.

The considerable increase in the allocation of funds to education sector in the current five year plans shows that the Government is interested in improving the system of education. It is the responsibility of every stakeholder to contribute in making higher education qualitative keeping in mind the paradigm shift in the national and global educational system. Conferences, seminars and workshops must be organized to disseminate knowledge and information among the academics, administrators, scholars, social thinkers on the issues related with quality and relevance in higher education and the new challenges of HEIs to respond to them effectively and to evolve different strategies for strengthening the higher educational institutions to sustain the momentum of the nation's growth.

References

Phillip, L. Matson, "Internal quality control and external quality assurance in the IVF laboratory", European Society for Human Reproduction and Embryology Human Reproduction, Volume 13, Supplement 4, 1998, pp. 156-65.

Annual Quality Assurance Report (AQAR), Internal Quality Assurance Cell, Jadavpur University, 2005.

Annual Quality Assurance Report (AQAR), Internal Quality Assurance Cell, Shri Shikshayatan College Year of the Report: June 2007-June 2008.

www.cauverycollege.ac.in/service.html

Prof. Kunhi Krishanan, a Report submitted to NAAC on Sri Subbaraya and Narayana College, Narasaraopet, Guntur District, Andhra Pradesh, 2006.

Pawan Agrawal, A working paper on "Higher Education in India—Need for a change, *ICRIER*, 2005.

Union Budget, 2009-10.

Department of Secondary and Higher Education, Ministry of Human Resources Development.

Website of University Grant Commission, www.ugc.gov.in

A Report of Internal Quality Assurance Cell (IQAC) of Sheth N.K.T.T College of Commerce and Sheth J.T.T. College of Art, Thane, 2006-07.

A Report of Internal Quality Assurance Cell (IQAC) of Union Christian College, 2008, Website : www.uccollege.edu.in

CHAPTER

32

Women Empowerment is a Key Constituent to Bridge the Gap of Gender Inequality in India

SHAZIA TABASSUM

ABSTRACT

The social phenomenon of being an educated person is a positive notion in post-colonial, Indian society. Girls' and women's education is regarded as important for their family and for the nation's progress. Academic research on asking educated women what do they think of themselves as being educated is hardly evident. Local and minority means of producing, knowing, and communicating are often undervalued in the face of modern development schemes, universal systems of education, and languages of wider communication. Through this study, I attempt to understand a local situation from local perspectives—specifically the education situation in India. Women in the light of their views on empowerment and their aims for the future are the main challenge which is faced by the society in India. My questions address Empowerment and education issues in India: (1) in relation to national policies and local ideologies, (2) as experienced and negotiated by young women. The purpose of the study is to explore how a variety of social issues and value systems impact the meaning expressed in their artwork. Gender gap exists regarding access to education and employment. The study concludes by an observation that access to education and employment are only the enabling factors to empowerment, achievement towards the goal, however, depends largely on the attitude of the people towards gender equality.

Keywords: Empowerment, Education, Indian, Social.

I. INTRODUCTION

Empowerment is now increasingly seen as a process by which the one's without power gain greater control over their lives. This means control over material assets, intellectual resources and ideology. It involves power to, power with and power within. Some define empowerment as a process of awareness and conscientization, of capacity building leading to greater participation, effective decision-making power and control leading to transformative action. This involves ability to get what one wants and to influence others on our concerns. With reference to women the power relation that has to be involved includes their lives at multiple levels, family, community, market and the state. Importantly it involves at the psychological level women's ability to assert them and this is constructed by the 'gender roles' assigned to her especially in a cultural which resists change like India. A nation that wants to progress cannot afford to ignore capacity building and empowerment of women. Women's development is inextricably linked with technology. Information Technology has revolutionized the world as never before. Rapid and dynamic transformations have taken place in the global world. Information technology has contributed significantly in terms of Income and Earnings, Growth and Employment generation. India has also witnessed extra-ordinary growth in the field of information technology. Due to the presence of world class educational institution in the country, large pool of trained manpower of international standards have been created.

Having been thrust into the globalized economy, the social environment in India has changed rapidly in the recent past. These changes are leading young people in India to begin questioning the traditional system (Kashyap, 1996). As Verma and Saraswathi (2002) observe, "Standing at the crossroads of technological advancement and a global market economy, it is an opportune time to examine how tradition and modernity in sociopolitical and cultural factors have shaped and continue to influence adolescence in India" (p. 106). The same could easily be said about emerging adulthood (Arnett, 2000a), the period between the ages of 18 and 25, in India. According to United Nation Article 13(1966), discrimination in education in any form is considered as violation of human right. Despite the recommendations and suggestions made by UNESCO (2003a), women are still facing enormous problems relating to access and enrolment of higher education in many countries especially in the developing countries. There have been several findings regarding gender inequalities in universities worldwide (Lie and O'Leary, 1990, Lie and Malik, 1994, Chamberlain, 1988, UNESCO, 1993, Acker and Piper, 1984) which indicate that women are underrepresented as students, faculty and administrators in most countries.

Modern development schemes often ignore time-tested local technologies and means of production. Universal education assumptions, as well, tend to undervalue local ways of knowing and learning. Similarly, local languages seem to lose their significance beside languages of wider communication. Often local ways of producing and learning and communicating are undervalued relative to more powerful ways, leading to a shift away from the traditional and the local. Certainly some change brings improvement. The problems arise when ideas about what brings improvement are assumed to be relevant for all people in any context. Decisions about what is best for a group of people are more likely to contribute to empowerment when they reflect the voices of the people.

Education significantly leads to the improvement of the productive capacity of all societies. It enables people to use their capabilities and better their livelihood. Again it empowers individuals to participate in the transformation of their own lives and the society as a whole. It is known that educated mothers tend to have healthier families than their counterparts who are not educated, a factor that contributes to an increase life expectancy and quality of live. This means that education is imperative to each and every individual irrespective of one's gender. Despite the fact that education is crucial to everyone and of course a right to everybody, it appears majority of girls are marginalized in accessing higher education in India.

Gender inequality in access to education has generally been seen as a major problem that needs to be addressed. This study investigates the factors that contribute to gender inequality in higher education in India. The study exposed some educational interventions by the government aimed exclusively at increasing girls' education in higher education, like the quota system and many others. In spite of these measures you would realize that the gap still persists. The study suggests to the government and other stakeholders in the higher education sector to embark on pragmatic and vigorous policies to curb the issue of gender inequality in the higher education sector. One such suggestion is that, there should be a policy which will enable girls to go back to school after delivering a baby and of course sex education needs to be openly and publicly discussed. The solutions for of implementing policies need also to be found in order to minimize the problem if not complete eradication. In addition, urgent attention is required in addressing poverty constraints. For proper economic take-off it is expected that both sexes must be given equal opportunity in accessing higher education in India.

2. REVIEW OF RELATED STUDIES

For accelerated development and growth to occur, both men and women must have equal access to education for the benefit of individual and national development. Gender and socio-economic issues are imperative when discussing distribution of education. Socio-cultural and social-economic factors that inhibit girl's education in India include:

- Persistence of negative traditional views on women's roles in society.

- Widespread poverty;
- Inadequate learning and achievement opportunities in schools;
- Lack of balanced national investment in education; and
- Lack of job opportunities for women with low levels of education (FAWE, 1993).

Studies conducted to investigate the factors affecting enrolment, persistence in schools and educational attainments in India were limited. Hence, an attempt is made in this paper to review some of the few literatures on Indian education and some other from others from the rest of the world especially from developing countries.

Mensah (1992), a positive correlation between parental education and parental attitudes towards education has been identified in a number of studies. A study which investigated societal attitudes towards female education in India reveals that parents without any educational background have little interest in educating their female children. There is preference for boys to go to school while girls stay at home to help with domestic chores, an indication of the division of gender role. Mfuo *et. al.* (1997) indicate that, most parents now appreciate the value of girls' education. However, when there are scanty resources, girls are sacrificed for their male counterparts. Akyeampong (1992) revealed that the educational status of parents is a benchmark for determining a child's aspirations and achievements. On the other hand, Oppong (1992) support this assertion in a study examining the educational performance of boys and girls in the Kwabeng area in the Ashanti region. Indeed, there are some exceptions and some children of parents with low educational levels aspire to reach at higher educational ladder. Owing to the growing awareness created of the benefits of education. There is a direct relationship between mothers' educational levels and children's participation in schooling. The higher the educational attainment of the mother, the more likely she is to understanding the importance and benefits of sending her children to school, especially the girl child. Some cultural and traditional practices such as early marriages particularly affect enrolment of girls. Marriage is seen as a priority in many communities, with the result that girls of school going age become wives and subsequently mothers at the expense of their education. These girls have almost no education or skills let alone having experience to enter into gainful employment. They are usually ill-informed to take part in decisions that border on their welfare as well as that of their children. Their children would of course miss out on the positive impact of mothers' education on children (Oppong, 1992).

Bunwaree (1999:135) conducted a study on gender inequality in Mauritius, focusing on higher education. The study involved various actors, including parents, female students, teachers, policy-makers, educational administrators and career advisers. The study used participant observation as well as structured and unstructured interviews. The findings of the study revealed that in times of financial constraint parents tended to favor boys as against girls. Some parents think that schooling is important for boys because girls will get married eventually. This implies that girls will get marry and depend on their husbands for survival. The researcher further elaborated that public higher education is not all that expensive, but an analysis of private tuition seems to highlight the overlapping of class and gender. Moreover, the study explained that there are many subtle mechanisms at work that push disadvantaged girls to the fringes of society. Exclusion from the labor market is a wider problem, affecting not only girls from disadvantaged homes. Girls from middle-class backgrounds are also marginalized in the labor market for various reasons. In assessing the findings, this study has revealed that gender inequality is caused by different factors that needed to be explored in order to address the situation.

Strong, Snell and Tooke (2002) support the arguments of Kader and Hochtritt by observing that modern approaches to Western art do not allow for a depth of understanding of the influences shaping art, hence, with greater diversified instruction students and teachers could benefit. Consequently, more purposeful teacher education and professional development programs are needed to assist in this process.

Kader (2005) notes that art educators often lack historical and contextual information needed to present lessons of meaningful multicultural value. Kader (2005) asserts art education is troubled by ineffective content and activities in its attempts to present culturally diverse content to satisfy education's requirements for diversity in the curriculum. Consequently, Hochtritt (2005) makes the point that more purposeful teacher education and professional development programs are needed to assist in providing more effective art instruction when presenting diverse cultures in the art education classroom.

Above review of the earlier studies, on the current position of Women Empowerment and education system for girls in India brings to the gap distinguishes the present work so far done. The pertinent literature scanned here in the form of books and articles, it relates to providing the remedial measures to take corrective action to improve the education system for girls and also provides the strategies to overcome or reduced this problem. The scope of the study is to explore how a variety of social issues and value systems impact the meaning expressed in their artwork. Gender gap exists regarding access to education and employment. The study concludes by an observation that access to education and employment are only the enabling factors to empowerment, achievement towards the goal, however, depends largely on the attitude of the people towards gender equality.

3. OBJECTIVES

The main objectives of this study are as under :

(1) To evaluate the current position of Women Empowerment in India in relation to national policies and local ideologies, and
(2) To examine Empowerment and education issues as experienced and negotiated by young women.

4. METHODOLOGY

Since the purpose of this study is to explore the degree of empowerment by observing the existing conditions of women's problems, it is important to note that empowerment should include the standards that lie outside the localized gender systems [Sen and Grown, 1987]. A number of studies have shown that women may be empowered in one area of life but not in others [Mather, *et. al.* 1997; Kishore, 2004]. However, it need not be presumed that if a development intervention promotes women's empowerment along a particular dimension then the empowerment in other areas would not necessarily follow.

5. GENDER

Gender is different from biological sex that we are naturally given at birth. Such biological difference between men and women clearly define sex. Gender deals with the "social construction of relationship between, people which shape their identity as men and women" (Mhina *et. al.*, 2004:37). It is worth-noting that gender is more complex, multifaceted, culture-specific construct that directs women and men's roles, access to productive resources, decision-making authority and power (Gupta, *et. al.*, 2002). In addition, as argued by Chikovore (2004:19), "whilst the gender axis involves a power advantage of men over women in virtually all societies, gender manifest itself in multiple forms, including relationship among groups of men and groups of women". This attests to the fact that, gender power is neither unproblematic, nor consistently uni-directional. Hence, the situation seems to be quite critical, as it points to the reality that there are in fact multiple or disaggregated masculinities and femininities which are contextually dependent.

I. Culture and Gender

The domain of "Culture" refers basically to essential aspects of collective social life, especially meaning and practices, "social customs, institutional ways of doing things and also person habits", McQuail (1994:62). Majority of researchers who investigate gender define sex as culturally constructed biological characteristics. Gender is accepted as a socially constructed, an ongoing culture process that constructs differences between women and men. Culture and society are twin factors which are seen as inseparable units; hence many researchers and theorists tend to associate these two terms together and try to explain gender as both a "culture" and "societal" phenomenon. Mies argues that 'patriarchy' signifies the historical emergence of particular forms of inequality between women and men, in contrast to the view that gender inequality is natural. All these three theoretical uses of the concept of patriarchy, the historical, material and psychoanalytic, have produced generalized explanations of the subordination of women. It is therefore imperative to examine gender inequality in access to higher education and to what extent the forms of cultural practices of the patriarchy contribute to this situation. The system brings about socio-economic inequalities between women and men, girls and boys within society with the result of enhancing class division between the rich and poor, educated and non-educated, urban and rural (Mansah, 1992). Burn (2000) was of the view that in many cultures, biological differences between men and women indirectly led to men's domination over women. In the same vein, psychologist Burn (2000) pointed out that women all over the globe continue to be overwhelmingly responsible for housework and child care, and this affect them negatively both economically and their political power. In India, families differ in the resources available to them for supplying their children with the basic necessities that would enable them, among others, to participate fully and successfully in schooling. The socio-economic means available within the family can be regarded as intermediate factors between family background and the students' educational achievement.

2. Gender Inequality and Poverty

Poverty has become a key area of focus for governments, development agencies and other international organizations for the past decade. Some commentators suggest that the poor are getting poorer and that the gap between the rich and the poor is alarming. Figures from World Bank (2001) indicate that actual number of people classified as poor are rising in most of the World. Poverty has several meanings and connotations but from sociological perspective, it can be seen as a relative deprivation defining levels of need in relation to other groups and individuals. Education has however become a privileged service for which households must pay. To this end, mass poverty means that many parents cannot afford to send their children to school especially in the higher education which it is believed that expenses are on the high side. Education charges take a variety of forms. They range from direct charges levied by both public and private institutions, the indirect comprises of expenses on the uniforms, tools of learning such as pens, pencils, books and other contingency expenses. Cost-sharing is a catch all phrases that describes the distribution of education cost between the two main actors: parents and the state. In reality, though, it is a euphemism for the privatization of education financing, and a tax on attendance. There are many reasons for the high cost of higher education to the poor households, but one near-universal factor is inadequate finance. The devastating interaction between household poverty and rising education cost hampers efforts to accelerate growth and reduce poverty, and exacerbating problems such as child labor. Public financing is not the only issue, but magnifies the other factors that are obstructing progress towards equal access to quality higher education. Where the quality of education is inadequate, or perceived as generating few benefits, poor households or parents are obvious not spend their scanty resources financing education. It is for fact that the children of the poor who account for those out of school, though there are other alarming sources of inequality based on gender, race, region and rural-urban divides. Under this circumstance women or the girl child becomes the victim because of our social structure which seems to favor men. Education charges interact with these factors, for instance, where low value is attributed to girl's education; charges are likely to reinforce gender inequalities in levels of attendance and completion.

6. WOMEN'S EDUCATION IN INDIA

Although in the Vedic period women had access to education in India, they had gradually lost this right. However, in the British period there was revival of interest in women's education in India. However, women's education got a fillip after the country got independence in 1947 and the government has taken various measures to provide education to all Indian women. As a result, women's literacy rate has grown over the three decades and the growth of female literacy has in fact been higher than that of male literacy rate. While in 1971 only 22% of Indian women were literate, by the end of 2001, 54.16% female were literate. The growth of female literacy rate is 14.87% as compared to 11.72% that of male literacy rate. Gender discrimination still persists in India and lot more needs to be done in the field of women's education in India. The gap in the male-female literacy rate is just a simple indicator. While the male literary rate is more than 75% according to the 2001 census, the female literacy rate is just 54.16%.

7. ECONOMIC AND SOCIAL EMPOWERMENT OF WOMEN

Since the beginning of this decade, much has been achieved in empowering women in the economic and social fields. An increasing volume of development financial resources has been devoted to achieving that objective. Consequently, many countries of the region have been able to report increased female literacy and enrolment rates, improved gender equality in education, reduced infant and child mortality rates, declining maternal mortality rates and expanding access to reproductive health services. The participation of women in formal economic activities has also registered a noticeable improvement.

1. Growing Economic Participation

Economic empowerment constitutes one of the fundamental building blocks in efforts towards the overall empowerment of women. Participation in formal economic activities on terms and conditions which reflect the productive capacity of women, and their control over their own incomes, are some of the important dimensions of economic empowerment. Although the increasing work participation of women has been viewed as part of the general employment boom created by the export-led economic expansion, female labour-force participation rates have tended to increase more than those for men in the Asian and Pacific region, suggesting that women's economic participation has been a critical feature of the region's quest for the economic empowerment of women.

2. Improvements in Social Development Indicators

Fertility rates have declined in the region, even though the total fertility rate and the average number of children per woman remain high (over four) in several countries in the region. The fertility rates on average remain high in those countries of Asia where female literacy is low and opportunities for outside work participation are limited. It is therefore increasingly accepted that, in addition to reflecting general conditions of economic growth and the availability of both health care and birth control facilities, fertility rates also serve as a proxy for women's general empowerment. This is because these rates are closely linked to the literacy and educational status of women, age at marriage, and other important features of women's status.

3. Access to Technology, Including Information Technology

Promoting access to productive resources and social support systems constitutes one of the fundamental building blocks in efforts to empower women in the region. Access to productive resources such as credit, technology, infrastructure, marketing links and networking facilities can significantly enlarge opportunities for women to engage in formal economic activities and improve their social status. In that regard, promoting access to new and emerging technologies, including information and communication technology, has become a powerful tool for women's empowerment.

8. WOMEN'S EMPOWERMENT IN INDIA— A REALITY OR MYTH

The Government of India had ushered in the new millennium by declaring the year 2001 as 'Women's Empowerment Year' to focus on a vision 'where women are equal partners like men'. The most common explanation of 'women's empowerment' is the ability to exercise full control over one's actions. The last decades have witnessed some basic changes in the status and role of women in our society. There has been shift in policy approaches from the concept of 'welfare' in the seventies to 'development' in the eighties and now to 'empowerment' in the nineties. This process has been further accelerated with some sections of women becoming increasingly self-conscious of their discrimination in several areas of family and public life. They are also in a position to mobilize themselves on issues that can affect their overall position. A review of government's various programmes for women empowerment such as Swashakti, Swayamsidha, Streeshakti, Balika Samrudhi Yojana and another two thousand projects reveal that little has been done or achieved through these programmes. The discrepancy in the ideology and practice of the empowerment policy of women in India constitutes its continued social, economic and social backwardness. Women make up 52% of our country's population. Hence there can be no progress unless their needs and interests are fully met. Empowerment would not hold any meaning unless they are made strong, alert and aware of their equal status in the society. Policies should be framed to bring them into the mainstream of society. It is important to educate the women. The need of the hour is to improve female literacy as education holds the key to development.

Empowerment would become more relevant if women are educated, better informed and can take rational decisions. It is also necessary to sensitize the other sex towards women. It is important to usher in changes in societal attitudes and perceptions with regard to the role of women in different spheres of life. Adjustments have to be made in traditional gender specific performance of tasks. A woman needs to be physically healthy so that she is able to take challenges of equality. But it is sadly lacking in a majority of women especially in the rural areas. They have unequal access to basic health resources and lack adequate counseling. The result is an increasing risk of unwanted and early pregnancies, HIV infection and other sexually transmitted diseases. The greatest challenge is to recognize the obstacles that stand in the way of their right to good health. To be useful to the family, community and the society, women must be provided with health care facilities. There is no doubt about the fact that development of women has always been the central focus of planning since Independence. Empowerment is a major step in this direction but it has to be seen in a relational context. A clear vision is needed to remove the obstacles to the path of women's emancipation both from the government and women themselves. Efforts should be directed towards all round development of each and every section of Indian women by giving them their due share.

9. IMPROVEMENT AND SUGGESTIONS

The empowerment of women refers to providing the necessary rights and responsibilities to women in order to make them self-reliant. Traditionally, Indian women have been brought to become workers or servants to serve the man-dominating world. Even in mythology, there is no gender equity and women were deprived of their legal rights, to get property, education privacy, social status and they were never treated as participants in any developmental works. Empowerment is the process of building capacities of women, creating an atmosphere which will enable people to fully utilize their creative potentials. Empowerment gives women, the capacity to influence decision-making process, planning, implementation and evaluation. The status of women empowerment in India using various indicators like women's household decision-making power, financial autonomy, freedom of movement, political participation, acceptance of unequal gender role, exposure to media, access to education, experience of domestic violence, etc. based on data from different sources. Gender gap exists regarding access to education and employment. Household decision-making power and freedom of movement of women vary considerably with their age, education and employment status.

Four of the main processes that could lead to women's empowerment, as defined by the IFAD evaluation, were:

- changes in women's mobility and social interaction;
- changes in women's labour patterns;

- changes in women's access to and control over resources; and
- changes in women's control over decision-making.

There was comparatively greater change reported in non-domestic productive tasks. Not all the changes in such labour patterns can be viewed as beneficial to women.

10. CONCLUSION

In the light of the expatiate study conducted it can be concluded that the education is a potent tool in the emancipation and empowerment of women. The greatest single factor which can incredibly improve the status of women in any society is education. It is indispensable that education enables women not only to gain more knowledge about the world outside of her hearth and home but helps her to get status, positive self-esteem, and self-confidence, necessary courage and inner strength to face challenges in life. Apparently, it also facilitates them to procure a job and supplement the income of family and achieve social status. Education especially of women has a major impact on health and nutrition as an instrument of developing a sustainable strategy for population control. Moreover, educated women can play an equally important role as men in nation-building. Thus, there is no denying the fact that education empowers women. Indeed the different organs of the United Nations and experts on women's liberation argue for women's education as the basic step to attain equality with men.

"When women move forward the family moves, the village moves and the nation moves". It is essential as their thought and their value systems lead the development of a good family, good society and ultimately a good nation. Indian government has taken several steps towards empowering women. Empowerment of women also requires participation and co-operation of men as they benefit by having educated mothers, wives, daughters and sisters. The economic empowerment will allow raising women's self-awareness, skill development, creative decision-making and it may also lead to produce better citizens and a new and modern India.

REFERENCES

Arnett, J.J., "Emerging Adulthood : A Theory of Development from the late teens through the twenties", *American Psychologist*, 55, 2000, pp. 469-80.

Arnett, J.J., "Learning to Stand Alone: The Contemporary American Transition to Adulthood in Cultural and Historical Context". *Human Development*, 41, 1998, pp. 295-315.

Burn, S.M., "Women Across Cultures : A Global Perspective", London: Mayfield Publishing, 2000.

Chikovore, J. (2004). "Gender Power Dynamics in Sexual and Reproductive Health: A qualitative study in Chiredzi District, Zimbabwe", (Doctoral Thesis) Umea University, 2004. http://publications.uu.se/umu/fultext/nbn_se_umu_diva_202.pdf. Accessed 21/04/08.

Gupta, G.R., "Gender, Sexuality and HIV/AIDS: the what, the why and the how", Washington, DC: International Center for Research on Women (ICRW), 2002.

Hochtritt, L., "Pre-Packaged Multiculturalism: A Cause for Concern in the Art Classroom", *Electronic Magazine of Multicultural Education*, 7(2), 18 paragraphs. Retrieved June 1, 2006, from http://www.eastern.edu/publications/emme/2005fall/lawton.html.

Kashyap, L., India, In J. Gibson-Cline (Ed.), "Adolescence: From crisis to coping; A thirteen nation study", London: Butterworth Heinemann Ltd, 1996, pp. 103-17.

Kader, T. (2005). "School Arts: DBAE and multicultural art education in the USA", *International Journal of Education through Art*, 1(1), 65-84.

McQuai, D., "Mass Communication Theory: An Introduction", Sage Publication, 1994.

Patrick, Maanu, "Gender Gap in Access to Higher Education in Ghana", Institute for Educational Research, Faculty of Education, University of Oslo, Unpublished Ph.D. Thesis, 2008.

UNESCO, "Gender and Education for All", The Leap to Quality. Summary Report, Paris: UNESCO, 2003.

Verma, S., and Saraswathi, T.S., Adolescence in India, In B.B. Brown, R.W. Larson and T.S. Saraswathi (Eds.), and "The World's Youth Adolescence in Eight Regions of the Globe", New York: Cambridge University Press, 2002, pp. 105-40.

Website References

http://azadindia.org/social-issues/Women-Empowerment.html

http://www.ifad.org/gender/learning/role/labour/in_tamil.htm

http://www.articlesbase.com/education-articles/analysing-the-current-scenario-of-women-status-1112712.html#axzz1RJ5V6HPI

http://www.lookforedu.com/education-is-the-foundation-for-womens-empowerment-in-india-prospects-challenges-and-remedies/

CHAPTER

33

Education for Women Empowerment, Especially Mathematics and Science Education in Morigaon District of Assam

A Study

SIMAREKHA BHAGOWATI AND JNANJYOTI SARMAH

ABSTRACT

It is always felt that women should be empowered and for this various governmental and non-governmental organizations has been implementing many policies. Women empowerment is possible in real sense if they are educated properly to work in different field. In general, it is observed that women workforce in the field of science and technology is much lesser compared to men. Through this paper it is tried to highlight the apathy of women towards mathematics and science confined to Morigaon district (a backward and tribal dominated district) of Assam. Also to study the existing facilities for mathematics and science study.

Key-words: Women empowerment, Mathematics and science learning

INTRODUCTION

Women Empowerment

In general women empowerment means—improvement of women's political, social, spiritual, and economic and health status. Further, women empowerment can be understood as to grow self-confidence among women to fight against any form of injustice to them. The extent to which empowering women in India can bring about improvements in nutrition outcome is yet to be explored. Measuring women's empowerment is challenging, because the term itself is often poorly defined (Gurumurthy, 1998; Kishor and Neitzel, 1996; Mason, 1986). The key underlying concepts that define women's empowerment, relate to choices, control, and power (Malhotra and Schuler, 2005). Women's empowerment is conceptualized as a function of women's access to and control over resources, which extends to their decision-making capabilities regarding household decisions, employment, income, household assets and expenditure, fertility, sexuality, and freedom of movement (physical mobility) and their control over material and intangible resources such as property, information and time; their position within the household *vis-à-vis* other male and female household members; their experience of domestic violence; and their education (Gurumurthy, 1998; Dyson and Moore, 1983).

Development of society depends upon the development of its people. Half of the total population of the world is women. In India ratio of female is 940 to 1000 males. In Assam the ratio is 954 to per 1000 male. So if a society is to develop both men and women should be developed equally. But despite many policies and provisions for equal development of women, they are unable to move forward with the men in some fields.

Further where women have been successful, their number is not high.

There are many reasons for this unfortunate condition. Major cause of under development is the lack of education for women in general. Education can uplift the status of women by providing opportunities for jobs or self-employment. Education can raise self-confidence among the women. Women has caliber of doing everything in every field if from the early age they are not restricted to do some specific tasks. The present mothers were girls earlier with lots of restrictions inside and outside the family. Similarly, the present girls will be future mothers. Women who are educated have fewer children than those who are denied schooling (some studies correlate each additional year of with a 10 percent drop in fertility). They delay their pregnancies, have healthier children and are far more likely to send their own children to school. According to the United Nations Population Fund, each additional year of schooling a woman has, is associated with a 5 to 10 percent decline in child deaths. (Women's Empowerment, CARE). So if our society is to progress, women must be educated to work in diversified field, to fight against the obstructions that arise not only to them but for girls of future generation. Presently it is observed that girls are coming out to work in various fields for their livelihood. But in the field of science and technology number of girls are very less in comparison to boys. As a result, they face many problems in their work field. Another fact is due to lack of proper science education; women face much other complexity in their daily life.

In case of Assam the scenario is rather more concerning. Our society needs women not only in the field of art and culture but also in the field of science and technology, economics and industry. Every year very less no. of girls appear for Assam Higher Secondary Council Examination in science stream.

From the Table 1 it is observed that only few girls go to the field of science and technology in Assam (students only under AHSEC). In general, mathematics is considered to be main cause of keeping girls away from science learning. Mathematics anxiety is very much prominent in all over the

TABLE I

Candidates Appeared in H.S. Final Examination under Assam Higher Secondary Council (AHSEC) (from 2006-2011)

Year	*Total students*	*Students in Arts*	*Students in Commerce*	*Students in Science*	*% of science students*	*Boys in Sc.*	*Girls in Sc.*	*% of girls in Sc.*
(1)	(2)	(3)	(4)	(5)	(6)	(7)	(8)	(9)
2006	148149	124882	8894	14373	09.70	10814	3559	2.402
2007	158407	135379	9190	13838	08.73	10407	3431	2.166
2008	162792	137270	10429	15093	09.27	11215	3878	2.382
2009	164632	140419	11682	12531	07.61	9334	3197	1.941
2010	194578	166311	13606	14661	07.53	10779	3882	1.995
2011	220999	186688	16776	17535	07.93	13054	4481	2.028

world. Gender difference is not prominent in mathematical abilities, but confidence of boys in mathematical abilities is more than that of girls as observed. Another fact is observed, in the countries where gender equity is more prevalent, performance of girls in mathematics is better than boys (*Science Daily*, Jan. 6, 2010). As mathematics is a compulsory subject for high school students, so most of the students specially girls give up the subject when they enter into higher secondary level of education due to mathematics anxiety. It is also observed that in every year due to fear for mathematics many girls even do not study economics as major subject in their graduate level (In the universities of Assam one mathematics paper of 100 marks is compulsory for economics major).

Women can be empowered without mathematics and science. Then why do we need mathematics and science? In fact in every field of life nobody can deny the importance of mathematics and science. Some important facts about mathematics and science are given below:

Study of Mathematics

- develops logical thinking ability in every sphere of life,
- increases problem-solving and analyzing capacity in everyday life problems,
- provides language and tool to explain everything of life scientifically,
- helps to understand the world, and
- increases career option.

Study of Science

- increases creativity to come up with changing society,
- develops inquisitiveness why things happen,
- develops thinking ability in every sphere of life including nature,
- increases analyzing capacity in everyday life problems, and

- develops thinking from the viewpoints of protecting our environments and teaches proper use of natural resources.

Apathy for science and technology is a vast topic for study. First step towards the field of science and technology is mathematics. If students face difficulty in mathematics, they cannot move to the field of science and technology. Therefore, study has been done in the field of mathematics especially in school mathematics.

Thus mathematics and science learning is most important for our future mothers.

Background

Morigaon district is located in the mid part of Assam. The district is almost plain and is flood prone. It is a tribal dominated district.

Population Data According to 2011 Census

Name of the district	*Total Persons*	*Total Males*	*Total Females*	*Sex ratio (Females per 1000 males)*
Morigaon	957,853	485,328	472,525	974

Literates and Literacy Rates

Name of the district	*Literate Total Persons*	*Literate Total Male*	*Literate Total Female*	*Literacy Rate Persons (%)*	*Literacy Rate Males (%)*	*Literacy Rate Females (%)*
Morigaon	554,143	297,422	256,721	69.37	73.66	64.99

The district is a place for religious superstitions. It is often seen, some thugs would make up stories sometimes claiming themselves as god to earn easy money. The innocence of the village folk specially women can be easily taken over by these fraud people. Besides negligence towards diseases, reluctance to obtain medical help during diseases or maternity periods, making issues out of menstrual periods in public are common among the women.

Some organizations are working for women empowerment in Morigaon district. But empowerment of women through the field of science and technology is not done at all by any organization. Assam Science Society and Assam Academy of Mathematics have been doing some activities regularly, to attract the young people towards science and technology. Any kind of special activity to motivate the girls towards science and technology is not visible.

But for learning science in higher level, adequate knowledge of mathematics is required. Because mathematics is a tool for the field of science and technology. If someone faces trouble in the subject at the lower level and proper rectification in not done accordingly, it closes the paths of further study in the field of science and technology. Mathematics anxiety is very much common among the students of Morigaon districts. Most of the students specially the girls are terrified even by the name of the subject. As a result, they flee away from the subject after class X. Thus their path for science study comes to an end. Without mathematics they cannot continue science subjects like physics, chemistry, etc. In Morigaon only a few women are doing higher study (doctoral study) in the scientific field. In the last 10 years not more than 15 girls are pursuing engineering degree and not more than five girls has gone for medical profession. Around 25 girls are studying paramedical courses after 10+2. Among these girls almost all are from town areas. As education up to secondary level is same for all students. After completion of this level they have to enter in to diversified field of study. To find the apathy of girls towards science and mathematics in particular a study has been done in the field of mathematics among the high school girls of Morigaon district of Assam.

OBJECTIVES

Main objectives of this paper are :

(1) To study the factors that affects the girls in learning mathematics,

    (a) Role of family
    (b) Role of teacher

(2) To study about the attitude of the girls towards mathematics, and

(3) To study about the awareness of the importance of mathematics in science learning in higher level.

METHODOLOGY

Survey method is adopted for the study. Primary data is collected for both girls and boys. Data is collected through survey and for that questionnaires are prepared. Primary data is also collected from school authorities, teaching faculties and parents by interviewing them. Secondary data is collected from various sources such as—office of the Inspector of schools, Morigaon; Assam Science Society, Morigaon Branch, Results of AHSEC (booklet), etc.

Sampling

For collection of data, 250 girls (class IX and X) of 14 schools situated in different locations of the district are selected randomly. Sample is confined to schools under state board (Secondary Education Board of Assam).

DISCUSSION OF THE TOPIC

Factors that Affects the Girls in Learning Mathematics: Role of Family

The main objective of this paper is to study about the factors that affect the learning process of mathematics for girls. Poor economic condition of the parents and lack of parents' consciousness affect the whole education system in many areas of Morigaon district. Students remain absent in their regular classes because they have to work in agricultural field especially during sowing and harvesting season. In rural areas it is observed that the whole responsibility of the family, specially bringing-up of the children and also looking after the parents (in-law) goes to the woman (mothers or the daughters-in-law). In villages though girls are sent to school but majority of the families keep the daughters busy with household works to help their mother. So they cannot spend much time in their studies. Sometimes they have to work in other people's house. As a result, they cannot attend regular classes. But mathematics is a sequential subject and needs lots of continuous effort. Further Morigaon district is a flood prone area. Regular occurrence of flood compel many girls to take their livelihood as first priority, education remain in cold storage. Another important fact that girls from some rural areas (Maanipur, Patidoria, Ghaguwa, etc.) of the district are hired as domestic servant in the town areas of Morigaon district and nearby districts. So in rural and interior places girls have to face many problems due to their poor economic condition. In many cases it is observed that parents consider education for their daughters is important only for marriage. Therefore, parents are not concerned about their daughters over all education. Thus learning of mathematics and science is meaningless for them.

The scenario is somehow different from place to place or depends on circumstances. In town areas the situation is better. Gradually parents have become conscious about the education of their daughters. So they try to provide facilities to the girls similar to that of boys. Another important fact about girls' mathematics learning is that most parents who are aware of their daughter's inability in mathematics feel, it is only enough for their daughters to secure the passing marks in class X examination. Because they are not going to pursue higher education in the subject. But if the same condition arises for their son they try to provide proper facilities for their son. This condition is also applicable in the educated families of rural areas.

ROLE OF TEACHER

Teaching-learning process of mathematics is not same with that of other subjects. Proper learning of mathematics is possible if the teacher teaches properly. Proper teaching of mathematics depends on many factors. Teacher must have sufficient knowledge in the subject. Without qualified teacher the learning cannot take place properly which affects the performance (Zaskis Rina, Zaskis Dov, 2010). The teacher must be helpful and he or she must have knowledge about the techniques or methods of mathematics teaching (Prediger Susanne, 27th August 2009). In this area many teachers do not have proper qualification. Most of the designated mathematics teachers were graduated without mathematics and do not have any training in mathematics teaching. Once a student is terrified by the teacher, he or she cannot follow the lesson taught by that teacher. The process of mathematics learning is such that if students face difficulty in the subject at early stages, he or she may not be able to understand the latter part of the topic. Thus the subject becomes a burden to him or her. If proper remedial measure is not taken, there is every possibility that students may flee away from the subject after class X or sometime drop out from the school. Teacher factor affects the girls much more than boys. In rural areas many girls cannot attend school regularly due to various socio-economic reasons. As a result they cannot cope up with the lesson taught by the teacher. Therefore, they require special care. But that type of care is not possible due to shortage of teacher, time shortage and irregularity in attendance of the girls. Teachers' attitude towards girls is very important for learning mathematics. Some teachers believe that girls are not good enough in mathematics. Therefore, they pay maximum attention to the boys thus learning of girls is affected a lot. Appreciation by teachers gathers enough confidence among the boys on the other hand feeling neglected by teachers, girls lose confidence in the subject. An article published in the U.S. newspaper 'Science Daily', Feb. 2008 shows that in U.S. schools, teachers are unaware of growing gender gap in the classroom. Except a few teachers, most of them emphasize that mathematics is not for girls.

Another important fact is that shortage of qualified teachers in school affects the girls more. Many girls have to appear in the examination without minimum amount of subject knowledge. Because boys can go for extra classes to a distant place but girls cannot. Many parents do not wish to send their daughters for extra classes for safety purpose, nor do they allow them to study under male teacher at home. Scarcity of female mathematics teacher is another small but important factor for many girls. This condition is applicable to primary and upper primary classes. In poor families generally girl's education is considered less important as stated earlier. So for the girls, no extra facility for learning the subject is provided due to poor economic condition though necessary. So availability of qualified teacher in their own school is an important factor of learning mathematics.

ATTITUDE OF GIRLS TOWARDS MATHEMATICS

Fear of mathematics leads to loss of interest in the subject. In general, mathematics anxiety is very much common in both boys and girls. This fear develops gradually from the lower classes. In the case of girls it develops easily due to improper environment especially in interior areas. Lack in pre-required knowledge of mathematics troubles them to study high school mathematics. As a result, they cannot cope up with the subject and it becomes a burden to them and gradually they lose interest in the subject. That results poor performance in examinations. Once fear for mathematics develops in the girls, performance declines (Yee, F.P., 1987)). But lack of basic knowledge is the result of poor teaching-learning environment in primary and upper primary level, as observed. The main cause of this condition is teachers' insufficient knowledge in the subject and inability to teach the subject properly in lower classes. In the primary and upper primary schools of Assam, teachers are not appointed as mathematics or language teacher. Every teacher has to teache all the subjects. Most of the teachers cannot give proper mathematical concept to students. There is a strong relation between fear of mathematics among girls and mathematics teachers. High mathematics anxiety is associated with low mathematics achievement (Das, N.R., Baruah, Karuna).

Awareness about the Importance of Mathematics in Science Learning in Higher Level

Most of high school going girls has no idea about the vast field of science and technology. Some girls from town area know about a few courses of scientific field. But most of them do not the requisite qualifications for different courses after higher secondary school. They study according to their parents or relatives' direction. Previous study shows that for selecting a career path, high school girls are more influenced by the advice of parents and teachers (Williams, F. Mary). Many educated parents even do not know the role of mathematics in science learning in class XII level. Many of them do not know that without sufficient knowledge of mathematics other science subjects cannot be learned properly. In the survey when the girls were asked about the importance of mathematics in their curriculum, most of them could not answer.

FINDINGS

(1) In rural and interior areas it was found that attitude of parents towards girls' mathematics learning is not good enough. For them it is sufficient if their daughter has passed matriculation examination. Thus they are marriageable. Parent's economic condition affects the learning process of girls more than boys. In rural areas many girls do not attend school at menstrual periods due to some restrictions from family and society. Thus they remain absent from classes for many days in a year and cannot take regular lessons. Further at time of occurrence of flood girls as well as boys remain absent from the classes. Every year in some areas (especially in Mayong area) schools remain close due to heavy flood for many days. This affects the education system as a whole.
In town areas, parents are however concerned about their daughters' education. Therefore, they take efforts to provide facilities in mathematics learning to their daughters; though the percentage of such parents is less.

(2) Mathematics learning environment is pathetic for girls especially in rural and interior areas. The reason for this is unavailability of proper qualified teacher. After the survey it was found that in majority of schools the teaching learning process was badly affected because of under qualified teachers. Teachers without mathematics subject in their graduate level were appointed as mathematics teachers earlier.

Many of them are still working without any training on mathematics teaching. But in August 2010, government has appointed temporarily competent teachers in mathematics, science, English and social study in all provincialized schools. Thus teaching-learning process has got a boost up in many schools. However, in non-provincialized schools the condition has not improved. In some areas it was observed that boys however manage extra classes but for girls it is not possible at all. In town areas situation is better.

(3) Lack in pre-acquired knowledge of mathematics affects high school mathematics. This lack of knowledge occurs due to improper teaching in primary and upper primary level. Many teachers expressed that girls as well as boys weak in mathematics, cannot perform simple multiplication or division problems of primary level. In the survey it was found to be true.

(4) After the survey it was found that only 15% of total girls' attitude for science learning is positive. Girls' love for mathematics is only 7%. Further it was found that performance of girls in mathematics is very poor. Only 4% were found to have basic concept of mathematics. It is also observed that girls from town areas are more interested to study science.

(5) Girls' awareness in the field of science and technology is negligible in interior villages compared to urban areas. Those who are willing to study science unaware of the fact that mathematics is essential for the study of science. Most of them think that the curriculum of science in high school is enough for the study of science in higher level.

(6) Number of girls' high school with proper mathematics learning facility is very less, as observed.

SUGGESTIONS

Therefore, it is essential that our girls should be provided proper knowledge of mathematics in school level so that they can prepare themselves for future study in science and technology. An environment is to be created so that maximum number of girls can be attracted towards mathematics and science. Some points to be consider as important in mathematics teaching-learning process.

(1) In case of appointments of teacher in primary and upper primary level, knowledge of mathematics should be stressed as important criteria. Minimum criteria for appointment of high school mathematics teacher must be mathematics honours graduate. Teaching of mathematics should not be considered same as other subjects. Liberalization of economy and subsequent development has created ample avenues for qualified people in various sectors. Consequence, impact has fallen on the teaching profession especially under government schools. A teaching job has become a last resort for a qualified person, when other options are closed. Mindset become such, the person will wait for the opportunity and leave the teaching job as soon as he gets his desired one. Thus his working period as a teacher is very casual. Teacher profession in government sector must be made lucrative and kept at par with other attractive job. Appointment of Mathematics teacher should not be on temporary basis.

(2) In-service short term training in mathematics teaching must made compulsory for every teacher (for both governments, private schools) at a regular interval of time.

(3) Mathematics laboratories should be set-up in every school with proper training facility for teachers.

(4) A good number of girls' high schools with proper mathematics and science learning facilities should be established to attract female students in rural areas.

CONCLUSION

(1) Mathematics learning stands on the way to science learning.

(2) Jumping away from mathematics is jumping away from science.
(3) Rural girl population is deprived of science learning due to the prevailing environment of mathematics teaching at primary and secondary level.
(4) This is standing as an obstacle to women empowerment.

References

Das, N.R., Baruah, Karuna, Secondary School Education in Assam (India) with Special Reference to Mathematics.

Desai, Manisha (July 2010), Hope in Hard Times: Women's Empowerment and Human Development, United Nations Development Programme, Human Development Reports.

Dyson, T. and M. Moore (1983), 'On Kinship Structure, Female Autonomy, and Demographic Behavior in India'. *Population and Development Review*, 9: 35-60.

Gurumurthy A. (1998), Women's Rights and Status: Questions of Analysis and Measurement'. Gender in Development Monograph 7.

Kishor, S. and K. Neitzel (1996), 'The Status of Women: Indicators for Twenty-five Countries'. Macro International. DHS Comparative Studies No. 21.

Malhotra, A. and S. Schuler (2005), 'Measuring Women's Empowerment as a Variable in International Development'. In D. Narayan (ed.) Measuring Empowerment. World Bank: Washington, DC.

Mason, K. (1986), 'The Status of Women: Conceptual and Methodological Issues in Demographic Studies'. Sociological Forum 1: 284-300.

Prediger Susanne, Published online: 27th August 2009. How to develop mathematics-teaching and for understanding: the case of meaning of the equal sign Springer Science +Business Media B.V., 2009.

Yee, F.P. (1987), Anxiety and Mathematics Performance in Female Secondary School Students in Singapore, *Asia Pacific Journal of Education*, 8(2), 22-31.

Zaskis, Rina, Zaskis, Dov (16 September 2010), The Significance of mathematical knowledge in teaching elementary method courses: perspective of mathematics teacher educators, *Educational Studies in Mathematics, An International Journal.*

APPENDIX

Girls' Data on Mathematics and Science Learning (Total No. of Girls)

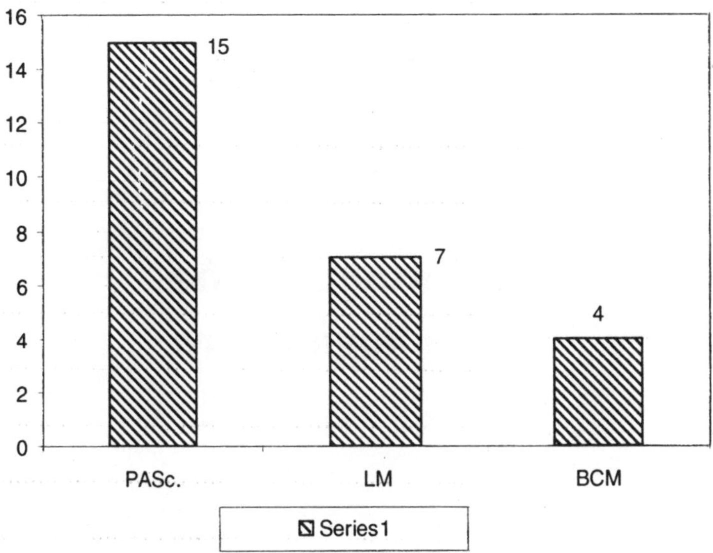

PASc.	:	Percentage of girls on Positive Attitude towards Science.
LM	:	percentage of girls with Love for Mathematics.
BCM	:	Girls' percentage having Basic Concept in Mathematics.

CHAPTER

34

Innovations in the Technological Era

SMRITI NAGI

INTRODUCTION

Technology is revolutionizing in our field of education by alerting it 'structure disregarding institutional walls developing new ways to access information and solve its problems. There has been a tremendous conceptual change in education. "Chalk and Talk" method to a great extent has been replaced by "Information Technology", "Teachercentered" learning by "Student Centered", "Passive learning" by "Creative learning". This is because education is holding a much greater importance than even before. Technology refers to the whole gamut of information and communication from computer, e-books, internet, system software, virtual learning environment, etc. The use of it is the new challenge to determine the best ways in promoting education, which plays an essential role in wealth creation. To be a successful learner in the digital era, individual must remain flexible, acquire new skills continuously and identify ways of managing knowledge and information.

It is needless to say that Information Technology (IT) is providing appropriate solution in promoting education and assuring reformation in respect of the quest for excellence in the area of promoting education too. What is imperative to note that IT adds value to the process of learning in the various learning institutions. The internet is the driving force for much development and innovation required in education. This is why the competencies are gaining importance from the view of increasing role of IT ensure excellence in promoting education:

1. Critical thinking.
2. Broad competencies.
3. IT competencies enabling expert work.
4. Decision-making.
5. Handling dynamic situation.
6. Working as a member of a team.
7. Communicating effectively.

Adequate preparation of teachers are needed for accepting the challenges of the three types of explosions—IT enables a teacher to respond to those challenges with careful preparation, management resourcing and continuing support. IT is helping in promoting educational system coping with all the challenges that calls for a change for excellence.

BENEFITS OF IT IN EDUCATION

(a) IT will improve the productivity of students and educators.
(b) Traditional classrooms can include technology to infuse and enhance learning with supplemental material and resources through online web pages.
(c) Learning can be extended beyond the classrooms to embrace the virtual domain of cyber space.
(d) With a learning time and distance factors will have less impact on the way instruction is delivered to students.

(e) IT provides various new possibilities on distance learning.

IT has widened the horizon of educational process. The new inventions and discoveries in IT has brought advancement that can be effectively used by learners. E-universities and e-learning are learning methodologies supported by IT, promoting solution to the challenges faced in teaching-learning process. Since traditional classroom teaching had many limitations associated with them. IT has brought a revolutionary change in the old educational set-ups in creating solutions through e-learning which not only supports the present methods of learning but also enhances the quality of educational system and meets learner's perspective. The new era of IT has the uniqueness of e-learning that is, it provides the learner the opportunity to learn anytime, anywhere. IT through it's e-learning is the only method of learning where the distinct learning styles of auditory learners, visual learners, and kinaesthetic learners are incorporated.

Today, a variety of IT can facilitate not only delivery of instructions, but also learning process itself. Morever, IT can promote international collaboration and networking in education and professional development. There's a range of IT options—from videoconferencing through multimedia delivery to web sites—which can be used to meet the challenges teachers face today. Infact, has been increasing evidence that IT may be able to provide more flexible and effective ways for lifelong professional development for even teachers of today. Rapid development in IT especially the internet, traditional initial training for teachers is undergoing a rapid change in the structure, contents and methods of their courses. Combining new technologies with effective pedagogy has become a daunting task for the teachers and the taught. IT is not just a weapon to change the way a teacher teaches but it is also useful in supporting more student searches approaches to instruction and in developing the higher order skills and promoting education along the collaborative activities.

With a rapid expansion of IT culture in education there is even pressure for governments to provide this education to all members of the population even in the face of scarce financial, physical and human resources—as a precondition for economic and social development. It's need of time, globalization and the shift to a 'knowledge-based economy' requires that educational institutions develop in individuals the ability to transform information into knowledge in dynamic, cross-cultural contexts. IT is the means for meeting these twin challenges. IT is improving access to and promote equity in education by providing educational opportunities to a greater number of people all ages including the traditionally un-served or undeserved. Second, IT is enhancing the quality of teaching and learning by providing access to a great variety of educational resources and by enabling partiapatory pedagogies. Third, IT is improving the management of education through more administrative processes, including human resource management, monitoring and evaluation and resource sharing.

There are many obstacles involved but keeping in mind the promises of IT, we need to be patient. IT will never fix a bad education system by using any switch. It's not only confined to purchasing computers in educational institutions but upgrading skills and knowledge, increasing motivation and changing attitudes of teachers and all involved. Education systems are developing e-content materials. In conclusion, IT in education is playing a vital role in promoting education and is also creating a positive impact on the community when the role of every stakeholder in education is clearly defined and effectively implemented. This can only be done by people with a sound knowledge of both Education and Information Technology (IT).

References

Jung, I. (2005). ICT-Pedagogy Integration in Teacher Training: Application Cases Worldwide. *Educational Technology and Society*, 8(2), 94-101.

Jung, I.S. (2003). A Comparative Study on the Cost-effectiveness of Three Approaches to ICT Teacher Training. *Journal of Korean Association of Educational Information and Broadcasting*, 9(2), 39-70.

UNESCO (2005). Proceeding of the UNESCO Sub-regional Seminar, Available at http//unesdoc.unesco.org/imagea.

International Bureau of Education (2003). Educational Innovation and Information. No. 114-15, August-December, Geneva, Switzerland.

Evart, Michel (1989). The International Encyclopedia Technology. London: Perganon Press.

CHAPTER

35

NGOs and Development

Analyzing their Role in Literacy and 'Education for All' Campaign in India

SUNIL KUMAR

'Give a man a fish and you feed him for a day. Teach a man to fish and you feed him for a life time'.

—A Chinese Proverb quoted in Subramaniam, 1998

INTRODUCTION

India has a long history of voluntary action spanning over different socio-economic and political fields. Voluntarism of the earlier era which used to be associated with 'welfarism' started changing into 'economism' during the early 20th century. Such a transformation from welfare activities into economic policies also laid the foundation of a change from voluntary organizations of the early period to the non-governmental organizations of the 20th and 21st centuries. With their 'meteoric rise' (Sen, 1999: 327) over the years, the NGOs have now come to be considered as the new developmental forces of the 21st century. The emergence of liberalization, privatization and globalization (called LPG) has further strengthened the growing realization that development would benefit more from NGOs' participation as 'non-state actors' rather than by State intervention in the developing economies across the globe.

However, with the changing nature of voluntarism, development also underwent change in the post-globalization phase thus effecting a transformation in the relationship between the two, viz., NGOs and Development. The paper, in fact, is an attempt to find out dynamics of development on the one hand and the increasing participation of NGOs as agents of development change, especially in the context of Literacy and Educational Campaigns called 'Sarva Shikhsha Abhiyan' undertaken vigorously by the state in India from 1980s on the other. The paper also attempts to analyze the state's policy on education along with the role played by NGOs as instruments of literacy promotion in contemporary India. The final section of the paper delineates the role and challenges of some leading NGOs to address the issues of literacy and education, and growth and development in global India.

DEVELOPMENT DISCOURSES : VARYING TURNING POINTS

Discourses on development have failed to be conceptualized with definite yardsticks, common parameters, defined pathways, universal approaches and uniform strategies. Viewed as an organic process of change, the term 'development' has come to be viewed differently and interpreted variously by social scientists from the beginning. During 1940-70 development came to be identified with 'employment' and 'basic needs'. The argument linking development with employment and basic needs gained ascendancy under the banner of United Nations and its affiliated agencies, especially the International Labor Organization. The post-economic depression phase led economists like Keynes to argue that development could be possible only with the help of the State. This laid the foundation of Bretton Woods System in forms of International Monetary Fund (IMF) and the World Bank emerging as important financial channels assisting and orienting state economies towards development. This was the period when discourses on development started witnessing a change from 'redistribution from growth' (Hans Singer) into 'redistribution with growth' (Hollis Chenery) (Quoted in Emmerij, 2006).

The decades of the late 1970s and 1980s constituted the first turning point in development which witnessed the emergence of Neo-Classical and Neo-Liberal School in social sciences. This period also set the stage for the birth of liberalization and privatization. Led by Margaret Thatcher and Ronald Regan as the two heads of the leading world nations, namely, Britain and the United States respectively, this phase was characterized by a 'competitive open market system'. Development during this period came to be characterized by the notion of a new 'Paradigm of Modernity'. During this period development got associated with 'growth' against income and poverty. Defined in terms of 'Washington Consensus', the period stated that policy reforms would automatically ensure better living standards. It set the stage for structural reforms undertaken by the developed world individually as well as collectively which actually led to the consolidation of economic blocks, e.g., European Union.

The decade of the 1990s constituted the second turning point in the history of development. It emerged with the popularization of the Human Development Index under the aegis of the United Nations Development Program (UNDP). The period emphasized regional, cultural and nationalist variations in development. The focus of this period was to broaden the concept of development and narrow the range of development models, especially in the context of developing economies. Amartya Sen (2000) was the key champion of this development model, called 'economic and social development model' which sought to bring on board political, cultural, social and human rights issues. The economic and social developmental model of Sen emphasized tolerance and pluralism as the important principles of democratic procedures.

Amartya Sen's (2000) approach to development focused on the following two points:

- *Individual capabilities*—Amartya Sen argues that 'the poor are poor because their set of capabilities is small, not because what they do not have, but because of what they cannot do'. The list includes being able to lead a healthy and productive life, to communicate and participate in community, to move about freely, etc.
- *Freedom* of choice as imbibed in the form of democracy. Amartya Sen argues that a 'country does not have to be deemed to be fit for democracy; rather, it has to become fit through democracy' (Sen, 1999). Democracy includes protection of liberties and freedoms, respect for legal entitlements, free discussions, etc.

Escobar (quoted in Emmerij, 2006) advocated 'Deconstructionist Approach' in development. Focusing on participation and empowerment, Escobar pleaded for differentiated development policies based on the cultural, institutional and historical characteristics of a given region. He thus emphasized the incorporation of local thinking and local constructions in development.

The concept of 'Development' thus revolves around different turning points the focus of which has shifted from economic aspects to non-economic dimensions like social development, human development and sustainable development. In case of India, development has addressed three significant concerns, viz., Poverty Eradication, Health Awareness and Educational Awakening. While the state has always been at the center of development—both at the level of policy formulation and the implementation level, it started delegating its work to non-state actors in the course of time. Non-Governmental Organizations (NGOs) have emerged important non-state agencies in this direction. Literacy and education as important planks of human development have remained the very bases in the formation of various voluntary organizations and NGOs across India in the post-independence era.

DEVELOPMENT OF EDUCATION : NGOs AS EFFECTIVE SOCIAL AGENTS

Education constitutes the essence of every model of development. Mass literacy campaigns are undertaken in the world with the purpose of bringing about major structural transformations in the economic, political and social lives of people either by the state or the non-state agencies. The UN Millennium Development Goals underlines six interrelated goals that together reflect a holistic conception of educational development across the globe. So far, the most dominant attention as emphasized by the United Nations Educational Scientific and Cultural Organization (UNESCO) in its report on 'Education for All' (EFA) has focused on the goals that pertain to schooling: universal primary education, gender parity and quality.

The role of NGOs in literacy and education for all campaign in developing economies has become a subject of greater concern over the years. In India, the campaign for mass literacy and education is seen as part of the modernization process. However, in India while NGOs have been rendering great service in the fields of health awareness and poverty eradication programs; their role in literacy and educational awakening has become all the more important, particularly in view of the state's national literacy mission called the Sarva Shiksha Abhiyan on the one hand and the Right to Education now constituting an important part of the list of the fundamental rights of Indian citizens in Part III of the constitution on the other.

LITERACY AND EDUCATION IN INDIA : COLONIAL LEGACY

Education during the colonial raj failed to get universal acceptance as the Britishers did not want to popularize education. The key objective of the British government was to prepare only an educated elite class from the Indian sections through the system of British English education. Education during the colonial India came to be identified according to Krishna Kumar (2005) as 'school knowledge'. And the job of deciding, selecting and shaping school knowledge was performed by the 'enlightened outsiders' called the British officers and Christian missionaries. Later on, the role of the enlightened outsiders according to Kumar was picked up by the educated Indians and voluntary agencies who became the 'enlightened outsiders' to the Indian masses.

During colonial India, Lord Macaulay established schools to promote literacy. Besides producing office clerks, the colonial system of education according to Krishna Kumar also produced 'political leaders, professional men and intellectuals' (Kumar, 2005: 25). Hence, 'the utilitarian doctrine of the colonial state kept India divided between elites and masses. Liberal democratic procedures were set in motion in the late colonial period, but liberalism as a political and social perspective failed to develop, especially in the context of education' (*Ibid.*, 9). As a result, voluntary organizations could not emerge as important social force to impart education to the masses in a comprehensive manner.

Nevertheless, educational discourse during the colonial period did acquire a nationalist slant in the writings of nationalists like Vivekananda, Sri Aurobindo, Dayanand Saraswati, Lala Lajpat Rai and Rabindra Nath Tagore. The nationalists and the social reformers emerged as the catalyst of social change in colonial India and championed the view that the West has to learn more from India than *vice-versa*. Education was emphasized as potential weapon of mass awakening by the national leadership. Hence, literacy movement was started in India during the last quarter of the 19th century by some social reformers in terms of conducting literacy classes, opening of libraries and reading rooms, etc. However, the social activities undertaken by social reformers and nationalist leaders got confined to few selected pockets in the country.

It was Gopal Krishna Gokhale who introduced an Educational Bill in the Imperial Legislative Council in 1911 to establish the provision of compulsory elementary education in the country. Gokhale advocated that increase in the state funds and compulsory elementary education would steer India's path towards progress. Later, Gandhi in the 1920s transformed literacy campaigns into mass movements. Gandhian critique of colonial education was based on the rejection of western civilization as Gandhi believed that the western education symbolized 'negation of the principles of non-violence and truth' (Kumar, 2005: 175). For Gandhi education was simply 'learning by doing' as he found organic links between education on the one hand and life and work on the other.

Gandhian ideas actually promoted opening of the national schools and colleges which were expected to take active part in literacy work at all India level. In fact, the literacy work took the shape of mass movement in 1937 after the installation of Congress ministries in the provinces. Publication of literature, establishment of village libraries, etc. were some of the outcome of this educational drive resulting into the increase in literacy figures by 6 per cent during 1931-41. Literacy work continued in Bombay and Mysore by non-official organizations with financial assistance from the state governments, cultural and social programs, reading clubs and libraries. Krishna Kumar (2005) argues that though Gandhi's basic education was implemented as a program for educational reconstruction, it soon died by leaving the 'structure of knowledge, values and opportunities embedded in the education system untouched' (Kumar, 2005: 21). The education system in post-independence India thus remained 'an agency contributing primarily to the maintenance of law and order' (*Ibid.*, 21).

LITERACY AND EDUCATION : POST-INDEPENDENCE ERA

Unable to revitalize primary education with the meager resources, mass education and literacy failed to attain priority in Nehru's system of administration after independence. However, Nehru did not want to abandon the rhetoric of free and compulsory elementary education for all. Hence, he brought education under the Directive Principles of State Policy (Article 45) rather than on the chapter of Fundamental Rights by leaving education at the discretion of state governments. With the adoption of *laissez faire* policy in school education, both state and private sector started investing in education during the first four decades in post-independence India.

The post-independence era also witnessed a phenomenal increase in the number of voluntary agencies, especially with the introduction of the Community Development Program in 1952. The successive five year plans too strengthened the state-voluntary organizations collaboration in literacy and educational development of India. For example, the First Five Year Plan (1951-56) recognized the role of voluntary organizations in the field of social welfare whereas in the Third Five Year Plan (1961-66) voluntary action was characterized as an essential aspect of public cooperation. Similarly, while the Sixth Plan (1979-84) witnessed a rise in grant-in-aid to the voluntary organizations associated with education; the Seventh Plan (1985-90), besides increasing their grant in a big way, also involved them in the poverty eradication and employment generated programs like Integrated Rural Development Program (IRDP), Jawahar Rozgar Program, etc.

Muttalib (1989) highlighted partnership between voluntary organizations and government as important linkage for educational growth during the post-independence era. According to him the state approached the voluntary organizations in this sector for various reasons, viz., 'flexibility, personal touch, easy accessibility, client groups, capacity to initiate experiments with new programs, stimulation and mobilization of the resources of the community, sensitivity to field problems, self-help and self-reliance' (*Ibid.*, 9). There has been tremendous growth in schools managed largely by voluntary organizations since independence. Their role has been innovative in the non-formal sector of education, especially adult education.

Siddhartha Sen (1999) in his study highlighted cooperation between the State and NGOs during the 1950s which got developed into antagonism during the 1960s and 1970s with an increasing state control over NGOs during the 1980s and 1990s. Cooperation and confrontation between the State and the NGOs according to Sen were actually based on motivations for forming NGOs, their attitudes towards the State and *vice-versa* as well as different socio-political context. Nevertheless, the State remained the key actor of development and its various policies and programs actually facilitated the emergence of various NGOs in the education sector.

JUXTAPOSING LITERACY AND EDUCATION : STATE AS KEY CATALYST OF EDUCATIONAL DEVELOPMENT

Realizing the potential of education as an instrument of social transformation, State in the post-independence era evolved national policies on education. There have so far been mainly two comprehensive statements of the National Policy on Education, viz. those of 1968 and 1986. While the former contained decisions of the Central Government on the recommendations of the National Commission on Education, 1964-66, the latter was a result of the renewed priority assigned to Education by Rajiv Gandhi Government during 1984-89. The 1986 policy was reviewed by a Committee constituted in 1990 under the chairmanship of Acharya Ramamurti. On the basis of the recommendations of this Committee, certain provisions of the 1986 policy were modified in 1992. Thus, in all, the following three comprehensive national policy statements exist on education:

- National Policy on Education, 1968
- National Policy on Education, 1986
- National Policy on Education, 1986, as modified in 1992

KOTHARI COMMISSION ON EDUCATION, 1964-66

In order to realize a well balanced, integrated and adequate system of national education capable of making a powerful contribution to all aspects of national life, the Government of India in October 1964 set-up an Education Commission, under Resolution of July 14, 1964. With its 12 Task Force and 7 Working Groups, the Kothari Commission in its voluminous report recommended free and compulsory education, vocationalisation of higher secondary stage and education for moral, social and spiritual values.

One of the important recommendations of Kothari Commission was the establishment of a Common School System for all children irrespective of their class, caste, religious or linguistic background. The commission stated that in order to fulfil this purpose, neighbourhood schools where parents from all educational, social and economic background are required to send their wards to a school in their neighbourhood, whether it is private or government school and the school cannot refuse admission, should be established in all localities .

Kothari's vision of education as reflected in the draft of the report entitled 'Education and National Development' was thus hailed as landmark in educational sectors in India and other developing countries.

NATIONAL POLICY ON EDUCATION, 1968

The National Policy on Education, 1968 marked a significant step in the history of education in post-independence India. It aimed to promote national progress, a sense of common citizenship and culture, and to strengthen national integration. It laid stress on the need for a radical reconstruction of the education system, to improve its quality at all stages, and gave much greater attention to science and technology, the cultivation of moral values and a closer relation between education and the life of the people.

The most notable development of the 1968 Policy was the acceptance of a common structure of education throughout the country and the introduction of the 10+2+3 system by most States. In the school curricula, in addition to laying down a common scheme of studies for boys and girls, science and mathematics were incorporated as compulsory subjects and work experience assigned a place of importance. A beginning was also made in restructuring of courses at the undergraduate level.

Since the adoption of the 1968 Policy, there has been considerable expansion in educational facilities all over the country at all levels. More than 90% of the country's rural habitations now have schooling facilities within a radius of one kilometer. There had been sizeable augmentation of facilities at other stages also. However, despite impressive achievements, the general formulations incorporated in the 1968 Policy did not get translated into a detailed strategy of implementation.

Besides, a variety of new challenges and social needs made it imperative for the Government to formulate and implement a new education policy for the country.

NATIONAL ADULT EDUCATION PROGRAM (NAEP), 1978 : FORMALIZING THE ENTRY OF NGOS

Launched in 1978 the National Adult Education Program envisaged a radical change in the socio-economic developmental process. The poor were sought to be drawn to the center of development activity as active participants rather than mere passive recipients. The NAEP recognized 'literacy as a political act and perceived the interlinked relationship between literacy and poverty' (Mukherjee, 2003: 10).

The movement started in the post-emergency era with lot of fanfare with the hope that the state alone would not be able to deliver the goods in the 'iniquitous market society'. Hence, need was felt to incorporate the non-state agencies like NGOs and social action groups to achieve the objective. The program was hailed not only as a progressive step but also an emancipatory tool designed to acquaint the adults with greater awareness, knowledge and skills leading them to a dignified human survival. The program was, however, wound up within a decade due to 'corruption, mismanagement of funds, and bureaucratization'.

In 1984-85 Rajiv Gandhi started 'Technology Missions' to undertake certain welfare measures on a war footing, including eradication of illiteracy. 'The distinction between literacy and education got an official legitimacy' (Mukherjee, 2003). In 1988, the government chalked out National Literacy Mission under the auspices of the Ministry of Human Resource Development which aimed at imparting 'functional literacy' to around 80 million unlettered persons in the age group of 15-35 by 1995. Later, the 9-15 age group was also included, raising the target by another 47 million. If NAEP opened the doors of education for the NGOs officially, the Technology Missions activated NGOs in the mass literacy campaigns which came to be known as 'Sarva Shiksha Abhiyan' subsequently.

NATIONAL POLICY ON EDUCATION, 1986

In order to ensure that the fruits of change reach all sections and education being considered as the highway to that goal, the Government of India formulated a new education policy in 1986. The policy advocated effective measures in the direction of Common School System recommended in the 1968 Policy. It recommended minimum levels of learning for each stage of education, promotion of the link language, translation of books from one language to another and to publish multi-lingual dictionaries and glossaries.

The 1986 Policy encouraged a new sharing of responsibility between the Union Government and the States in respect of the vital area of national life. Education for women, Scheduled Castes, Scheduled Tribes, Minorities, Handicapped and the other backward sections of the society assumed significance in the education policy of the state. Day-care centers were advocated as support service for universalization of primary education, to enable girls engaged in taking care of siblings to attend school and as a support service for working women belonging to poorer sections.

The new thrust in elementary education emphasized two aspects, viz., universal enrolment and universal retention of children up to 14 years of age, and a substantial improvement in the quality of education. A phased drive, symbolically called—Operation Blackboard was advocated to improve primary schools all over the country with the involvement of government, local bodies, voluntary agencies and individuals. A large and systematic program of non-formal education was launched for school drop-outs, for children from habitations without schools, working children and girls who could not attend whole-day schools. Besides, the Act also advocated Navodaya Vidyalaya in each district, Peace Setting Schools for children with special talent or skill and Anganwadi and adult education centers specially to literate household women.

The education policy 1986 thus laid the foundation of three important terms in academic and planning discussions, viz., 'access, participation and achievements'.

NATIONAL LITERACY MISSION AND NGOs AS EMERGING 'NON-STATE ACTORS' FOR LITERACY CAMPAIGNS

The most important aspect of all the education policies, however, was the involvement of the non-government and voluntary effort including social activist groups in the educational programs of the state. With the state introducing National Literacy Mission as one of the five key Technology Missions, the NGOs as 'non-state actors' were called upon by the state to assist in its mission of universalization of education. The Seventh Five Year Plan (1985-90) which actually led to the formal beginning of the NGOs defined development not in terms of factories, dams and roads but basically about the 'people'. The plan defined goal in terms of 'people's material, cultural and spiritual fulfilment'. The government realized that the very success of its national literacy mission should be based on the active support and involvement of the NGOs.

Following were the aims as devised by the National Literacy Mission:

- Achieving self-reliance in literacy and numeracy.
- Generating awareness about the causes of deprivation.
- Improving conditions through organization and participation in the process of development.
- Acquiring skills to improve the economic status and general well-being.
- Imbibing the values of national integration, conservation of environment, women's equality and observation of small family norms.

To achieve the above objectives the state launched Total Literacy Campaign (TLC) which made district as the basic unit of operation to fulfil the goal of learning through center and state funding, monitoring, internal and external evaluating, etc. The state banked upon the NGOs towards the fulfilment of total literacy campaign.

NGOs AS 'THIRD ACTOR'—FROM 'POLITICAL ENTREPRENEURS' TO 'DEVELOPMENT AGENTS'

Viewed as 'para professional support agencies', NGOs have constituted the 'third actor' of development in contemporary India. In view of their all-encompassing presence from small grassroots groups working in small areas among the people to intermediary agencies operating at the global level, the emergence of NGOs is equated with 'global associational revolution' (Nawani, 2002: 121). NGOs have come to be defined as organizations serving and working with the poor by 'channeling financial support to community-based or grassroots organizations of the poor' (Sen, 1999: 332). They work towards ensuring radical transformation of Indian politics and society. Being the offspring of the post-emergency phase which got formal recognition during the 7th Five Year Plan (1985-90), one of the important objectives of the NGOs has been their efforts to reach out both to the grassroots and the policy-makers. Harish Sethi (1998) attributed two reasons in the growth of NGOs movements in post-independence India.

- Decline of institutional politics (formal institutions)—elections, legislatures, parties and trade unions. No internal elections were conducted by political parties in India since mid-1960s.
- Exclusion of dalits, tribals, backwards amongst OBCs, poor and landless amongst minorities. Their struggle for dignity and survival failed to come to the mainstream politics resulting into the emergence of NGOs.

Hence, inability of state, bureaucracy and institutional politics led to the rise of activist groups called NGOs. Over the years the NGOs have been trying to combine in themselves the role of both 'political entrepreneurs' and 'development agents' (Chhotray: 2008). 'As political entrepreneurs, NGOs have been known to act as catalyst of radical and transformative social change, through their association with grassroots struggle in various forms. As development agents, NGOs have increasingly become key partners of both governments and donor agencies in implementing development programs' (*Ibid.*, 261).

Since the mid-1980s NGOs have been rendering a great helping hand in the education sector in both rural and urban India. 'Their aim is not to create structures parallel to those of the government but to supplement and strengthen government's initiatives in providing education to all its citizens' (Nawani, 2002: 126). The selfless devotion of the social workers and the state's motivation in its mission of Sarva Shiksha Abhiyan led to a significant rise of NGO activities across nation.

NGOs IN EDUCATION SECTOR : A COMPARATIVE STUDY

Though it is difficult to analyze and present the working of different NGOs in the education sector in India, one can still cite some of the leading NGOs and their special initiatives exclusively in the field of education and literacy in contemporary India.

(1) Sewa Bharti—'Education as Expansion of Knowledge'

Working on the principles of 'sewa, sanskar, samrasta, samriddhi' (denoting service, values, coexistence and prosperity respectively) Sewa Bharti is one of the leading NGOs working especially in the education sector in different parts of Delhi and its vicinity since the 1970s. The locus and focus of Sewa Bharti has been the street children. The schools run by Sewa Bharti in various cluster colonies and slums actually cater to the needs of the street children who are deprived of the formal education. Children in the age-group of 5 to 10 are given elementary and primary education respectively, with emphasis on 'morality, character, etiquette and nationalism'. The various centers of Sewa Bharti work with the street children and provide them basic education, vocational training, moral education, and finally link them to the formal system of school education.

Besides imparting education through its Balwadi Schools, Primary Schools, Residential Schools, Sewa Bharti also runs a school for the destitute and orphans called Gopal Dham. Gopal Dham and Sewa Dham are set-up to accommodate children from all walks of life, i.e. socially backward communities, OBCs, orphans, financially backward and victims of terrorism. Its Prodh Vidya Niketan taps the potential of students, who belong to socially and economically weaker sections and prepare them for various competitive examinations like IIT-JEE, DCE and other engineering colleges. Sewa Bharati run schools thus impart both technical and moral education to children, belonging to different castes, religions, regions and languages and try to bring them to the mainstream civil society.

(2) Amar Jyoti Charitable Trust—'Enlightening the Gifted Children'

Set-up in 1981, Amar Jyoti has been 'reaching out to persons with disability using a holistic approach to provide a wide range of rehabilitative service including inclusive education, medical care, vocational training, capacity building courses and employment opportunities'. The schools run by Amar Jyoti are integrated schools where children with and without disabilities study together in equal number from nursery to class VIII. The children with mental challenges and socially disabled are integrated with special education facilities in Amar Jyoti schools. Integrated sports and cultural activities are also part of the educational curriculum of its schools. Besides providing counseling through its social work department, Amar Jyoti also gives medical and therapeutic facilities, vocational training to its children.

Starting from the time of admission, a team of psychologists, special educators, orthotists, social workers and doctors work together for assessment and allocation of classes at Amar Jyoti. The assistive devices are provided as per need of the children with different type of disabilities. Under the stewardship of Amar Jyoti 40 Indians with disability participated in the 7th International Abilympics ('Ability + Olympics') in November 2007 in Japan. In its quest for a rights-based society and equal opportunities for persons with disability, Amar Jyoti has forged partnerships with a number of NGOs and civil society groups.

(3) Pryas—'Restoring the Childhood of Children in Need'

Established in 1988 Pryas has been working for the welfare and development of street and working children in Assam, Arunachal Pradesh, Andaman and Nicobar Islands, Bihar, Delhi, Gujarat and Haryana. It believes in the principle that 'rights and needs of a child are synonymous'. Some of its aims and objectives are:

- Fulfilment of basic needs and rights of the neglected children.
- Sensitization of the government and society about the needs of such children.
- Networking and synergy with Government, Community and the Voluntary Sector for providing effective services to the street children.
- Action-based and policy research on juvenile justice, child rights, child labor and issues related to the marginalized under-privileged children.
- Awareness generation and advocacy for the implementation of the Juvenile Justice Act and other child-related legislations.
- Promotion and dissemination of proactive knowledge and information on various child-related issues.

Some of the programs and activities of Pryas include shelter homes for both boys and girls, alternative education and life skills programs, vocational training, mid-day meal, rehabilitation and restoration, etc. It caters to dropouts, out of school children, working children. It provides linkages with formal education by preparing children to enter the formal system of education. It also runs distance education through national institute of open schooling.

Pryas has hands-on experience in alternative education for more than a decade and half, 'developed its niche through tested models of education for the marginalized children by adopting an educational management system'. Its approach is comprehensive, focused and greatly integrated with the community.

(4) Prayatan—'Empowering the Marginalized through De-School'

Prayatan, a Delhi-based NGO established in 1991, has been associated with the development of the disadvantaged sections of the society. It was set-up with the objective of empowering the marginalized by building up their capacities through education and skill development. 'It has developed, designed, implemented and managed developmental projects through participatory approach involving all stakeholders'. Some of its activities include participation of community in developmental projects, strengthening community structures, building the capacities of its staff and beneficiaries and collaboration and networking for resource mobilization with other partner NGOs and individuals, donors, funding organizations.

Supported by the Seth Foundation, Prayatan has come out with a noble idea in education and literacy mission called De-school which attempts to educational facilities to slum children. The low cost, quality education emphasizing on mainstreaming children in MCD/Sarvodaya schools have been significant contribution of Prayatan which seeks to focus on the holistic development of the children.

(5) Nirantar—'Constantly Working towards Gender Sensitive Educational Change'

With its formation in 1993 Nirantar has been working towards fulfilling its mandate of empowering women through education—by enabling access to information, promoting literacy and engendering education processes. It seeks to achieve this objective through direct field interventions, creating educational resources, research and advocacy, and training. Actively involved with the women's movement and the democratic rights movements, Niranatar brings concerns central to these movements into its educational field.

Nirantar develops and produces a range of gender sensitive educational resources—reading material for newly literate readers that is simple, entertaining and informative, teaching-learning materials that are interactive and developed through sustained field interactions, reports, pamphlets, etc. It believes that literacy is a right that women and socio-economically disadvantaged communities have been denied. They have the right to read and write not only to get information, but also for entertainment and engagement with a world beyond their own. It believes that 'literacy and education should enable marginalized women to take control of their lives by developing skills of critical reflection and ensuring that education process connects with their lived realities'. And once they have entered the world of letters they should have access to an environment that sustains their skills.

For Nirantar education is actually a feminist issue. Concerns central to the feminist movement should be included in any agenda for women's education. It believes that 'structured teaching-learning spaces—both formal and non-formal—are vital arenas through which gender equality can be promoted'.

(6) Utsaah—'Changing Society by Changing the Self'

Beginning with the basic question 'can society be changed without changing the self' some young, dynamic and committed students of Shyam Lal College (Evening), University of Delhi soon after their graduation set-up a voluntary organization called Utsaah in Shahdara, East Delhi in 1998. The main objective of Utsaah has been to assist the poor, dalit, girl students and other backward children of government schools in East Delhi both financially and socially.

The energetic members of Utsaah have been working hard amongst the poor sections of the society for nearly a decade by adopting the educationally sound children who can not afford school education due to financial constraints. Utsaah conducts special coaching classes for the poor students of East Delhi studying in their board classes in subjects like Maths, Science, English, Accounts, by ensuring that they also get inducted into higher education.

By conducing various extra curricular activities like debates, speech, extempore, essay competitions as well as social awareness programs like traffic awakening, ecological protection, sustainable development, etc. throughout the year, Utsaah volunteers keep on steering school children towards self-reliance and social commitment. Though Utsaah is a registered NGO, it functions on the voluntary contribution of all its members without taking any donation from the state as it believes in the principle that every single positive step contributes towards success.

NGOs, EDUCATION AND GLOBAL CHALLENGES

The decade of the 1980s which sometimes is characterized with the phase of 'NGO Decade' or 'NGO Boom' witnessed a huge increase in NGO activities across the globe. Though concepts like Global Civil Society have yet to become part of the mainstream scholarly discourse, there is no denying the fact that the forces of globalization have actually shaped and reshaped both the NGOs and the ideas about NGOs. This has transformed some NGOs into what Anthony Bebbington, Samuel Hickey and Diana C. Mitlin (2008) have characterized as 'transnational community' (Bebbington, Hickey and Diana, 2008: 7). The authors argue that the current global NGOs are finding it difficult to work outside the neo-liberal market system which incorporates core NGO terminology like democracy, rights, empowerment, participation, poverty and livelihoods. Unlike the larger NGOs which have been successful in raising funds from the international donors, the smaller NGOs are finding it difficult to crack the state-bureaucracy nexus to ensure a fair deal of the donor countries.

Despite the world passing through the phase of globalization with India achieving creditable success in many areas such as industrial growth, emergence of a large scientific community, and agricultural revolution, etc.; India has fared rather poorly in the area of elementary education. It is true that literacy rates have gone up since independence, but it is equally correct that the 'absolute number of illiterates has also gone up during 1981-91 (from 300 million to 301 million)' (Mukherjee, 2003:9). Mukherjee (2003) argues that even after about half a century of independence the adult literacy rate in India revolves somewhere around 60 per cent which is far below the average of even the least economically developed countries in the world. This can be corroborated from Table 1.

Education today stands at the crossroad. While there has been reduction in the growth of illiteracy, the quality education has considerably declined. With the privatization of higher

TABLE I
Literacy Rates in India from 1951-2001

Year	*Literacy Percentage*	*Percentage Decadal Growth*
1951	18.3	—
1961	28.3	10.0
1971	34.4	6.1
1981	43.5	9.1
1991	52.2	8.7
2001	64.8	12.6

Source : Innovative Approaches to Functional Literacy for Poverty Alleviation. National Case Study, India, New Delhi and UNESCO, 2008: 11, Updated from data 2001.

education and the big corporate houses taking up the larger chunks of the educational cake in our society, the role of voluntary agencies has further diminished. Vocationalization of secondary education has yet to make headway. Muttalib (1989) states that the primary task is to 'harness the human resources and to improve the capability of development with equity' (Muttalib, 1989: 18). Accordingly the development of education itself would take care of the problems and challenges like poverty, inequalities and rural-urban disparities. Jean Dreze and Amartya Sen (1995) make a dialectical relationship between educational progress and social change by arguing that the spread of education helps to overcome the traditional inequalities of caste, class and gender by the simple logic that the removal of these inequalities contributes in the spread of education.

With market overpowering the state and governance replacing government in an era of globalization, NGOs too have come under intense critical scrutiny from both supporters and opponents alike. In the current globalized competitive market society, the real challenge for the NGOs is to have 'considerable financial skills to manipulate the global market situation to their advantage, pursue an alternative agenda and still be seen as competent' (Bebbington, 2008: 17). Bebbington and others argue that while NGOs are facing challenges of successful sustenance, endurance and management in the global society; it is also feared that their attempt to strive to the global mainstream would actually cut them off from their base thereby undermining their comparative advantage as agents of alternative development at the grassroots level.

Despite a mushroom growth of NGOs across globe particularly dealing in primary education of the State called Sarva Shiksha Abhiyan, education has not witnessed a spectacular growth during the past one decade. According to UNESCO's Education for All Global Monitoring Report, 2007 adult literacy rate in India is less than 65 per cent. Worse, approximately 35 per cent of the world's adult illiterates live in India. Of the 200 million children in the age group of 6-14 years, 59 million do not attend the school. Rather than targeting the elementary education, NGOs are focusing only on the basic education or first five years of school education. Critics argue that such an attempt by the NGOs as well as the State actually deflected from the 'constitutional objective of providing free and compulsory education to every child up to 14 years of age' (Chanana, 2004: 50).

There is need to understand and analyze the organizational complexities and social realities existing at the grassroots level to ensure effective coordination between the State and the NGOs towards educational development in global India.

REVOLUTIONIZING EDUCATION IN INDIA : CONSTITUTIONAL AMENDMENTS AND NGOs

The decade of the 1990s and early 21st century witnessed remarkable turning points in terms of constitutional amendments providing both opportunities and challenges to the non-state actors in different fields of social development. The *73rd Constitutional Amendment* (1992-93) is considered to be a milestone in the history of democratic decentralization in India. The amendment sought to equip the Panchayati Raj Institutions (PRIs) with power, authority and responsibilities. Broadly defined in terms of Triple Fs reflecting 'Functions, Functionaries and Funds', the amendment sought to give the panchayats 'functional, administrative and financial autonomy'

(Sumathi and Sudarsen, 2005) with the objective of ensuring their 'political survivability, administrative credibility and economic viability in grassroots governance' (Sunil, 2009).

The 73rd amendment not only empowered Panchayati Raj Institutions by transferring education at the local level, it also offered great opportunities to the NGOs to reach the specific target groups like the child labor, street children, dalits and other downtrodden sections of the society. The amendment in this way actually facilitated the emergence of NGOs as real catalyst in education as they started playing a direct role in running the schools as well as supporting existing schools at grassroots level.

To universalise quality education and to envisage increasing accountability of schools to the community through greater involvement of village education committees and parent-teacher associations, the government formally initiated the Sarva Shiksha Abhiyan in 2001. Inability of the state to reach the poorest of the poor and other downtrodden strata of society, the services of the NGOs and various other voluntary agencies were encouraged to implement the objectives of universalization of elementary education in India.

The 87th Constitutional Amendment act, 2002 inserted Article 21A by amending Articles 45 and 51A of the Constitution by declaring that the state shall provide right to education to all until the age of fourteen and early childhood care until the age of six. This set the stage for the Right to Education Act in 2009. The amendment contained several features including ensuring a school in every neighbourhood, free education to all admitted children with 25 per cent reservation to economically weaker sections to private schools, prohibition of capitation fee as well as screening tests, etc. The 86th amendment in this way facilitated the NGOs' reach as social catalyst to the literacy and educational development of children at the grassroots level.

It was only in August 2009 that education got its legitimate constitutional status with the passage of the Right of Children to Free and Compulsory Education Bill, 2008. The bill came into force on 1 April 2010. The passing of the bill allows children aged between 6 to 14 years to avail free and compulsory education as a fundamental right. The bill also earmarks 25 per cent seats to weaker sections in private schools. Described as the landmark legislation in the last 62 years of India's political history, the bill came to be described as the 'harbinger of a new era for children to meet the challenges of the 21st century'.

Following are the salient features of the Act:

- Free and compulsory education to all children of India in the six to 14 age group;
- No child shall be held back, expelled, or required to pass a board examination until completion of elementary education;
- A child who completes elementary education shall be awarded a certificate;
- Calls for a fixed pupil-teacher ratio (PTR) of 30:1;
- Provides for 25 percent reservation for economically disadvantaged communities in admission to Class One in all private schools;
- Mandates improvement in quality of education;
- School teachers will need adequate professional degree within five years or else will lose job;
- School infrastructure (where there is problem) to be improved in three years, else recognition cancelled; and
- Financial burden will be shared between state and central government.

Various provisions of the bill have received great applause across the board. For instance, Section 3 talks of right to free and compulsory education and admission in a neighbourhood school whereas Section 4 emphasizes admission of child in class appropriate to his or her age. Similarly, while Sections 8 and 9 advocate obligations of the government to provide compulsory education to children; Section 12 focuses on the obligation of the unaided recognized private schools to provide free seats to the extent of 25% to the children of the economically weaker sections. Further, Section 13(1) prohibits 'capitation fee' and 'screening procedure' for admission, Section 14 underlines admission without insisting upon production of age proof. Section 16 talks of 'no expulsion of a child' whereas Section 17 bans corporal punishment. Recruitment of only qualified teachers, Pupil-Teacher Ratio of 30:1 and grievance redressal mechanism are some of the landmark features of the bill highlighted by advocate and social activist Ashok Agarwal (2009).

The government also brought about a subsequent amendment to the bill ensuring the inclusion of children with disabilities within the ambit of the draft bill. The bill thus is considered to be a 'giant leap towards universalization of education in India' (Mukul, 2010). It legitimizes the role of the NGOs as the third actor in social development. With the public-private schooling gap getting widened over the years such an innovative step on the part of the state would actually strengthen the role of the NGOs by brining deprived children to the mainstream education. From this perspective NGOs can still play a crucial role in the literacy and educational development of such children who according to Partha Chatterjee (2004) are neither outside the state's reach nor are treated as citizens or as members of civil society.

Though the amendment has taken care of the primary education at a war footing, it has still left out children below 6 years of age. It is estimated that nearly '17 crore children below six years of age will be losing their fundamental right to balanced nutrition, health care and preprimary education' (Sadgopal, 2009). Further, the bill lacks provision to compel the State to provide adequate funds in this direction. The act further distorts the concept of Neighborhood School recommended by the Kothari Commission (1966) thereby authorizing the government to compel the poor children to study in inferior quality schools. It is criticized on the ground that it 'legitimizes inequality through a multi-layered school system'.

Viewed thus, the amendment according to Poonam Batra (2005) does not address two broad issues, viz. :

- It fails to make a difference between literacy and education. Literacy has remained the key objective of the amendment rather than educational awakening. There are various disturbing areas like attitude of recognition regarding public and private schools, recognition of parrot teachers, quality *vs.* quantity debate, etc. which the amendment has not able to address effectively.

- Education produces inequalities in society. It has yet to replace the caste and religious ridden social system, e.g., madarsa education. Curriculum revision has been introduced without taking into consideration ground socio-economic realities. Education has not been linked with the market society. By providing for shifting of public funds to private schools, the draft bill seems to have become 'an instrument of the market forces' (Sadgopal, 2009).

The success or failure of the act according to Arun Mehta (2009) would largely depend upon how effectively it is implemented and whether sufficient funds are allocated for its implementation. Nevertheless, despite some limitations the act provides great opportunities to the NGOs to ensure schooling to those children who work as domestic labor, paid or unpaid children. NGOs have the larger accessibility in this connection and they can alone address the social problems and the livelihood concerns of such children in their respective areas. From this perspective the NGOs can actually work as an effective lynchpin between the public and the private schools in terms of universalizing the primary education on the one hand as well as by acting as a strong force of sustenance encompassing early childhood care and pre-primary education as 'third actors of development' on the other.

CONCLUDING OBSERVATIONS

The changing nature of development concomitant with the changing orientation of voluntarism has necessitated a changing perspective of the NGOs in global India. With the issues like human rights, development, dignity and survival, gaining ascendancy in the educational curriculum, there is need for the NGOs to actually delve into such issues to remain as true third actors of social change. The literacy *vs.* education controversy needs to be addressed by the NGOs through strengthening the educational consciousness and awakening among the masses. The competitive market system has thrown open several challenges to the NGOs. Their success as non-state actors of development actually lies in their adequate grasping of this change in their objectives and working.

In the changed socio-economic and political milieu, NGOs have started moving from the institutions of charity to the organizations of productive activities. The public-private partnership of the present global era can also steer the path for State-NGOs collaboration in the field of promoting literacy and 'education for all' campaign in India. In view of their multifaceted roles in several sectors of economy, polity and society NGOs have become the real intermediaries of global Indian society. With education now constituting the fundamental right, NGOs can truly act as significant catalyst by transforming primary education into 'universalization of education'.

References

Agarwal, Ashok (2009). "The Right of Children to Free and Compulsory Education Bill Fails the Test of Constitutional Mandate".

Atal, Yogesh (2008). Education: Meeting the Challenge of Social Development. Professor M.V. Mathur Memorial Lecture. Jaipur: Institute of Development Studies.

Amar Jyoti: Reaching Out. *Newsletter*. February 2008.

Batra, Poonam (2005). "Universalization of Education", Lecture delivered at the Center for Professional Development in Higher Education, University of Delhi, 28 March.

Bebbington, Anthony J., Samuel Hickey and Diana C. Mitlin (eds.) (2008.). Can NGOs Make a Difference: The Challenge of Development Alternatives. London: Zed Books.

Chanana, Karuna (2004). "Exploring the Links of Higher Education with Basic Education" in Karuna Chanana (ed.) Transforming Links between Higher and Basic Education: Mapping the Field, New Delhi: Sage Publications.

Chatterjee, Partha (2004). The Politics of the Governed: Reflections on Popular Politics in Most of the World. New York: Columbia University Press.

Chhotray, Vasudha (2008). "Political Entrepreneurs or Development Agents: An NGO's Tale of Resistance and Acquiescence in Madhya Pradesh, India" in Anthony J. Bebbington, Samuel Hickey and Diana C. Mitlin (eds.) (2008.). Can NGOs Make a Difference: The Challenge of Development Alternatives. London: Zed Books.

Dreze, Jean and Amartya Sen (1998). Economic Development and Social Opportunity. New Delhi: Oxford University Press.

Education for All Global Monitoring Report (2007). Paris: UNESCO.

Education for All: Literacy for Life (2005). Paris: UNESCO.

Emmerij, Louis (2006). "Turning Points in Development Thinking and Practice", United Nations University-World Institute for Development Economics Research, Research Paper No. 2006/08.

Kumar, Krishna (2005). Political Agenda of Education: A Study of Colonial and Nationalist Ideas. New Delhi: Sage Publications.

Innovative Approaches to Functional Literacy for Poverty Alleviation. National Case Study, India (2008). New Delhi and UNESCO.

Jolly, K.G. (1992). Literacy for All by 2001. Delhi: B.R. Publishing Corporation.

Mehta, Arun C. (2009). "Right to Education Act, 2009, Estimations: A Few Points of Consideration". November.

Mohanty, Jagannath (1999). "Non-Formal and Adult Education in India" in B.M. Sankhdher (ed.). Encyclopedia of Education System in India, Vol. 12. India's Independence to the Present Day, 1947-98. New Delhi: Deep and Deep Publications.

Mukherjee, Aditi (2003). Literacy in India: The Present Context. Shimla: Indian Institute of Advanced Study.

Mukul, Akshyay (2010). "Passed by House in August, Right to Education Yet to be Law", TNN, 6 January.

Muttalib, M.A. (1989). Voluntary Action in Education. New Delhi: Sterling Publishers.

Nawani, Disha (2002). "Role and Contribution of Non-Governmental Organizations in Basic Education" in R. Govinda (ed.) India Education Report: A Profile of Basic Education. New Delhi: Oxford University Press. Published in association with National Institute of Educational Planning and Administration and UNESCO.

Nirantar: A Center for Gender and Education. New Delhi.

Prayatan: A Developmental Effort. Annual Report, 2003-04, New Delhi.

Pryas: An Alternative Education Program. New Delhi.

Rajput, J. S. (1999). Education in a Changing World: Fallacies and Forces. New Delhi: Vikas Publishing House.

Sadgopal, Anil (2009). An Appeal to the Speaker. New Delhi: Lok Sabha.

Sen, Amartya (1999). "Democracy as Universal Value", *Journal of Democracy*, Vol. 10, No. 3.

———, (2000). Development as Freedom. New Delhi: Oxford University Press.

Sewa Bharti: A School for Street Children. New Delhi.

Sen, Siddhartha (1999). "Some Aspects of State-NGO Relationships in India in the Post-Independence Era", *Development and Change*, Vol. 30, No. 2.

Sethi, Harish (1998). "Micro Struggles, NGOs and the State" in Manoranjan Mohanty, Partha Nath Mukherji, Olle Tornquist (eds.), People's Rights: Social Movements and the State in the Third World. New Delhi: Sage Publications.

Soundarapandian, M. (2002). Literacy Campaign in India. New Delhi: Discovery Publishing House.

Sumathi, S. and V. Sudarsen (2005), "What does the New Panchayati System Guarantee? A Case Study of Pappapatti", *Economic and Political Weekly*, Vol. XL, No. 34.

Sunil Kumar (2009). "Democratic Resurgence of Panchayati Raj Institutions: Coping with the New Challenges of Grassroots Governance", *Indian Journal of Social Enquiry*, 1(1) March.

Subramaniam, S. (1998). Literacy Accelerates the Pace of Development. Anand : Institute of Rural Management.

The Right of Children to Free and Compulsory Education Act, 2009, Ministry of Law and Justice, New Delhi, 27 August 2009.

Tilak, Jandhyala B.G. (ed.) (2003). Education, Society and Development: National and International Perspectives, New Delhi: A.P.H. Publication Corporation.

CHAPTER

36

Women as Agents of Change in Adult Education

ZAHID RAZA KHAN AND KAMRAN MOHAMMAD KHAN

ABSTRACT

Women are worst affected by poverty, which means not only material shortages but also lack of opportunities, whether in the field of education or in the enjoyment of cultural, political and social rights. Zahid Raza Khan and Kamran Mohammad Khan jointly presents the results of a study which PRIA carried out with three voluntary development organizations. The study was intended to explore the impact of educational practices on women's collectives in terms of their ability to gain control over economic, social and political resources. It forms part of a study by the Institute for International Cooperation of the German Adult Education Association (IIZ/DVV) on 'Adult Education and Poverty Reduction: A Global Priority'.

Key Index: Women, education, agents, NGO, adult, government schemes.

INTRODUCTION

Out of an estimated 1.2 billion poor people in the world, over two-thirds are women. They face abject poverty in want of adequate food, clean water, sanitation, and health care. They often lack access to the critical resources of credit, land and inheritance. They are denied opportunities, choices, access to information, education, and skills. Without any sense of power whatsoever, their participation in decision-making is minimal, both at home and in the community.

Women are found extending their working hours inordinately at home and outside, to earn enough to meet the subsistence requirements of their households. Yet, their labor goes unrewarded and unrecognized, in most cases. Given the plight of women, it becomes important to redefine poverty. This calls for a concept of poverty that doesn't only take into account the absence of minimum basic needs, but also includes denial of opportunities and choices. Poverty reduction implies enhancing resources, choices, capabilities and the power necessary to enjoy an adequate standard of living and other rights (civil cultural, political and social).

When provided with access to economic and educational opportunities, as well as the autonomy needed to take advantage of such opportunities, poor women are enabled to make strategic life choices to negotiate their poverty. The provision of credit, especially micro credit, is increasingly being recognized as an effective strategy for poverty eradication. Self-Help Groups (SHGs) formed to encourage savings and credit activities are one of the effective methods of socio-economic development of women.

SHGs usually have 15-20 members from a poor socio-economic background. These groups begin with savings. Regular meetings of members are held where members contribute a saving deposit, an amount decided by the group. When these savings build up after about a year, members are able to access credit through their pooled resources. Members are allocated loans based on group solidarity, instead of formal collateral. The group takes independent loan decisions on issues relating to selection of borrowers, fixing the amount of loan or the rate of interest, and the terms of repayment, etc.

The profits, however small, are either distributed among the members, or jointly disposed as desired by the group. This strategy promotes self-sufficiency and independence amongst the poor women. SHGs also take up income generating activities for their members. Savings, credit, and enterprise build the capacities of women's collectives to generate their own capital, meet their credit needs, and expand options for livelihood.

However, most SHGs are ill-equipped to effectively tackle the livelihood/poverty issues. They require educational support for enhancing the knowledge and skills of women members, and for improving the efficacy of their poverty eradication activities.

The role of education in empowering women's collectives assumes greater significance in this context. Information dissemination, raising awareness, capacity building, and translation of skills into practice increases women's economic options and promote their sense of worth. Basic literacy skills help them to acquire knowledge and skills required for improving and developing their tasks in all fields. Vocational education and training go a long way in facilitating their economic base. Enhanced organizational and social leadership skill empowers them socially and politically.

Poor women lack resources, skills, education and collective strength to break the cycle of their oppression and exploitation. External facilitation through voluntary development organizations plays a crucial catalytic role by creating a platform for learning.

This paper aims to put forward (a) the ways in which savings and credit, enterprise and basic literacy are used as tools for building the capacity of grassroots women's collectives to enhance their livelihood and improve their quality of life; and (b) the impact of these on women's collectives.

The research was carried out with women's SHGs in Medak district, Andhra Pradesh, Naugaon, Uttarkashi district in Uttaranchal, and Kasargod district, Kerala. In Andhra Pradesh, women's groups received basic literacy skills and training in livelihood enhancement, while women's groups in Uttaranchal received substantial formal training in entrepreneurship skills—such as marketing, accounts keeping, etc. The women's collectives in Kerala, formed primarily for savings and credit purposes, received extensive training on enterprise development, leadership skills, decision-making, financial management, loaning, etc.

The study was carried out in collaboration with three voluntary development organizations: *HARC* (Himalayan Action Research Center) in Uttaranchal, *PEACE* (People's Action for Creative Education) in Andhra Pradesh, and *SAHAYI* (Centre for Collective Learning and Action) in Kerala. Our collaboration with the organizations allowed us to not only understand their attempts to organize and educate, but also helped access to different self-help groups on a basis of trust. We used a combination of focus group discussion and in-depth, open-ended interviews for the purpose, as we wanted to understand the impact on women from their own personal perspectives.

THE CONTEXT AND THE ORGANIZATIONS

Agriculture is an important sector of the Indian economy. In Andhra Pradesh, Kerala and Uttaranchal, agriculture is constrained by low productivity, lack of an assured supply of inputs, lack of technologies, poor resources and inadequate extension and support services.

In Andhra Pradesh, only 10% of the population holds agricultural land. Roughly 60% of the gross cropped area falls in the category of rain fed dry lands. Telengana, one of the poorest and least developed regions in the State, is in the rain fed dry land region. Nearly 50% of Kerala's population depends upon agriculture. The shift in cropping patterns from labour intensive paddy cultivation to commercial crops has resulted in the decline in the share of agricultural workers. Subsistence farming is the most common form of agriculture in Uttaranchal. Most landless, small and marginal farmer households in these states belong to backward groups (Scheduled Castes and Tribes).

Poor women have neither an independent income, nor many assets. They rely on their labour power to meet their subsistence requirements. Women in Telengana, Andhra

Pradesh, are some of the worst affected by chronic hunger and poverty. Their main source of income is wage labour in agriculture. Given the low wages and declining productivity of agriculture in the rain fed dry lands, it is very difficult for women to break out of the declining spiral of indebtedness and poverty. Women in Uttaranchal perform 80 per cent of agricultural activity and play a significant role in providing food security to their families. Despite a high social capability (high literacy rates and good health status), women in Kerala are invisible in the public domain. Severe unemployment in Kerala has discouraged women from actively seeking employment. Changes in the structure of employment have further lowered their participation rate. For instance, the shift in cropping pattern from the female labour intensive paddy cultivation to commercial crops has resulted in the decline in the share of women agricultural workers. The crisis in the cottage industries has resulted in the decline in the share of cottage industries in the female work force.

Highly unequal relationships of class and gender also influence the social status of women. Women in Telengana, Andhra Pradesh, are predominantly from SC/ST communities belonging to landless or marginal farmer families. Absence of basic education has left them unaware of their minimum legal rights, while their lack of exposure to alternative values and ideas has prevented them from questioning the *status quo*. Moreover, women's voice in local governance and decision-making is conspicuously absent.

From the outset, these voluntary organizations did not look at the problem of poverty simply as lack of resources. They felt that lack of voice, agency and organization also explained the poverty of women. Hence, their broad focus was the empowerment of women instead of limited goals of poverty alleviation. The formation of self-help groups (SHGs) was recognized as a successful mechanism for the organization, mobilization and self-development of women. Organizing poor women in self-help groups and empowering them with capacities would enhance their competence to access and manage resources, expand their options for sustainable livelihoods and enable them to participate actively in community development. They could also be instruments of social empowerment through awareness generation, and convergence of delivery of schemes. Women's collectives, however, needed education, training, analytical and practical skills to be able to exercise their agency efficiently. Each of these voluntary organizations is facilitating the process of change in favour of poor women by organizing them as SHGs.

PEACE (People's Action for Creative Education), which has been working with the rural poor since 1986 in the severely drought prone Telengana region of Andhra Pradesh, aims to create awareness among the poor rural women and empower them through literacy and livelihood improvement programmes. It works in 12 mandals covering 120 villages in Bhongir and Nalgonda revenue division in Nalgonda district, and Siddipet revenue division of Medak district in Andhra Pradesh (AP).

PEACE has organized poor women into groups at three levels. Up to 20 women are brought together into one SHG at rural community level. The group members make regular savings and lend to each other. 10 to 20 SHGs are brought together into a cluster called Sangam at village level. 10 Sangam villages come together under a federation called Mutually Aided Credit Societies (MACS) at Mandal (district) level. PEACE has initiated three MACS: Vasundhara, Manjira and Maitri. These institutions run democratically to serve the needs of their members. The MACS have 4,093 members consisting of 90 groups who have a regular saving habit. (Manjira MACS = 1640 members, 65 groups; Vasundhara MACS = 1161 members, 14 groups; Maitri MACS = 1292 members, 11 groups).

All women who are members of SHGs become members of the General Body of MACS. The members initially pay an amount of Rs. 100 towards the Share Capital of the proposed society from the savings amount. The General Body or representatives of the General Body elect Managing Committee members for a period of 3 years by rotation. A retired committee member is eligible for re-election. The President is elected from the Committee members every year. The Chief Executive is an employee of the Society and is the person responsible for day-to-day functions. Selected volunteers work on facilitating loan disbursement, recovery transactions, and assisting the manager. These volunteers are selected from among the Managing Committee to promote accountability and transparency.

SAHAYI (Centre for Collective Learning and Action) has been working since the 1990s towards capacity building of small and medium sized development-oriented NGOs, VDOs, and citizens' groups such as women's collectives in Kerala. It has two resource centers in Kasargod and Kollam districts of Kerala. These two district resource centers work for the cause of the marginalized people, strengthen their capacity, work for the best practices in governance, strengthen the governance institutions, build the capacity of the people to ensure the effective participation in Gramsabha/Wardsabha, influence the policy-making bodies for pro-poor policies by conducting studies, and work for keeping social cohesion and peace in the community. SAHAYI also provides short-term entrepreneurship development training to women's collectives in market analysis, marketing skills, marketing strategies, salesmanship, production, and inventory and financial management. The training programmes aim towards making the enterprises of women's collectives sustainable profit-making units. SAHAYI's interventions have largely focused on capacity building of SHGs and consequently have had little role to play in building coalitions in terms of federation.

HARC (Himalayan Action Research Center) has been engaged in the community empowerment process in Uttaranchal since 1988. It is promoting sustainable livelihood alternatives by developing opportunities and choices for women. It helps them to increase their incomes and improve their well-being by strengthening their capacity for collective entrepreneurship.

HARC began the process of building women's SHGs in 2000, in Naugaon. Once the groups were oriented and trained, it facilitated the process of the formation of a federation of SHGs for collective business. Rawain Women SHG Federation came into existence on October 3, 2002. It was decided that the federation would act as a trading organization, which would help the SHGs in marketing their products. 160 women of 14 SHGs contributed a share value of Rs. 500 to get life membership, and started a collective business. HARC is helping them to deal with banks and other financial institutions. The federation has not taken any loans yet. It runs purely on the shareholders' investment.

EDUCATION FOR EMPOWERMENT OF POOR WOMEN'S COLLECTIVES : CAPACITY BUILDING STRATEGIES

Capacity building of poor women's collectives is an essential input to reduce the vulnerability of group members to poverty, and to enhance their participation in economic growth through improved livelihoods. The organizations have strengthened the organizational capabilities of women members through education and training for knowledge and skill development in the savings and interloaning process, record management for group and finance management, livelihood enhancement, income generating activities and entrepreneurship development.

CAPACITY BUILDING SUPPORT FOR THRIFT AND CREDIT

Managing savings and credit groups is a highly skilled task. PEACE, SAHAYI and HARC have focused on perspective building orientation, leadership training, report writing, accountancy, self-development, courses in SHG management, book-keeping and project planning.

CAPACITY BUILDING SUPPORT TO ENHANCE LIVELIHOODS

PEACE has adopted a livelihood enhancement approach. This approach involves upgrading of livelihoods through environmentally sustainable agricultural methods. It provides information and training on improved management of animals, developing local breeds of cattle fodder, vermicomposting, and non-pesticide management.

Both SAHAYI and HARC have focused on promoting micro-enterprise development. Besides providing entrepreneurship development training to the members of

SHGs, they give information on project planning, identification of resources, problems in the way of setting up an industry, marketing management and developing linkages with other organizations. But they have different approaches towards micro-enterprise development. While HARC has motivated the groups to start collectively an enterprise based on local available resources, SAHAYI has provided training to the group members in numerous enterprise activities such as bee-keeping, dairy, banana and pineapple plantation, vermicomposting, snacks and bag making, etc.

INTEGRATED LEARNING MODEL

PEACE realized that women needed to be educated and trained to efficiently play diverse roles such as members of Boards of Directors, Chairpersons, MACS managers, Sangam and SHG leaders, or simply as borrowers of credit. Therefore, it associated itself with a holistic education package called WELLD (Women's Empowerment through Literacy and Livelihood Development) project designed for the poorest and least educated women. The WELLD project assumed that women could manage the SHG independently once they acquired basic skills of reading, writing and arithmetic. The

TABLE I
Key Capacity Building Areas of PEACE, SAHAYI and HARC

SHG	Formation, management, leadership development, problem-solving and conflict resolution.
Federation	Financial management, resource mobilization, decision-making.
Accounts and documentation	Maintenance of records, annual plans, budgets, documenting the minutes of meetings.
Enterprise development	Enterprise promotion, feasibility, other technical and management aspects, information and training on techniques to enhance existing livelihoods.
Empowerment	Awareness raising on women's issues.
Basic literacy	Reading, writing and numeracy skill enhancement.

project aimed to help women acquire basic knowledge and skills to make informed financial and livelihood decisions. PRIA, in collaboration with World Education (WE), was involved in coordinating this pilot project. Self-help groups initiated in Medak district were covered under this programme.

Key Capacity building areas of PEACE, SAHAYI and HARC are summarized in Table 1.

PARTICIPATORY LEARNING TOOLS

The capacity building initiatives were participatory, interactive and inclusive in nature. The organizations created a variety of learning opportunities for women. Practical learning through study tours, visits to best practice projects, hands-on training and demonstration projects, face-to-face interactions with experts, practitioners, and government officials, are some of the ways in which women's groups have been trained. These activities have played a significant role in exposing women to new ideas and strategies, building self-confidence, and creating an enabling environment for experimentation and innovation. HARC, for instance, organized exposure trips to different small-scale industries, which gave women a practical orientation on grading and packaging. Members of the purchasing committee were taken to an international trade fair in Delhi where they could get an opportunity to sell their products and build marketing linkages with big traders from all over the country. Training on food processing was given at the food processing unit at HARC. The aim was to upgrade the technical knowledge and skills of the members of the federation and the fruit processing committee so that they could utilize the practical knowledge for income generation activities.

WOMEN AS AGENTS OF CHANGE

This section discusses the impacts, resulting directly or indirectly, from the education and training of women as members of SHGs. The analysis goes beyond the concern with incomes, profit and productivity and focuses on the changes at the individual, household and community level. These changes concern the non-economic dimensions of poverty. The changes considered in the study include cognitive and behavioural change (changes in knowledge, attitudes, perceptions and behaviour); material change (changes in access to a variety of tangible resources such as the standard of living, access to and ownership of resources, etc.); and changes in the terms on which women interact with each other, including the terms on which they access resources at various institutional levels like the household, the SHGs, the market and politics.

Findings of the study suggest that the collectives, when empowered with information, skill and awareness were able to exercise independent agency and challenge established power relations.

Women's collectives reported a number of changes in their lives, which could be deemed empowering. These changes were linked to their level of participation in the programme and included an improved sense of independence; an enhanced social position as their levels of assets or incomes rose; increased participation in household decision-making; bank accounts and land in their own names; and higher levels of political and community activity. The changes may be seen as challenging deep-seated social norms and being truly transformative.

COGNITIVE AND BEHAVIOURAL CHANGES

The capacity building programme helped women change their attitudes, behaviours, and styles of communication. They have become efficient, confident and actively participate in various public activities. Training in SHG management has helped them to manage their group efficiently. All their activities and transactions are documented and recorded.

A case in point is the Anjali SHG that has been trained to organize its activities. They now maintain systematic records, and follow streamlined accounting and reporting procedures. The Gram Panchayat in Balal audited their accounts and certified them to be well documented and transparent. It has declared Anjali SHG the best savings group. Anjali SHG, which was earlier confined to small savings and microcredit, is now participating in social development activities to improve the quality of life of their village.

Practical learning allowed women's groups to reflect on their everyday experiences and articulate their needs and priorities. More importantly, they were able to move beyond the limited realm of the household. Women who had never stepped out of their homes took part in learning activities such as study tours, exposure visits, interactive sessions within learning centers, etc. Each learning forum brought them out of their homes and villages, exposing them to alternative ways of being. They had to break many rules, and face taunts from family members. To convince their detractors, the women argued that their newly acquired skills would contribute to the economic and social betterment of their families and communities.

The members of Rawain Women Trading Federation in Naugaon, Uttaranchal reported that the village elders had constantly pressurized them, before the formation of the federation. They doubted the viability of an all women's federation, saying, 'Nothing will happen. HARC is going to take away all the money.' Now, they seem to understand that the federation is functioning.

Women's groups have moved from being mere participants to resource persons facilitating other learning groups. Mary Thomas from Aishwarya SHG in Vellarikund in Kerala, and Jagdamba Parmar from Bhagirathi SHG in Kotyal, Naugaon in Uttaranchal, are resource persons today, and give training on food processing and group finance management.

The women have become more efficient and have reported a change in their attitudes. Women SHGs as members of Rawain Women Trading Federation in Naugaon, Uttaranchal claim to have developed capacity and confidence to work. They have graduated beyond thinking at the SHG level to think at the federation level. Their sense of ownership towards their own enterprise has developed.

We do the processing of fruits, extract juice and prepare squash. This is our skill. HARC has enabled us to play this role...we decide our target production and fix the price. Earlier we depended on HARC for fixing the rate of product. Now it's different. HARC only gives us advice...(Women members,

Rawain Women Trading Federation, HARC, Naugaon, Uttaranchal)

Though they understand that they will eventually manage their enterprises on their own, they look forward to HARC's support.

We have benefited a lot from the trainings received from HARC. If tomorrow it withdraws support we can manage on our own. But our federation is just two years old. We need more understanding; therefore we'll need guidance from HARC. (Women members, 134 Rawain Women Trading Federation, HARC, Naugaon, Uttaranchal).

Members have demonstrated confidence. Their mobility has increased. Exposure visits, and interaction with experts as part of their capacity building exercise, has brought a change in their own stereotyped mindsets.

Women have acquired literacy skills. They can read and write, and do simple calculations. They are using their skills to write provisions lists, read scraps of paper and bus numbers. They have internalized the importance of education and are sending their children, including daughters, to school.

After attending the learning centre I understood the importance of education. I can now read the signboard, weight and price of commodities. Once after reading the price of a commodity I went to shopkeeper and told him that he had overcharged me. The shopkeeper returned me the balance. I realized that basic literacy helped me to negotiate with people for just practices; if my children become educated they could transform their lives. (Pochamma, Daulapur WELLD Learning Center, PEACE, AP)

Women members of Rawain Women Trading Federation in Naugaon, Uttaranchal are applying the acquired knowledge in their day-to-day lives.

We have learnt to make use of every product. Earlier ripe tomatoes would go to waste since we didn't know the way to preserve them. Now we make puree at home for personal consumption at home. Nothing is wasted... (Women members, Rawain Women Trading Federation, HARC, Naugaon, Uttaranchal)

Women have found the entrepreneurship development training programme useful. They are able to identify viable micro-enterprises. Sneha SHG runs a bag-making unit, Aishwarya SHG a food preservation unit, while members of the Anjali group individually pursue a number of income generating activities such as bee-keeping, dairy, and banana and pineapple plantation.

MATERIAL CHANGES

Incomes have increased. Women have gained control over produce and income. Self-earned income has instilled in them a sense of pride and confidence in managing on their own. Women's bargaining and decision-making power within the family has increased.

Earlier when we had to deposit Rs. 20 as part of the SHG saving scheme, we were constantly under pressure. We had to ask from our husbands and in-laws. Now there is no such tension. We are earning and we are saving... we can spend without having to ask from anyone. (Women members, Rawain Women Trading Federation, HARC, Naugaon, Uttaranchal)

Some of the women's collectives are managing independent enterprises. Loans from groups have reduced the dependency on moneylenders. Women are taking loans for investment in land and for livelihood enhancement. They have invested in household asset building, milch animals, and good quality seeds, etc. Lifestyles have changed with purchase of consumer items such as a television set, a refrigerator, etc. Membership of SHG and easy accessibility to loan and skill support from the respective organizations has made this possible. For instance, after receiving information from PEACE on biological pesticides and bio-fertilizers, women have begun using non-chemical fertilizers like tobacco juice and vermin compost in their fields.

During a class discussion, a debate on the benefits of organic farming took place. On realizing the benefits of organic farming I requested PEACE staff to hold a meeting in the village for all women and men. I experimented with light traps to control pests in my pigeon pea field. I did not use chemical pesticides. Not only has my crop quality improved, the yield has also increased. I replicated this experiment on the cotton crop. I used vermin compost on the field and implemented non-chemical interventions to control pests. As a result, I harvested higher yields and income. The village sarpanch visited my field and appreciated my work. Now village elders have requested support from PEACE for similar interventions in their fields. (Swaroopa, Gollapally WELLD Learning Center)

RELATIONAL CHANGES

Membership of SHG and easy accessibility to loans and engagement in micro-enterprises have facilitated the women's inclusion in household decision-making. They are able to negotiate with their husbands on crucial matters. Husbands are taking keen interest in their enterprises, often actively helping them in their economic ventures. Men are beginning to understand the linkages in the programme (literacy-saving-livelihood enhancement).

We participate in the decision-making... after all we are contributing to many of the household expenses such as paying school fees for children, buying books for them, getting things that are needed at home, bringing rations, and other things from the market. (Women members, Rawain Women Trading Federation, HARC, Naugaon, Uttaranchal)

There is a change in the mindsets of husbands and in-laws. They now understand that women are running a trading federation, therefore they need to go out for work.

... On the days when I have to come to the center for meetings and work, my father-in-law says that I shouldn't be late for the meetings or when I am resting he tells my mother-in-law, let her rest she works so hard... (Beena Bandhani, Federation processing unit in-charge, Rawain Women Trading Federation, HARC, Naugaon, Uttaranchal)

GROUP SOLIDARITY

The training programmes have reinforced a collective identity among members. The learning and exchange between women's groups has enhanced their confidence. The federation of SHGs has instilled in them a sense of solidarity—a 'we' feeling. Meetings and sharing of experiences have made them sensitive to each other as well as to the community's needs.

They have allowed women's groups to pool their equity/ savings and test their credit-worthiness in the face of credit institutions. They have helped women's groups to access funds, and at the same time allowed them to explore community enterprises based on the combined strength of groups. All SHGs in the project area of PEACE in AP are members of MACS. SHGs in the project area of SAHAYI at Kasargod district, Kerala, are members of the Sneha federation. They meet regularly to share experiences. They celebrate festivals together. The federation has instilled in them a sense of solidarity and security. Fourteen SHGs in Naugaon, Uttaranchal, are members of Rawain Women Trading Federation. Members meet regularly to share experiences of trainings and information that any particular member has received. Sharing of experiences also enhances their awareness. Professional rivalry between the SHGs exists, because the groups do not want to lag behind any other group with respect to training, and access to information. They are concerned over why a particular group has been asked to come to the center, chosen for training or given particular information. They are fiercely competitive; yet feel that the competitiveness is good because they are constantly upgrading their skills.

PARTICIPATION IN PUBLIC/POLITICAL LIFE FOR COLLECTIVE ACTION

Women's groups are emerging as strong power groups. They negotiate confidently with government officials, moneylenders and outsiders. Women are playing a key role in local governance. They have come out with strategies to elect the sarpanch of their choice. Many of them are ward members in the gram panchayat. Women learners from Medak district, AP, have taken up issues of minimum wages, intervening in village panchayats and safeguarding citizens' rights. Some of them have taken up public offices such as members of Village Education Committees.

As part of Janmabhoomi program in our village we demanded that officials lay down water pipelines. As a result officials got pipelines laid within one month of the Janmabhoomi meeting. The entire village is getting water connection. We constructed three small tanks and distributed the water in these three tanks. The problem of drinking water supply is solved now. We also demanded streetlights be put up on the road that they take to attend the night literacy center. We also raised our voice against the appointment of the former chairman of the Village Education Committee (VEC) and for new leadership. We selected the leader from Sangam. (Women Board of Directors, Manjira MACs).

Women's groups from Naugaon, Uttaranchal, have actively participated in the planting of trees that would give fodder. They have raised the issue of a liquor ban in Gram Sabha meetings. They have taken the initiative in the cleaning of the panchayat house, and repairing damaged and broken roads. Women's groups from Kasargod district, Kerala, have raised issues relating to basic needs of the community such as access to drinking water, construction of roads, houses for the poor, old age pensions and cleaning of hospitals. Anjali SHG for instance, has articulated the specific disadvantages faced by poor widows and has demanded old age pensions and housing. They are also participating in local self-governance as ward members and members of gram panchayats. In this way, they are transforming the agenda of governance by ensuring that the survival needs of the poor are given priority.

IMPACTS AT MARKET

The intervention of PEACE has indirectly made a significant impact on the wider financial and labour market. Women report that the role of moneylenders declined after formation of the group. Knowledge of legal rights has helped them in getting land entitlement and minimum wages in agricultural labour.

We know how much work we are doing and how much we should be getting. Earlier we used to get Rs. 10 for our fieldwork. We fought for higher wages. Now we are getting Rs. 20. We decided the revised rate in the night school. We can challenge the Reddy—the dominant caste in our village. (Lakshmi, Gollapally WELLD Learning Center, PEACE, AP).

The Rawain Women Self-help Group Federation in Naugaon, Uttaranchal is a two-year-old enterprise with a turnover of Rs. 300,000. The increase in share value has raised women's confidence. This federation is dealing with 18 products such as pulses, millet, and fruit processing items. The federation understands that it is weak in marketing. It is looking towards developing more linkages and contacts with other retail outlets. It is conscious of the fact that with good quality products, it can build a brand identity in the market.

The federation has no previous experience of trading; it is developing systems from practical experience. For instance, the executive committee of the federation decided that the entire group would do the grading, but found that not all women could do it. So they changed the strategy, calling on the group as per their abilities. Even distribution of profit to shareholders was difficult. Some women members objected as to why a few groups were getting a share of the profit, despite no contribution in the production process. Here, with HARC facilitation, they were able to resolve the conflict by explaining how shareholders get the profit equally, but how some groups could earn more than the other groups on the basis of their contribution.

EMERGING LESSONS

Poverty as Capability Deprivation

The study looks at non-economic aspects of poverty. Access to resources, the ability to define and articulate needs and priorities, and to act upon them, constitute capabilities. Capabilities help people achieve their valued goals. Poverty reflects the underlying capability deprivation.

Sustained or chronic deprivation of the resources, capabilities and choices necessary for an adequate standard of living and enjoyment of economic, political and social rights, make poor women vulnerable, powerless and dependent. A social understanding of poverty takes into account these deficits, which sometimes matter to people more than money. Poverty reduction, therefore, implies increasing capacities and choices and decreasing the vulnerability of the people. This study is based on women SHGs' analysis of the impact of education and training on poverty alleviation. Their analysis goes beyond concern with incomes, profit and productivity. A strong organization of their own, access to resources and opportunities, strong capabilities built through education, information, skills and confidence have empowered them and provided them freedom of choice and action.

SELF-HELP GROUPS : A MICRO-FINANCIAL APPROACH TO POVERTY REDUCTION AND EMPOWERMENT OF POOR WOMEN

Availability of credit is the basic requirement for poor women to meet the exigencies of extreme poverty. Micro-finance for the poor/women is an important strategy for poverty reduction and for economic empowerment. Micro-finance implies savings, credit, insurance and other financial services for the poor/informal sector communities. However, poor women find it difficult to access credit programmes due to high transaction costs. Organization of women in small self-help groups to collectively generate their own capital can touch the core of poverty. Participation in thrift and credit activities brings improvement at the level of subsistence. SHGs also take up income generating activities to ensure their members' sustainable livelihoods. Ownership of wealth—the capital fund through savings and credit as well as enterprise and access to resources for sustainable livelihoods can effectively alleviate their poverty and also mitigate the psychological consequences of being poor.

ADULT EDUCATION AND EMPOWERMENT OF WOMEN

Adult education can make a difference to the lives of poor women. Case studies have pointed out that skill enhancement in finance management, and SHG management, like book-keeping, accounting, record-keeping, micro-enterprise management, has enabled many women to take up leadership roles in their respective SHGs and also run their respective trades confidently. Credit with education improves the chances of well-being in the household, simultaneously leading to enhanced self-confidence.

The impact of educational inputs has been all-encompassing. They have brought women into the public arena; engaged them with the power structures in society; enhanced their skills to take on leadership roles and take decisions; improved their capabilities to contribute to the family well-being; and provided them with the security of solidarity in women's groups formed for the same purpose. All these have contributed in reducing poverty.

The learning programme has had a significant impact at three levels of empowerment: power within, power to, and power with. At the power within level, a key impact is the observation that women have developed an awareness of their own potential to fight against poverty. They are confident, sensitive and informed persons. At the power to level, the projects have expanded women's control over their labour, resources and decision-making processes. Access to their own savings, access to networks of women outside their family and access to leadership positions have empowered them. At the power with level, women have intervened collectively in many institutions: family, market (labour and financial), community and local self-governance institutions.

CATALYTIC ROLE OF EXTERNAL FACILITATORS

Poor women lack resources, skills, education and collective strength to break the cycle of their oppression and exploitation. External facilitators such as NGOs in such a context play a catalytic role by educating, organizing and mobilizing women purposively and consciously around a common or shared concern for reducing poverty.

The organizations in this study are not micro-finance organizations. They do not take loans or give credits. They are only promoting and supporting the SHG model of micro-finance. They are facilitators of group formation around perceived needs and common goals. The key capacity building areas at the level of SHGs include group management, leadership development, and problem-solving and conflict resolution. At the level of the federation the training component includes financial management, resource mobilization legal aspects, and decision-making. For accounts and documentation, the training component includes maintenance of records, annual plans, budget, project proposals and writing minutes of meetings. Enterprise development involves training in enterprise promotion, feasibility, and other technical and management aspects. Empowerment implies raising awareness on women's issues and convergent action. Basic literacy skills include teaching of basic reading, writing and numeracy skills.

The organizations took different strategies to empower the adult learners as per their need requirements. In Andhra Pradesh, female literacy rates are low. Absence of basic literacy skills prevented women SHG members playing their role efficiently. Hence, PEACE adopted the WELLD project with a view to equipping women with basic literacy skills along with training in SHG management and livelihood enhancement. In Kerala, despite the high literacy rates women are economically not independent. To break the constraints of economic dependency SAHAYI decided to strengthen women SHGs not only with income generating activities also with awareness about their political rights. The topography of hilly Uttaranchal brings about low-income opportunities. Women perform 80 per cent of agricultural activity and play a significant role in providing food security to their families. Poverty increases the work burden of women. Hence, HARC focused on training women SHGs for collective entrepreneurship and provided the members with alternative viable livelihood opportunities.

RECOMMENDATIONS

- Issues relating to basic needs are important to women. Capacity building strategies should emerge to meet the basic needs of women. They should be based on local manpower, local resources and local opportunities. Hence, vocational education policy for adults should take into consideration the needs of particular localities in order to ensure that livelihood enhancement training actually results in higher productivity, incomes and well-being.
- Women as marginalized groups form a substantial section of adult learners. Poor women do not

perceive the immediate relevance of literacy in their daily struggle for survival. Literacy *per se* may seem meaningless to them when livelihood concerns take primary importance. The policy-makers of adult education should develop an integrated educational package that is integrated with savings and credit group activities and livelihood enhancement programmes.

- Any transformative learning has a political perspective. Adult education as a transformative learning tool needs to strengthen poor women's self-esteem, their analytical skills, competencies and consciousness so that they gain a sense of their rights and are able to question inequitable relations of power.
- The content of adult education should place women's empowerment and reduction of feminization of poverty firmly on its agenda. It should integrate the issues relating to gendered power relations, access and control over resources, and rights and entitlements. It should educate and train women with the necessary information to make choices that will lead to breaking the dependency syndrome and eventually to the reduction of their poverty qualitatively.
- Participatory teaching methods tend to be more effective than didactic approaches. Adult education policy should promote active, participatory and interactive forms of instruction and learning.
- Voluntary development organizations have played catalytic roles in strengthening the struggles of poor women. There is a great need to document the positive cases so that sensitive rights-based policy can be evolved out of it. Adult education policy should identify and document empirical positive experiences and expertise of local organizations and make these widely available to all interested readers. It must also develop a meaningful rights-based policy.

REFERENCES

Anand, Jaya S., 2002. Self-Help Groups in Empowering Women: Case study of selected SHGs and NHGs, Discussion Paper No. 38. Thiruvananthapuram: Kerala Research Programme on Local Level Development Centre for Development Studies.

Dash, Anup, 2003. 'Strategies for Poverty Alleviation in India: CYSD's Holistic Approach to Empowerment through Self Help Group Model. *IDS Bulletin*, Volume 31, Number 4, October: 133-42.

Gopalan, Prema, 2001. The Many Faces of Micro Credit. *Humanscape Magazine*, August.

Kabeer Naila, 2003. Assessing Wider Social Impacts of Microfinance Services: Concepts, Methods and Findings. *IDS Bulletin*, Volume 31, Number 4, October: 106-14.

PRIA, 2002. Effect of Capacity Building Interventions to Strengthen WELLD Programme on Partner NGOs and Women Learners, A Participatory report of the Pilot Project: WELLD. New Delhi: PRIA.

Mayoux, Linda, 2003. Sustainable Learning for Women's Empowerment: Ways Forward in Micro Finance. New Delhi: Samskriti Murthy Ranjani. 2001. 'Building Women's Capacities'. New Delhi: Sage Publications.

Narayan, Deepa (*et. al.*). 2000. Voices of the Poor: Crying out for Change. Oxford: Oxford University Press.

Oxenham, John (*et. al.*). 2001. Strengthening Livelihoods with Literacy—A Draft Report. Bonn: IIZ/DVV.

UNDP, 2000. Overcoming Human Poverty : A Poverty Report, New York: UNDP.

CHAPTER

37

Emotional Intelligence among Youth in Technological Era

KIRAN LATA DANGWAL

ABSTRACT

Present technological era is offering new opportunity and new potential to the youth. It offers knowledge, personal growth, extended relationships and fun. Most of the time youth are engaged in the technological world of imagination, curiosity, exploration and experimentation, which has a myriad of attractions for them. Directly or indirectly this technological world is influencing the emotional intelligence of today's young generation along with its impact on society. Education and parenting about emotional intelligence in the technological era are presented with a new set of challenges that needs new solutions for the youth. This new challenge of educating and parenting requires immediate and effective responses from a socially responsible system of education. Educating and training youth in emotional intelligence would play a vital role in increasing their awareness about the problems arising from the technological world and ways to deal with them. Edifice up important emotional intelligence will help the youth to translate knowledge and attitude in a positive direction and acquire healthy behavior to improve their lives in general. The need of the hour is to empower youth with strategies to make healthy choices that contribute to a meaningful life. The present paper may bring new ideas and facts about enhancing emotional intelligence among youth in technological era, which will explore the abilities that will help to promote the mental well-being and competence in young people as they face the realities of life.

"Technology and our human potential are the two great challenges and adventures facing humankind today".

Above said line by Naisbitt (1984) depicts that, as we progress technologically the emotional, physiological, and the behavioral level become more prevalent. Whenever new technology is introduced into society, there needs to be a counterbalancing human rejoinder. Technology, which includes computers, software, telecommunications and consumer electronics, underpins the rest of the knowledge industries because technology manages and move knowledge. In the present technological era Internet communication, especially instant messaging has become an essential feature of young generation's social lives. These technologists are creative, smart, hard-working problem-solvers, but they are also techno-centric, unbalanced, and lacking in social imagination (Castells, 1998; Cringely, 1996; Delbecq and Weiss, 2000; Goleman, 1998b; Rosenberg, 1995).

YOUTH IN TECHNOLOGICAL ERA

Youth is a time of new social demands, which in turn have an impact on psychological development. In the Age of the Computer the qualities of thinking that permit youth to succeed in a tecnological world, is actually the process of learning, an empowering, connective, exploratory, creative process, which youth need to learn rather than a specific knowledge content. Technology offers a way that can encourage this empowered type of learning rather than stifled, regulated, regimented thinking. Younger Generations are both capable and ready to work within a technological environment i.e. one that is based on computer, web and mobile phone technologies. Face-to-face interaction and some telephone conversations have been partially replaced with facebook, email and instant message communication. Most of the times, it is seen that the youth involve themselves emotionally in virtual world which are many times create problems and difficulties in their lives. These difficulties are giving rise to many psycho-somatic problems such as anxiety, tensions, frustrations and emotional upsets in day-to-day life. So, the study of emotional life is now emerging as a descriptive science, comparable with anatomy.

EMOTIONAL INTELLIGENCE : IMPORTANCE IN PRESENT ERA

Emotional intelligence has become a convenient term to describe the emotional and social abilities one can apply to being successful in life and work. Practical skills and the ability to handle people that include a part of the art of managing emotion contribute a lot towards any success. D. Daniel Goleman (1995) called it emotional intelligence. Daniel Goleman (1995) popularized the term when his book of the same name suggested that EQ is just as important, if not more important, as IQ. Emotional intelligence, in its broadest meaning, can have impact on a culture.

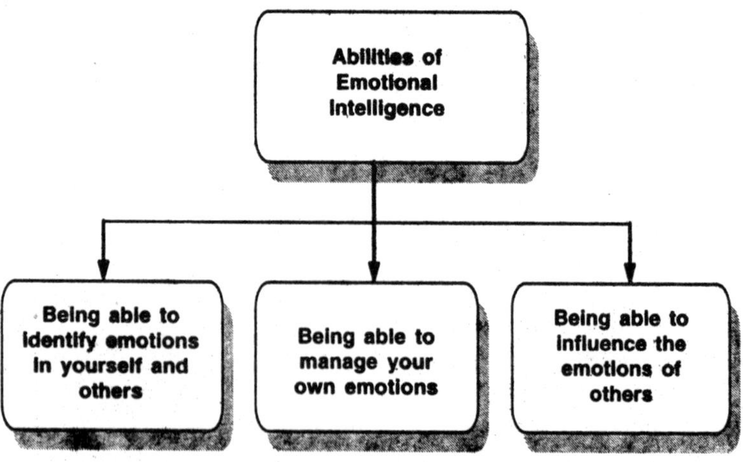

Emotions contain histories, every chapter and verse of energy, experience, deep understanding and relationship in our lives that is why they are vaster than our minds. Emotions shape our mind as well as the entire personality pattern. They enter our human system as a source of energy that radiates and reverberate.

Emotions are reactions consisting of physiological reactions, subjective cognitive states and expressive behaviours. Every emotion has a cognitive component and every thought is influenced by emotional factors. Both emotion and thought are basic attributes, which in the human being are intimately meshed in a dialectical unity (Thomas and Chess, 1980).

People who have control over their lives can manage and know their feelings well and read and deal effectively with other people's feelings. While the people who do not have control over their emotional life fight inner battles that sabotage their ability to focus on work and think clearly (Goleman, 1995). Emotional intelligence is a type of social intelligence which involves the capacity for recognizing our own feelings and those of others for motivating ourselves and for managing emotions well in ourselves and in our relationships.

At present this is one of the important issues that young generation who are living in technological era are emotionally how much mature. This is all show that young generation when do internet they starts traveling in the sky of virtual world which take them away from real world and attach themselves emotionally also with virtual friends. These youths take advantage of the Internet's ability to interact virtually with anyone around the world. As visual, touch, and voice modalities become prevalent and instantaneous language translation becomes a reality, there is diverse opportunities to learn social interaction skills.

E-mail and instant message systems also allow youth to maintain long-distance relationships if they move or when students go away to different schools and colleges. However, recent studies show that the Internet is causing many people to spend less time with friends and family. Sara Kiesler, a professor of social and decision sciences at Carnegie Mellon's Human-Computer Interaction Institute, hypothesizes, "Many users may be substituting Web browsing or chat rooms for their stronger, real-life relationships." Too much involvement in technological enhanced world is somewhere affecting their mental capabilities.

STRENGTHEN OF EMOTIONAL INTELLIGENCE AMONG YOUTH

Day-by-day technology is influencing today's youth and also affecting their emotional intelligence. Parents help children to connect feelings and emotions to social situations. Though all parents interact with their children, the opportunities they provide for learning emotional skills are not same. At times they may provide incorrect lessons about emotions or may feel inadequate to handle their children's emotions. These variations suggest that individuals operate from different emotional starting point i.e., the basis of emotional understanding is different for different people.

We can play a key role in supporting youth's emotional intelligence by encouraging them to be in touch with their emotional selves. The emotional lessons about cultivating inner strength that youth learn from the adults in their lives are powerful and long-lasting. When we ignore youth's feelings, youth come to believe their feelings are not important. When we repeatedly threaten or punish youth for a display of emotion, youth learn that emotions are dangerous things that need to be held inside and hidden—an invitation to later depression or rage.

It is needed to create real social and emotional assistance to improve social interaction abilities among young generations. Following are the suggestions to develop emotional intelligence among young generation:

- Try to make face-to-face interaction with people don't encourage young generation to get into the virtual world.
- Try to see yourself as others see you. Ask important people for feedback about your behavior. Face your reality and deal with it.

- Use internet for enjoyment doesn't make it the part of your life.
- Don't make emotional relations with virtual friends.
- Practice acting selfish and unselfish, and notice how people react.
- Parents should share their child's email account and password.
- Parents should interact with their young children about the people he or she is meeting online.
- Always place the computer in a busy part of the house, avoide young children to indulge them too much in virtual world.

There is need to create life-long learning opportunities for youths that take advantage of different time, different place education made possible by e-learning. Those opportunities need to reinforce social and emotional learning, as well as knowledge acquisition, as opposed to further isolating from each other.

References

Agarwal, J.C. (1966): Research in Education-An Introduction: Arya Book Depot: New Delhi.

Anastasi, A. (1968): Psychological Testing, MacMillan Company, London.

Bernet, M. 1996. Emotional intelligence; Components and correlates. Paper presented at the annual meeting of the American Psychological Association, Toronto, Canada.

Best, J.W. (1982): Research in Education: Prentice Hall: New Delhi.

Brubacher, T.S. (1947): History of the Problem of Education, McGraw Hill,. New York.

Gardner, H. (1995): Cracking open the IQ box. The American Prospect, (2), 71.

Garrett, H.E. (1962): Statistics in Psychology and Education, Allied Pacific Pvt. Bombay.

Goleman, D., Emotional Intelligence, Bantam Books, New York, 1995.

Good, C.V. (ed.) (1959): Dictionary of Education, McGraw Book Co.: New York.

Guildford, J.P. (1965): Fundamental Statistics in Psychology and Education, McGraw Hill Book Co., New York.

Mitra, A. (1998): Categories of Computer use and their Relationships with Attitude Toward Computers. *Journal of Research on Computing in Education,* Vol. 30(3), 281-92.

Sherman, R.C., End, C., Kraan, E., Martin, J. Cole, A., and Gardner, J. (1998): Sex Differences in Internet Use: Attitudinal and Experiential Correlates. Presented to the American Psychological Society Convention, Washington, May 1998.

http://www.country-day.com/philosophy2.htm (Accessed on 10.5.2011).

CHAPTER

38

Education for Empowerment of Women

NAGA RAJU ALLURI

ABSTRACT

Women's education in India has been one of the major issues of concern of the Government of India as well as the society at large. It is because of the fact that today the educated women play a very significant role in overall development and progress of the country. Women hold a prominent position in the Indian society as well as all over the world. Although in the Vedic period women had access to education in India, they had gradually lost this right. However, in the British period there was revival of interest in women's education in India. During this period, various socio-religious movements led by eminent persons like Raja Ram Mohan Roy, Iswar Chandra Vidyasagar emphasized on women's education in India. Mahatma Jyotiba Phule, Periyar and Baba Saheb Ambedkar were leaders of the lower castes in India who took various initiatives to make education available to the women of India. However, women's education got a fillip after the country got independence in 1947 and the government has taken various measures to provide education to all Indian women. As a result, women's literacy rate has grown over the three decades and the growth of female literacy has in fact been higher than that of male literacy rate. Education is a potent tool in the emancipation and empowerment of women. The greatest single factor which can incredibly improve the status of women in any society is education. It is indispensable that education enables women not only to gain more knowledge about the world outside of her hearth and home but helps her to get status, positive self-esteem, and self-confidence, necessary courage and inner strength to face challenges in life. A woman can only empower herself; organizations and, governments can play a role in supporting the journey and providing an enabling environment.

INTRODUCTION

Women's education in India has been one of the major issues of concern of the Government of India as well as the society at large. It is because of the fact that today the educated women play a very significant role in overall development and progress of the country. Women hold a prominent position in the Indian society as well as all over the world. There has been rapid increase in education of girls and women in recent decades in rural and urban areas. Discrimination in access to education does exist but with economic progress of the family, while the boy is given the first opportunity to go to school, the girl follows the same path. Again the notion of man being the primary earner has not been dismantled and is still embedded in the cultural value system of middle class; in poor families women make equal or more than half contribution towards the household economy. However, women's right and need to pursue their career and to have their own independent income and personality development has begun to be accepted and respected even by the middle classes. The effect of rapid increase in the education of girls is still to be felt because of almost decade and a half of gestation period required between changes in the attitude towards education of girls and expansion of facilities for education. But increase in the number and proportion of girls at different levels of education and tremendous drop in dropout rates indicate a strong trend in education of girls not only as a social obligation, of getting educated grooms (as found in my research in villages in 1961), but with a long-term need for their developing into empowered human beings. The Indian society is convinced about the empowering role of education, training and skill development for women at the individual level, and there is enormous expansion in the infrastructure for education in the public and the private sector, particularly in the urban areas. The urban and rural divide in provision of facilities for education is partly responsible for migration of young people to the urban areas. The demand for more educational facilities and of better quality is being met by more and more expansion in the private educational institutions.

WOMEN EDUCATION IN INDIA : A HISTORICAL PERSPECTIVE

Although in the Vedic period women had access to education in India, they had gradually lost this right. However, in the British period there was revival of interest in women's education in India. During this period, various socio-religious movements led by eminent persons like Raja Ram Mohan Roy, Iswar Chandra Vidyasagar emphasized on women's education in India. Mahatma Jyotiba Phule, Periyar and Baba Saheb Ambedkar were leaders of the lower castes in India who took various initiatives to make education available to the women of India. However, women's education got a fillip after the country got independence in 1947 and the government has taken various measures to provide education to all Indian women. As a result, women's literacy rate has grown over the three decades and the growth of female literacy has in fact been higher than that of male literacy rate.

In ancient India, women and girls received less education than men. This was due to the set social norms. Interestingly, in the Vedic period women had access to education, but gradually they had lost this right. Women education in ancient India prevailed during the early Vedic period. In addition to that Indian scriptures Rig Veda and Upanishads mention about several women sages and seers. Women enjoyed equivalent position and rights in the early Vedic era. However, after 500 B.C., the position of women started to decline. The Islamic invasion played a vital role in restricting freedom and rights of the women. A radical change attended and there was a terrific constraint for Women education in India.

Women education in medieval India further deteriorated with the introduction of Purdah system. Different customs and conventions of diverse religions like Hinduism, Islam, and Christianity further deteriorated the state of women in the country. A range of socio-religious movements contributed to the development of women literacy in the country. Many leaders took several initiatives to make education available to the women of India. The ordered form of women education in India was incorporated in the early centuries of the Christian era.

The position of the women education in India revived with the invasion of the British in the country and with the advent of Bhakti movement. The colonial period also introduced the institutional form of imparting learning. Women education in Colonial India witnessed an essential expansion. Various movements were launched to make women of the country literate. Furthermore, this progress journeyed through the years and influenced the modern Indian education system.

WOMEN EDUCATION IN MODERN INDIA

Women Education in Modern India is traced back to the years after the independence of the country. In the present times, the government of India takes measures to provide education to all women of the country. Women literacy rate seemingly rose in the modern days. This has actually helped women to achieve top positions at work place and also at society. Education is a potent tool in the emancipation and empowerment of women. The greatest single factor which can incredibly improve the status of women in any society is education. It is indispensable that education enables women not only to gain more knowledge about the world outside of her hearth and home but helps her to get status, positive self-esteem, and self-confidence, necessary courage and inner strength to face challenges in life. Apparently it also facilitates them to procure a job and supplement the income of family and achieve social status. Education especially of women has a major impact on health and nutrition as an instrument of developing a sustainable strategy for population control. Moreover, educated women can play an equally important role as men in nation-building. Thus, there is no denying fact that education empowers women. Indeed the different organs of the United Nations and experts on women's liberation argue for women's education as the basic step to attain equality with men.

The 2001 Census report indicates that literacy among women is only 54 percent. It is virtually disheartening to observe that the literacy rate of women in India is even much lower to national average, i.e. 65.38. The growth of women's education in rural areas is very slow. This obviously means that still large womenfolk of our country are illiterate, the weak, backward and exploited. Moreover, education is also not available to all equally. Gender inequality is reinforced in education which is proved by the fact that the literacy rate for the women is only 54% against 76% of men as per 2001 Census.

One of the recommendations of National Policy on Education (1986) by the Government of India is to promote empowerment of women through the agency of education and it is considered to be a landmark in the approach to women's education of illiterate. The National Literacy Mission is another positive step towards eradication of illiteracy in the age group of 15-35 years. Women's education has assumed special significance in the context of India's planned development, as it is incorporated in every five-year plans as the major programme for the development of women. This proves that educated women promote education in their family. Further, learned women can also help in the lessening of child death rate and expansion of population. In the modern era, women education is the replica of a Vedic model for instructive inspiration.

WOMEN EMPOWERMENT

Empowerment is not both a process and a result, that cannot be measured nor can it be taken by some individual or institution/organization and given to some body else. A woman can only empower herself; organizations (through logistic support) and, governments (through their gender just policies) can play a role in supporting the journey and providing an enabling environment. Women are empowered when they become aware of the unfair power relations they face and are able to take the challenge to overcome inequality. Empowerment enables women to take control over their lives and builds self-confidence and self-reliance. In order to build self-confidence and to evolve a female agenda, besides education, formation of coalitions to have a united strong voice is equally important.

Women are still unequal to men, but the last quarter of a century has seen tremendous improvement in their status through progress in education, in having better health and longevity of life and entry into jobs in the organized sectors. While we have found no direct correlation between increase in education with female work participation rate and representation in legislatures, education does lead to individual development and creates awareness about individual rights and is thus empowering at the individual level.

CAUSES FOR LOW LITERACY AMONG WOMEN IN INDIA

Women education is a multi-dimensional phenomenon. No single factor or cause can be held responsible for very low literacy rate of women in India. Subsequently it is associated with combination of many factors including social, cultural, economic, educational, demographic, political and administrative and so on. The following are some of the important factors which could be attributed for the present poor state of affairs of womenfolk in education.

- In many families girl children play the role of second mother by shouldering the responsibilities of household work such as looking after the sibling, fetching water, collecting firewood, bringing fodder for cattle, cleaning and cooking, etc. In rural India especially in poor families this traditional sex role makes girl child handicapped and conditioned by the attitude of mother and the family and discourages girl child to go school as it becomes secondary.

- Dowry system and other social practices act as main causes of the neglect of the girl child and discrimination against girl child including the deprivation of right of education. In many families especially poor and down-trodden think that if their daughters are educated more, they have to accumulate more assets and properties to provide as dowry in large proportion at the time of marriage, so prefer rather to either stop their children with average education and so on but never higher education. This prevails more in underprivileged families and communities
- In general, the school environment for girls in India is not really interesting and encouraging. The subjects taught in schools are also not related to the environment of girl children. The methods of teaching are mostly out-dated, rigid and uninteresting. There are still hundreds of schools with poor basic amenities such as drinking water, latrine and toilet facilities, improper building, and inadequate number of teachers' especially female teachers preferable for any parents for safety of their girl children from different types of exploitation and abuse.
- The lower enrolment of girls in schools is one of the foundational factors which stand as stumbling block for women empowerment in India. Reliable sources indicate that more than 50% of the Non-Starters (those who have never been to school) are girls. According to the latest statistics, two out of every ten girls in the age group of 6-11 are still not enrolled in schools.
- The incidence and prevalence of drop-outs among girls especially in rural, tribal and slum areas seem to be quite high. According to available sources, occurrence of drop-out and stagnation amongst girls is nearly twice that of boys all over India.

- Indian constitution and various legislations pertaining to education to children assure free and compulsory education all children of this nation but unfortunately the enforcement machinery fail to discharge its duties and responsibilities to the satisfaction of the public interest and welfare of women

MEASURES TO IMPROVE THE LITERACY LEVEL OF WOMEN IN INDIA

The following measures can be considered for bringing phenomenal change in the plight women's education and empowerment in India.

- The female child in every Indian family irrespective of socio-economic status should be moulded to overcome the challenges of inferiority; subservience and domesticity which place several limitations on her education and development. Every family irrespective its socio-cultural and economic background can take it a challenge to bring up their girl children as dignified human being with empowerment in physical, mental, economic and social dimensions of life.
- The Ministry of Education both at Centre and State level should work out strategic steps to stop firmly the ongoing high drop-outs among girls especially in rural, tribal and slum areas with the serious involvement of voluntary organisations in every locality to realize zero drop-out among girls.
- Appropriate steps should be taken by the educational authorities with the participation of communities in order to bring the girl children to the mainstream of education and development at every level including family and community.
- The Mid-day meal scheme and other educational supportive services like free text books, Note books, Free uniforms, Free Bicycles, Scholarships Free bus pass and so on can be provided in all states and

union territories to lift up the literacy level among girls.

- Government, voluntary sector and philanthropic organisations and individuals should come forward to provide free education for poor girls and provide free hostel facilities for girls studying in schools and colleges in every state of India. This will certainly encourage children of poor families to pursue good and higher education without much impediments.
- The parents of children belonging to poor, underprivileged families must be specially educated with proper social formula to help them to understand the significance of education for their girl children as foundation for empowerment.
- The law enforcing machinery should be made really effective with efficient monitoring vigilant system to implement the constitutional and legislative provisions and administrative measures to assure free and compulsory education for all children of this nation without any gender discrimination.

CONCLUSION

Women's education in India has been one of the major issues of concern of the Government of India as well as the society at large. It is because of the fact that today the educated women play a very significant role in overall development and progress of the country. Women hold a prominent position in the Indian society as well as all over the world. Education is a potent tool in the emancipation and empowerment of women. The greatest single factor which can incredibly improve the status of women in any society is education. It is indispensable that education enables women not only to gain more knowledge about the world outside of her hearth and home but helps her to get status, positive self-esteem, and self-confidence, necessary courage and inner strength to face challenges in life. A woman can only empower herself; organizations and governments can play a role in supporting the journey and providing an enabling environment.

References

Durant, Valerie L. and Sather, Zeba A., "Greater Investment in Children through Women's Empowerment: A Key to Demographic Change in Pakistan".

Gopalan, S., "Towards Equality—The Unfinished Agenda—Status of Women in India 2001", National Commission for Women, Government of India, 2002.

Government of India, Census of India, 2001.

Hamilton Roberta (1978), Liberation of Women, London, George Allen Publishers.

Jaya Kothai Pillai (1995), Women and Empowerment, Gyan Publishing House, New Delhi.

N.L. Gupta (2003), Women's Education Through Ages, Concept Publications Co., New Delhi.

R.K. Rao (2001), Women and Education, Kalpaz Publications, Delhi.

Saraswathi Mishra, Status of Indian Women, Gyan Publishing House, New Delhi, 2002.

CHAPTER

39

Empowerment for Backward Women Through Education

GHAZALA RASHID

INTRODUCTION

Education is the key factor in any social change. All educationists, social reformists agree with the statement that without education one society cannot be liberated from darkness. Empowerment of women is actually the empowerment of the society. By educating women we are actually educating a family. Woman is the companion of man, gifted with equal mental capacities. She has the right to participate in every minute detail in the activities of man and she has an equal right of freedom and liberty with him...By sheer force of a vicious custom, even the most ignorant and worthless men have been enjoying a superiority over women, which they do not deserve and ought not to have. Many of our movements stop halfway because of the conditions of our women.

If women are ignored and not educated enough then how is our country going to progress? There is a need to rehabilitate them to a place of honour. To focus attention on the problem concerning women all the world over, the decade 1975-86 was declared the International Women's Decade. In the same spirit 2001-02 was dedicated to Women's Empowerment stressed on seeking meaningful equality in social rights, elimination of discrimination in employment and universal education of women, the lack of which tends to perpetuate the unequal *status quo*. Empowerment of women, meaning thereby adequate access to resources, power and decision-making is a prerequisite towards gender justice. Such a situation can come about when there is equal participation in decision-making at family, society and other institutions of government. It needs to be recognized that any strategy which aims to empower women must be based on an understanding of, and to overcome the causes of the lack of power which lie behind it.

The draft National Policy for the Empowerment of Women (1996) observes that "A synergy of development measures will be affected and affirmative action designed for the holistic empowerment of women. Women will be given complete and equal access to and control over, factors contributing to such empowerment, particularly health, education, information, life-long learning for self-development, vocational skills, income earning opportunities, technical services, land and other forms of property, including through, common property resources, credit, technology and market, etc." "Equal access to education for women and girls will be ensured. Measures will be taken to eliminate discrimination, universalize education, eradicate illiteracy, create a gender-sensitive educational system, increase enrolment and retention rates of girls and improve the quality of education to facilitate to life-long learning as well as development of skills by women."

The social trend of India leave the vestige of sheer discrimination of sex. Women in Indian society irrespective of religion, territory and language suffer from sex discrimination and find themselves placed in subordination of men. They become the men's possession or property. This sex discrimination has been deep-rooted in society from time to immemorial. The position of all women of India is not the same in society. The problems of women of backward community are not the same as of women of upper caste community. There is need for improving the condition of women in the weakest sector—the rural, slum Muslim and tribal population (Hasan and Menon, 2005).

POLICIES/PLANS/PROGRAMMES AND ACTS SUPPORTING THE EDUCATION FOR WOMEN

Women have always been given a privileged status in law. Be it criminal law, constitutional law or family law, women have always found favour from Indian Law-makers. It was always believed that women need to be given special status so as to ensure its upliftment and prosperity which would bring prosperity for the whole society. The concept of women empowerment is enshrined in the Indian Constitution in its Preamble, Fundamental Rights, Fundamental Duties and Directive Principles. The number of articles of Indian Constitution guarantee greater freedom for women empowerment. It contains a number of provisions for the empowerment of women such as the following:

Article 14: Equality before Law

Article 15(1) provides for no discrimination by the state on the grounds of religion, race, caste, sex and place of birth.

Article 15(3) makes it mandatory for the state to make special provision for women and children.

Article 16 envisages equality of opportunity and gives status to women or workplace and in the matter of seeking empowerment.

Article 39(a) speaks out about state policy to be directed to securing the right to an adequate means of livelihood for men and women.

Article 39(d) guarantees non-discrimination in payment of salary and wages for women on the principle of equal pay for equal work, irrespective of sex.

Article 42 requires state to make provisions for securing just and humane condition of work and for maternity relief.

Article 51(A)(e) ensures to promote harmony and to renounce practices derogatory to the dignity of women.

The Indian Penal Code lists out various offences against women and ensures that due justice should received by aggrieved women and provides for exemplary deterrent punishment for the guilty.

The Indian Criminal Law guarantees safety to women against marital crimes, physical crimes and crimes against her modesty.

The Indian Succession Act, 1956 provides equal right to women to inherit property from her father and her father-in-law.

The Indian Marriage Act, 1955 was also directed to strengthen the rights of the women in matrimony.

The government made a number of efforts to raise the status of women. It enacted legislations to improve the condition of women and provide better opportunities for their development. There were the main acts passed by the government.

1955 : The Hindu Code Bill
1961 : The Dowry (Prohibition) Act
1961 : The Maternity Benefits Act
1971 : M.T.P. (Legalizing of Abortion)
1976 : Equal Remuneration Act
1986 : The Child Labour (The Prohibition and Regulation Act)

NATIONAL POLICY FOR THE EMPOWERMENT OF WOMEN, 2001 INDIA

The development of Women and Child Department of the Indian Government evolved a comprehensive policy in 2001, aiming at empowering women towards social justice, gender equality, developing capabilities, including those related to professional, science and technology and entrepreneurship. It highlights areas such as education, health nutrition, legal system, institutional mechanism, resource management, panchayatiraj institutions, etc., which can enable women in all walks of life.

EDUCATION AND RESERVATION : GIVING SAFETY, SECURITY IN SOCIETY

For quite some time, we are hearing of 33 percent reservation for women in different spheres like political/ education/employment fronts. At the panchayatiraj level, the government has already made amendments and the women have been given 33 percent reservation at the panchayat level.

The place of women in Free India is becoming more and more secure with the change of times. Women have a significant role in shaping the behavior and mental make up of the younger generation. Vivekanand said, "If you want the nation to prosper include women in every aspect of life." It is necessary to create an environment for women to seek knowledge and information in order to make informed choice at the own place.

But in spite of many efforts from government side, not enough progress has been made with regard to the education of minorities especially muslims, ST, SC. Now the question arises *why women are backward in education.*

There are many reasons for their backwardness in education.

1. Low Level of Girls' Education

Most Muslim girls have been to school; close to 60% of Muslim women report themselves to be illiterate and the school enrolment rate for Muslim girls is less than that of scheduled castes. Hardly 17% Muslim women (enrolled in schools) completed 8 years of schooling and less than 10% completed higher secondary schooling, which is below the national average. On the whole, Muslim women lag behind Hindus in enrolment and educational achievement for many reasons.

The enrolment of girls for vocational and special education is still not impressive. Some facilities are being provided to educational institutions but they are inadequate. Funds for women education are available but proper utilization is needed. Today there are more than 1,200 institutions (out of 9,200) for women in different disciplines. But a large number of them is still don't get entry into the higher education because of the limited opportunities, facilities and family problem.

2. Low Standard of Living

Poverty of parents is the chief cause of not sending their children to school. Saiyyid Hamid, a former vice-chancellor of AMU and a prominent member of the Sachar Committee says it is poverty not conservatism, which to an extent, is stopping Muslim parents from educating their children, both boys and girls, in a big way. They are too poor to afford expenses of travelling to school and the costs of clothes, books, etc.

3. Child Marriage

Puberty and early marriage are an effective brake on girls' education factors that never come in the way of boys' schooling. The girls are considered as a burden on their parents until they are married. Child marriage also exists in our rural as well as urban society. Therefore, the question of their education is hardly thought of.

4. Child Labour

Girls in rural areas from lower economic strata of the society do not attend schools and the educational level of such families whose girls do not attend schools is very low. Girls from such families either help their parents in work or earn their own livelihood.

Successful introduction of free and compulsory education up to the age of 14 will no doubt accelerate the pace of women's education and will be helpful in eliminating child labour.

5. Male Dominated Society

The society as a whole is male dominated and patriarchal in nature. The family system was paternal and the eldest male member was the final authority. This aspect subjugated the role of woman in social life. The role of women was limited and restricted to home life, especially looking after children, elders and their husbands.

6. Discrimination against Women by Birth (Bhrun Hatya)

If a female is murdered before her birth, how can we say that there is empowerment to women in India? It is unimaginable that any civilized society will actually kill the baby girl at birth. When a girl child is born, the gender bias is evident and this need is to be eliminated. There is a need of change of the outlook of the parents and the society towards the birth of girl child.

7. Unemployment

Women are in a disadvantageous position in social milieu and they are often prevented from carrying out a job successfully. They are treated unfairly. Women earn less than men in spite of similar qualifications and positions. After getting higher education Muslim women do not get satisfying jobs because of discrimination between different religions. That's why they do not want to get higher education. Some of them are deprived of higher education.

SUGGESTIONS

How to Improve Women's Status?

The past experience of Indian politics proves that political reservation for women is not essential to improve the status of women. Even without reservation we had many dynamic women politicians in pre-independence and post-independence period in India. Even without political reservation women in Indian society can improve their personalities and achieve equal status and rights in every field with men only when they become competent in education, will power, courage and adaptability. These aspects are discussed as follows:

(a) Education

History of civilization of the world has proved that education is the first and foremost requirement of human development of personality and status. Hence women can equalize themselves with men if they excel in education. Without proper education even if they enjoy the rights and facilities will hardly be benifited. The present state of women population in India clearly indicates that they need education first. Education helps the women to maintain high morale character and warns them against the ensuing oddities, educatiion helps in improving the economic status also. Children of educated mother prosper fast and maintain social etiquette better than others.

(b) Will-Power

Discrimination can make a person improved and able to raise status equal to others. If Indian women create will power, i.e. the power of determination in them they can reach to a peak of elevation. Hence, women can not aspire for betterment without determination.

(c) Courage

In India Hindu as well as Muslim societies in remote areas, women lose courage from the childhood and become dependable on man. In many occasions women are found displayed indomitable courage and velour which is no less than a man can play. This genius is common in all the females but the surrounding environment suppresses them from development. The women of the day need to develop their genius not by suppressing the genius but by generating in them the bravery.

(d) Adaptability

They are indolent or reluctant to accommodate themselves in the new disposition. The women should develop in them adaptability because adaptability contributes lot to a person's success and a successful woman in all respects commands reverence, dignity and high status in society equivalent to man.

The status of women's education is not merely an issue for pedagogic or academic discussion but a sociological problem. The women and men still live in different worlds with different access, opportunities incentives, rewards and legal protection. Experience around the world shows that educating women and empowering them with a stronger rule enhances the quality of not merely their own lives but also contributes to economic growth, survival, health of all members of the family, reduces fertility and helps slow population growth.

Education is thought not merely as an investment for

future exchange to employment but as an important tool to develop the growth of the person, with ability to develop rationality and to ask how and why of things and to wield the power to choose.

References

Giri, V. Mohini (2002), Emancipation and Empowerment of Women, pp. 215-16, 252, Gyan Publishing House, New Delhi.

Hasan, Z., and Menon, R. (2005), Educating Muslim Girls: A Comparison of Five Indian Cities. New Delhi: Women Unlimited.

Mandal, Jyotirmay (2004), Women and Reservation in India, pp. 253-56), Kalpaz Publications, Delhi.

Shah, Beena (2006), Women Higher Education and Empowermrnt (Challenges and Prospects) pp. 6-8, Y.K. Publishers, Agra.

Soni, J.K. (2008), Women's Education: Harnessing the Gender Power. New Delhi: Author's Press.

Wajihuddin, Mohammad, (6, June, 2011), *The Times of India*, New Delhi, p. 12.

CHAPTER

40

Social and Cultural Inclusion in Education

KUSUM LATA KAPOOR

ABSTRACT

Quality education is an education that is inclusive. It is an education that aims at the full participation by all learners, teaches attitudes and behaviours of tolerance and is therefore a vehicle for the construction of an inclusive and participative economy and society. Concern with educational inclusion cannot be dissociated from the need to ensure relevant quality education as a vehicle for the construction of an inclusive and participative society. Focusing on quality education for enhanced social inclusion implies identifying strategies for overcoming or eliminating the barriers to full participation in quality education for individuals and groups which experience discrimination, marginalisation and exclusion or which are particularly vulnerable. The teacher sees teaching as pulling out knowledge—"like mining". but Ladson-Billings contrasts this with the traditional, factory-based model of education as a process of assimilation, through which the teacher deposits knowledge into the child. Multicultural education is one of our most pressing necessities. Within our modern society of individualization, globalization, interculturality, completely different worldviews live together. All around us are different cultures.

SOCIAL AND CULTURAL EFFECT

A person's culture and upbringing has a profound effect on how they see the world and how they process information. Learning styles differ from culture to culture or from background to background. Learning habits also depend on the nature of a particular environment. A child's upbringing also has a profound effect on the way they learn, and this involves many aspects, including opportunities for play and interaction with other children, having access to books and other resources, having the chance to acquire a range of skills and interests and experiencing success, achievement, confidence, self-esteem and resilience. If a child is brought up in a secure, loving and encouraging environment, they will have a much more positive attitude towards learning. If a child has a healthy lifestyle they will also be much more capable of learning. Families may be a source of positive motivation within a children's life, encouraging them to believe in their abilities, and to have the confidence to meet different challenges at schools to facilitate learning.

HISTORY OF OUR INDIAN SOCIAL AND CULTURAL EDUCATION

Lets have a glance on the History of our Indian social and culture education system after British took hold of our education system :

In 1835, Lord Macauley laid successfully the foundation of modern education in India. The sole purpose was to educate Indians in such a way that they "should through western education get Anglicised in terms of both cultural and intellectual attainments".

Lord Macauley clearly said that, "we must at present do our best to form a class, who may be interpreters between us and the millions whom we govern; a class of persons, Indians in blood and colour, but English in taste, in opinions, in morals and in intellect." The reason was that it was too costly and practically impossible to import a large number of Englishmen to fill up the large and increasing number of subordinate or lower posts in administration.

The atmosphere was completely ready. Missionaries and their supporters as well as National leaders, intellectuals and Reformers not only welcomed but exerted pressure on the company to encourage and promote western education in India. Missionaries believed that modern education would lead the people to adopt Christianity. Humanitarians, intellectuals and nationalist leaders considered modern education "the key to the treasures of scientific and democratic thought of the modern West" and the best remedy for social, political and economic ills of the country.

The emphasis of British rulers was on English medium education system. In 1844 through an Declaration knowledge of English was made compulsory for Government employment. It made English medium schools very popular. The traditional Indian system of education gradually withered away for the lack of official support. Western literature and philosophy opened up the doors of knowledge and widened the mental horizons of Indian intelligentsia and gave Indians the understanding of liberal, and humanitarian ideas thought of Western World. It also equipped them with the intellectual tools, with which they could fight the oppressive British Raj.

Modern education also highlighted the weaknesses, rigidity and harshness of society towards the weaker sections of the society. It had attracted the attention of the people towards social evils, that had developed in the system. It gave access to all sections of Indian society to get educated irrespective of caste or creed. It brought social awakening and awareness amongst masses about their rights. But at the same time, it disassociated Indian people from their traditional way of learning, classical roots and knowledge. With it, faded Indian values, philosophies and traditions. It divided the

Indian people. It loosened the bonds of caste system. It also made them to loose their faith in social values. A group of Indian intelligentsia started feeling the social practices in India to be indefensible.

Modern education not only provided personnel to fill the lower levels in administration, as desired by the rulers, but also produced national leaders, intellectuals and reformers like Raja Ram Mohan Roy, Dadabhai Naoroji, Ferozeshah Mehta, Gokhale, Gandhi, Jinnah, Ambedkar, Tilak, Lala Lajpat Rai, Moti Lal Nehru, Jawahar Lal Nehru, Netaji Subhash Chandra Bose, Patel and many more. They took upon themselves the responsibility to build a modern, open, plural, culturally rich, prosperous and powerful India out of a fragmented, poverty stricken, superstitious, weak, indifferent, backward and inward looking society.

Social Reformers advised people to remain firmly rooted to the Indian Culture. They tried to revive their own rich ancient culture and prevent the masses from being swayed away by the glamour and materialism of alien culture. Organisations like Brahma Samaj (1928) in Bengal, Prarthana Samaj in Maharashtra (1867), Arya Samaj in Northern India, Rama Krishna Mission, Theosophical Society of India (1879), Dev Samaj in Lahore and Servants of India Society took up the job to awaken the masses. They talked about the greatness of Hindu Vedic culture and about Vedas as the source of all knowledge and truth. Swami Vivekanand founded the Rama Krishna Mission tried to reveal to the world Indian Philosophy and culture. Some reform institutes like Vivekanand's or Rama Krishna Mission or Theosophical Society of India tried to familiarize the Western World, too, to the charm and graciousness of Indian Culture.

Swami Vivekanand and many others gave a call to "Return to Vedas". He said, "Each nation like each individual has a theme in this life, which is its center, the principle note, around which every other note comes to form the harmony. If any nation attempts to throw off its national vitality, the direction, which has become its own through the transmission of centuries, the nation dies."

CONFLICTING VIEWS OF CULTURE

The question of developing student's cultural competence is a complex one due to the conflicting definition of culture within the field of multicultural education. These definitions range from symbolic analysis understanding of culture as representational, constructivist, and changing to a socio-cultural systems analysis understanding of culture as a fixed set of shared beliefs and practices passed down from generation to generation. Within literature relating to culturally Relevant Pedagogy in particulars, Mcintyre *et. al.*, (2001) take a definitively symbolic stance with regards to culture and its transmission and that no list can be flexible and dynamic enough to describe an individual's point of view, let alone the points of view of a group of individuals. A different point of view can be found in the Ladson-Billings (2004), who draws upon the work of Foucault (1991) and Bennet (1992) in her assertion that "culture is created through the processes of social management, and that it is both the object the instrument of government". This definition views culture as material changeable and interactive, but also as a political entity with direct relationships to the power hierarchy of a given society. Ladson-Billings goes on to assert that measures towards standardization of curriculum and assessment reinforce the mythology of the dominant culture as superior and underline the reliance of dominance on subjugation. As such the hierarchical nature of culture can be understood as a necessity for the maintenance of power and privilege.

Gaye (2000) uses culture to refer to "a dynamic system of social values, cognitive codes, behavioral standards, worldviews, and beliefs used to give order and meaning to our own lives as well as the lives of others. This definition also views culture as one element of an inter-subjective realty that evolves over time and place. It is important to understand that each individual is slightly different, and sometimes radically different. When they refer to culture and cultural competence.

THE EDUCATIONAL IMPACT OF CULTURE AND CULTURAL LEARNING

Culture has a powerful role to play in delivering effective educational outcomes. Local authorities, schools and partners can use culture to offer young people, families and the wider community personalised and universal experiences across the curriculum and extended services.

Working in partnership with cultural organisations can develop the workforce and expand the expertise that an integrated children's service can draw on. BSF provides opportunities for schools and local authorities to forge new partnerships with cultural organisations or strengthen existing ones. Cultural practitioners such as artists, musicians, archivists and librarians can make a valuable contribution to the learning workforce.

QUALITY EDUCATION FOR SOCIAL INCLUSION

While the traditional conception of inclusive education aims at the mainstream participation of individual learners with special educational needs, concern with social inclusion focuses on all learners. Indeed, many vulnerable groups of children and youth, including girls and young women, those who are working, who are forced to seek refuge or are displaced, orphans, those who belong to linguistic, cultural or religious minorities, and those living in situations of extreme poverty, insecurity and of conflict, and those infected or affected by HIV/AIDS, continue to be excluded from quality education. Additionally, little attention has been paid to a new kind of vulnerability that results from the inability of well-educated people coming from medium or even high-income backgrounds to insert themselves productively and/or socially in the society, generating the so-called disaffiliation. If social inclusion is to be taken into consideration, then a change of attitude would seem to be required, turning from a demand-based approach to a need-based one. Additionally, it is necessary that the most privileged of the society—who are usually also at the top of the decision-making process—be willing to act towards social integration.

Last, but not least, the marginalized and vulnerable populations are not always consulted or included in the search for good alternatives for ensuring the quality of education for social inclusion. However, it seems that the degree of consultation and stakeholder participation in policy dialogue, formulation and implementation and linkages to other sector policies (health, youth, labour, finance, etc.), are both very important to guarantee quality education for all adolescents and young people. It is now recognised that the challenge of achieving education for all is not solely one of access and initial enrolment, but also of regular attendance, retention, attainment and achievement. This implies not only that marginalized and vulnerable groups of children and youth actually have equitable access to educational opportunities, but also, that equitable participation in quality education be ensured for all individual learners and groups. Moreover, a social inclusion perspective on quality education is also concerned with the need to ensure that learning opportunities contribute to effective inclusion of individual and groups of youth into the wider socio-economic, civic and cultural fabric of society.

Quality education is therefore an education that is inclusive. It is an education that aims at the full participation by all learners, teaches attitudes and behaviours of tolerance and is therefore a vehicle for the construction of an inclusive and participative economy and society. Concern with educational inclusion cannot be dissociated from the need to ensure relevant quality education as a vehicle for the construction of an inclusive and participative society. Focusing on quality education for enhanced social inclusion implies identifying strategies for overcoming or eliminating the barriers to full participation in quality education for individuals and groups which experience discrimination, marginalisation and exclusion or which are particularly vulnerable.

LEARNING ENVIRONMENT AND SCHOOLING PROCESS

To take the learner's background into account means to address the issues of learning contents, processes and learning environments in a very different way as it was done in the past.

Now, the teacher sees teaching as "pulling out knowledge—'like mining'". But Ladson-Billings contrasts this with the traditional, factory-based model of education as a process of assimilation, through which the teacher deposits knowledge into the child.

In the past it was thought that the learning contents, processes and environments had to be homogeneous and could be defined in an abstract way. In fact, diverse problems arose. In many cases the learning contents were biased. Stereotyping or mono-cultural and monolingual approaches were—and still are—widespread. The concern with the relevance of learning content to changing societal realities and needs was insufficient. Nowadays there are many efforts to promote the integration of rights education, gender equality, HIV/AIDS and preventive education, respect for human dignity and diversity and also concepts and skills linked to the emergent new economy. However, these efforts are still not always reflected in the day-by-day educational practices in schools for adolescents and young people. Perhaps one of the reasons for this imbalance between innovation in the prescribed learning contents and reality might be that processes of education are an often overlooked dimension of quality. How knowledge, skills, competencies, values and attitudes are transmitted and shaped are as important as the content of the officially prescribed curriculum.

CULTURALLY RELEVANT PEDOGOGY

Practitioners of Culturally Relevant Pedagogy posses a wide range of pedagogical skills that directly reinforce their belief in the importance of developing students cultural competence. The teacher in Ladson-Billings (1994) study enacted this belief in at least three essential ways :

- The teacher helps students make connections between their community, national, and global identities. Teachers accomplish this by bringing the student's backgrounds to the centre of the classroom curriculum and pedagogical practices.

- Before teachers can recognize and affirm student's cultural heritage, they need to be comfortable with their own cultural selves. This competence can be developed through, pre-service home-stay with a family in the community where this will be placed. Additionally, cultural competence among teachers should be furthered throughout the teaching year through a service learning partnership with a local non-profit agencies, churches, and community centers. A third component of developing personal cultural competence involves interacting with students in their home and community settings.
- The third tenet of Culturally Relevant Pedogogy is "critical multiculturalism". She cites McLaren (1994) as putting forth the idea that "multiculturalism without a transformative political agenda can be just another form of accommodation to the larger social order".

Bennet describes the characterstics of an effective teacher as including pride in teaching, awareness of societal conditions of discrimination and injustice and non-assimilationist pedagogical stances. Their teaching, the defining elements of which are high levels of academic success across all areas, student cultural competence, and the "drawing out" of the child's valuable, and valued home culture, clearly reflects their axiological orientation. This definition fits closely with the three tenets at Culturally Relevant Pedagogy as put forth Ladson-Billings in Crossing over to Canaan. She asserts that culturally relevant pedagogy is based on three propositions about what contributes to success for all students. These propositions are :

- Successful teachers focus on student's academic achievement.
- Successful teachers develop student's cultural competence.
- Successful teachers foster student's sense of sociopolitical consciousness (Ladson-Billings, 2001, a.144).

MULTICULTURAL EDUCATION

In two diverse conceptual frameworks for multicultural education, Christine Bennett and George Bank both describe Equity pedagogy as one of the four major tenets of multicultural Education (Bank, 2004; Bennett, 2001). Bank and Bennett both include Equity pedagogy as an integral dimension of multicultural education. Banks' description focuses on a paradigmatic understanding of ways to teach minority. Children, ranging historically from a cultural deficit model to the current struggle between the more empowering cultural difference model and the "at-risk" model that has reintroduced cultural deprivation theory using new terminology. He touches upon both learning styles and teaching styles, and includes a special emphasis on language within the domain of seconds language acquisition and application (Banks, 2004). The foci of Bennett's Equity Pedagogy cluster are broader, including school and classroom climate, student achievement, and cultural styles in teaching and learning. The emphasis of the first genre in this cluster is on the exploration of positive school and classroom climate in terms of the etiological orientation of teachers and administrators using student achievement, and inter-group relations as corollaries. The second genre other discussion of student achievement focusing on effective teaching of historically underserved children. The third genre, Cultural Style in Teaching and Learning, further emphasizes the role of culture in effective pedagogy and specifically the role of the teacher in understanding student culture and implementing relevant pedagogy.

AIM OF MULTICULTURAL PEDAGOGY

The aim of multicultural pedagogy is to create stimuli, so that every single person can build up his/her own identity. In practice, how do we try to do that? Dr. Schmeltzer listed the following fundamental characteristics of an multicultural school:

1. A fear-free learning environment.
2. Learning in mixed groups.

3. Whole-day school. This is a very important factor for intercultural togetherness: the children must have a lot of time to be together.
4. An International College of Teachers. Teachers with direct experience of immigration or an immigration background can better understand the condition of their pupils.
5. In the classes there should always be an atmosphere of multilingualism.
6. Presentation of Social Projects, etc.

CONCLUSION

Finally, updating educational contents and improving educational processes only will be effective if the learning environment is also improved accordingly to the needs of each context. Both the physical environment of learning (adequate attention paid to the promotion of physical and mental health, safety and security), as well as the psycho-social environment of learning (absence of gender or minority discrimination, bullying, corporal punishment) will enable or hinder learning the needed contents through the adequate processes to form competencies for inclusion, thanks to inclusive education.

References

David, J. Sousa, Mustafa, Ozcan, The Impact of Culture on a Child's Learning, ECSWE Newsletter No 24, Nov. 2010, Kusum Lata Kapoor, Cultural Relevance and Montessori, July 2008.

Lata Sinha, Sept. 2009, Impact of Modern Education on Indian Society.

Matthew Lynch: Examining the Impact of Culture on Academic Performance, June 30, 2011.

NVQ Level 3, Supporting Teaching and Learning in Schools.

Quality Education and Social Inclusion, Discussion Paper: IBE, in collaboration with OEI and UNESCO.

CHAPTER

41

Knowledge Management

An Organizational Approach

OSMAN BIN SALAM, S. VENKATESHWAR RAO
AND G. SRINIVAS

ABSTRACT

Knowledge Management efforts typically focus on organizational objectives such as improved performance, competitive advantage, innovation, the sharing of lessons learned, integration and continuous improvement of the organization. KM efforts overlap with organizational learning, and may be distinguished from that by a greater focus on the management of knowledge as a strategic asset and a focus on encouraging the sharing of knowledge. KM includes courses taught in the fields of business administration, information systems, management, and library and information sciences more recently, other fields have started contributing to KM research; these include information and media, computer science, public health, and public policy.

Key Words: Knowledge Management, Competitive Advantage, innovation, public health.

INTRODUCTION

Knowledge Management (KM) comprises a range of strategies and practices used in an organization to identify, create, represent, distribute, and enable adoption of insights and experiences. Such insights and experiences comprise knowledge, either embodied in individuals or embedded in organizational processes or practice.

Many large companies and non-profit organizations have resources dedicated to internal KM efforts, often as a part of their 'business strategy', 'information technology', or 'human resource management' departments. Several consulting companies also exist that provide strategy and advice regarding KM to these organizations.

KNOWLEDGE AND INFORMATION ARE DIFFERENT

The different operational purposes of knowledge and information in the enterprise are quite clear, albeit explicated knowledge is typically communicated as information in one form or another. When considering how knowledge affects personal decision-making and reasoning, we need to understand what knowledge is and how it relates to information.

Knowledge consists of facts, perspectives, concepts, mental reference models, truths, beliefs, judgments, expectations, methodologies, and know-how. The purpose of knowledge is to determine and implement effective action, partially by providing people with capabilities with which to reason. In part, knowledge also consists of understanding of how to juxtapose and integrate seemingly isolated information items to develop new meanings to create new insights with which to approach effective handling of target situations. Knowledge is used to evaluate and handle situations, that is, assess, decide, problem solve, plan, act, and monitor. As such, knowledge is mostly tacit, implicit, difficult to examine, and, for the most part, cannot be managed directly, only indirectly by managing knowledge-related processes.

Information consists of data organized to characterize a particular situation, condition, context, challenge, or opportunity. The purpose of information is to describe and specify conditions, things, concepts—any kind of describable concrete or abstract objects. As such, information is explicit, readily examined, and its management requires conscientious and detailed attention to mechanical manipulation, storage, presentation, and distribution. Since both the purpose and nature of information is different from knowledge, it implies that KM is fundamentally different than information management. Knowledge and information are not part of a continuum and need to be managed separately and diligently by separate disciplines.

INFORMATION IS SUBORDINATE TO KNOWLEDGE

The different roles of knowledge and information in support of work of any kind are indicated, which also illustrates why KM and information management are both separate and necessary. However, one very important issue that has been overlooked in many organizations is the need for information and knowledge to match, and, in particular, for information to match the situation-handling that is governed by the application of available knowledge. For knowledge to be fully applicable, it must have access to information that matches in timeliness, granularity, and all other dimensions of concern. Ideally, information must also be accessible in ways that do not impede situation-handling.

Taking into account the literatures on knowledge management and organisational learning, the Knowledge Processes Wheel, a framework of knowledge processes has been defined (see Figure 2). It addresses the possible knowledge management practices that an organisation might implement to continuously maintain and develop its knowledge assets.

Fig. 1
Difference between Information and Knowledge

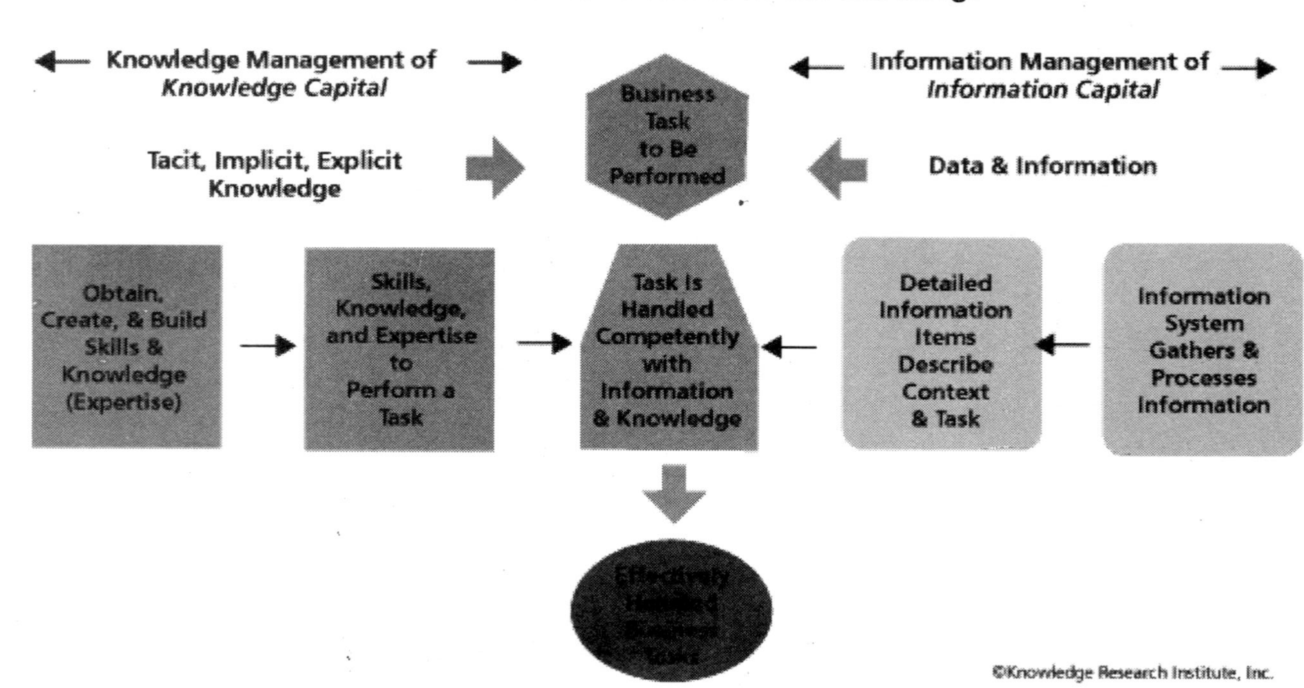

FIG. 2
The Knowledge Processes Wheel

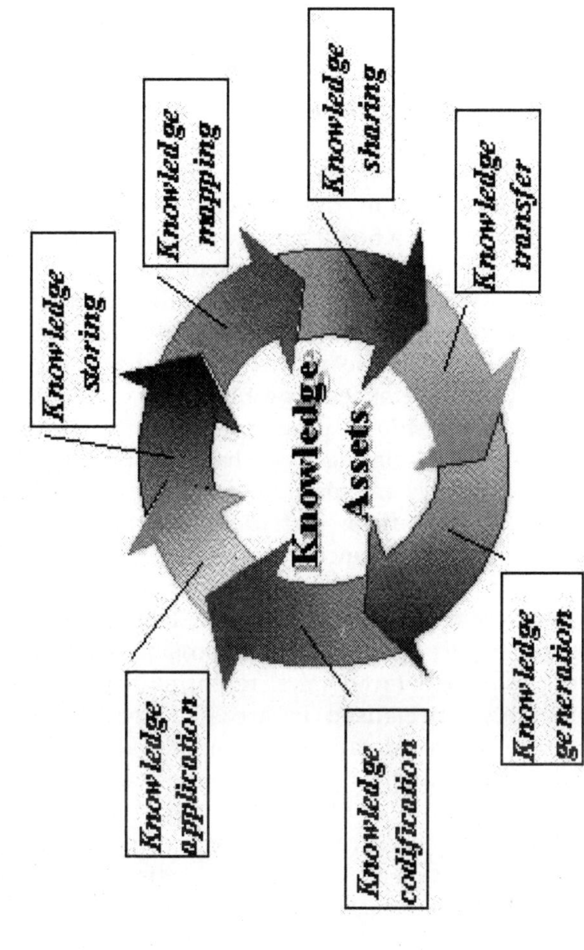

Source : Marr and Schiuma, 2001; Carlucci *et. al.*, 2004.

Each of the knowledge processes will be explained in the following :

Knowledge generation includes a set of processes executed in order to increase the stock of corporate knowledge assets. Its aim is to allow organisation to develop knowledge assets. It is possible to recognize two main sub-processes of knowledge generation, which are the knowledge acquisition and the knowledge creation.

Knowledge acquisition is the process of capturing and bringing knowledge from the external environment into the internal context of a company. The most direct way to acquire knowledge assets from the external environment of the company is to buy it. Knowledge acquisition can be performed by scanning the external environment and identifying and capturing knowledge for instance in the form of patents, practices and technologies. Alternative methods are either to acquire knowledge assets or to rent them, e.g. paying consultants to resolve specific problems, or to obtain them by building up relationships, e.g. setting up joint ventures or other forms of agreements aiming to exchange knowledge.

Some companies are specialised in providing a support to acquire knowledge from outside the organisation; these companies perform the function of knowledge brokers. Teltech for instance is a company helping other organisations to get access to external technical know-how. It provides four main services: the expert network, i.e. the possibility to be linked to a network of experts (academics, recent retirees from industry, or consultants) specialised in areas of specific knowledge expertise; the assisted database searches, i.e. access to over 1600 online databases with support of knowledge analysts; the vendor service, i.e. a service to search particular products or services; and the technical alert service, i.e. a system that provides information about the most significant technical developments from researches around the world (Davenport, 1998).

Knowledge creation is the process of developing new knowledge assets within the company. Adopting a cognitive approach it can be considered as the result of an information interpretation process performed by individuals within the organisation. Knowledge creation within a company is then strictly tied to individual learning processes and can be the result of either a fortuitous individual activity or a planned organizational policy. The most effective way to create knowledge within an organisation is to motivate employees to be creative and learning-oriented, as well as to dedicate specific resources to these processes. A common way to generate knowledge is to establish organizational units specifically for the purpose of knowledge generation, such as a R & D departments.

Knowledge mapping is the process of identifying knowledge assets within the organisation and of defining ways of getting them. Often, much of the knowledge people require to solve problems already exists within an organisation, but it is not easily available when needed. All organisational knowledge has to be accessible, as this makes the process of creating new knowledge assets more efficient and effective. Knowledge mapping is usually supported by knowledge storing technologies that make knowledge either available when it is necessary or enable employees to locate where the knowledge resides and how it can be acquired.

Knowledge sharing is the process by which the knowledge is disseminated across the organisation. Knowledge sharing contains two process dimensions, formal and informal processes used to distribute by knowledge throughout the organisation. For example, knowledge can be shared in formal processes such as meetings, seminars and workshops, by using co-workers, company knowledge data-bases and internal documents. On the other hand, informal processes consist mainly of informal discussions between individuals that can be encouraged by the organisation which can define time, space and social initiatives for this purpose. This can be achieved by defining suitable places to socialize or scheduling tea/coffee breaks to encourage people to meet. Specific knowledge projects aimed to support knowledge sharing processes can be implemented within organisation. For example, internal benchmarking practices allow identifying organizational best practices and strategic know-how as well as finding approaches to better spread and exploit them. Further knowledge sharing can be supported by the use of ICT, e.g. Groupware, on-line databases, data warehousing/knowledge repositories, intranets, decision-support tools. The strategy to adopt ICT appears to be one of the most followed managerial practices within the organisation, but just the implementation of ICT does not ensure knowledge sharing. Individuals generate knowledge and they have to be encouraged to share their knowledge, ICT can just be a facilitator. Therefore, an investment in ICT that disregards the human dimension of the knowledge sharing process will inevitably fail.

Knowledge transferring is the process of passing on knowledge between cognitive systems. When it takes place within a firm among different units, groups or individuals, it overlaps with knowledge sharing. Instead, when it involves the inter-organizational dimension, it has common characteristics with many knowledge acquisition processes. The main difference between the two knowledge transfer processes is the disparity in their intention. The former endeavors to make individual or team knowledge organizational knowledge. The latter works towards creating a channel and context to enable the organisation to acquire knowledge which has been generated outside the firm's borders. Both processes, intra and inter-organisational knowledge transfer, are based on a communication process that involves both information and interpretation processes in order to allow the knowledge owned by the sender to be acquired and absorbed by the receiver. It is important to point out that the nature of the transferred knowledge should determine the communication characteristics. For instance, when the knowledge is tacit the communication is better performed by socializations or facilitated by multimedia communication technology. The effectiveness and efficiency of knowledge transfer processes is affected by the absorptive capacity of the receiver, which is related to a shared knowledge background between sender and receiver. If they share a common technical and cultural experience the performance of the knowledge transfer process is improved by reducing the ambiguity of the information interpretation process.

Knowledge Codification is the process that aims to formalize knowledge into appropriate codes. It involves three main dimensions: capturing knowledge, which consists of identifying the knowledge related to a specific ability; knowledge externalization, which involves changing the nature of knowledge from tacit to explicit; and knowledge representation, which involves a description of the explicit knowledge with an appropriate set of information codes.

Knowledge storing is the process of saving knowledge within the organisation, meant to make knowledge available anytime and anywhere. Knowledge storing is at the heart of knowledge mapping and can take the form of either knowledge databases, in which codified knowledge is stored in appropriate information codes, or of yellow pages, which provide links to people with specific know-how. The former is based on the idea that knowledge can be codified and made available to be retrieved electronically. This is an approach followed by many consultant companies such as Arthur Andersen, Andersen Consulting and Ernst and Young which have developed and adopted best practices databases to support the activities of consultants spread out around the world. In the latter only some information about potential knowledge resources are stored that assist in identifying the people and the places where knowledge resides. For example, Hoffmann-LaRoche, as a part of its overall Drug Approval Process knowledge map, included a Yellow Page catalogue of relevant experts, arranged according to know-how, questions and issues.

Knowledge application is the process of applying knowledge within the organisation. The knowledge is a value-added resource only if it is applied within the organisation and its processes. Knowledge becomes an organisational innovation only if it is applied to improve business performance. The knowledge application is most of the time a question of turning knowledge into action. Often the differences in organisational performance come not only from differences in what companies know, but rather from their ability

CONCLUSION

The growth in developed as well as developing countries is a function of the inclusion of knowledge, every organization has to work for obtaining knowledge, so as to bring a good and fruitfull result the organization need to work on bringing the knowledge assets to the organization, knowledge as a strategic resource can also if it knows how to attract, retain and motivate superior knowledge workers.

References

Addicott, Rachael; McGivern, Gerry; Ferlie, Ewan (2006). "Networks, Organizational Learning and Knowledge Management: NHS Cancer Networks". *Public Money and Management*, 26(2): 87–94. doi:10.1111/j.1467-9302.2006.00506.

Alavi, Maryam; Leidner, Dorothy E. (1999). "Knowledge Management Systems: Issues, Challenges, and Benefits". *Communications of the AIS*, 1(2).

Alavi, Maryam; Leidner, Dorothy, E. (2001). "Review: Knowledge Management and Knowledge Management Systems: Conceptual Foundations and Research Issues". *MIS Quarterly*, 25(1): 107–36. doi:10.2307/3250961. JSTOR 3250961.

Andriessen, Daniel (2004). "Reconciling the rigor-relevance dilemma in intellectual capital research". *The Learning Organization*, 11(4/5): 393–401.

Andrus, D. Calvin (2005). "The Wiki and the Blog: Toward a Complex Adaptive Intelligence Community". *Studies in Intelligence*, 49(3).

Benbasat, Izak; Zmud, Robert (1999). "Empirical research in information systems: The practice of relevance". *MIS Quarterly*, 23(1): 3-16. doi:10.2307/249403. JSTOR 249403.

Bontis, Nick; Choo, Chun Wei (2002). The Strategic Management of Intellectual Capital and Organizational Knowledge. New York: Oxford University Press. ISBN 019513866X.

Booker, Lorne; Bontis, Nick; Serenko, Alexander (2008). "The Relevance of Knowledge Management and Intellectual Capital Research". *Knowledge and Process Management*, 15(4):

Capozzi, Marla M. (2007). "Knowledge Management Architectures beyond Technology". *First Monday*, 12(6).

Davenport, Tom (2008). "Enterprise 2.0: The New, New Knowledge Management?". *Harvard Business Online*, Feb. 19, 2008.

Ferguson, J. (2005). "Bridging the Gap between Research and Practice". *Knowledge Management for Development Journal*, 1(3): 46-54.

CHAPTER

42

Knowledge Management

Issues and Challenges for Developing Countries

Sadaqat Ali, Javed Khan and Mohd. Taqi

ABSTRACT

The present study is an attempt to analyze of issues and challenges in Knowledge Management in developing countries. Knowledge has always been viewed from multiple perspectives—abstract, philosophical, religious and practical throughout the history. Active management of their knowledge assets is mandatory for success. Drawing from reported private sector experiences, some issues, challenges and opportunities for government services provision are examined. A suggested implementation approach highlights leadership, culture, technology, and measurement as critical success factors. Examining some Indian government early practices, the paper advocates for "communities of practice", cautions on "best practices" and concludes with recommendations. In the knowledge-based society, organizations often encounter problems as they seek to manage knowledge. Consequently, they try to identify the causes of these problems and find solutions. In this article, we develop a knowledge management problems-causes-solutions framework that encompasses: problems associated with knowledge creation, retrieval, transfer and application; causes, including organizational, human-related and technical dimensions; and both IT and non-IT solutions.

Keywords: Knowledge assets, Knowledge management, Communities of practice, e-Government.

INTRODUCTION

Knowledge management research and practice have grown at a dramatic pace in the last few years. Given the intensively competitive climate, organizations position themselves as knowledge-driven companies, seeking to leverage their knowledge resources in order to achieve competitive advantage. However, organizations are confronted by a variety of knowledge management (KM) problems. These problems can be addressed both by identifying the causes and by developing solutions. Prior research in the KM arena has tended to focus on organization-level initiatives, as well as senior management and their strategic application of KM.

It seems strange to talk about the new economy perhaps because there isn't a readily agreed upon definition of what it is, when it first appeared or just what we are supposed to do differently. Some might describe the new economy in terms of new products or services that have recently become available—palm pilots, cell phones, the Internet, etc. Others might define the new economy in terms of the new tools and technologies that permit us to manage data and information faster and better than ever enabling us to discover if not create knowledge. Enterprise Resource Planning systems that enable new businesses such as ecommerce, data mining tools that help us manage tremendous amounts of data so as to better understand customer behavior and supply chain management systems that help us to better manage our supply chains are but a few examples. While we have always been concerned with managing data and information in order to improve organizational efficiency and effectiveness, today the Internet and related technologies have enabled us to make data, information and even knowledge available to anyone at anytime. This has resulted in not only more efficient business processes but also in more effective learning and innovation. One thing that distinguishes the new economy from the old one is speed—the speed of data capture, processing, and dissemination. The speed of learning and innovation enable firms to more effectively compete in today's highly competitive global economy. Perhaps the most important distinguishing feature of the new economy, however, is that it has become a knowledge economy where "knowledge, not labor or raw material or capital, is the key resource" of production. As customers demand and receive more customization at ever diminishing costs from knowledge-oriented private sector firms, they have also come to expect similar benefits from the public sector. Public sector organizations generally do not operate as private sector organizations. Consequently, fulfilling the needs of customers in the new economy is not an easy task. Poised to operate in a reasonable manner, just as private organizations, governments are now embarking on e-Government and even e-Commerce. However, they might not succeed in these endeavors without actively engaging in managing their key resources. The rest of this paper contributes to an understanding of how this can be achieved through knowledge management (KM).

Knowledge sharing networks and especially CoPs provide an easy entry point in KM with enormous benefits. They readily overcome cultural barriers to knowledge sharing. They offer the opportunity and ability to manage organizational knowledge, on which the level of social capital can be released. Furthermore, they act like gene pools within which the ability to evolve future solutions lie. Through such communities the issues of trust and motivation essential to ensuring continuity in KM can also be addressed. Governments should set-up CoPs for webmasters and helpdesks as suggested earlier. These CoPs can support and ensure e-government and government E-Commerce services.

Government can and should replicate instances of successful KM practices from the private sector. The payoff is a smarter government, offering veritable government e-Commerce and e-Government services to its citizens and customers. KM systems are much more complex than traditional IM systems. With a history of high IM system failure rate in governments [44], KM projects should be initiated and carried out in small manageable phases. In these phases, reinvention should be avoided at all costs. It is important to reuse what is known or available, to the limit possible. There should be a focus on organizational culture and norms, external knowledge, past experience and technologies. Considering the wide array of activities involved, an incremental approach as suggested in this paper is highly recommended. In this process, a street light analogy can be made: Technology is the green light, leadership is the yellow (amber) light and culture is the red light. Unlike in other business areas, where technology is a major barrier to success, technology has a minimal effect on KM compared to the other CSF. Technological solutions are already available for veritable KM efforts that can handle all the technical and soft aspects but care must be exercised in selecting and putting in place an appropriate infrastructure.

Capabilities for leadership in KM, required for roles of the CKO come from various backgrounds. Success depends on how much the CKO can understand the intricacies of all the processes and CSF involved and how he/she can respond to the challenges. Culture as the red light is the biggest barrier to KM. Its impact is often under estimated or even ignored. If an organization is unable to handle cultural issues properly, it should probably stay with IM, rather than attempting KM.

Finally, "Best practices" are a good starting point, but organizations should be conscious of the pitfalls of using them. These practices should not be used in isolation. They should be integrated with other endeavors such as CoPs. Award winning state organizations such as the CTG, which act as enablers and catalysts for innovative application of technology in government agencies should be transformed.

GOVERNMENT KNOWLEDGE CENTERS

This will give them the opportunity to be more involved in KM while still performing their current activities. This means they would not be confined to producing "Best Practices" that might soon become outdated or not used at all as they are doing now, but they would effectively help government agencies to implement KM, which is an imperative for governments in the 21st century and the new economy.

THE IMPORTANCE OF KNOWLEDGE MANAGEMENT (KM)

Interest in KM has surged in recent years. Scholarly publications have increased. Courses, certificate or degree programs are being introduced in some universities, for example. Many more organizations are now engaged in it. Research conducted by Teltech Corporation three years ago, showed that KM was taken seriously. The results of the research reported in concluded that forty-five percent of the respondents had no major interest in KM. Forty percent indicated only an unconscious readiness. Nine percent indicated some formal leadership support for KM, and only six percent indicated they had integrated KM into their performance appraisal. Another report by on a subsequent Teltech study barely a year later indicated that fifty percent of the companies were engaged in KM, and doing so because of expected savings. The other fifty percent was concerned with growth and quality of service. The importance and necessity of KM cannot be overemphasized. Its timeless nature has been discussed by [4], illustrating its role in the construction of the pyramids at Giza. Research carried out at the National Defense University involving public and private sector participants concluded that as far as the necessity and importance of KM is concerned, not much has changed from what it was during the days of the construction of the pyramids. The necessities to develop organizations' social and structural capital, innovate, transfer knowledge across time, space and boundaries as well as satisfy customers remain in place. We contend that the reason why the above needs have remained uncharged is that the task of building and maintaining various structures—nations by governments and businesses by firms is analogous to that of building the pyramids. One conclusion that can be drawn from the research is that regardless of whether it is a new or old economy KM is essential. From this conclusion, the rationale for KM is fully justified. Furthermore, due to the influence of various technologies and the globalization of world trends, KM presents a viable alternative for firms to create and maintain competitive advantage in turbulent economies. A compelling reason for this is the fact that unlike physical goods that are subject to decreasing returns, knowledge appreciates and consequently yields increasing returns. Many governments are still living in the 'apparent' luxury of non-competitive environments. The INDIA government sees the situation quite differently and is poised to be a major player in the expected knowledge-based economy. While embracing e-Government and e-Commerce, the hope is that KM will help agencies meet some critical requirements as the Clinger-Cohen Act of 1996 and the Government Performance and Results Act. Many agencies are already engaged in some form of KM while others are already reaping some benefits. Whatever the case, if governments are not pursing KM now emerging conditions will ultimately force them to do so. For example, it is estimated that by the year 2004 thirty percent of the INDIA federal workforce will retire, and by 2005 upwards of sixty percent of its Senior Executive Service members will also retire. These statistics are not confined to the INDIA alone, most governments are facing the same problems. KM implementation presents the greatest challenges, and is what we consider next.

CAUSES OF KNOWLEDGE MANAGEMENT (KM)

Most organizations have recognized the existence of Knowledge Management problems, the causes of problems need careful analysis if organizations are to conduct corrective actions. Our findings indicate that the causes attributed to the KM problems identified can be classified into three dimensions as below.

ORGANIZATION RELATED CAUSES

Many respondents mentioned that "lack of training", "limited resources" and "lack of dedicated time for discussion" contribute to knowledge creation, storage and transfer problems. The lack of organizational incentive to create and transfer knowledge appears to be the major explanation for KM problems. One respondent pointed out that "The management does not apply the encouragement/punishment system properly".

The organizational structure is another root cause of KM problems. One respondent indicated "The hierarchy of my company is too flat and is not well managed. Such a structure makes knowledge transfer difficult". Similarly, "the bureaucratic way of work" is also considered as evidence for the establishment of barriers to knowledge creation and transfer. The inherent organizational culture is a critical factor contributing to KM problems. Some respondents indicated that "there is no good communication atmosphere in the company, so there is not enough sharing among colleagues". "Inter-departmental conflicts hinder knowledge retrieval and transfer, especially for the knowledge transfer among different departments".

HUMAN RELATED CAUSES

The respondents recognize that, in KM systems (KMS), the facilitator plays an important role. When this role is missing, the KMS is doomed to fail: "no specific person is responsible for the knowledge updating work. The information in the system is outdated and no longer applicable to current work practice".

Another significant concern related to the knowledge conversion problems lies in the knowledge externalization processes. The respondents thought that "staff feels too difficult to express their experiences, although they know their experiences are very useful for junior staff. Knowledge is too difficult to be translated to text". In China, guanxi or personal relationships, is a determining influence in most areas of human activity, including KM (Fu *et. al.* 2006). Respondents pointed out that "inter-personal conflicts", "competition among staff", "lack of trust and relationships" and "intra-departmental conflicts" complicate knowledge transfer.

TECHNICAL RELATED CAUSES

The respondents agree that IT is useful in managing knowledge and consider it as an enabler for KM. However, it appears that from the junior knowledge workers' perspective, IT-based KMS have not yet been adopted in Hong Kong organizations, at least for low-level or operational-level work, as illustrated by the following quotations. "The system is outdated and some work has to be done manually" which contributes to KM storage problems. "The current IT system cannot facilitate the changes of KM concepts in the company". "Organizational IT systems do not support knowledge management". Although some organizations have used information systems (usually intranets), the poor ease of use and the non-usefulness of the KMS contribute to the lagging KM practice, as indicated by the quotations: "The capacity of the hardware and software support is not enough". "The system is slow and always busy; sometimes it hangs". "Security of the KMS is a big concern". "The flow of using the KMS is not convenient". "The KMS is too complex to use".

PROBLEMS AND ISSUES OF KNOWLEDGE MANAGEMENT

The problems identified cover the four KM processes of creation, storage/retrieval, transfer and application. As junior knowledge workers, most respondents expressed the importance of KM and KM problems in their organizations from a knowledge receiver perspective. As knowledge receivers, they desire standardized procedures and specific guidance from supervisors or the organization. In general, explicit knowledge is helpful but usually missing in their work, so the KM problems identified through this viewpoint are more related to explicit knowledge creation, storage, transfer and application.

KNOWLEDGE CREATION

"Work procedures of work are not standardized"; "Staff seldom share knowledge"; "The information in the system is not enough"; "The skill of selling various products can only be learned by new employees when they face the clients".

KNOWLEDGE STORAGE/RETRIEVAL

"Staff always repeat the same mistake in issuing credit letter; this kind of mistake should be stored in the system or as a working guideline. However, we did not have such practice"; "General staff cannot access Internet for work purposes. Only senior colleagues have Internet or email functions"; "The company loses knowledge after retirement of staff"; "The special selling skills cannot be learned from colleagues because of the high turnover rate".

KNOWLEDGE TRANSFER

"Mentees can't get enough information from mentors in coaching"; "There is a wide communication gap between the senior and junior staff. They (senior staff) do not provide us (junior staff) sufficient knowledge"; "There is no training provided in the work, which leads a long time for new employees to catch up the job"; "Employees in different divisions have different work practices, so there is a lack of inter-division communication"; "Most of our colleagues are very dependent on me. I always spend a lot of time to communicate with them or answer their questions several times. They feel convenient and have developed the habit of asking me questions by phone again and again"; "The company lacks a well organized computer system for checking or updating information".

KNOWLEDGE APPLICATION

"There are different departments in my law firm. Staff cannot identify the major activities performed by each lawyer. For example, in a commercial department, there are different cases like trademark and patent, mortgage, listing, etc. Different lawyers are responsible for different practices although all these practices are classified into commercial cases.

It is difficult for us (legal secretaries) to locate experts and apply different kinds of expertise in different contexts".

"Each officer possesses unique and specialist knowledge, but it is difficult for junior employees to understand and apply them to their work".

CONCLUSION AND RECOMMENDATIONS

In this paper, we have attempted to contribute to developing an understanding of the underlying foundations and processes associated with KM by examining some of the issues, challenges and opportunities associated with this new discipline and especially how governments can get engaged and benefit from it. The main ideas and recommendations presented can be summarized as follows: The purpose of KM, in the "new economy" is to provide on line, real time access to knowledge, information and data throughout the organization and to its customers in that order. The organization's slogan in KM should be: Anyone, Anytime, Anywhere and Anything for organizational performance, efficiency and competitive advantage. For governments, this requires a radical change in mindset—stripping away unnecessary bureaucratic procedures that cause delays and hamper information and knowledge flow, putting in place the appropriate networks (human and technical) and above all recognizing that they must "compete" with private sector organizations in the quality of services rendered to customers/citizens. To this end, governments must understand that the stakeholders in any KM initiative include: management, employees, partners, customers and even other governments; and their roles are to participate, collaborate and learn in all stages of KM. Furthermore, with the looming retirement of a large number of civil servants, KM initiatives would be beneficial in preserving and extending organizational knowledge. Knowledge sharing networks and especially CoPs provide an easy entry point in KM with enormous benefits. They readily overcome cultural barriers to knowledge sharing. They offer the opportunity and ability to manage organizational knowledge, on which the level of social capital can be released. Furthermore, they act like gene pools within which the ability to evolve future solutions lie. Through such communities the issues of trust and motivation essential to ensuring continuity in KM can also be addressed. Governments should set-up CoPs for webmasters and helpdesks as suggested earlier. These CoPs can support and ensure e-government and government E-Commerce services. Government can and should replicate instances of successful KM practices from the private sector. The payoff is a smarter government, offering veritable government e-Commerce and e-Government services to its citizens and customers. KM systems are much more complex than traditional IM systems. With a history of high IM system failure rate in governments, KM projects should be initiated and carried out in small manageable phases. In these phases, reinvention should be avoided at all costs. It is important to reuse what is known or available, to the limit possible. There should be a focus on organizational culture and norms, external knowledge, past experience and technologies.

Finally, "Best practices" are a good starting point, but organizations should be conscious of the pitfalls of using them. These practices should not be used in isolation. They should be integrated with other endeavors such as CoPs. Award winning state organizations such as the CTG, which act as enablers and catalysts for innovative application of technology in government agencies should be transformed into Government Knowledge Centers. This will give them the opportunity to be more involved in KM while still performing their current activities. This means they would not be confined to producing "Best Practices" that might soon become outdated or not used at all as they are doing now, but they would effectively help government agencies to implement KM, which is an imperative for governments in the 21st century and the new economy.

References

Alavi, M., and Leidner, D.E. "Review: Knowledge Management and Knowledge Management Systems: Conceptual Foundations and Research Issues," *MIS Quarterly* (25:1), 2001, pp. 107-36.

Bock, G.W., Zmud, R.W., Kim, Y., and Lee, J.N. "Behavioral Intention Formation in Knowledge Sharing: Examining The Roles of Extrinsic Motivators, Social-Psychological Forces, and Organizational Climate," *MIS Quarterly* (29:1), 2005, pp. 87-111.

Fu, P.P., Tsui, A.S., and Dess, G.G. "The Dynamics of Guanxi in Chinese High-tech Firms: Implications for Knowledge Management and Decision-making," *Management International Review* (46:3), 2006, pp. 277-305.

Gold, A.H., Malhotra, A., and Segars, A.H. "Knowledge Management: An Organizational Capabilities Perspective," *Journal of Management Information Systems* (18:1), 2001, pp. 185-214.

Gray, P.H., and Meister, D.B. "Knowledge Sourcing Methods," *Information and Management* (43) 2006, pp. 142-56.

Joia, L.A. "Information Technology for Intelligent Metabusiness," in: Knowledge Management and Business Model Innovation, Y. Malhotra (ed.), Idea Group Publishing, London, 2001, pp. 95-113.

Kankanhalli, A., Tan, B.C.Y., and Wei, K.K. "Contributing Knowledge to Electronic Knowledge Repositories: An Empirical Investigation," *MIS Quarterly* (29:1), 2005, pp. 113-143.

Ko, D.-G., Kirsch, L.J., and King, W.R. "Antecedents of Knowledge Transfer from Consultants to Clients in Enterprise System Implementations," *MIS Quarterly* (29:1), 2005, pp. 59-85.

Pentland, B.T. "Information Systems and Organizational Learning: The Social, Epistemology of Organizational Knowledge Systems," Accounting, *Management and. Information Technology* (5:1), 1995, pp. 1-21.

Sambamurthy, V., and Subramani, M. "Special Issue on Information Technologies and Knowledge Management," *MIS Quarterly* (29:1), 2005, pp. 1-7.

Wasko, M.M., and Faraj, S. "Why Should I Share? Examining Knowledge Contribution in Electronic Networks of Practice," *MIS Quarterly* (29:1), 2005, pp. 35-57.

CHAPTER

43

Do Family and Experience Matter to Access Finance?

A Test on Women Entrepreneurs of Dhaka

M. SAYEED ALAM, SABINA SHARMIN
AND OMAR FARUQ

ABSTRACT

Research on women entrepreneurs is mostly available from developed world. The picture of women entrepreneurs from the developing world perspective is scanty. Research on women entrepreneurs is at an exploratory stage in Bangladesh. According to BWCC (Bangladesh Women Chamber of Commerce and Industry) there is lack of field-based data as well as finished information on women entrepreneurs of Bangladesh. A stratified sampling based on three business category strata (boutique, food and others) is used for this study to test relation of two variables (family support and experience) to get institutional support. From this study of thirty samples it is found that family support will be helpful to get institutional support whereas experience matter little. This study is concentrated only within Dhaka city and one limited sample so extended areas and more sample size are suggested to generalized the findings.

Key words: Women entrepreneur, Family support, Experience, Institution support

INTRODUCTION

Pine *et. al.* (2010) in their paper said that until the late 1970s, the role of women entrepreneurs was rarely considered (Humbert *et. al.*, 2009). Nowadays, however, as Carter and Shaw (2006) noted, research on entrepreneurship is moving from looking at whether gender makes a difference to how it makes a difference. Naser *et. al.* (2009) in their paper cited although a number of studies were undertaken to examine factors that influence women entrepreneurs in the developed world (DeLollis, 1997; Christopher, 1998; Goldenberg and Kline, 1999; Inman, 1999; Smith-Hunter, 2003; Smith-Hunter and Englhardt, 2004), a limited number of studies have been undertaken to investigate these factors in the Arab World in general and in the Arab Gulf region in particular (Dechant and Al-Lamky, 2005). In Bangladesh situation, research on women entrepreneurs is at an exploratory stage. It is evident from the BWCC's (Bangladesh Women Chamber of Commerce and Industry) there is lack of finished information on the situation of women entrepreneurs. There is lack of field-based data. Most of the financial institutions, public institutions do not have any gender disaggregated data (BWCC, 2008). Bangladesh Women Chamber of Commerce and Industry (BWCC, 2008) conducted an exploratory study aiming at having an overview of the situation of women entrepreneurs in Bangladesh. The covered issues in this report are—socio-demographic profile, types of women owned business and the nature of common barriers. The survey is based on 130 women entrepreneurs from 11 districts (BWCC, 2008).

DEFINITION OF A WOMEN ENTREPRENEUR

An entrepreneur is a person who starts a new business

venture. He/she is a person who can find opportunities and has the ability to develop those opportunities into profit-making businesses (Naser *et. al.*, 2009). Studying women-owned businesses has presented some methodological problems for researchers (Stevenson, 1990). A major difficulty is definition of a woman-owned business (Mattis, 2004). There is no specific definition is available for women entrepreneur in South Asia. Sinha (2005), in her study on "Developing Women Entrepreneurs In South Asia: Issues, Initiatives And Experiences" a preliminary definition set as "women running their own SMEs within the formal sector in South Asia". But because of lack of statistics it is not always possible to concentrate only one formal sector or the differences between formal and the informal sectors is not very clear, or even it is not clear what size of organizations (women entrepreneur) we can consider for analysis.

The National Directory of Woman-Owned Business Firms uses the following criteria to define a woman-owned business (Business Research Services, 2001):

- one or more of the principal owners, or the majority, of shareholders are women;
- as a group, the woman owners or shareholders own at least 51 percent of the business;
- the woman owners or shareholders have dominant control over the business; and
- participate in day-to-day operations; and the business is a going concern.

FINANCE AND WOMEN ENTREPRENEURS

Another problem that might confront women entrepreneurs is availability and use of fund. Owing to woman social position and family commitment, it is difficult to obtain the required fund run a business (Naser *et. al.*, 2009). Furthermore, research has shown that it is particularly difficult for women to acquire satisfactory start-up capital (Brush *et. al.*, 2000; Shaw *et. al.*, 2000). It has also been suggested the "barriers" to finance might be more acute for female-owned SMEs as there is a perception that financial institutions discriminate against female business owners (Riding and Swift, 1990; Breen *et. al.*, 1995; Brush *et. al.*, 2001).

A. Family and Women Entrepreneurs

Women entrepreneurs might encounter is lack of time needed to run a business. Arab women are responsible for many household chores in addition to raising children. Spending time on household chores and raising children leaves little time for a woman to develop her entrepreneurial knowledge and skills. This also restricts a woman from running a business, visiting banks, attending training courses seminars and conferences, attracting customers or looking for diversified suppliers (Naser *et. al.* 2009). Women may also fear or face prejudice or sexual harassment, and may be restricted in their ability to travel to make contacts (Sinha, 2005).

On this study we proposed first hypothesis :

H_1: There is no relation between family support and Institution support.

B. Experience and Women Entrepreneurs

According to Nilufer (2001), socio-cultural factors in developing countries influence women's decision to become an entrepreneur. Socio-cultural factors include religious values, ethnic diversity and marital status. Naser *et. al.* 2009 stated in their paper that as it may, the success of any business in the Arab countries depends on the entrepreneur's social position and the network they can create and access. In societies dominated by men, like the Arab Gulf, women entrepreneurs find it difficult to reach men's social positions. Given the nature of women and cultural restrictions on their movements, establishing an effective network and accessing them are not an easy task for women entrepreneurs. Naser *et. al.*, 2009 arguments has been documented by previous studies who found that women participation in network is less than men and even the network that they may develop is different than that formed by men (Granovetter, 1985; Aldrich and Zimmer, 1986; Burt, 2000). Based on this literature we can form the following hypothesis :

H_2: There is a relation between experience and Institution support.

Research Focus: Women have to play dual role while they are in business. At the same time it is learned from the literature that social network for women entrepreneurs are not that strong like male counterpart. In addition to these two variables (dual role and absence of social network) they face third problem that is access to finance is a problem for women. The specific focus of this research is to identify whether family support and experience has any impact and or relation to gain support from the Institution. More specifically if any woman entrepreneur has family support whether it is easy for her to gain support from the institution and if any woman with experience has advantage to support from the institution. In this paper by institution authors means financial institutions (Banks, Leasing companies, Merchant banking who can provide or issue loans to its clients and all of these institutions, it is not mandatory of these institutions to be listed in the stock markets). A sample of 30 women entrepreneurs constitutes the sample of this study.

Boutique alone represents around 70% of the total women entrepreneurs in Bangladesh (Alam, Biswas and Faruqui, (2009). It is learn from Faruqui, 2009 that boutique, food business, custom jewelry/flower business are more common business sectors for women in Bangladesh. Based on these studies a stratified sampling is used for this study. Three strata called Boutique, Food and others are selected and on the basis of random sampling 30 samples are chosen from the three strata. A structured questionnaire is used to collect the information. And a total of 120 samples are selected and out of this 120 a total of 40 questionnaires were collected and it is found 30 were completely filled up.

RESEARCH METHODOLOGY

Result

A. *Reliability Analyses*

The reliability of the scales is satisfactory, as the majority of them have alpha coefficients above 0.6 (Table 1). According to Cronbach, 1990, and Kim,2001 an alpha coefficient of 0.6 and above is considered good for research in social sciences. Family Support, Experience, institutional support are measured in terms of opinion on a five point Likert scale (1 = Strongly disagree to 5 = Strongly agree, where 3 = neutral)

TABLE I
Reliability Analysis

	Cronbach's Alpha if Item Deleted
Family support	0.977
Experience	0.700
Institution Support	0.690

B. Descriptive Statistics

	Family Support	*Experience*	*Institution Support*
Mean	3.47	3.60	3.53
Maximum	5	5	5
Minimum	2	2	2
Std. Dev.	1.074	0.770	1.008
Sum	104	108	106
Observations	30	30	30

Five-level Likert item is used: where 1 = strongly disagree, 2 = disagree, 3 = Neither agree nor disagree, 4 = agree, 5 = Strongly agree. The questions are :

Family : Without family support (either from parents/ husband) no woman can start any business.

Experience : Without experience it is almost difficult to start any business for women.

Institution support : Major barrier to start a business as a woman is no cooperation from the financial institution regarding loan or any form of financial service.

C. *Hypothesis test*

Hypothesis 1

H_1: There is no relation between family support and Institution support.

Institution support as dependent variable and Family support as independent variable, the result is :

$$Y_{\text{Institution Support}} = 0.371 + 0.912\ X_{\text{Family support}}$$

Variables	*Coefficient*	*Std. Error*	*t-Statistic*	*Prob.*
Constant	0.371	0.150	2.467	0.020
Institution support	0.912	0.041	22.014	0.000

Value of r^2 is 0.945, so the relation between Institution support and family support is very strong. P value is < 0.01 so null is rejected in favor of alternative hypothesis. There is a strong relation between family support and Institution support.

Model Summary

Model	*R*	*R-Square*	*Adjusted R-Square*	*Std. Error of the Estimate*
1	.972(a)	.945	.943	.240

a Predictors: (Constant), Without family support (either from parents/ husband) no woman can start any business.

Hypothesis 2

H_2: There is a relation between experience and Institution support.

Institution support as dependent variable and experience as independent variable, the result is :

$$Y_{\text{Institution Support}} = 2.822 + 0.198\ X_{\text{Experience}}$$

Variables	*Coefficient*	*Std. Error*	*t-Statistic*	*Prob.*
Constant	2.822	0.900	3.137	0.004
Institution support	0.198	0.245	0.808	0.426

Value of r^2 is 0.023, so the relation between Institution support and experience is very weak. P value is > 0.01 so null is rejected in favor of alternative hypothesis. There is no relation between experience and Institution support.

Model Summary

Model	*R*	*R-Square*	*Adjusted R -quare*	*Std. Error of the Estimate*
1	0.151	0.023	-0.12	1.014

a Predictors: (Constant), Without family support (either from parents/ husband) no woman can start any business.

Correlations matrix

From the correlation matrix it is learned that there is a strong correlation between family support and Institution support. But the relationship strength between experience and Institution support is not significant.

	Family support	*Experience*	*Institution support*
Family Support	1.000	.173	.983(**)
Experience	.173	1.000	.122
Institution Support	.983(**)	.122	1.000

** Correlation is significant at the 0.01 level (2-tailed).

CONCLUSION

In Bangladesh the study on women entrepreneurship is at exploratory stage. Data scarcity and cooperation from the sample population side are the major problem to do research in this area. From this study we learn that women entrepreneurs think that family support is important than experience to get institutional support for access to finance. Welsch and Young (1984) also observe that women owners had less business experience than their male counterparts. Stevenson (1986) notes that, while male founders are able to gain experience from past work roles, women are less able to do this and only begin to obtain such experience from their own business.

Women have to play dual role so if they have support from the family it will be a great help not only to enter into business, the sample of this study believes that it will be a great help to get access to finance and this sample group believes that this support is more vital than experience. This study is based on very small sample and concentrated area so this study is suggested for extended area and more sample size for generalize this finding.

References

Aldrich, H. and Zimmer, C. (1986), "Entrepreneurship through social networks", in Sexton, D.L. and Smilor, R.W. (Eds.), The Art and Science of Entrepreneurship, Ballinger Publishing Company, Cambridge, MA, pp. 3-24.

Breen, J., Calvert, C. and Oliver, J. (1995), "Female entrepreneurs in Australia: an investigation of financial and family issues", *Journal of Enterprising Culture,* Vol. 3, No. 4, pp. 445-61.

Brush, C.G., Carter, N., Gatewood, E., Greene, P.G. and Hart, M.M. (2001), An Investigation of Women-led Firms and Venture Capital Investment, A Report for the US Small Business Administration, Office of Advocacy National Women's Business Council.

Brush, C., Carter, N., Greene, P., Hart, M., Gatewood, E. and Weeks, J. (2000), Women and Equity Capital: An Exploration of the Factors Affecting Capital Access, available at:www.babson.edu/entrep/fer/XI/XIA.

Business Research Services (2001), National Directory of Woman-owned Business Firms, 11th ed., Business Research Services, Washington, DC.

Burt, R.S. (2000), "The Network Entrepreneur", in Swedberg, R. (Ed.), Entrepreneurship: The Social Science View, Oxford University Press, Oxford, pp. 281-307.

Carter, S. and Shaw, E. (2006), Women's Business Ownership: Recent Research and Policy Developments, Report to the Small Business Service, DTI Small Business Service, London.

Christopher, J. (1998), "Minority Business Formation and Survival: Evidence on Business Performance and Viability", *The Review of Black Political Economy,* Vol. 26, No. 1, pp. 37-72.

Dechant, K. and Al-Lamky, A. (2005), "Towards an understanding of Arab women entrepreneurs in Bahrain and Oman", *Journal of Developmental Entrepreneurship*, Vol. 10, No. 2, pp. 123-40.

DeLollis, B. (1997), "Today's female passion for entrepreneurship", *The American Enterprise*, Vol. 8, pp. 42-5.

Goldenberg, S. and Kline, T. (1999), "An exploratory study of predicting perceived success and survival of small businesses", *Psychological Reports*, Vol. 85, No. 2, pp. 365-77.

Granovetter, M. (1985), "Economic action and social structure: the problem of embeddedness", *American Journal of Sociology*, Vol. 9, No. 3, pp. 481-510.

Humbert, A.L., Drew, E. and Kelan, E. (2009), "Gender identity and ICT entrepreneurship in an Irish context", in Pines, A.M. and Ozbilgin, M.F. (Eds.), Handbook of Research on High-Technology Entrepreneurs, Edward Elgar, Cheltenham.

Inman, K. (1999), Women's Resources in Business Start-up: A Study of Black and White Women Entrepreneurs, Garland Publishing, New York, NY.

Mattis, C. Marry (2004), "Women entrepreneurs: out from under the glass ceiling", *Women in Management Review*, Volume 19. Number 3, pp. 154-63.

Naser, Kamal, Mohammed Rashid Wojoud, Nuseibeh Rana (2009), "Factors that affect women entrepreneurs: evidence from an emerging economy", *International Journal of Organizational Analysis*, Vol. 17, No. 3, pp. 225-47.

Nilufer, A. (2001), "Jobs, gender and small enterprises in Bangladesh: factors affecting women entrepreneurs in small and cottage industries in Bangladesh", *SEED Working Paper No. 14*, International Labor Office, Geneva.

Pines Malach Ayala, Lerner Miri, Schwartz Dafna (2010), "Gender differences in Entrepreneurship Equality, diversity and inclusion in times of global crisis", *Equality, Diversity and Inclusion : An International Journal*, Vol. 29 No. 2, pp. 186-98.

Riding, A. and Swift, C.S. (1990), "Women business owners and terms of credit: some empirical findings of the Canadian experience", *Journal of Business Venturing*, Vol. 5, No. 5, pp. 327-40.

Sinha, Shalini (2005), "Developing Women Entrepreneurs in South Asia: Issues, Initiatives And Experiences", Trade and Investment Division, UNESCAP, Bangkok, Thailand.

Shaw, E., Carter, S. and Brierton, J. (2002), "Unequal Entrepreneurs: Why female enterprise is an uphill struggle", The Work Foundation.

Smith-Hunter, A.E. (2003), Diversity and Entrepreneurship, Successful Women Entrepreneurs, University Press of America, Lanham, MD.

Smith-Hunter, A.E. and Englhardt, W. (2004), "Determinants of economic success for women entrepreneurs: an analysis across racial lines", *Journal of the Academy of Business and Economics*, January.

Stevenson, L. (1986), "Against all Odds: The Entrepreneurship of Women", *Journal of Small Business Management*, Vol. 24, No. 4, pp. 30-6.

Stevenson, L. (1990), "Some Methodological Problems Associated with Researching Women Entrepreneurs", *Journal of Business Ethics*, 9 April/May, pp. 439-46.

Welsch, H. and Young, E. (1984), "Male and Female Entrepreneurial Characteristics and Behaviours: A Profile of Similarities and Differences", *International Small Business Journal*, Vol. 2, No. 4, pp. 11-20.

CHAPTER

44

Access and Issues of Education for Minorities

A Case for Affirmative Action

IFTEKHAR AHMED, ASMA PARVEEN AND IRAM FEROZ

INTRODUCTION

Education is one of the important parameters of judging the human development index of a community. Since the independence of the country and especially after the introduction of new economic reforms there has been phenomenal expansion in the field of education. Nevertheless, the Muslim community as a whole seems to be left untouched by the great strides made by education in both digitalised and conventional forms. Various reports published from time to time have stood testimony to the bitter truth that Muslims are deprived of the fruits of development. The authors try to investigate the lack of educational attainment among the Muslims especially the Muslim children and the Muslim women. They further peruse the reports available to ascertain the reasons behind the laggardness in education especially the access of Muslim masses to education and the availability of infrastructure and facilities to encourage the growth of literacy among Muslims. The authors also do a field survey to find the impact of education on the political empowerment of Muslim women by virtue of their political participation in Uttar Pradesh. The authors find that although the access and availability of educational means and resources to Muslims of UP are at nadir, to say the least, yet the women are actively participating in politics through elections and election generated rallies and meetings. This paradoxical situation emphasises the desire in the community to break free from the shackles of poverty and backwardness in the hope that their action will result in improvement of their lot but for education without which such desire to break free are just a wishful thinking.

Even though Islam emphasizes the rights and importance of education unequivocally, access to education for Muslim women has been deeply severed. The Prophet stated: "Whosoever follows a path to seek knowledge therein, Allah will make easy for him/her a path to Paradise."[1] Similarly, the Quran asks, "Are those who know and who do not know equal?"[2] Great emphasis is placed on education and no distinction is made between men and women.

Muslim women have played an important and historic role as scholars and leaders in education. For instance, the princess Fatima Al-Fihri established the first degree-granting university in the world, University of Al Karaouine, in Morocco in 859 CE. Similarly, throughout the Ayyubid dynasty, 26 mosques and madrasas that were established in Damascus were funded by women through the Waqf, charitable trust or trust law, system. Half of all the royal patrons for these institutions were also women.

However, Muslim women face restrictions in accessing education that differ greatly from one region to another. There are underlying challenges that Muslim women face in trying to receive education. One such example is the traditional patriarchal interpretation of qiwamah, the notion that men are guardians of Muslim women. Although the Quran stipulates that both men and women are protectors of one another, the concept of qiwamah has been used to justify various restrictions on women that in turn hinder Muslim women's education. For instance, limiting women's right to free movement is a great impediment to free and equal access to education. In various regions Muslim girls are also forced to marry at a very early age and thus kept at homes instead of in the classrooms. They are taught that their only role is that of a wife and of a mother and are discouraged from seeking educational and professional opportunities.

Other factors, such as poverty and shortage of nearby schools, also impact girls' education, particularly in remote areas.

METHODOLOGY

In the present study the authors investigate the issues of access of education to Muslim women and also some of the issues that are intricately woven with it like choice of educational institution, enrolments, levels of educational attainment and issue of language. Besides, some independent variables other factors like beliefs and psychological/ attitudinal aspects were also examined by assessing the joint impact of all these variables on political behaviour of Muslim women of Uttar Pradesh.

Sample

The sample was selected from amongst the whole of the state of Uttar Pradesh, consisting of 18.5% of Muslim population. The total number of 600 samples was drawn from the different parts of the state. In all 300 OBC (Other Backward Classes), Muslim women and 300 OBC Hindu women were sampled.

To find the impact of education on political behaviour of both the Muslim and Hindu females, further two groups—education up to high school and education above high school—were made.

POLITICAL BEHAVIOUR QUESTIONNAIRE

The questionnaire measuring the behaviour of Muslims political aspects was consisted of seventeen dimensions. The psychological orientations contained twelve dimensions. Besides these twelve dimensions, five more dimensions were measured to encompass the political behaviour in totality.

The answers of the respondents were meticulously tick marked in the questionnaire sheet itself. The answer options ranged from simple 'Yes' or 'No', 'agree' or 'disagree', to 'fully agree', 'somewhat agree', 'somewhat disagree', 'fully disagree' and 'a great deal', 'somewhat', 'not at all'.

STATISTICAL ANALYSIS

For converting the questions on political behaviour into numerals, first of all, the various answer options to a question were graded according to number of answer options available in a question in a descending order, with answer option showing greater political behaviour given more numbers. Thus, all the questions were graded and total marks were obtained. Similarly, individual respondent's marks were obtained and tabulated in already categorized groups.

In the first phase, the tables so obtained were combined with the dimensions as was required, and thus, various dimensions were permuted and combinations were calculated. In this way, percentages of all the dimensions were calculated.

ACCESS AND ISSUES OF EDUCATION FOR MUSLIM WOMEN

In Uttar Pradesh, it was found that among the Muslim OBC females school enrolment rates continue to be low: 39.6%, as compared to 61.2% in the case of 'upper' caste Hindus. In eastern U.P it is only 11.5%, in western U.P 22.1%, and in south India, above 70%, which is above the all-India average for all girls.

Only 14.1% of Muslim girls from poor families attend schools, while 75% of Muslim girls from economically better-off families do so, thus clearly suggesting that low levels of education of Muslim girls owes not to religion but to poverty. 98% of Muslim girls are said to study in government or private schools and only 2% in Madrasas, the majority being from poor families. Less than 15% of Muslim girls finish eight years of schooling and less than 8% complete higher secondary education. In the eastern U.P. the corresponding figures are 4.5% and 4.75% respectively, compared to the national female average of 17.8% and 11.4% respectively. Only 1.3% eastern U.P Muslims, both boys and girls, and 5.1% western U.P Muslim children are enrolled in senior secondary schools. The average number of years that Muslim girls study is a dismal 2.9 years, as compared to 4.1 years in the case of Hindu girls. In other words, on the whole, Muslim girls are characterized by a very high drop-out rate from the formal schooling system.

LITERACY LEVELS

The most common indicator of educational attainment is literacy. In the absence of any other source providing data on the literacy levels of OBCs, in particular Muslim-OBCs, the authors have used NSSO data to compute literacy levels. Literacy levels among the population aged 6-years and above shows marginal differences at the all-India level (Table 1). However, disaggregated analysis by place of residence reveal sharp differences across SRCs (Social Religious Communities) in urban areas; Muslims, and in particular Muslim-OBCs, are lagging behind Hindu-OBCs. The literacy levels among the Muslim-OBCs is the least in rural areas as well but the difference is not as sharp between them and other SRCs (Social Religious Communities) in urban areas.

TABLE I

Literacy Levels of SRCs by Place of Residence

SRCs	*India*	*Urban*	*Rural*
Hindu-OBCs	65.7	80.8	61.7
M-Gen	66.0	75.6	61.2
M-OBCs	61.9	70.1	57.8
India	67.3	82.6	61.9

Source : Estimated from NSSO (2004-5) 61st Round, Sch. 10.

LEVELS OF EDUCATION

Table 2 shows the proportion of persons in each SRC analyzed according to the highest level of education attained. A comparison across SRCs suggests that the educational levels of Muslim-OBCs (M-OBC) and Muslim-Gen (M-Gen) are lower than those of Hindu-OBCs (H-OBCs). In general, educational levels among Muslim-OBCs are lower than the other two SRCs; the illiteracy is the highest among this group and a lower proportion of persons in this group complete school education or undertake graduate studies.

TABLE 2
Distribution of Persons (aged 6+ years) in each SRC by Levels of Education

Educational Level	*H-OBCs*	*M-Gen*	*M-OBCs*	*Total*
Illiterate	33.4	33.3	37.4	31.6
Just Literate	1.2	2.2	2.9	1.4
Below Primary	0.8	1.7	1.5	1.0
Primary	15.9	18.0	17.5	15.4
Middle	16.0	18.6	16.0	15.7
Secondary	15.0	12.6	13.1	14.2
Higher Secondary	7.4	5.9	5.1	7.8
Diploma/Certificate	3.9	2.8	2.5	4.4
Graduate and above	3.2	2.4	1.9	4.3

Source : Estimated from NSSO 61st Round (2004-5), Sch. 10.

ACHIEVEMENTS IN HIGHER EDUCATION

Finally, the status of the three SRCs (Table 3) is examined with respect to their attainments in the field of higher education. Three levels of education have been used for this purpose—general graduates and above, technical graduates and technical diploma and certificate courses.

It can be seen that all the three SRCs have a lower proportion of persons holding a technical/non-technical degree

TABLE 3
Proportion of Persons aged 20 years+ with Higher Education in each SRC

SRCs	*General Graduate*	*Technical Graduate*	*Tech. Dip/Cert.*	*Higher Education*
H-OBCs	3.7	0.2	2.3	6.2
M-Gen	3.5	0.2	1.4	5.2
M-OBCs	2.3	0.1	1.7	4.1
Total	5.5	0.3	2.6	8.5

Source : Estimated from NSSO 61st Round (2004-5), Sch. 10.

or technical diploma/certificate compared to the Hindu-OBCs. Except in the case of technical diploma/certificate courses, Muslim-OBC has the lowest level of achievements in higher education; in general, Hindu-OBCs do better than the other two SRCs. Thus, in terms of higher education also, the Muslim-OBCs lag behind the other SRCs namely, Hindu-OBCs and Muslim-Gen.

The authors note an enthusiasm for modern education among many Muslim parents, although this is generally thwarted by widespread poverty and the fear that well-educated girls might find it difficult to find suitable match because of the relative paucity of well-educated Muslim men. Another problem is the shortage of Urdu schools, which many parents would prefer to send their girls to. When students pass out from these schools they are faced with either being forced to enroll in Hindi-medium secondary schools or drop-out from the formal schooling system.

There is lack of interest in promoting Muslim education. There are some privately managed Urdu-medium primary schools in some districts like Aligarh, Saharanpur, Moradabad, Rampur, etc. but these are confined to big cities and that to in the western part of U.P., though a large number of Muslims live in this part of the state. On the whole, Urdu schools in the state suffer from shortage of funds, trained teachers, textbooks and inadequate infrastructure.

EDUCATION AND POLITICAL BEHAVIOUR

The purpose here is to find whether education determine political behaviour of the people to the extent that *Almond and Verba*[3], *Lerner*[4] and others claim it does? Unfortunately, the research conducted in the Asian countries does not support the western premise. Different studies have shown that in Asian region particularly in India, education is very strongly related to cognitive aspects of the political orientation like—political interest, political information index, issue and problem awareness, symbol and heritage awareness, etc. A positive correlation is witnessed in these aspects.

And those political activities where affective orientation aspects of the masses are involved like—voting participation, campaign participation, communal activity, political activity, etc., a negative correlation is observed. The study done by *Goel (1974)*[5] on Indian Gallup polls on 1961, 1964 and 1967 proves the contention. The following Table 4 regarding the political behaviour of Muslim and Hindu females in U.P. further elaborates and proves the above point.

On measuring various dimensions of political behaviour in education upto high School category, it was found that Hindu OBC women are more politically active than their Muslim OBC counterparts in most of the dimensions. Voting participation (VP)-50%, campaign participation (CP) -28.37% along with political information index (PII) -26.28% and political interest (PI) -23.03% all seem to be fairly higher among Hindu women having education up to high school as compared to those of Muslim women with literacy level below high school (Table 4). In some dimensions like symbol and heritage awareness (SHA), attitude towards system (ATS), political action (PA), political efficacy (PE) and political trust (PT) the percentage of difference narrows down to that of less than 2 per cent otherwise in rest of the dimensions the difference remains fairly high.

Similarly, in the other category of females of those above high school it was found that the Hindu females are much more politically active than Muslims in the almost all the political dimensions measuring cognitive, affective and evaluative aspects of behaviour. It clearly emphasises the fact

TABLE 4
Education and Political Behaviour

Dimensions	*Upto HS Muslim%*	*Upto HS Hindu%*	*Above HS Muslim%*	*Above HS Hindu%*
VP	40.01	50.00	35.54	45.78
CP	20.03	28.37	15.34	23.14
PI	18.63	26.28	23.56	28.15
PII	16.26	23.03	18.56	28.55
IPA	12.23	18.38	22.12	24.13
CA	20.12	26.4	15.23	19.56
SHA	18.22	20.3	23.34	25.54
ATS	17.23	18.78	20.67	22.34
ATC	12.29	17.2	12.45	18.23
PA	17.18	18.56	19.14	20.13
PE	16.00	17.00	18.43	22.24
PT	16.34	17.61	16.12	18.23
M	16.05	26.89	15.34	20.34
MME	11.14	16.13	18.56	20.36
P.aff.C	20.06	13.32	20.56	14.34
P.aff.SP	45.02	55.98	48.78	59.17
P.aff.BSP	25.04	23.4	26.00	24.00
V.pref.C	12.34	22.23	13.13	24.67
V.pref.P	60.09	50.65	62.23	58.64
O.D.fm	44.56	45.56	45.00	46.00
O.D.f	8.08	10.3	10.01	11.34
O.D.c	15.56	25.56	17.38	28.18
O.D.cw	3.03	6.87	4.00	8.00
O.D.s	55.05	57.07	50.00	56.00

that Muslim women on the whole are less politically active than the Hindu females. (Figure 1).

Educational Impact

When we analyse the impact of education on the two groups—Muslim and Hindu females, the data becomes more

FIG. 1
Educational Impact

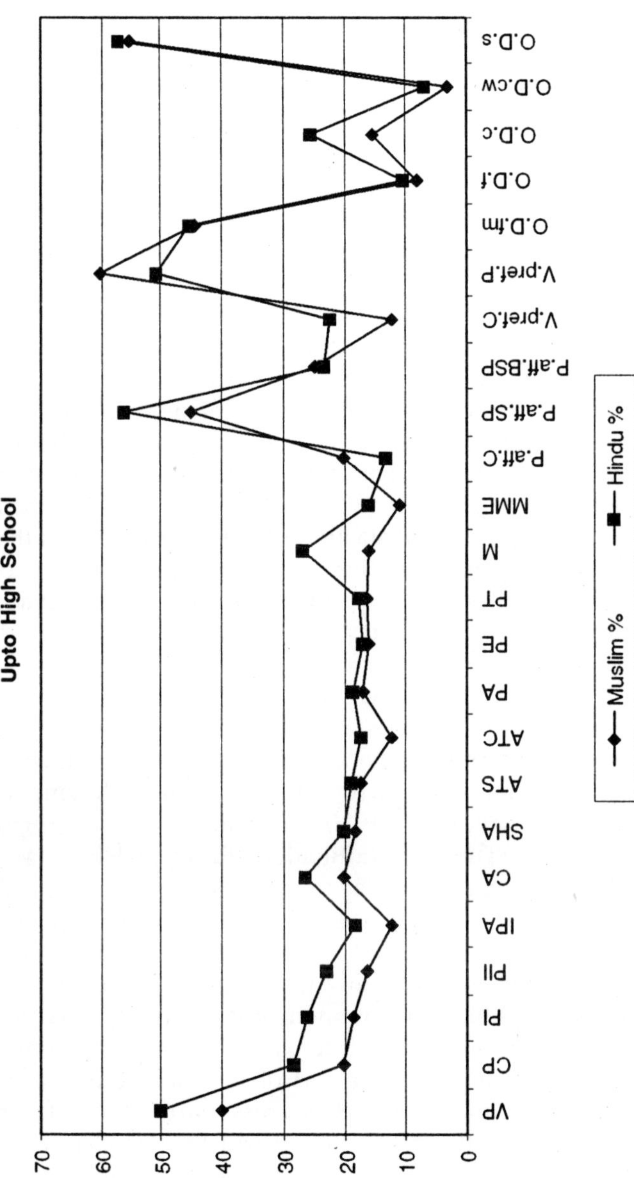

revealing and highly interesting. Amongst the Muslim female it was found that with increase in education, the cognitive orientation depicted in dimensions like political interest (PI), political information index (PII), issue and problem awareness (IPA) and symbol and heritage awareness (SHA) reveals an increasing trend whereas affective orientations like voting participation (VP), campaign participation (CP), communal activity (CA) shows a downward trend. The case of Hindu females is not different. They also show increase in cognitive activities but affective aspect is muffled. It clearly shows that education prepares them for greater political participation but owing to social restrictions they are not forthcoming in actively participating in politics. (Figure 2)

With regard to dimensions like political efficacy (PE) and political trust (PT) which are considered to be depicting acceptance of system and its functioning, here democratic system, it is found that female of the species are not too happy with it. The prevalence of corruption was one of main reasons cited for such dissatisfaction. What is surprising is that when it comes to channelling this dissatisfaction into mass mobilization (M), education, contrary to its role in western democracies, is proving to be a hindrance. That shows societal restrictions on the free movement of females.

The voting preference (V.pref.) among both the groups Hindus and Muslims and in both the categoriesup to high school and above school is heavily loaded in favour of party than in candidate, with Muslim females having preference greater than that of Hindu females in supporting party candidate. The party affiliation (P.aff.) in Hindu and Muslim OBCs shows a clear bias towards Samajwadi party. Here again the point to be emphasised is that the increase in the level of education has not led to any diminish in the passion for supporting one's own caste group, however, the percent increase is not in commensuration with increase in other dimensions. What is interesting is that the preference for Congress party shows a sort of revival in the form of support from Muslim women. Congress party (20%) finds favours among both the categories of Muslim females. However, the story is not so pink for Congress as more and more support is forthcoming for BSP in both Hindu and Muslim females and

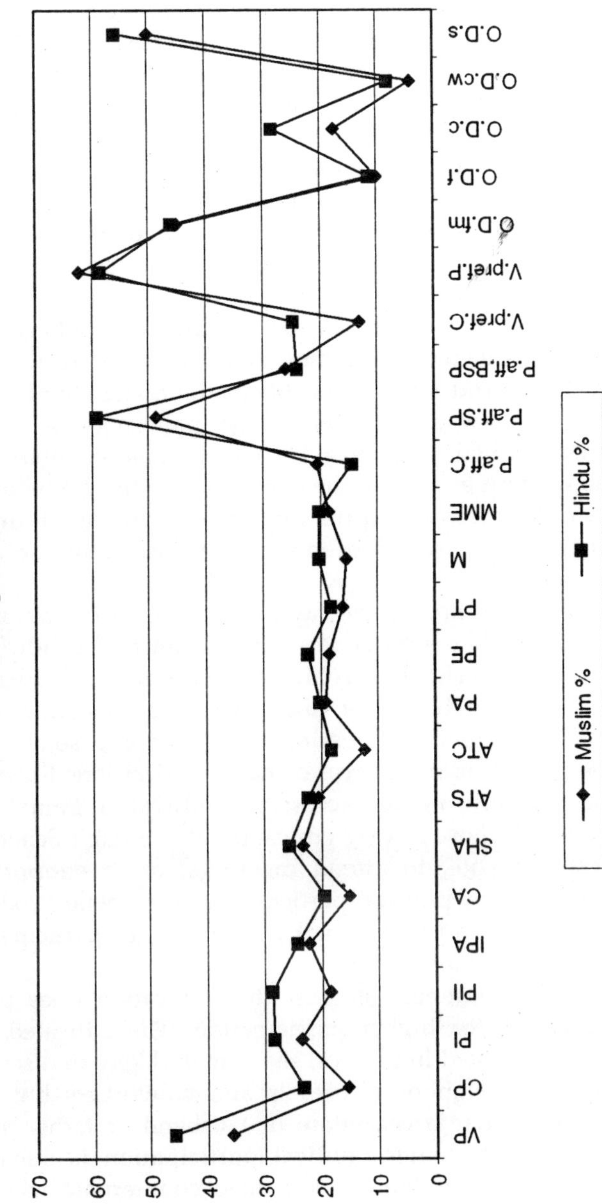

FIG. 2
Educational Impact
Above High School

less and less support is for Congress party. In opinion decider (OD) dimension, family members (fm) play a more meaningful role whereas the opinion of Spouse (ODs) play a decisive role in political behaviour of both the Hindu and the Muslim females in both the categories of education up to High School and education above High School. However, in both the categories the combination of friends, caste and co-workers play an ineffective role in making up of mind for voting.

Most polls show a curvilinear relationship in India especially among Males; that is turnout rises with rise in literacy, but decreases with a further rise in the level of education and continues to decrease with college education. Masses in general have shown the same pattern with regard to education and their political behaviour. Here the Female of the species show an entirely similar pattern of behaviour even when studied separately from their male counterparts. Thus, the western belief that the change in the level of education will lead to commensurate change in the level of political participation rate does not prove correct in the context of Females.

To sum up, we can say that the higher education does not lead to higher turnout rates in Muslim and Hindu females of Uttar Pradesh. The relationship between education and participation holds for such activities as taking interest in political matters, discussing politics, doing something in an attempt to influence local or national decisions like the case in the Western democracies, the educated Female of U.P., especially those having education above High School, are less likely to vote, to attend meetings, or to support partisan campaigns by physical participation or monetary contributions. Overall education does not lead to higher participation in all political activities.

The evidences suggest that education does prepare an individual for higher participation. The educated female is more interested in politics, she is more likely to discuss politics with her neighbours, friends and co-workers but vote only under the patriarchal glare of Husband or father as the case may be. Thus, her political participation is subject to the participation of that of her male counterpart which studies have revealed leans towards curvilinear trajectory.

EXPLANATIONS

Recent studies point to the conclusion that higher education in India is not instrumental in breeding strong love for the country, or patriotism or inculcating a belief that voting is a civic obligation. For instance, a study by **Alex Inkeles,**[6] of six developing countries, i.e. India, Israel, Nigeria, Bangladesh, Chile and Argentina, came to the conclusion that in some countries the "participant" or "good" citizens (i.e. persons who were informed, knowledgeable, participant and rational) were also more hostile and unpatriotic.

Another study by *Eldersveld, S.J, et. al.,*[7] found that in their survey in 1968 the city of Delhi and the nearby rural areas, that in general the upper, more educated classes were much less supportive of public authority than were the lower classes.

Various Government reports and recently the *Sachar Committee Report (2007)*[8] have revealed that there is a significant disparity between the educational status of Muslims and that of other socio-religious categories. Different and periodical riots have broken the will of the Muslim masses. So the educated masses are more concerned with formal jobs and struggle for bread and butter than election and turnout.

In a study of Luckow and Madurai, *Joseph Elder*[9] also discounts the common presumption prevalent in some circles that increasing education is the bulwark of parliamentary institutions. The parliamentary system based on universal adult suffrage has given rise to what *Weiner*[10] calls "a mass political culture"—which is the bane of all the problems in India since it has given rise to parochial ties of caste, region, language, religion and community which are misused by hungry power seeking petty politicians to further their personal agenda, at the cost of nation and development. This may explain why the educated people develop disliking for politics.

Notes and References

1. Sahih Muslim, Book 35, Number 6518.
2. Sura Zumar, Ayat 9.
3. Almond, G. and Verba, S. (1965), *The Civic Culture,* Boston: Little Brown and Company, 318-19.

4. Daniel Lerner. (1958). *The passing of Traditional Society,* N.Y.: The Free Press, p. 64.
5. Madan Lal Goel, *op. cit.*
6. Alex Inkeles, 1969, *op. cit.*
7. Eldersveld, J. Samuel; Jagannadham,V. and Barnabas, A.P. (1968). *The Citizen and the Administrator in a Developing Democracy,* Glen View, III: Scott, Foresman, 58.
8. Sachar Committee Report, 2007. www.nationalarchives.nic.in
9. Joseph Elder (1966). *Religious Beliefs and Political Attitudes: South Asian Parties and Religion.* Princeton: Princeton University Press, Chapter 12, 249-76.
10. Weiner, M. and Kothari, R. (1965). *Indian Voting Behaviour,* p. 32, Calcutta: F.K.L. Mukhopadhyay.

Index